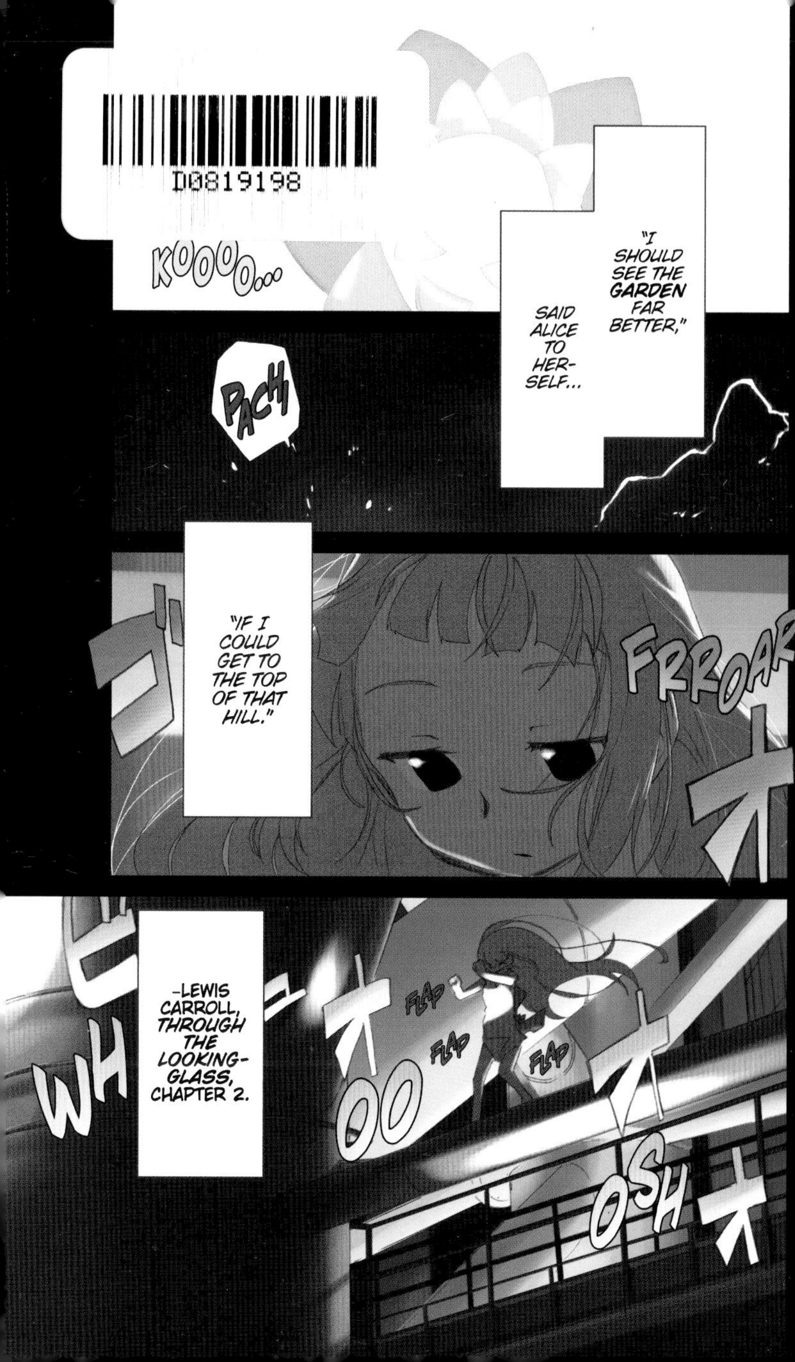
KOOOO...
"I SHOULD SEE THE **GARDEN** FAR BETTER,"
SAID ALICE TO HER-SELF...
PACHI
FRROAR
"IF I COULD GET TO THE TOP OF THAT HILL."
FLAP
FLAP
FLAP
WHOOSH
-LEWIS CARROLL, THROUGH THE LOOKING-GLASS, CHAPTER 2.

Chapter.1
The Red Queen Escapes

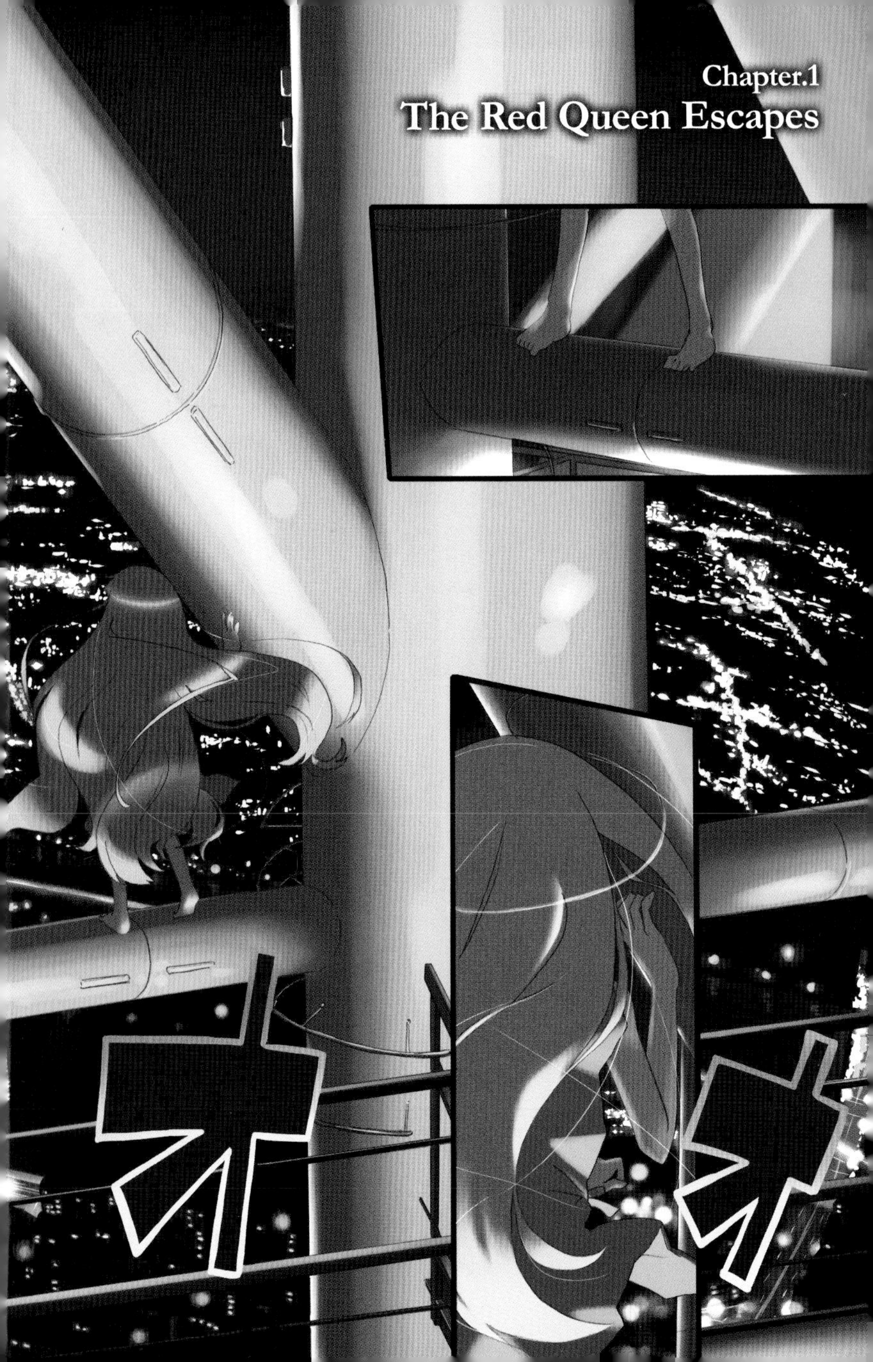
オ
オ

Alice & Zoroku 1

story & art by TETSUYA IMAI

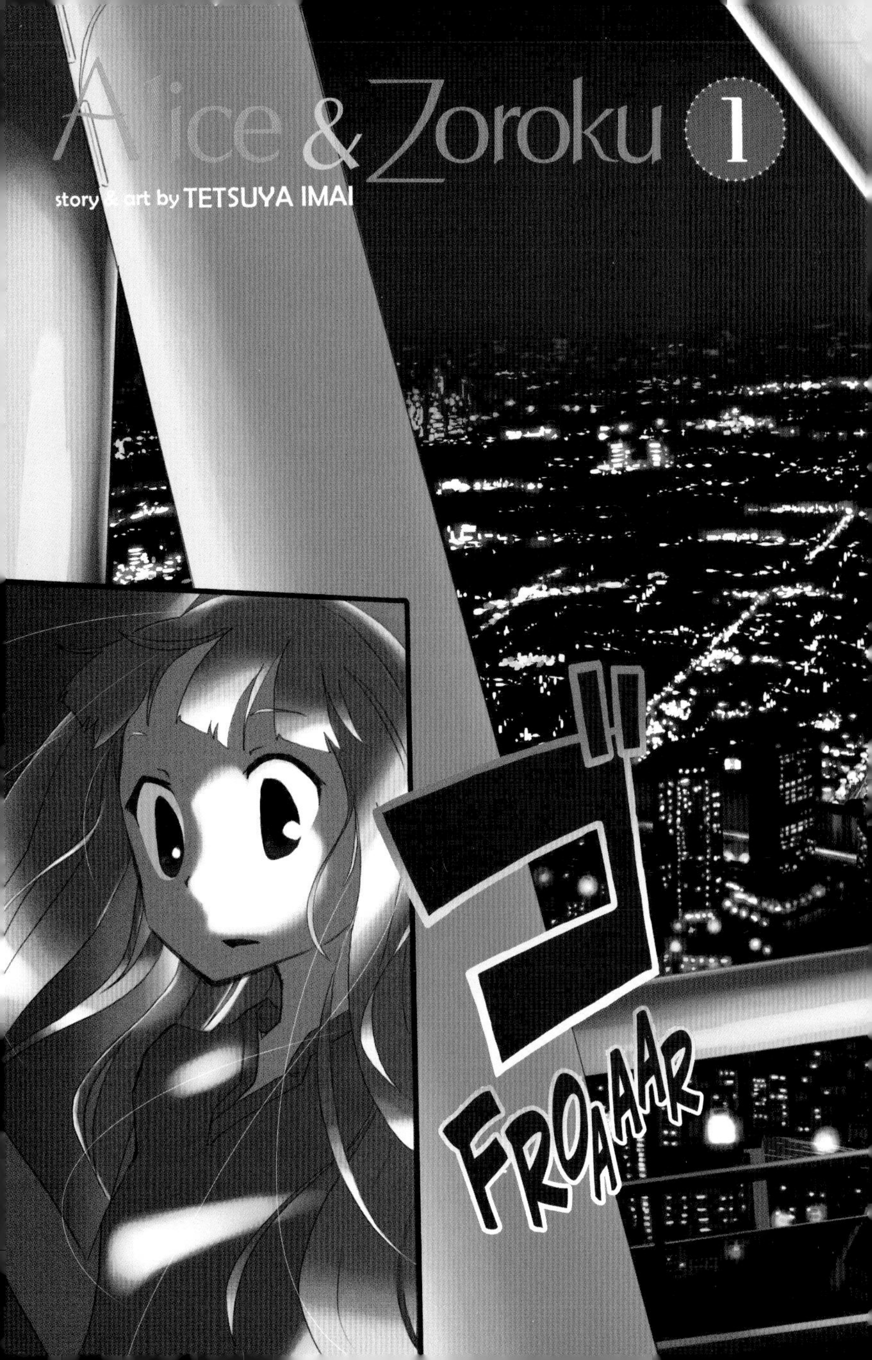
ゴ
FROAAR

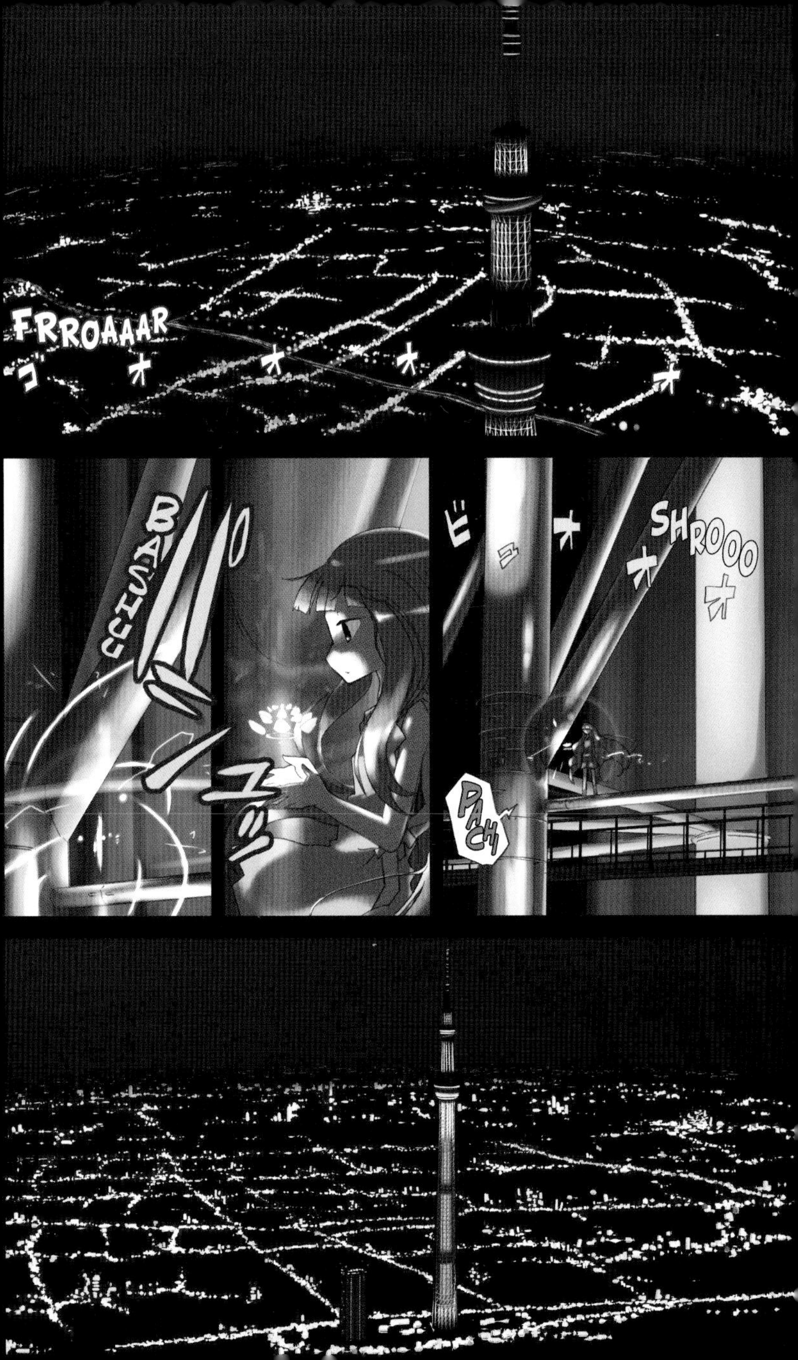
FRROAAAR
SHROOO
PACHI
BASHUU

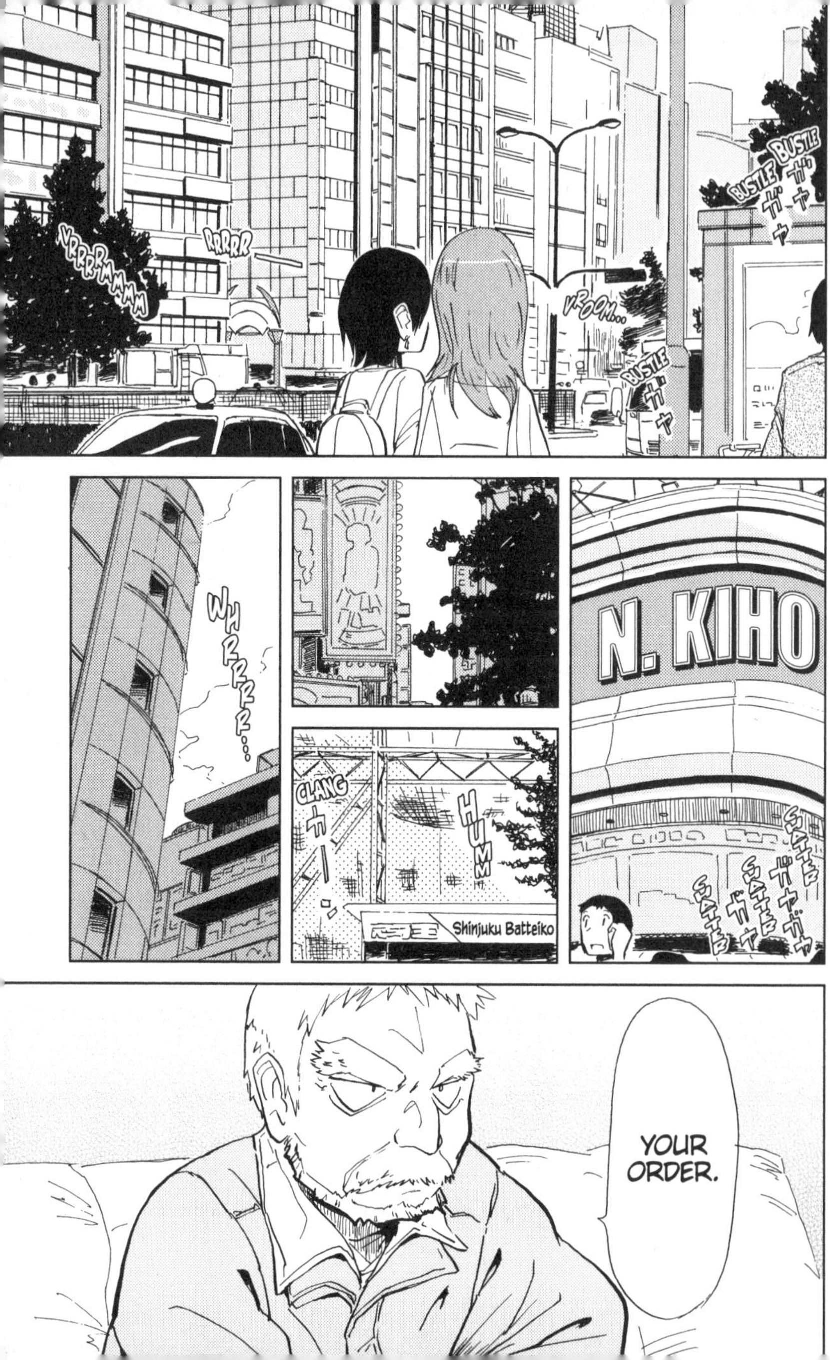
BUSTLE BUSTLE
ガヤガヤ
VROOM...
BUSTLE
ガヤ
RRRRR
VRRRRMMMM
N. KIHO
SHATTER
ガヤガヤ
SHATTER
ガヤ
SHATTER
HUMM
CLANG
ウィー…
Shinjuku Batteiko
WHRRRR...
YOUR ORDER.

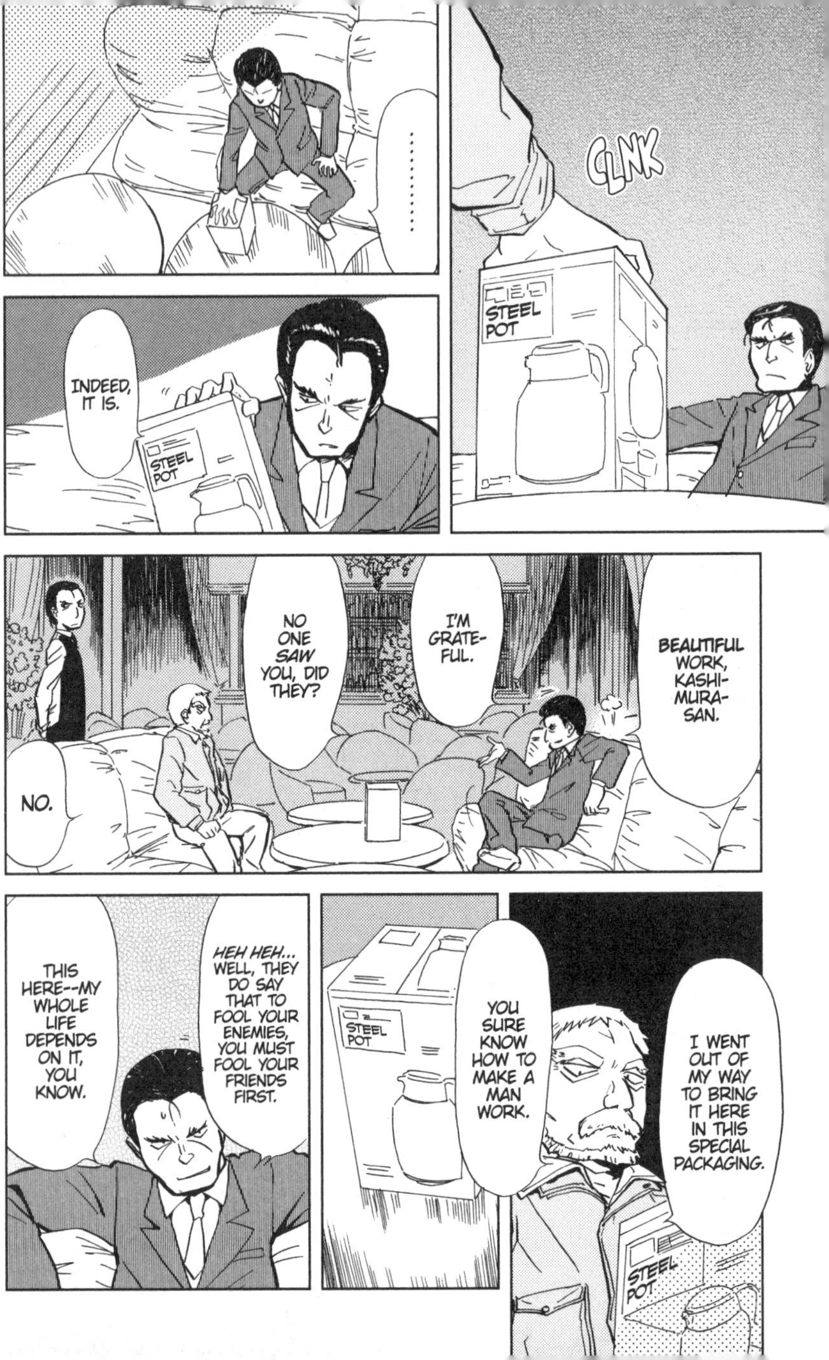
CLNK
STEEL POT
......
INDEED, IT IS.
STEEL POT
BEAUTIFUL WORK, KASHIMURA-SAN.
I'M GRATEFUL.
NO ONE SAW YOU, DID THEY?
NO.
I WENT OUT OF MY WAY TO BRING IT HERE IN THIS SPECIAL PACKAGING.
STEEL POT
YOU SURE KNOW HOW TO MAKE A MAN WORK.
STEEL POT
HEH HEH... WELL, THEY DO SAY THAT TO FOOL YOUR ENEMIES, YOU MUST FOOL YOUR FRIENDS FIRST.
THIS HERE--MY WHOLE LIFE DEPENDS ON IT, YOU KNOW.

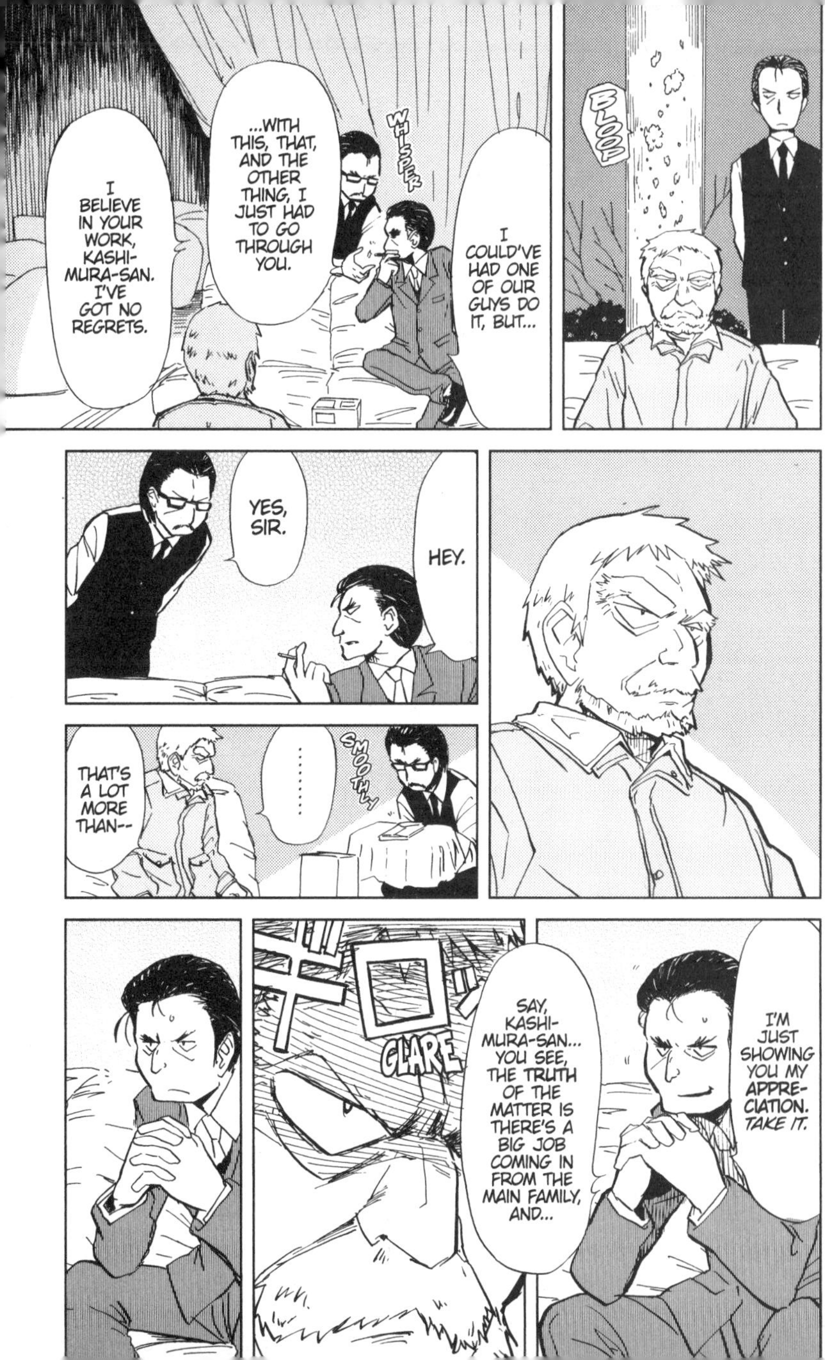
BLOOP
I COULD'VE HAD ONE OF OUR GUYS DO IT, BUT...
WHISPER
...WITH THIS, THAT, AND THE OTHER THING, I JUST HAD TO GO THROUGH YOU.
I BELIEVE IN YOUR WORK, KASHIMURA-SAN. I'VE GOT NO REGRETS.
HEY.
YES, SIR.
SMOOTH
......
THAT'S A LOT MORE THAN--
I'M JUST SHOWING YOU MY APPRECIATION. *TAKE IT.*
SAY, KASHIMURA-SAN... YOU SEE, THE TRUTH OF THE MATTER IS THERE'S A BIG JOB COMING IN FROM THE MAIN FAMILY, AND...
GLARE

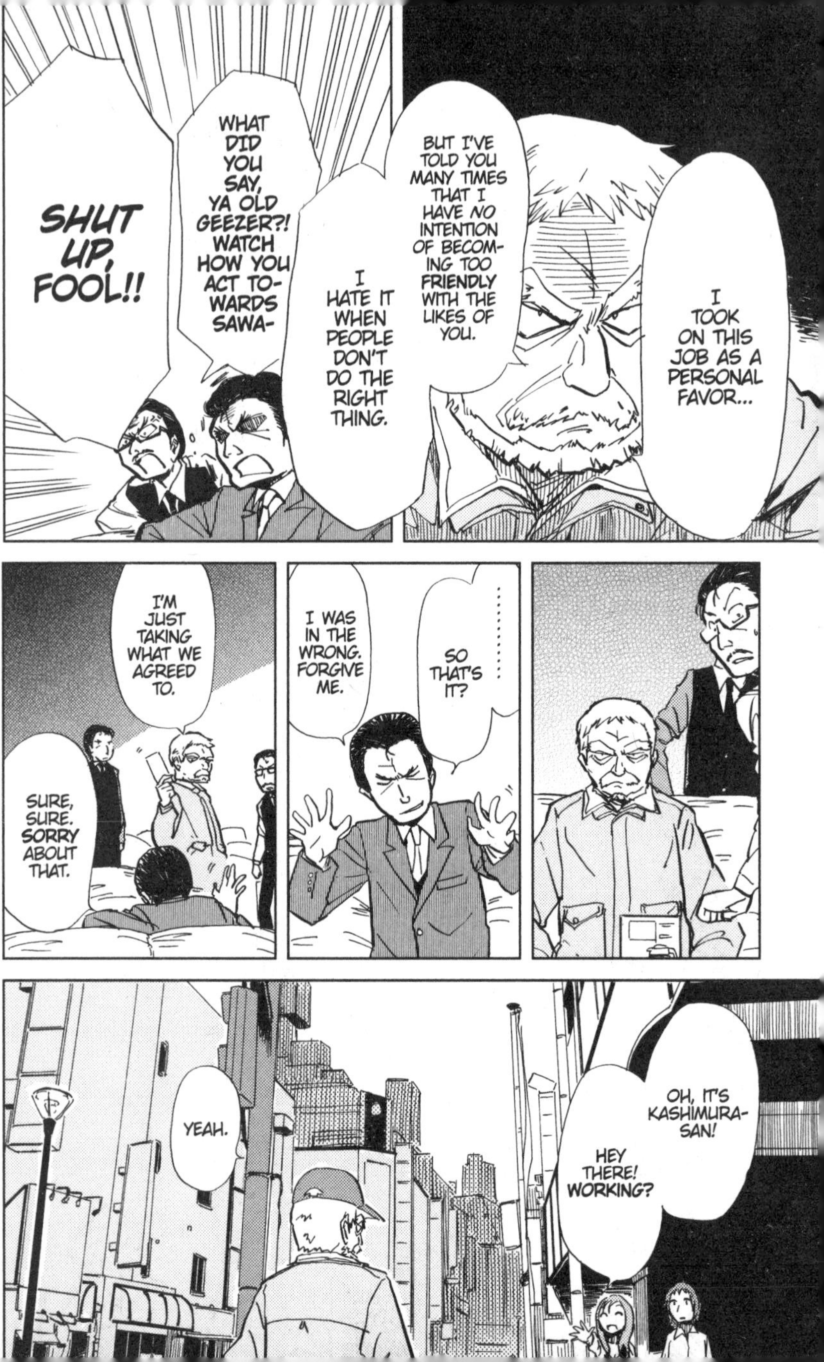
I TOOK ON THIS JOB AS A PERSONAL FAVOR...
BUT I'VE TOLD YOU MANY TIMES THAT I HAVE NO INTENTION OF BECOMING TOO FRIENDLY WITH THE LIKES OF YOU.
I HATE IT WHEN PEOPLE DON'T DO THE RIGHT THING.
WHAT DID YOU SAY, YA OLD GEEZER?! WATCH HOW YOU ACT TOWARDS SAWA-
SHUT UP, FOOL!!
......
SO THAT'S IT?
I WAS IN THE WRONG. FORGIVE ME.
I'M JUST TAKING WHAT WE AGREED TO.
SURE, SURE. SORRY ABOUT THAT.
OH, IT'S KASHIMURA-SAN!
HEY THERE! WORKING?
YEAH.

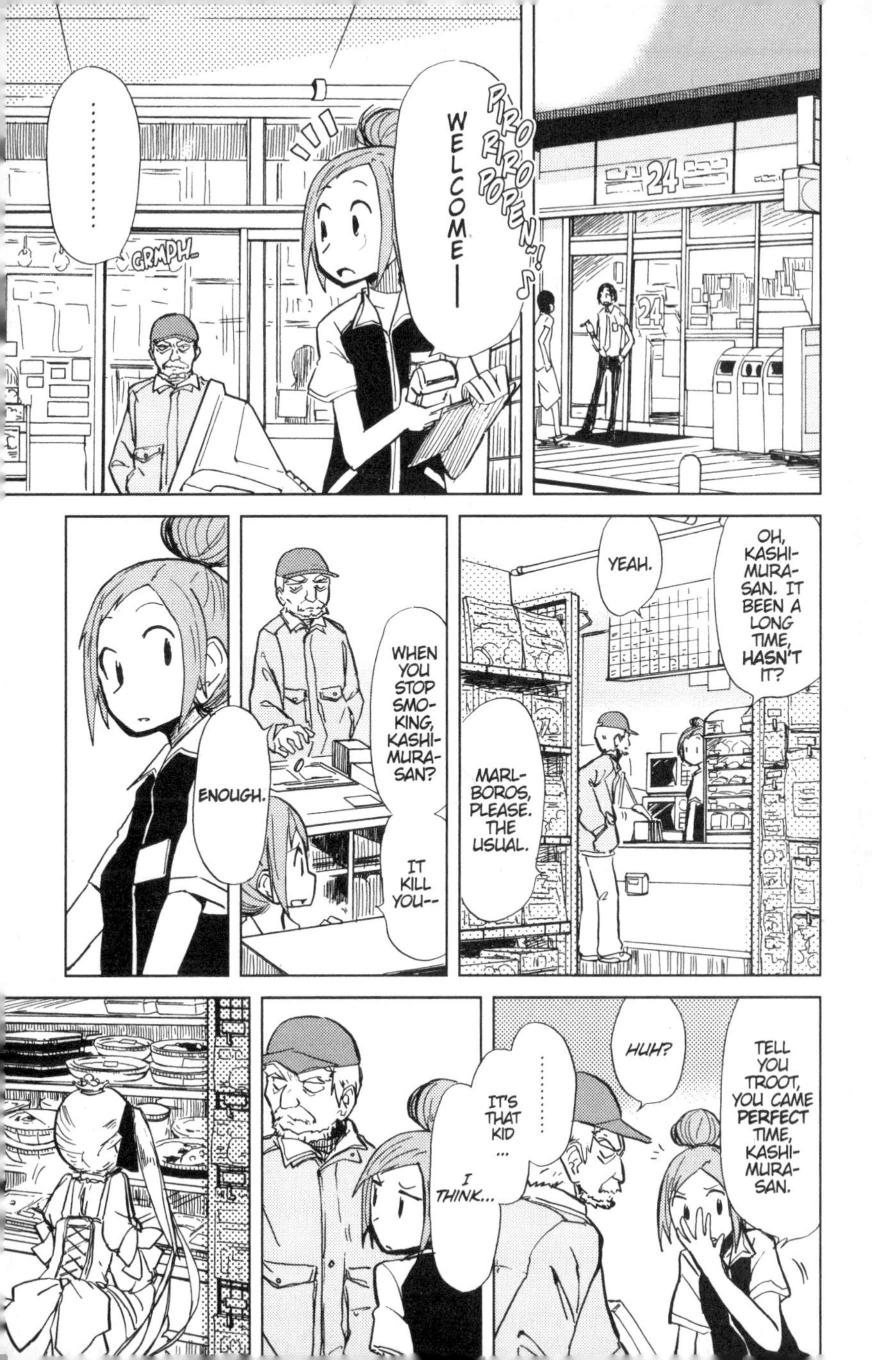
PIRO RIRO POPEN~!♪
WELCOME—
......
GRMPH...
OH, KASHIMURA-SAN. IT BEEN A LONG TIME, HASN'T IT?
YEAH.
MARLBOROS, PLEASE. THE USUAL.
WHEN YOU STOP SMOKING, KASHIMURA-SAN?
IT KILL YOU--
ENOUGH.
TELL YOU TROOT, YOU CAME PERFECT TIME, KASHIMURA-SAN.
HUH?
......
IT'S THAT KID ...
I THINK...

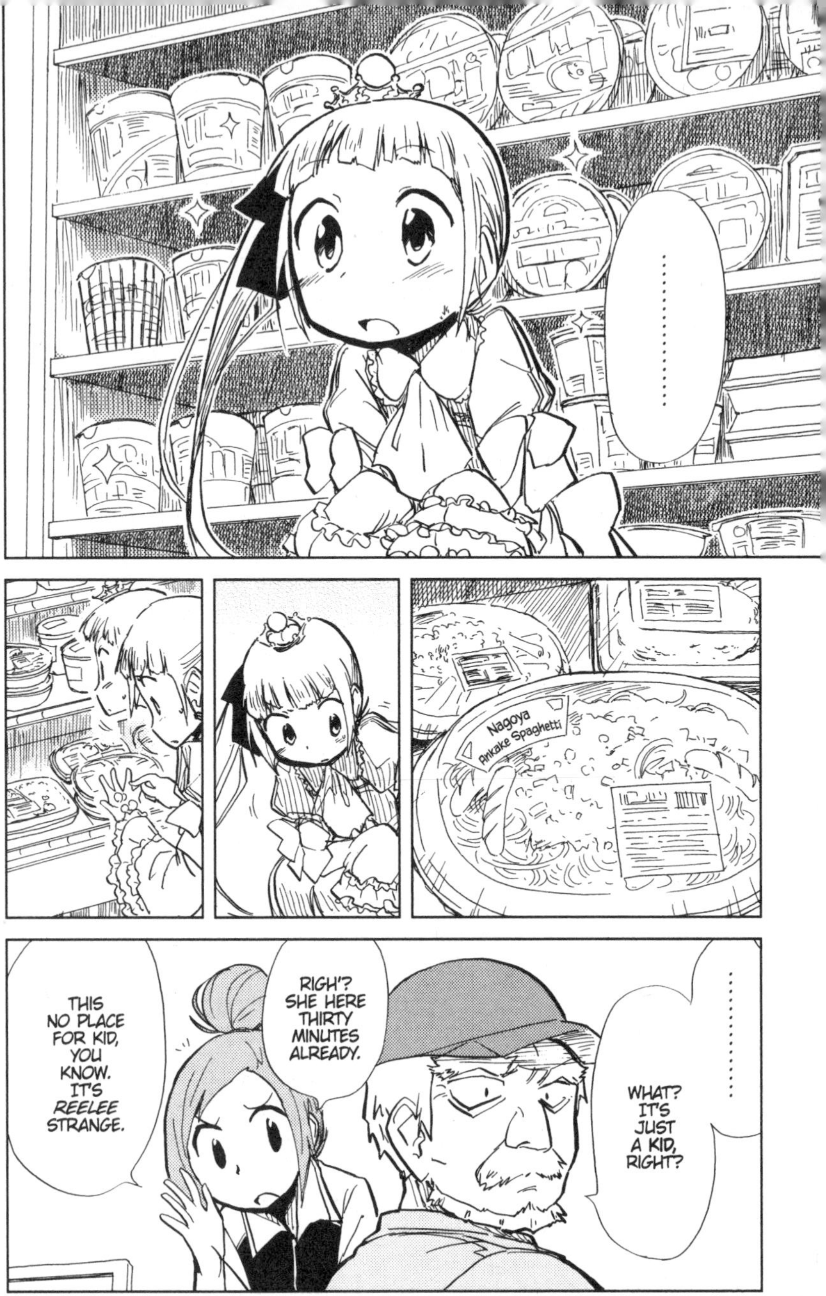
……
Nagoya Ankake Spaghetti
……
WHAT? IT'S JUST A KID, RIGHT?
RIGH'? SHE HERE THIRTY MINUTES ALREADY.
THIS NO PLACE FOR KID, YOU KNOW. IT'S *REELEE* STRANGE.

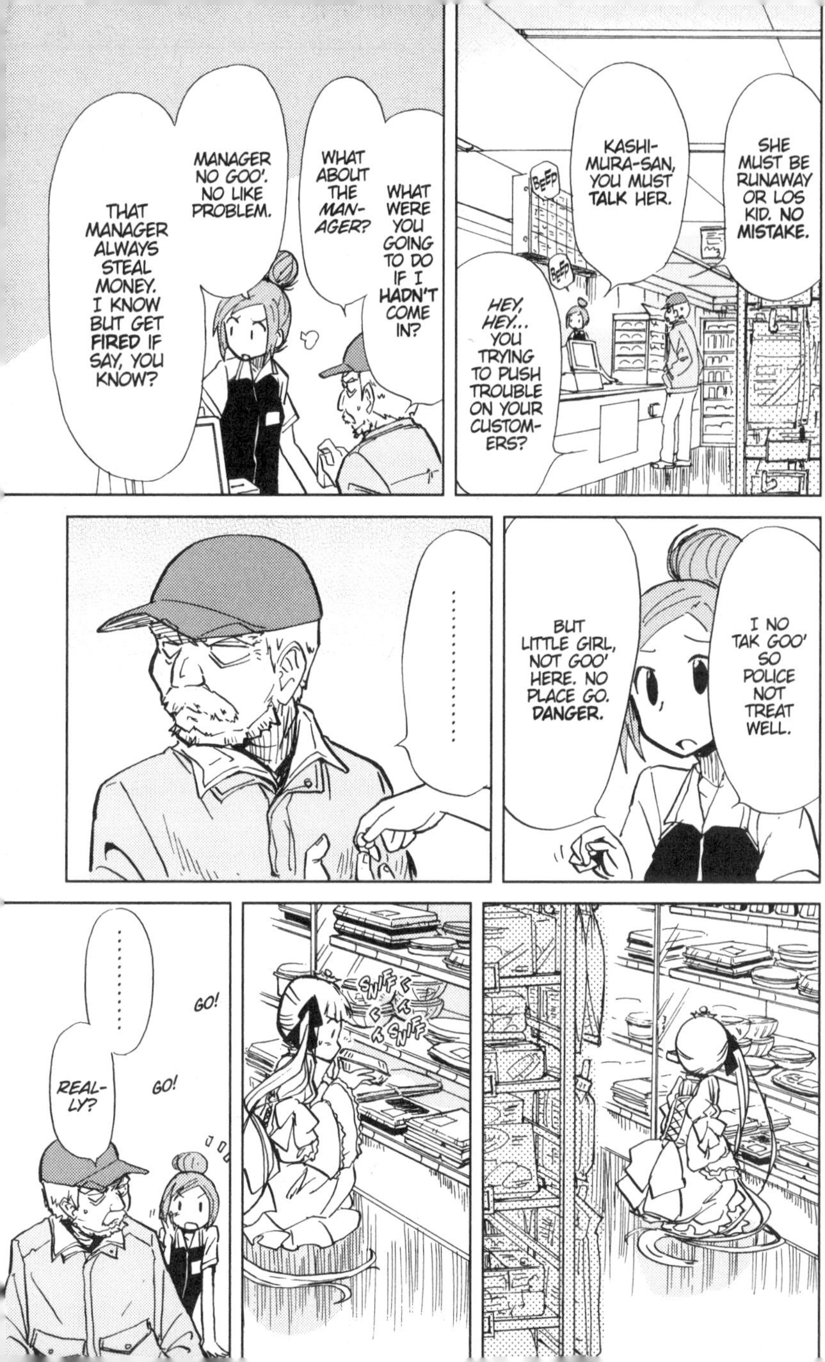

SHE MUST BE RUNAWAY OR LOS KID. NO MISTAKE.
KASHI-MURA-SAN, YOU MUST TALK HER.
BEEP
BEEP
HEY, HEY... YOU TRYING TO PUSH TROUBLE ON YOUR CUSTOM-ERS?
WHAT WERE YOU GOING TO DO IF I HADN'T COME IN?
WHAT ABOUT THE MAN-AGER?
MANAGER NO GOO'. NO LIKE PROBLEM.
THAT MANAGER ALWAYS STEAL MONEY. I KNOW BUT GET FIRED IF SAY, YOU KNOW?
I NO TAK GOO' SO POLICE NOT TREAT WELL.
BUT LITTLE GIRL, NOT GOO' HERE. NO PLACE GO. DANGER.
......
SNIFF
SNIFF
......
GO!
GO!
REAL-LY?

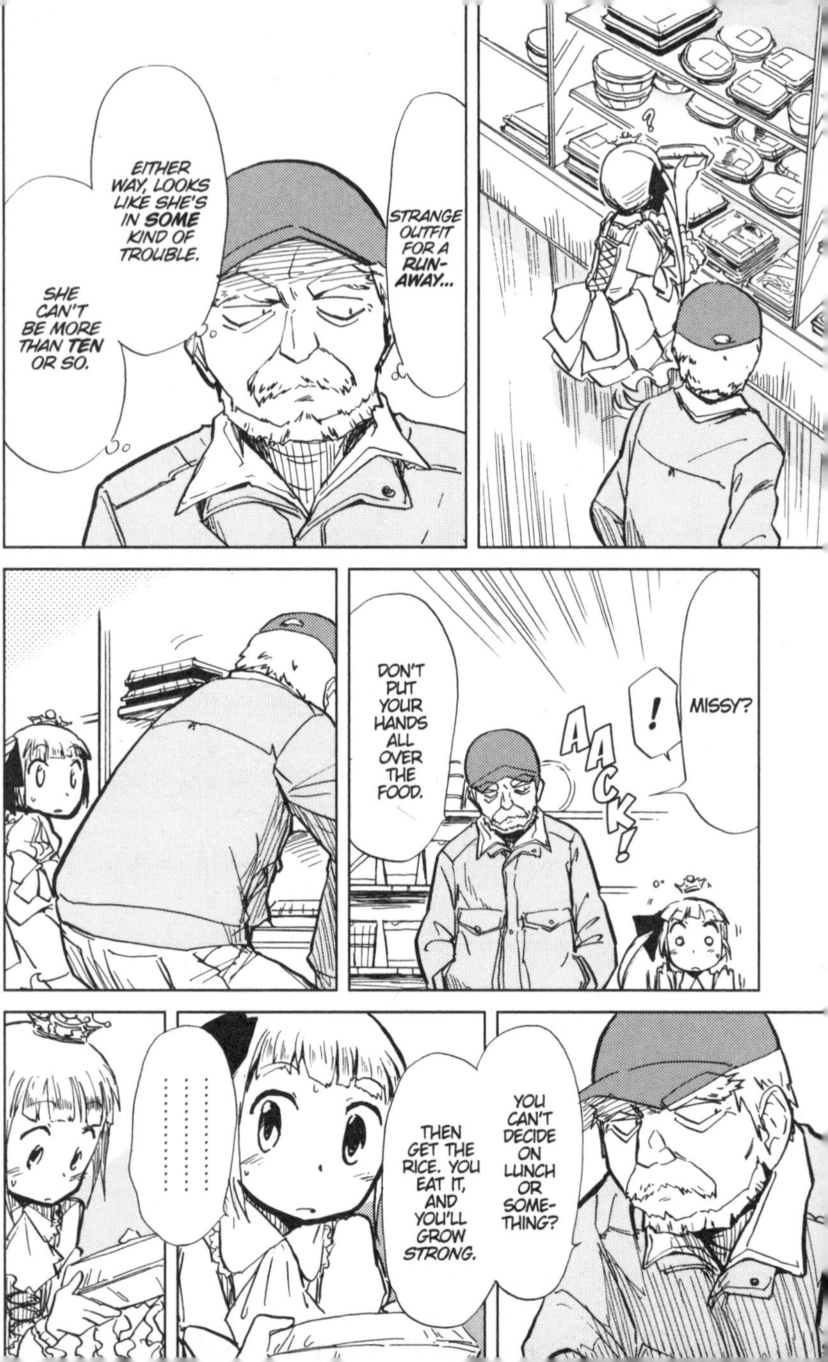
?
STRANGE OUTFIT FOR A RUN-AWAY...
EITHER WAY, LOOKS LIKE SHE'S IN **SOME** KIND OF TROUBLE.
SHE CAN'T BE MORE THAN **TEN** OR SO.
MISSY?
!
AACK!
DON'T PUT YOUR HANDS ALL OVER THE FOOD.
YOU CAN'T DECIDE ON LUNCH OR SOME-THING?
THEN GET THE RICE. YOU EAT IT, AND YOU'LL GROW STRONG.
......

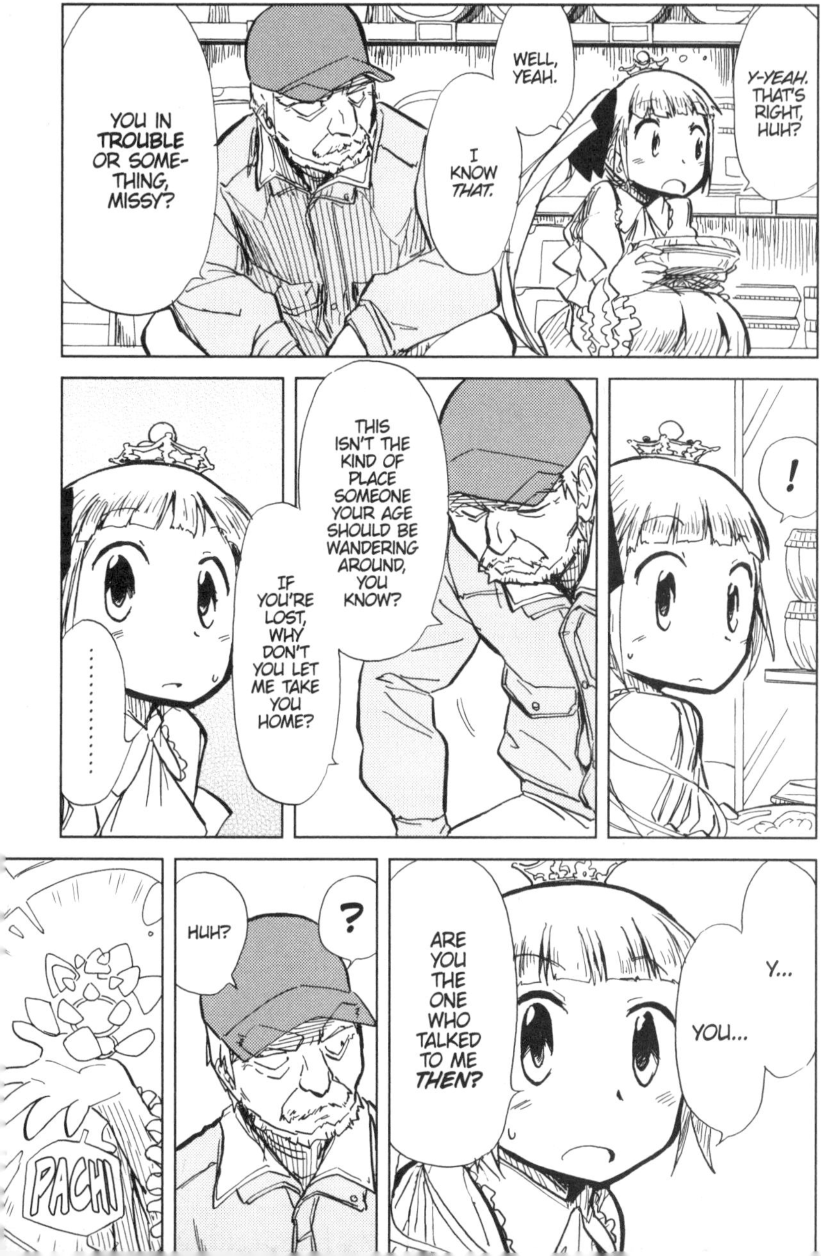
Y-YEAH. THAT'S RIGHT, HUH?
WELL, YEAH.
I KNOW *THAT.*
YOU IN TROUBLE OR SOME-THING, MISSY?
!
THIS ISN'T THE KIND OF PLACE SOMEONE YOUR AGE SHOULD BE WANDERING AROUND, YOU KNOW?
IF YOU'RE LOST, WHY DON'T YOU LET ME TAKE YOU HOME?
......
Y...
YOU...
ARE YOU THE ONE WHO TALKED TO ME ***THEN?***
?
HUH?
PACHI

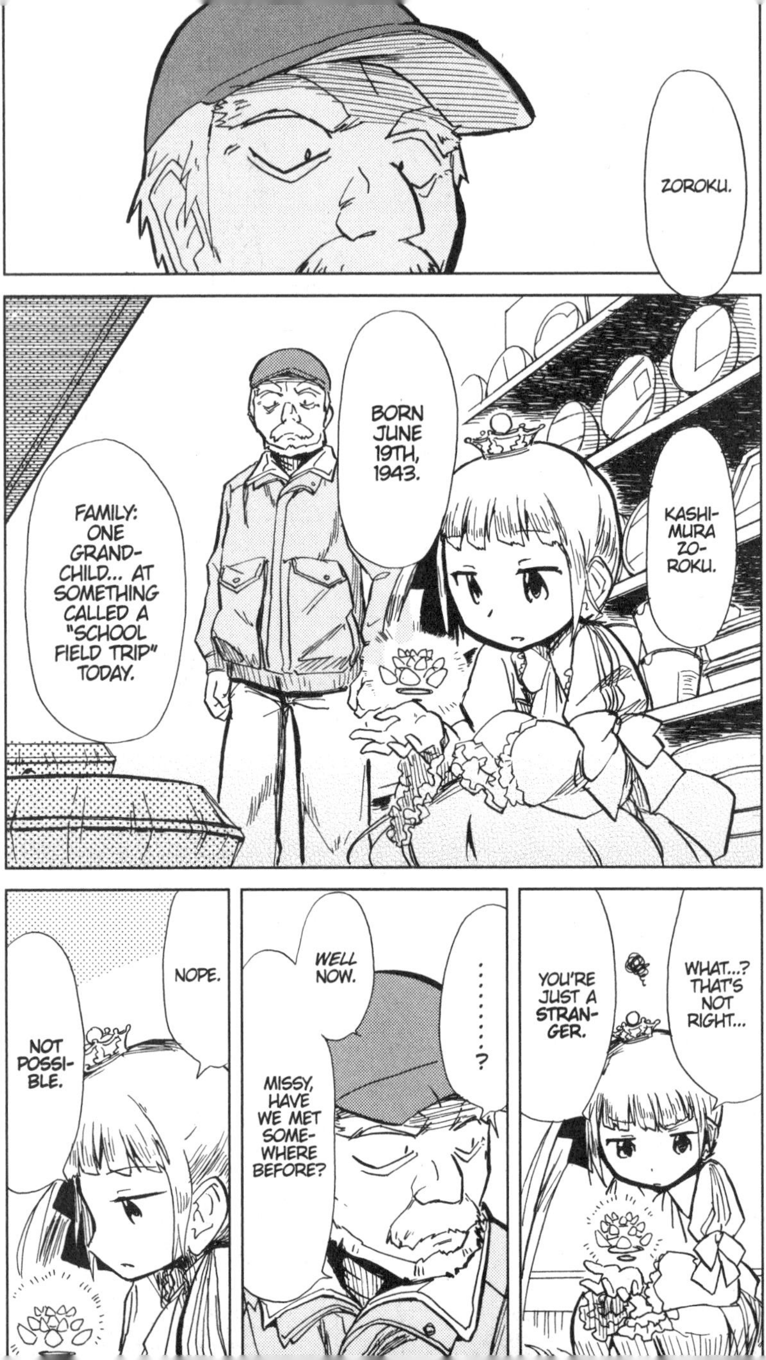
ZOROKU.
KASHIMURA ZOROKU.
BORN JUNE 19TH, 1943.
FAMILY: ONE GRANDCHILD... AT SOMETHING CALLED A "SCHOOL FIELD TRIP" TODAY.
WHAT...? THAT'S NOT RIGHT...
YOU'RE JUST A STRANGER.
......?
WELL NOW.
MISSY, HAVE WE MET SOMEWHERE BEFORE?
NOPE.
NOT POSSIBLE.

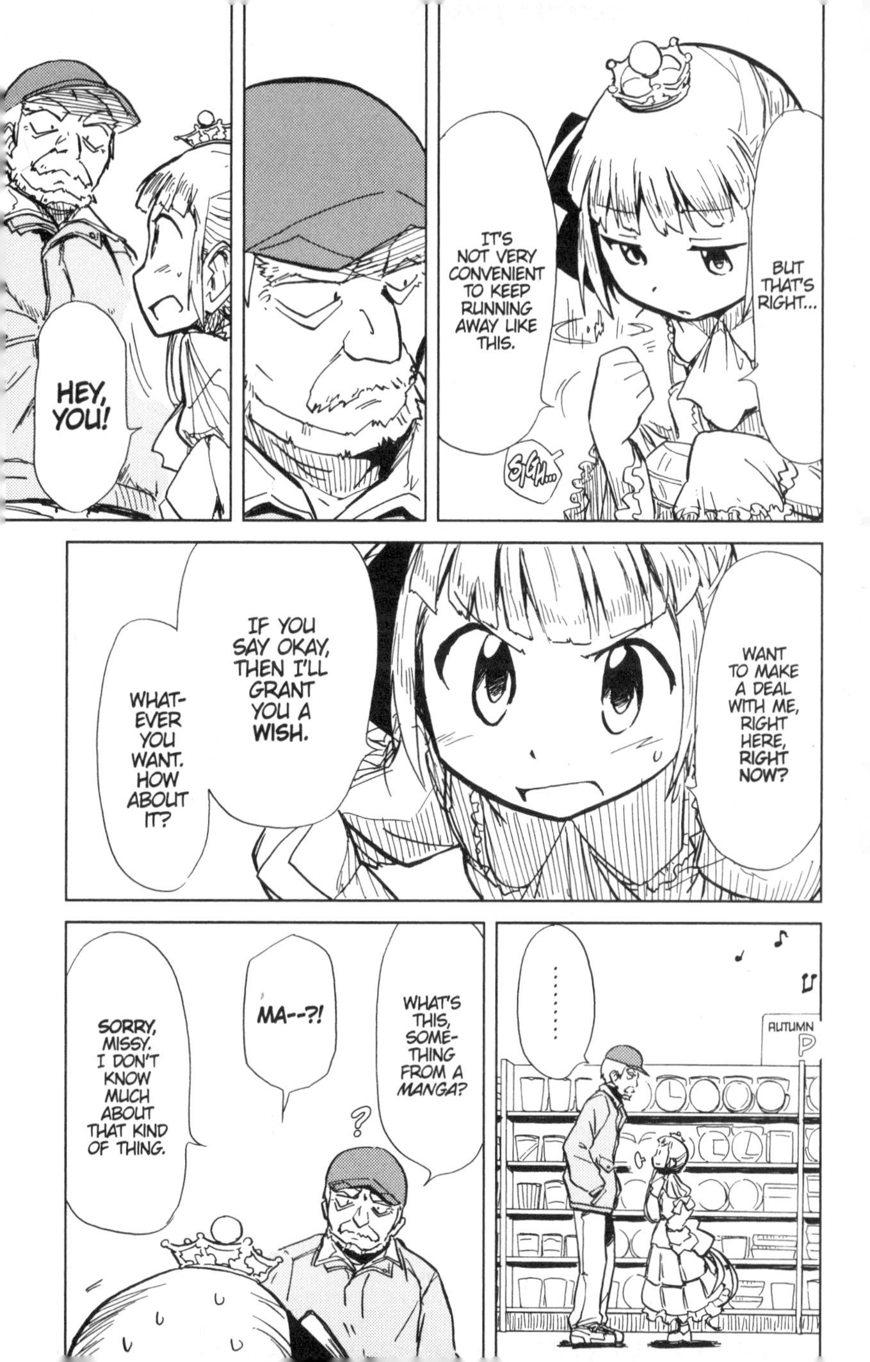
BUT THAT'S RIGHT...
IT'S NOT VERY CONVENIENT TO KEEP RUNNING AWAY LIKE THIS.
SIGH...
HEY, YOU!
WANT TO MAKE A DEAL WITH ME, RIGHT HERE, RIGHT NOW?
IF YOU SAY OKAY, THEN I'LL GRANT YOU A WISH.
WHAT-EVER YOU WANT. HOW ABOUT IT?
....
AUTUMN
WHAT'S THIS, SOME-THING FROM A MANGA?
MA--?!
SORRY, MISSY. I DON'T KNOW MUCH ABOUT THAT KIND OF THING.

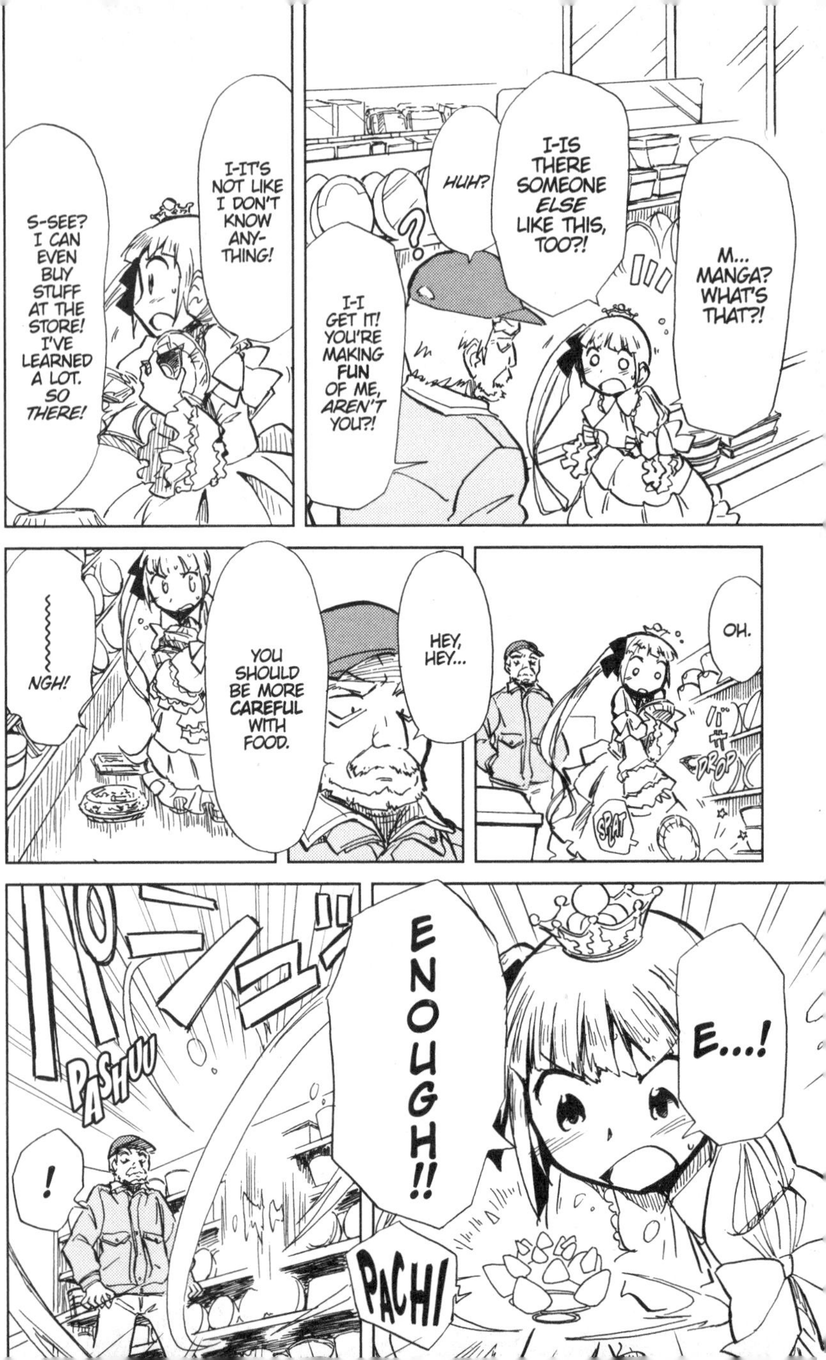
M... MANGA? WHAT'S THAT?!
I-IS THERE SOMEONE ELSE LIKE THIS, TOO?!
HUH?
I-I GET IT! YOU'RE MAKING FUN OF ME, AREN'T YOU?!
I-IT'S NOT LIKE I DON'T KNOW ANYTHING!
S-SEE? I CAN EVEN BUY STUFF AT THE STORE! I'VE LEARNED A LOT. SO THERE!
OH.
DROP
SPLAT
HEY, HEY...
YOU SHOULD BE MORE CAREFUL WITH FOOD.
NGH!
E...!
ENOUGH!!
PACHI
PASHUU
!

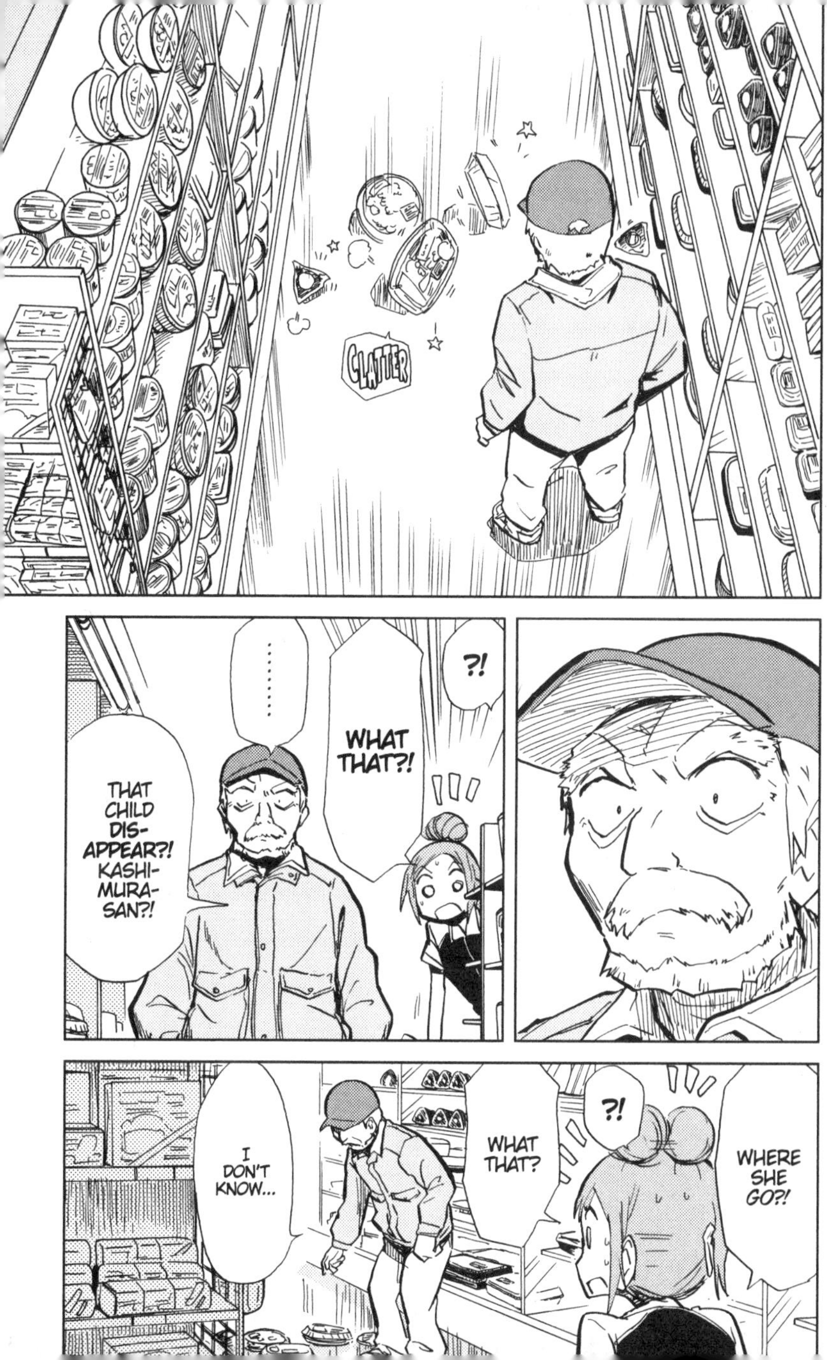
CLATTER
?!
WHAT THAT?!
......
THAT CHILD DIS-APPEAR?! KASHIMURA-SAN?!
WHERE SHE GO?!
?!
WHAT THAT?
I DON'T KNOW...

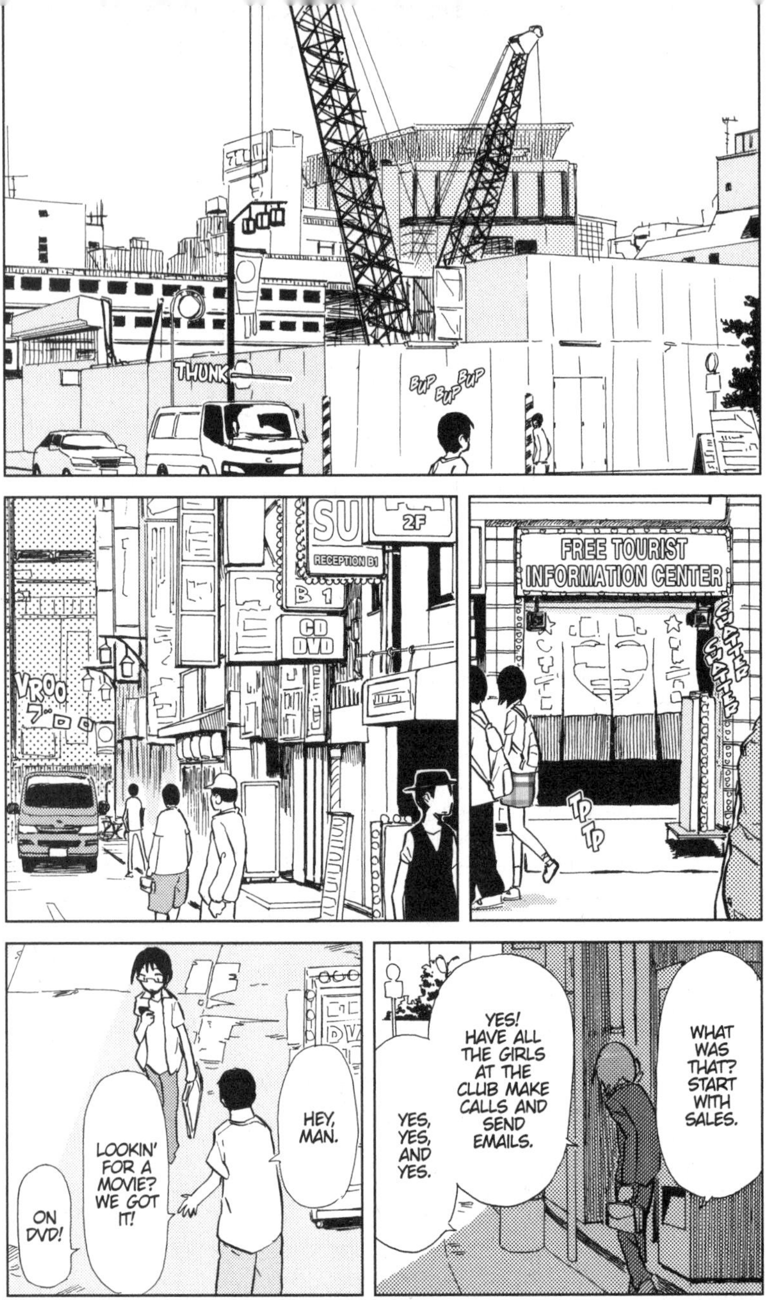
THUNK
BUP BUP BUP
FREE TOURIST INFORMATION CENTER
CLATTER CLATTER
TP TP
2F
SU
RECEPTION B1
B1
CD DVD
VROO
WHAT WAS THAT? START WITH SALES.
YES! HAVE ALL THE GIRLS AT THE CLUB MAKE CALLS AND SEND EMAILS.
YES, YES, AND YES.
HEY, MAN.
LOOKIN' FOR A MOVIE? WE GOT IT!
ON DVD!

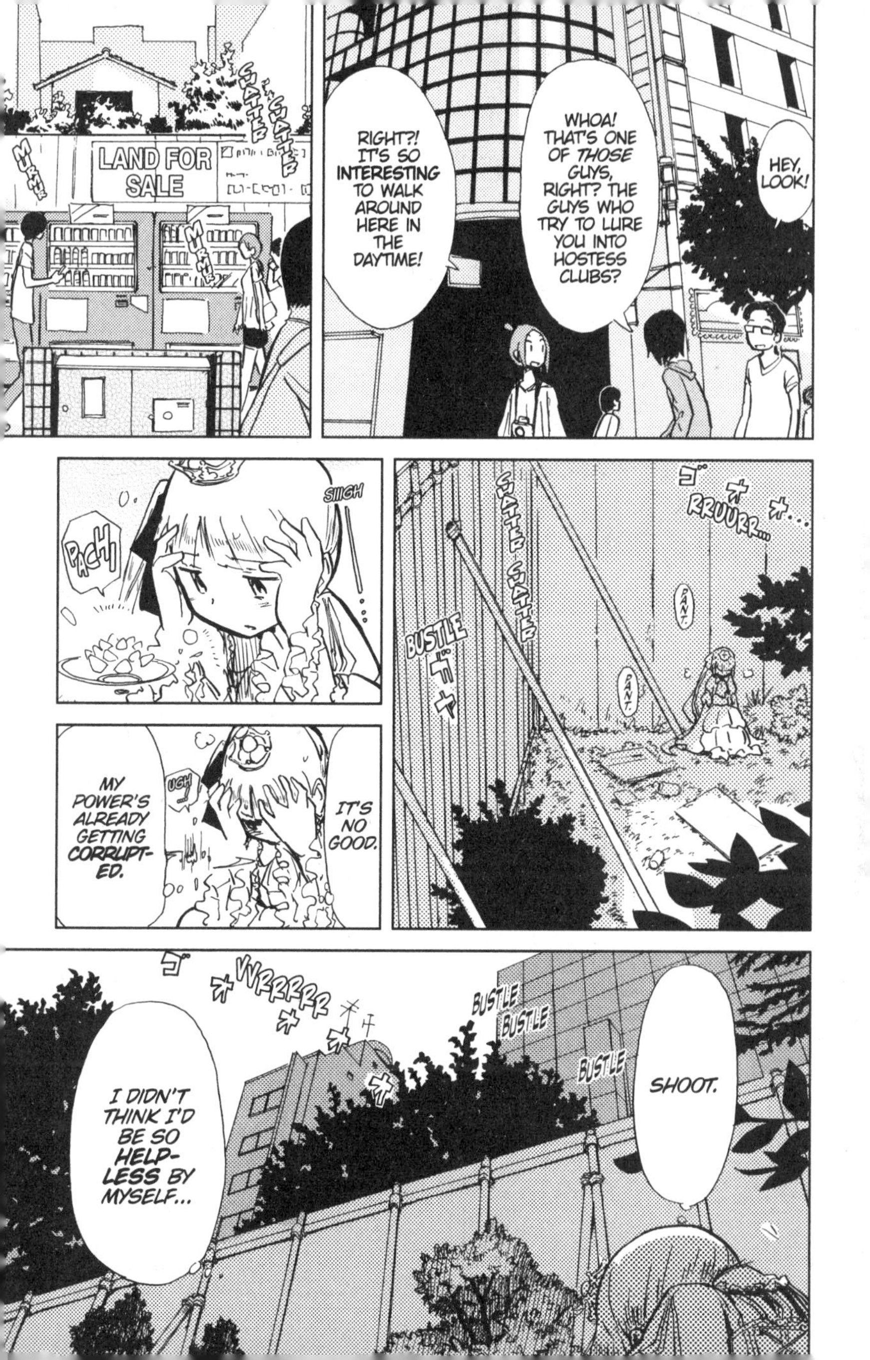
HEY, LOOK!
WHOA! THAT'S ONE OF THOSE GUYS, RIGHT? THE GUYS WHO TRY TO LURE YOU INTO HOSTESS CLUBS?
RIGHT?! IT'S SO INTERESTING TO WALK AROUND HERE IN THE DAYTIME!
CHATTER CHATTER
LAND FOR SALE
MURMUR
MURMUR
ゴオオ… RRUURR...
PANT.
PANT.
CHATTER CHATTER
BUSTLE ガヤ
SIIGH
PACHI
IT'S NO GOOD.
UGH...
MY POWER'S ALREADY GETTING CORRUPTED.
SHOOT.
BUSTLE BUSTLE
BUSTLE
ゴオオオ VVRRRRR
I DIDN'T THINK I'D BE SO HELPLESS BY MYSELF...

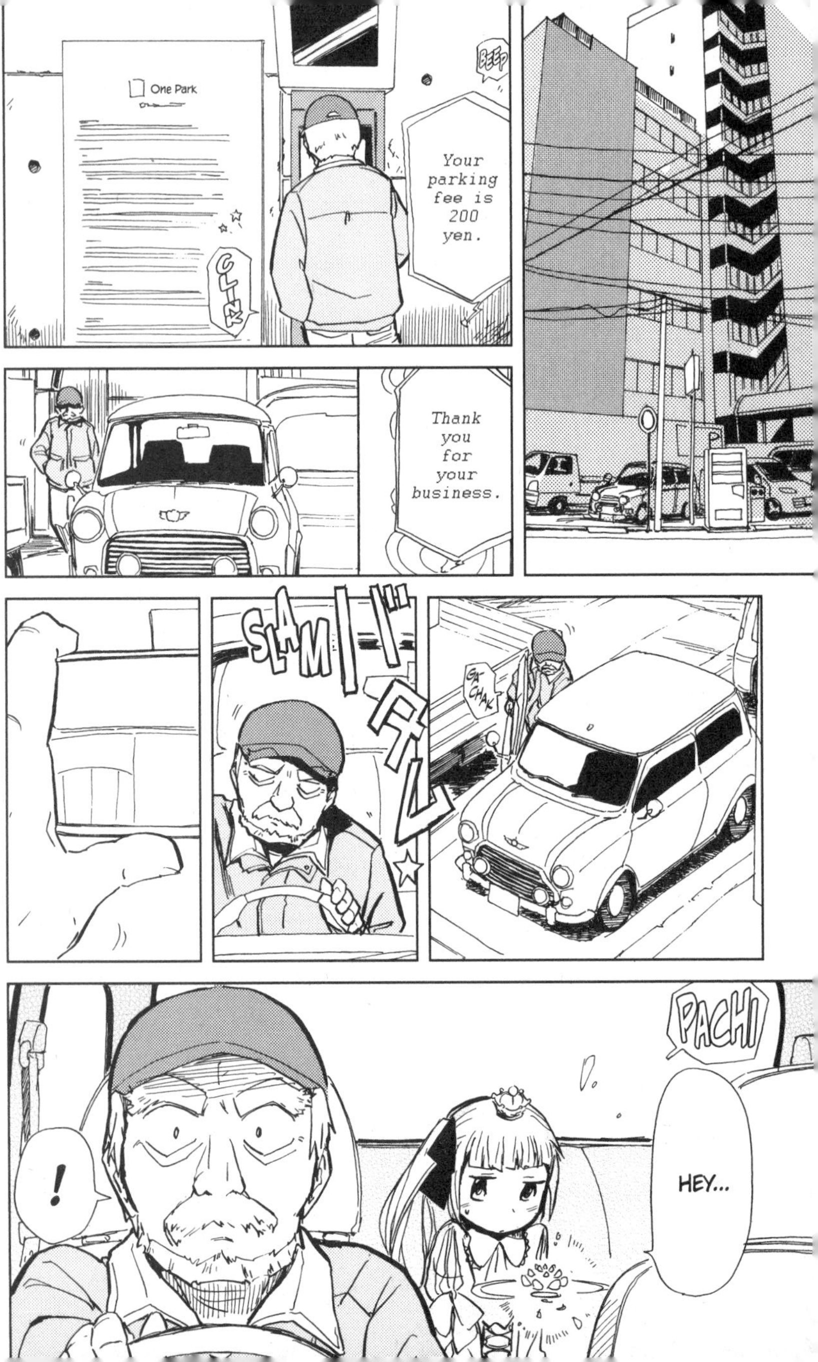
BEEP
Your parking fee is 200 yen.
One Park
CLINK
Thank you for your business.
GACHAK
SLAM
PACHI
HEY...
!

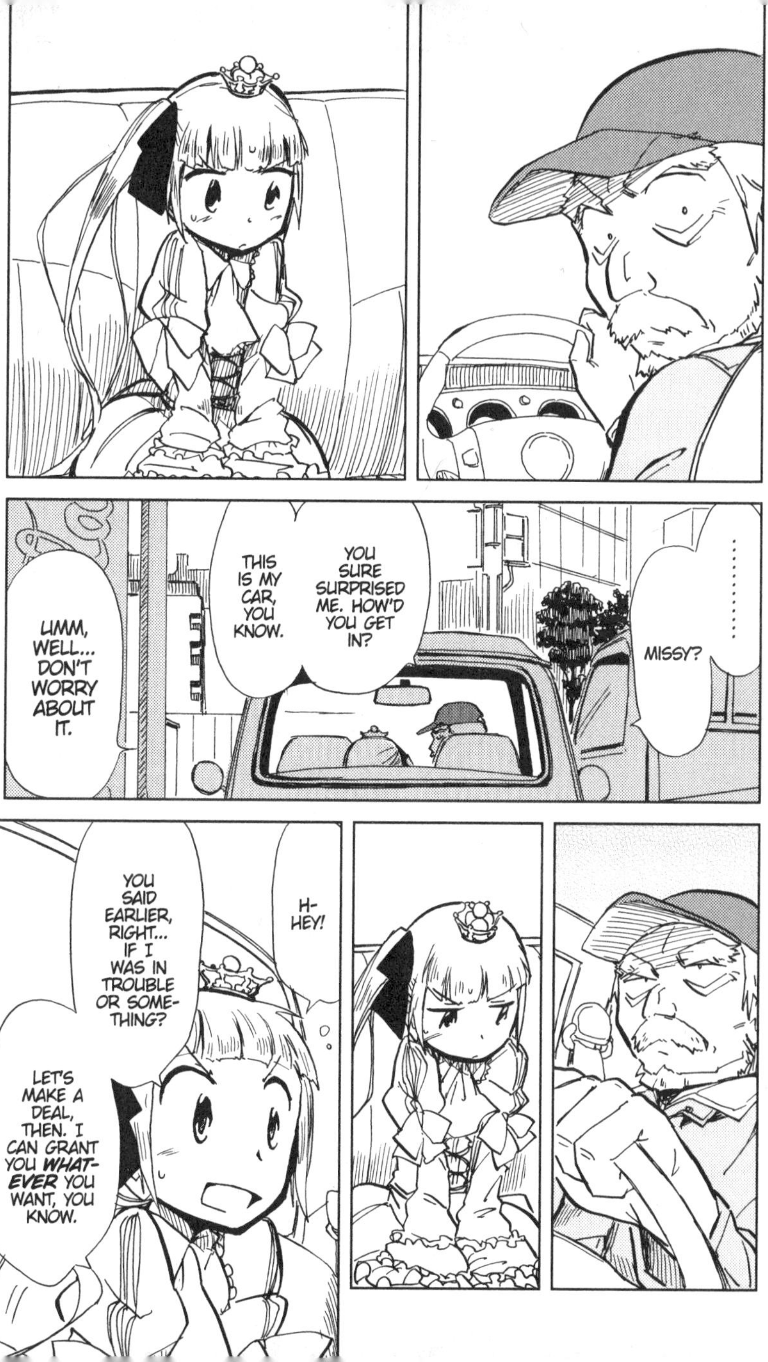
......
MISSY?
YOU SURE SURPRISED ME. HOW'D YOU GET IN?
THIS IS MY CAR, YOU KNOW.
UMM, WELL... DON'T WORRY ABOUT IT.
H-HEY!
YOU SAID EARLIER, RIGHT... IF I WAS IN TROUBLE OR SOME-THING?
LET'S MAKE A DEAL, THEN. I CAN GRANT YOU ***WHAT-EVER*** YOU WANT, YOU KNOW.

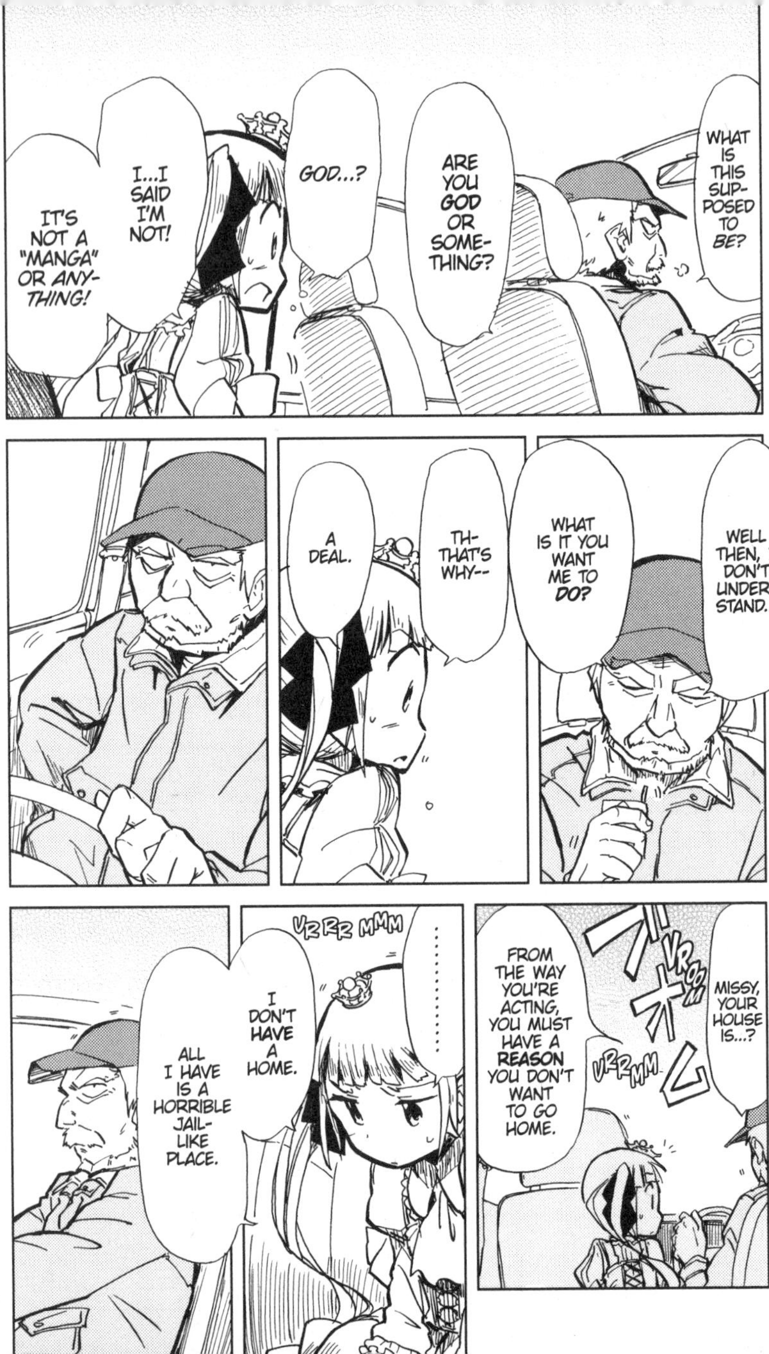
WHAT IS THIS SUPPOSED TO BE?
ARE YOU GOD OR SOMETHING?
GOD...?
I...I SAID I'M NOT!
IT'S NOT A "MANGA" OR ANYTHING!
WELL THEN, I DON'T UNDERSTAND...
WHAT IS IT YOU WANT ME TO DO?
TH-THAT'S WHY--
A DEAL.
MISSY, YOUR HOUSE IS...?
VROOM
FROM THE WAY YOU'RE ACTING, YOU MUST HAVE A REASON YOU DON'T WANT TO GO HOME.
URRMM
URRR MMM
......
I DON'T HAVE A HOME.
ALL I HAVE IS A HORRIBLE JAIL-LIKE PLACE.

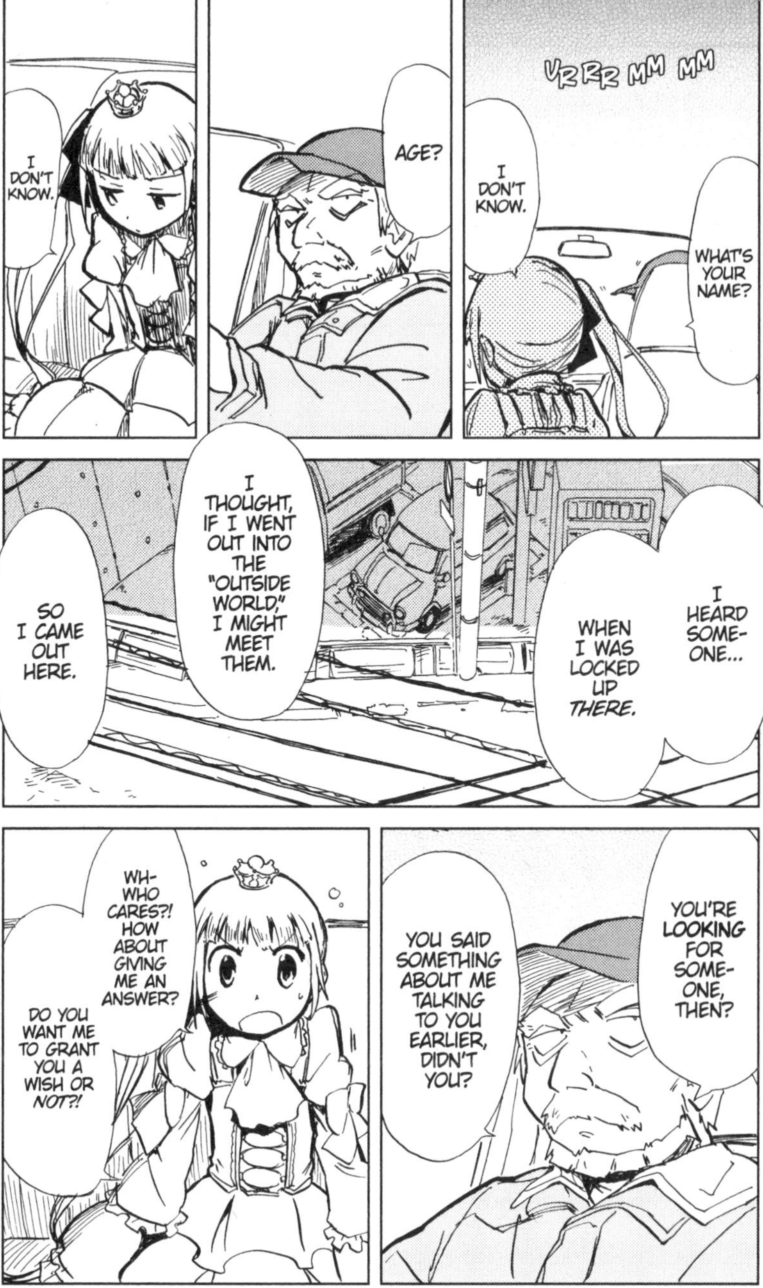
VRRR MM MM
WHAT'S YOUR NAME?
I DON'T KNOW.
AGE?
I DON'T KNOW.
I HEARD SOME-ONE...
WHEN I WAS LOCKED UP *THERE.*
I THOUGHT, IF I WENT OUT INTO THE "OUTSIDE WORLD," I MIGHT MEET THEM.
SO I CAME OUT HERE.
YOU'RE **LOOKING** FOR SOME-ONE, THEN?
YOU SAID SOMETHING ABOUT ME TALKING TO YOU EARLIER, DIDN'T YOU?
WH-WHO CARES?! HOW ABOUT GIVING ME AN ANSWER?
DO YOU WANT ME TO GRANT YOU A WISH OR *NOT?!*

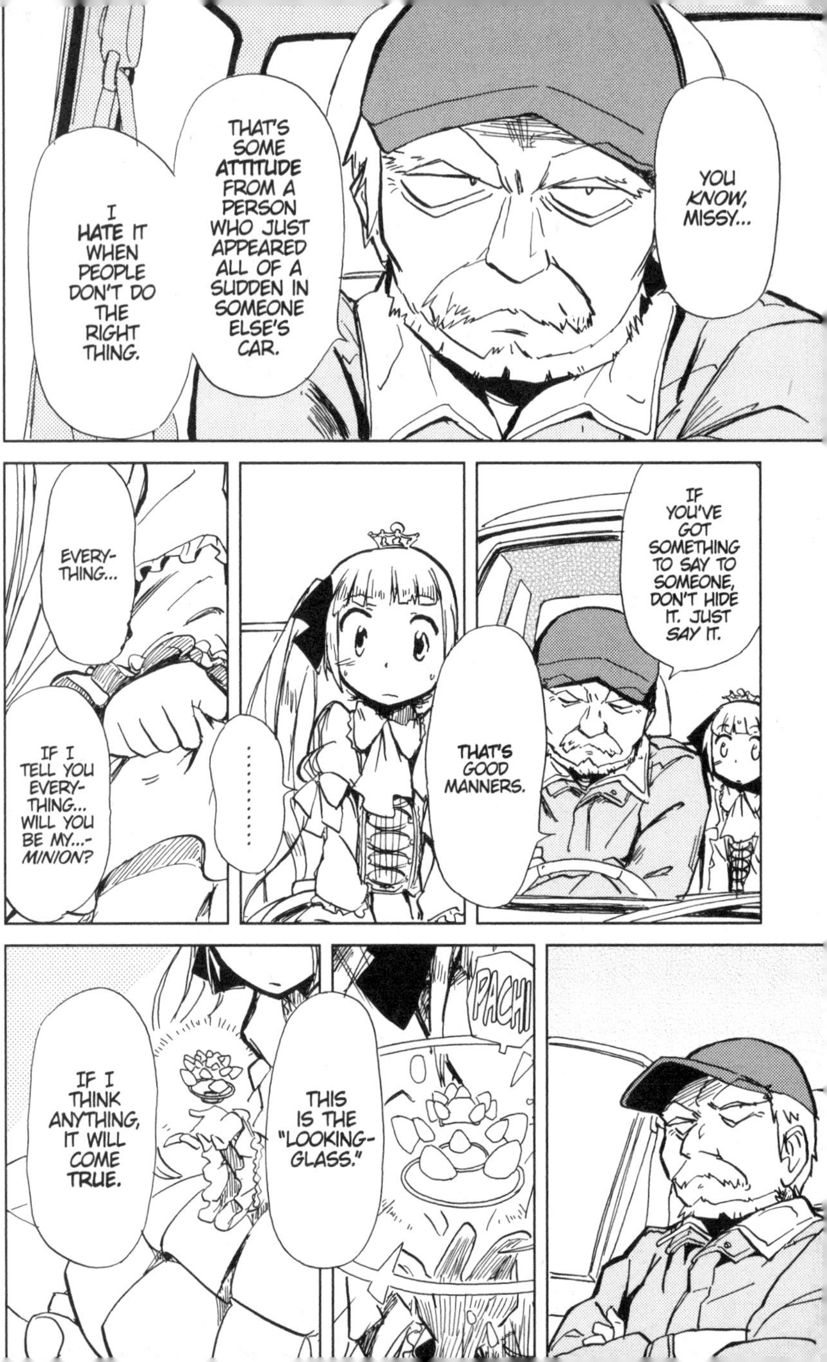
YOU KNOW, MISSY...
THAT'S SOME ATTITUDE FROM A PERSON WHO JUST APPEARED ALL OF A SUDDEN IN SOMEONE ELSE'S CAR.
I HATE IT WHEN PEOPLE DON'T DO THE RIGHT THING.
IF YOU'VE GOT SOMETHING TO SAY TO SOMEONE, DON'T HIDE IT. JUST SAY IT.
THAT'S GOOD MANNERS.
......
EVERY-THING...
IF I TELL YOU EVERY-THING... WILL YOU BE MY...-MINION?
PACHI
THIS IS THE "LOOKING-GLASS."
IF I THINK ANYTHING, IT WILL COME TRUE.

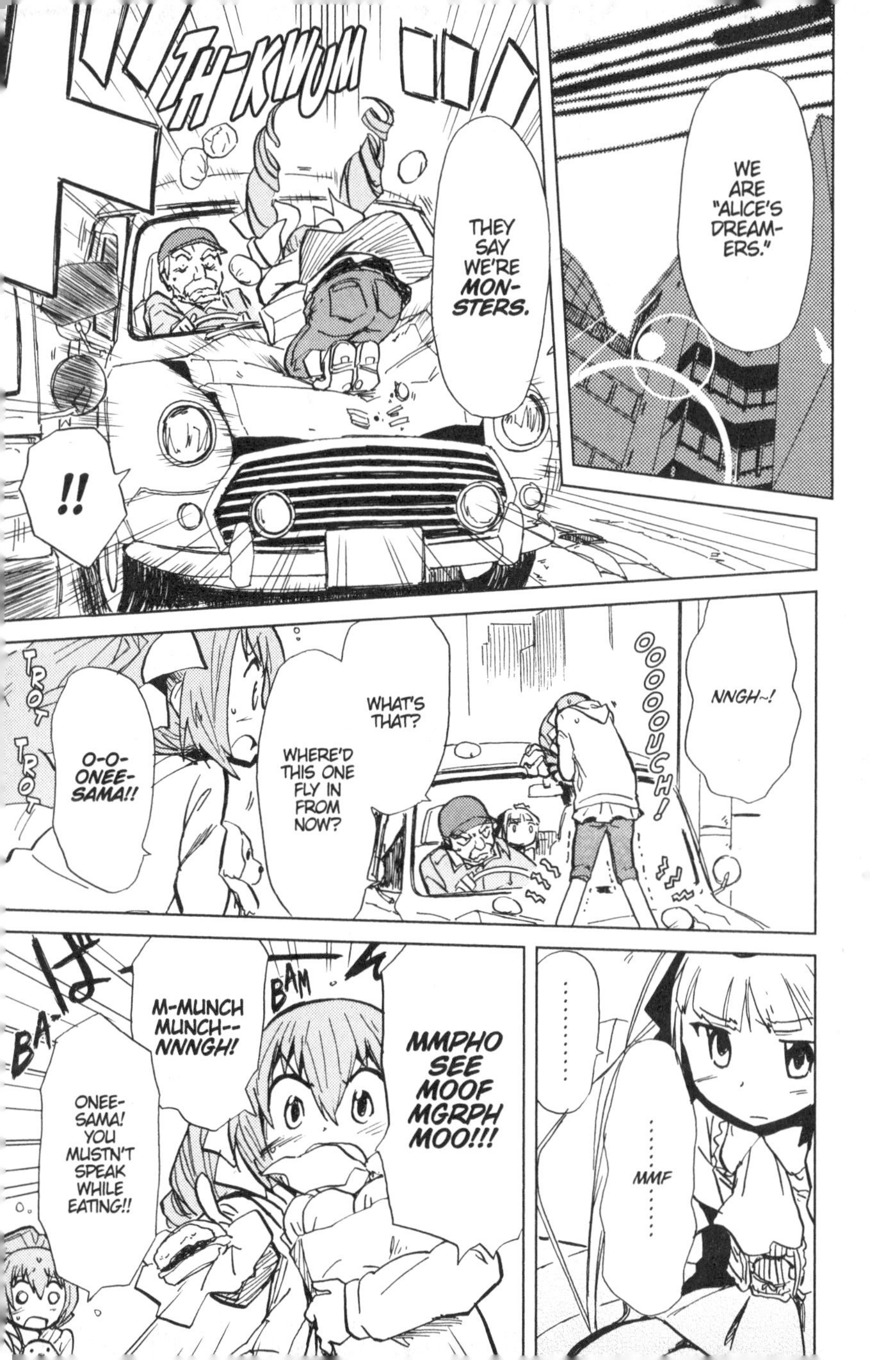
WE ARE "ALICE'S DREAMERS."
THEY SAY WE'RE MONSTERS.
TH-KWUM
!!
NNGH~!
OOOOOOUCH!
WHAT'S THAT?
WHERE'D THIS ONE FLY IN FROM NOW?
O-O-ONEE-SAMA!!
TROT TROT
......
......MMF
BAM
MMPHO SEE MOOF MGRPH MOO!!!
M-MUNCH MUNCH--NNNGH!
BA-
ONEE-SAMA! YOU MUSTN'T SPEAK WHILE EATING!!

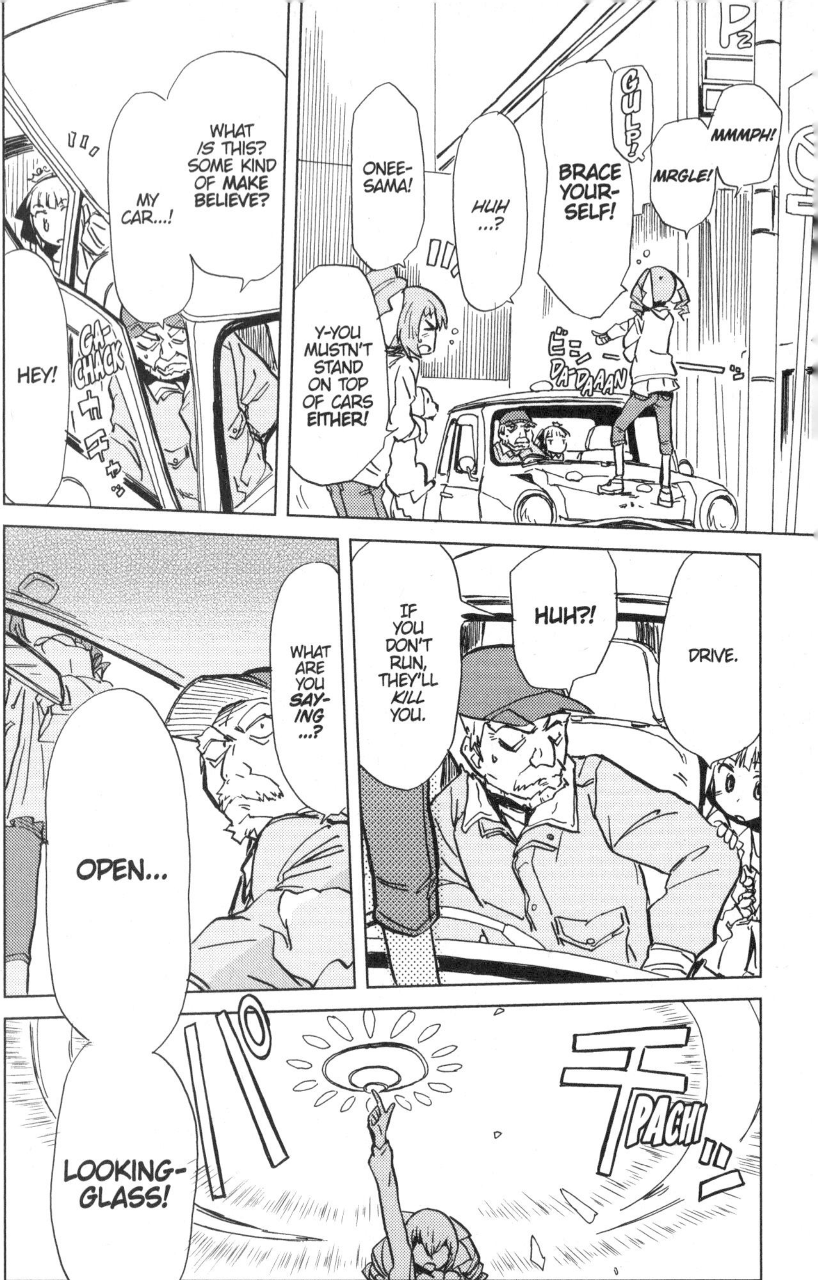
MMMPH!
MRGLE!
GULP!
BRACE YOUR-SELF!
HUH ...?
ONEE-SAMA!
Y-YOU MUSTN'T STAND ON TOP OF CARS EITHER!
DA-DAAN
WHAT IS THIS? SOME KIND OF MAKE BELIEVE?
MY CAR...!
GA-CHACK
HEY!
DRIVE.
HUH?!
IF YOU DON'T RUN, THEY'LL KILL YOU.
WHAT ARE YOU SAY-ING ...?
OPEN...
PACHI
LOOKING-GLASS!

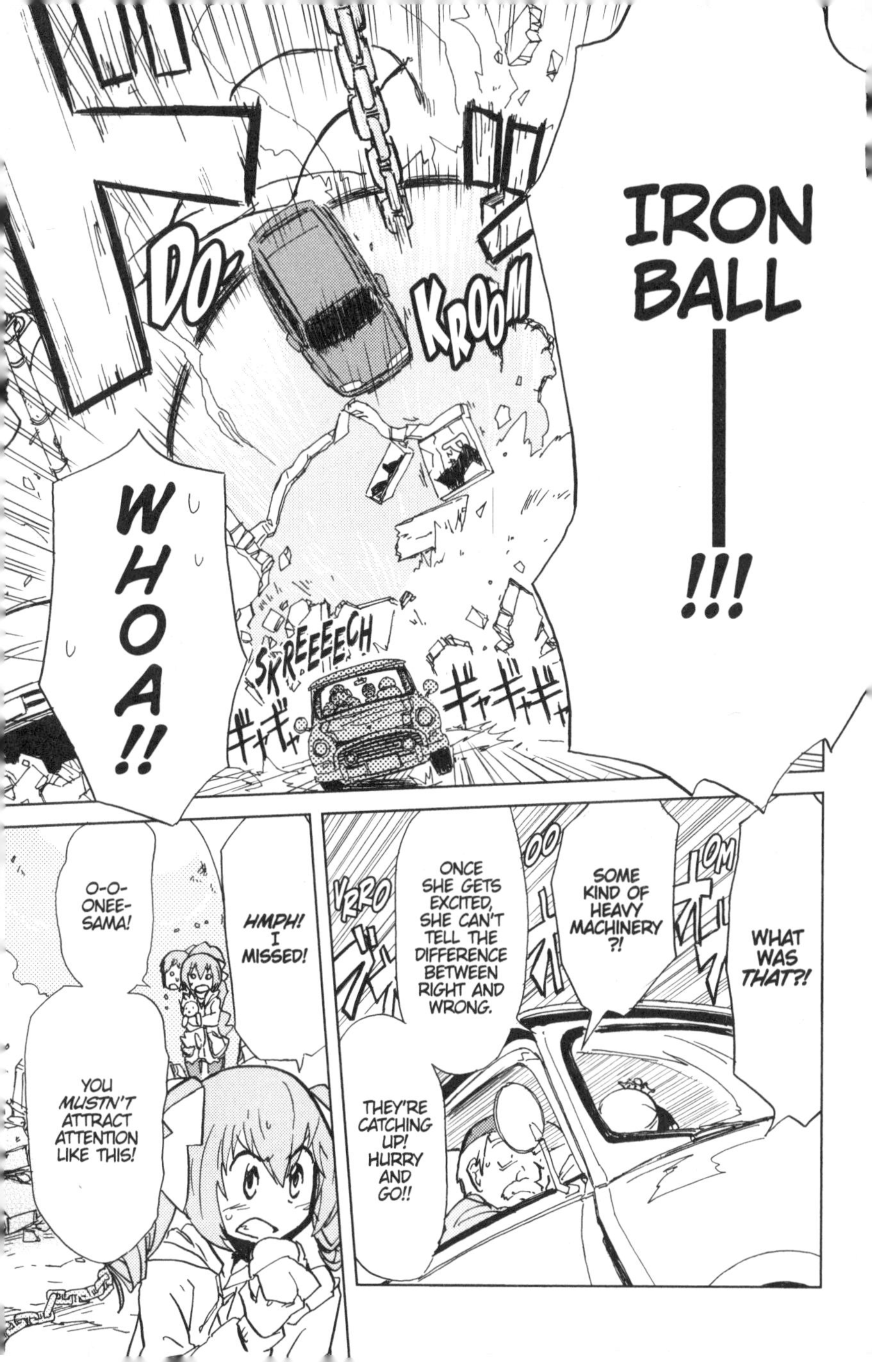
IRON BALL—!!!
KROOM
DO-
WHOA!!
SKREEEECH
WHAT WAS THAT?!
SOME KIND OF HEAVY MACHINERY?!
ONCE SHE GETS EXCITED, SHE CAN'T TELL THE DIFFERENCE BETWEEN RIGHT AND WRONG.
THEY'RE CATCHING UP! HURRY AND GO!!
HMPH! I MISSED!
O-O-ONEE-SAMA!
YOU MUSTN'T ATTRACT ATTENTION LIKE THIS!

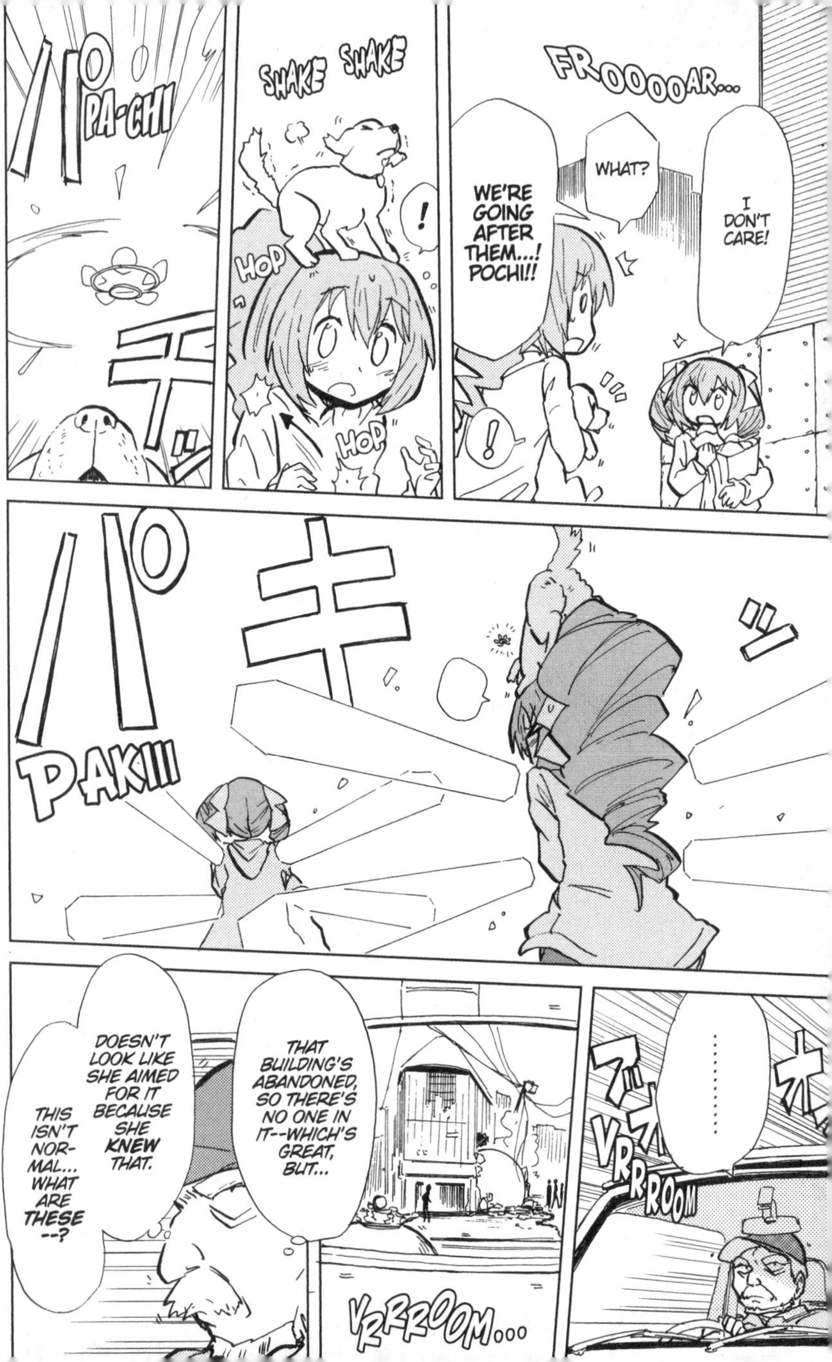
FROOOOAR...
I DON'T CARE!
WHAT?
WE'RE GOING AFTER THEM...! POCHI!!
!
SHAKE SHAKE
!
HOP
HOP
PA-CHI
PAKIII
......
VRRROOM
THAT BUILDING'S ABANDONED, SO THERE'S NO ONE IN IT--WHICH'S GREAT, BUT...
VRRROOM...
DOESN'T LOOK LIKE SHE AIMED FOR IT BECAUSE SHE KNEW THAT.
THIS ISN'T NOR-MAL... WHAT ARE THESE --?

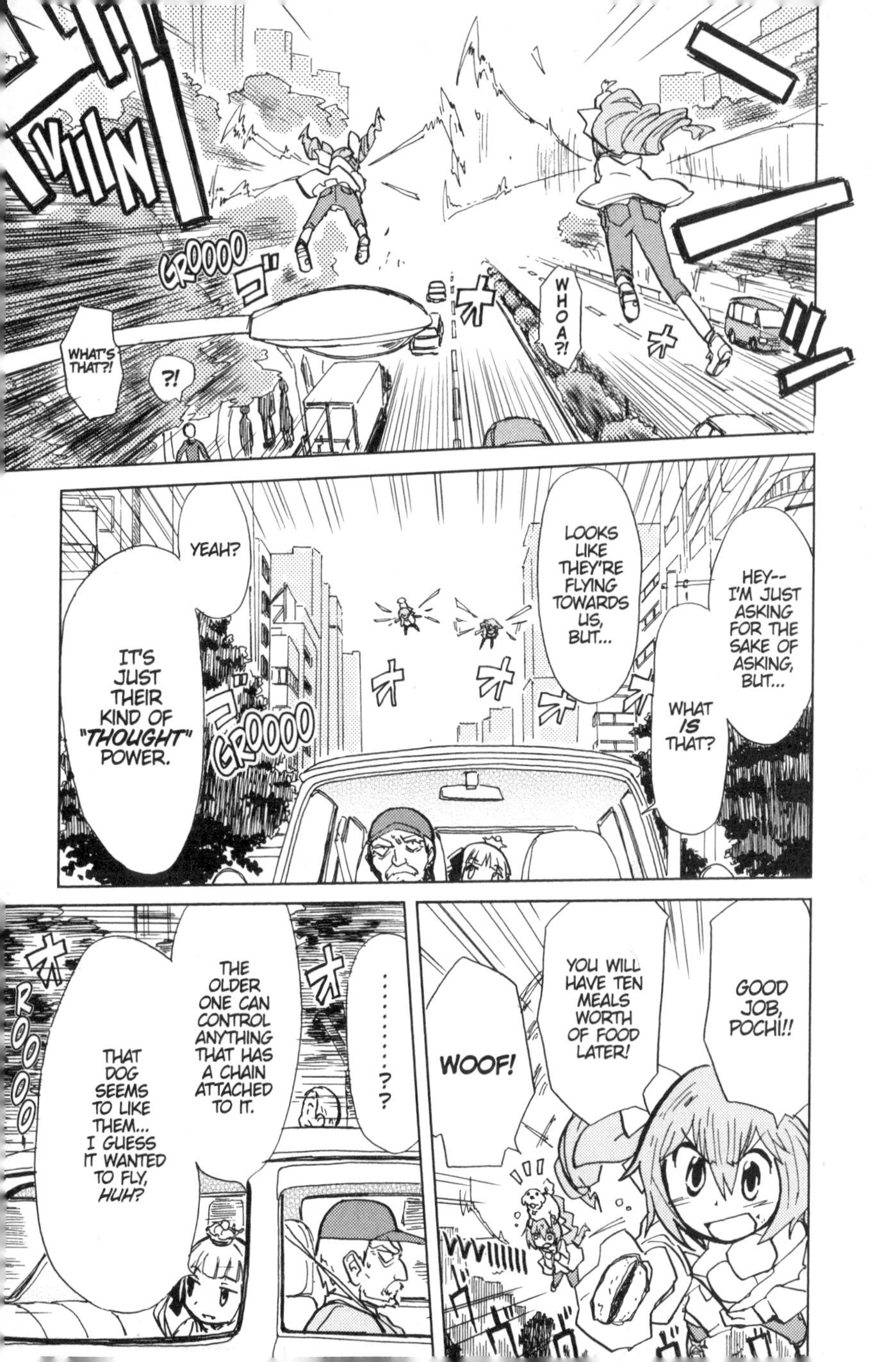
WHOA?!
GROOOO
WHAT'S THAT?!
?!
HEY-- I'M JUST ASKING FOR THE SAKE OF ASKING, BUT...
WHAT *IS* THAT?
LOOKS LIKE THEY'RE FLYING TOWARDS US, BUT...
YEAH?
IT'S JUST THEIR KIND OF "*THOUGHT*" POWER.
GROOOO
GOOD JOB, POCHI!!
YOU WILL HAVE TEN MEALS WORTH OF FOOD LATER!
WOOF!
........??
THE OLDER ONE CAN CONTROL ANYTHING THAT HAS A CHAIN ATTACHED TO IT.
THAT DOG SEEMS TO LIKE THEM... I GUESS IT WANTED TO FLY, *HUH*?
ROOOO

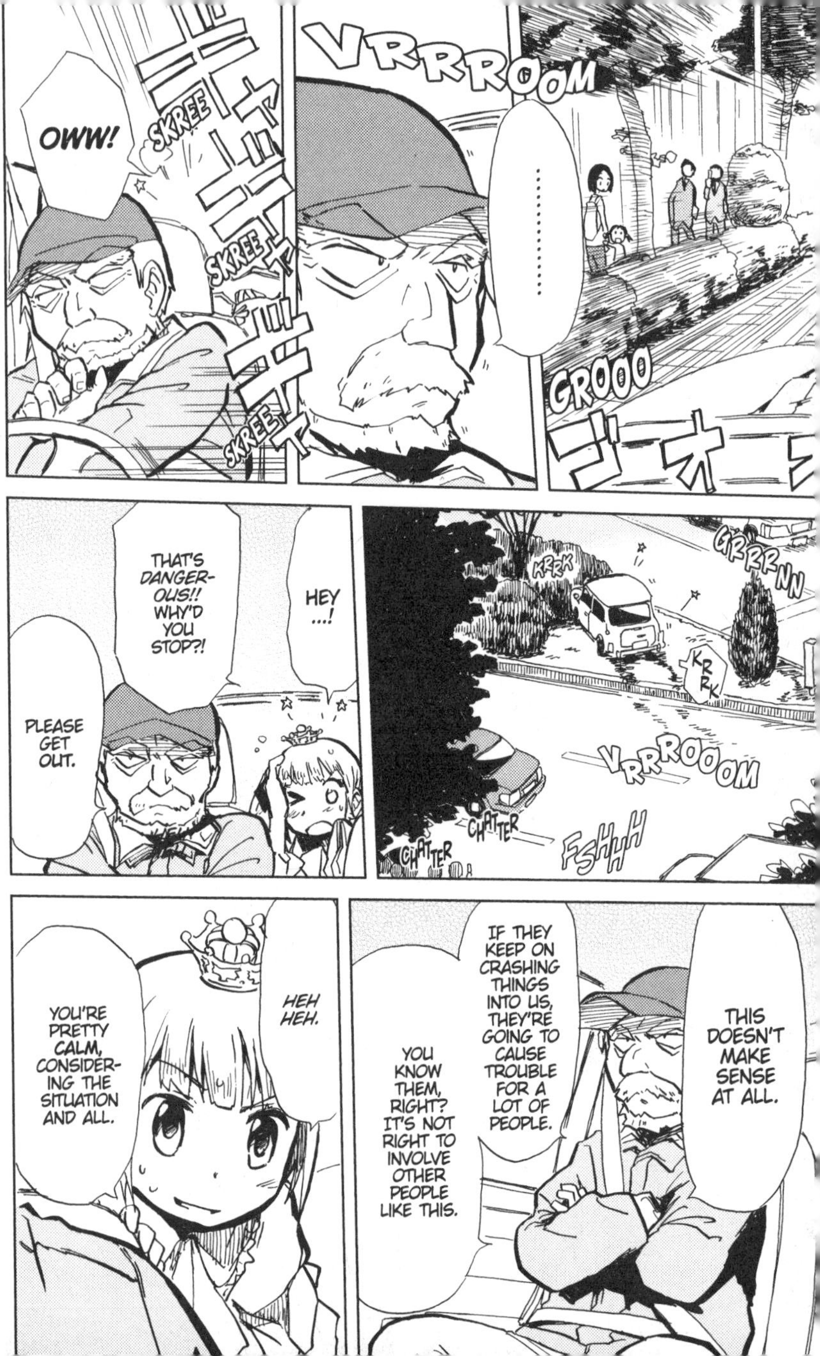
GROOO
VRRROOM
......
SKREE
SKREE
SKREE
OWW!
GRRRNN
KRRK
KRRK
VRRROOOM
CHATTER
FSHHH
CHATTER
HEY ...!
THAT'S DANGER-OUS!! WHY'D YOU STOP?!
PLEASE GET OUT.
THIS DOESN'T MAKE SENSE AT ALL.
IF THEY KEEP ON CRASHING THINGS INTO US, THEY'RE GOING TO CAUSE TROUBLE FOR A LOT OF PEOPLE.
YOU KNOW THEM, RIGHT? IT'S NOT RIGHT TO INVOLVE OTHER PEOPLE LIKE THIS.
HEH HEH.
YOU'RE PRETTY CALM, CONSIDER-ING THE SITUATION AND ALL.

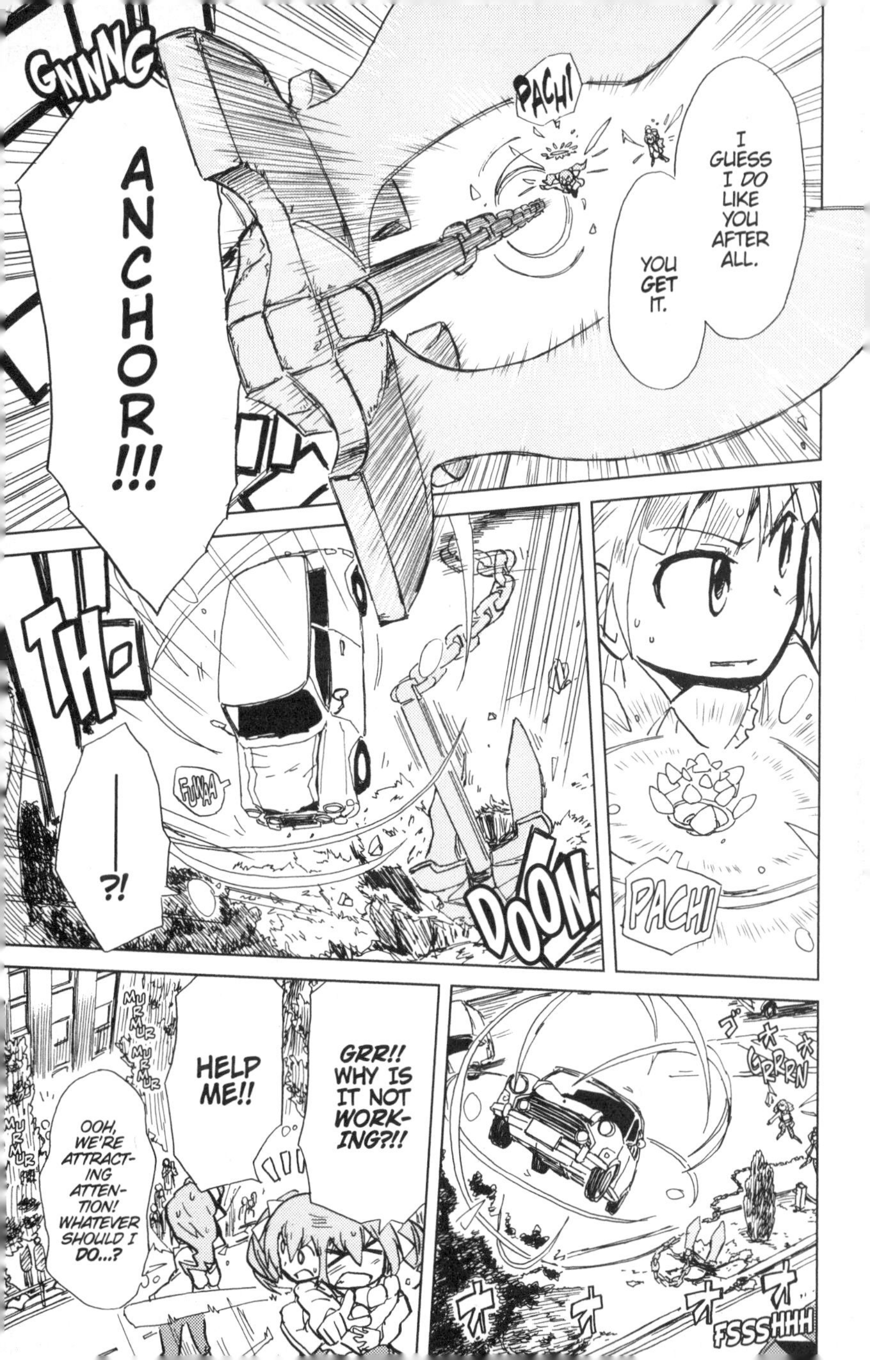
PACHI
I GUESS I DO LIKE YOU AFTER ALL.
YOU GET IT.
GNNNG
ANCHOR!!!
PACHI
DOON
FUWAA
TH-
——?!
GRRRN
FSSSHHH
GRR!! WHY IS IT NOT WORKING?!!
HELP ME!!
MURMUR MURMUR MURMUR
OOH, WE'RE ATTRACTING ATTENTION! WHATEVER SHOULD I DO...?

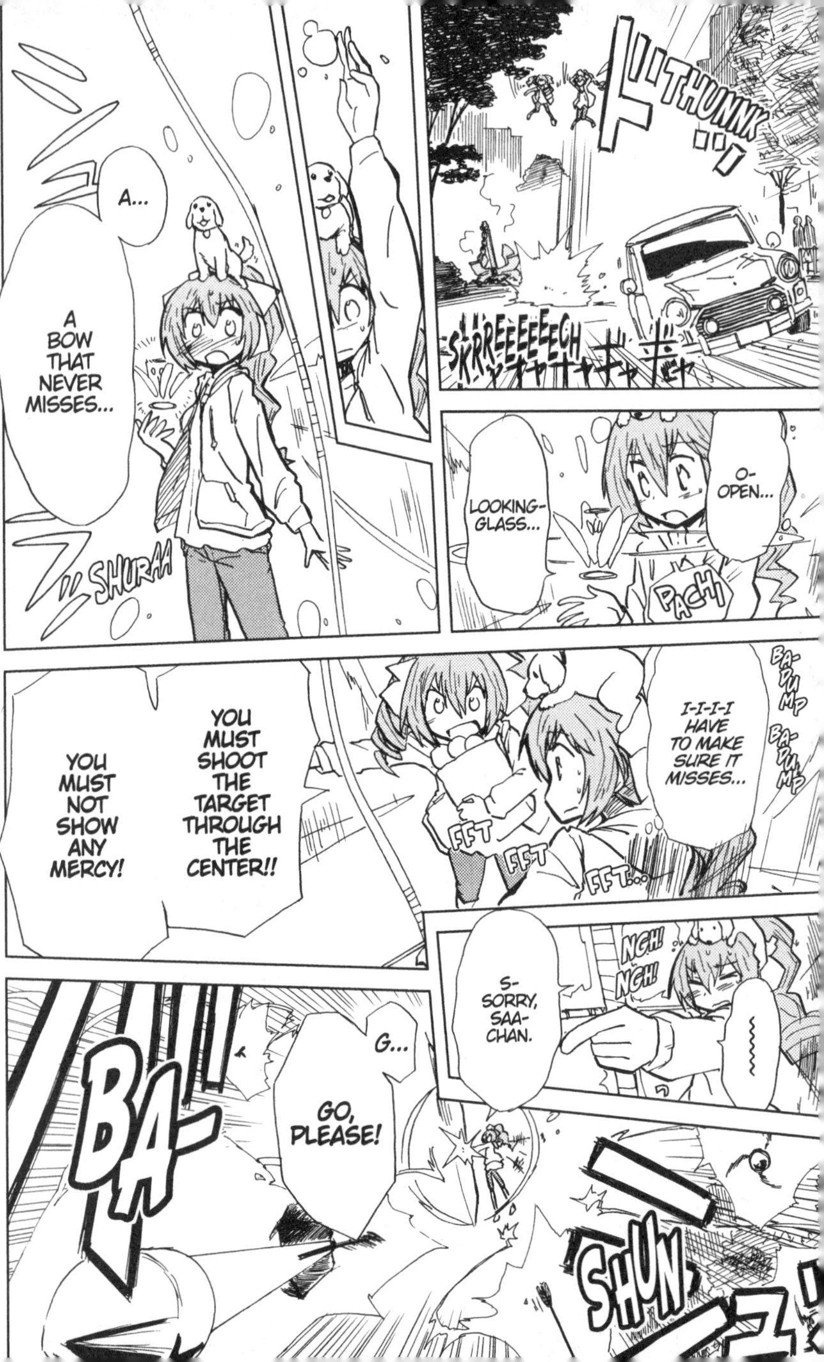
THUNNK
SKRREEEEEEECH
O-OPEN...
LOOKING-GLASS...
PACH
A...
A BOW THAT NEVER MISSES...
SHURAA
BA-DUMP BA-DUMP
I-I-I-I HAVE TO MAKE SURE IT MISSES...
FFT FFT FFT...
YOU MUST SHOOT THE TARGET THROUGH THE CENTER!!
YOU MUST NOT SHOW ANY MERCY!
NGH! NGH!
S-SORRY, SAA-CHAN.
SHUN,
G...
GO, PLEASE!
BA-

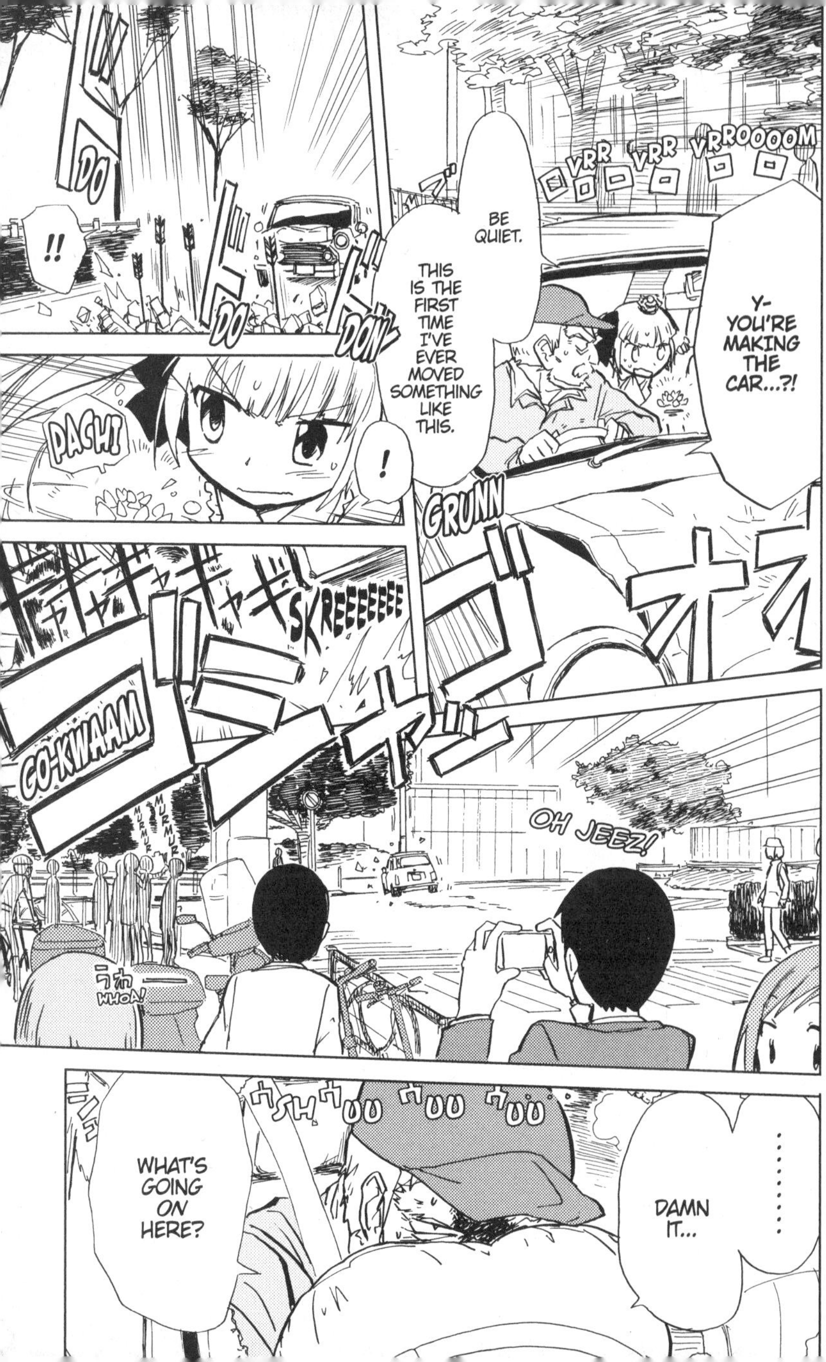
VRR VRR VRROOOOM
Y- YOU'RE MAKING THE CAR...?!
BE QUIET.
THIS IS THE FIRST TIME I'VE EVER MOVED SOMETHING LIKE THIS.
!!
DO
DO
DON
PACHI
!
GRUNN
SKREEEEEEE
CO-KWAAM
OH JEEZ!
MURMUR MURMUR
WHOA!
USH UU UU UU
....
DAMN IT...
WHAT'S GOING ON HERE?

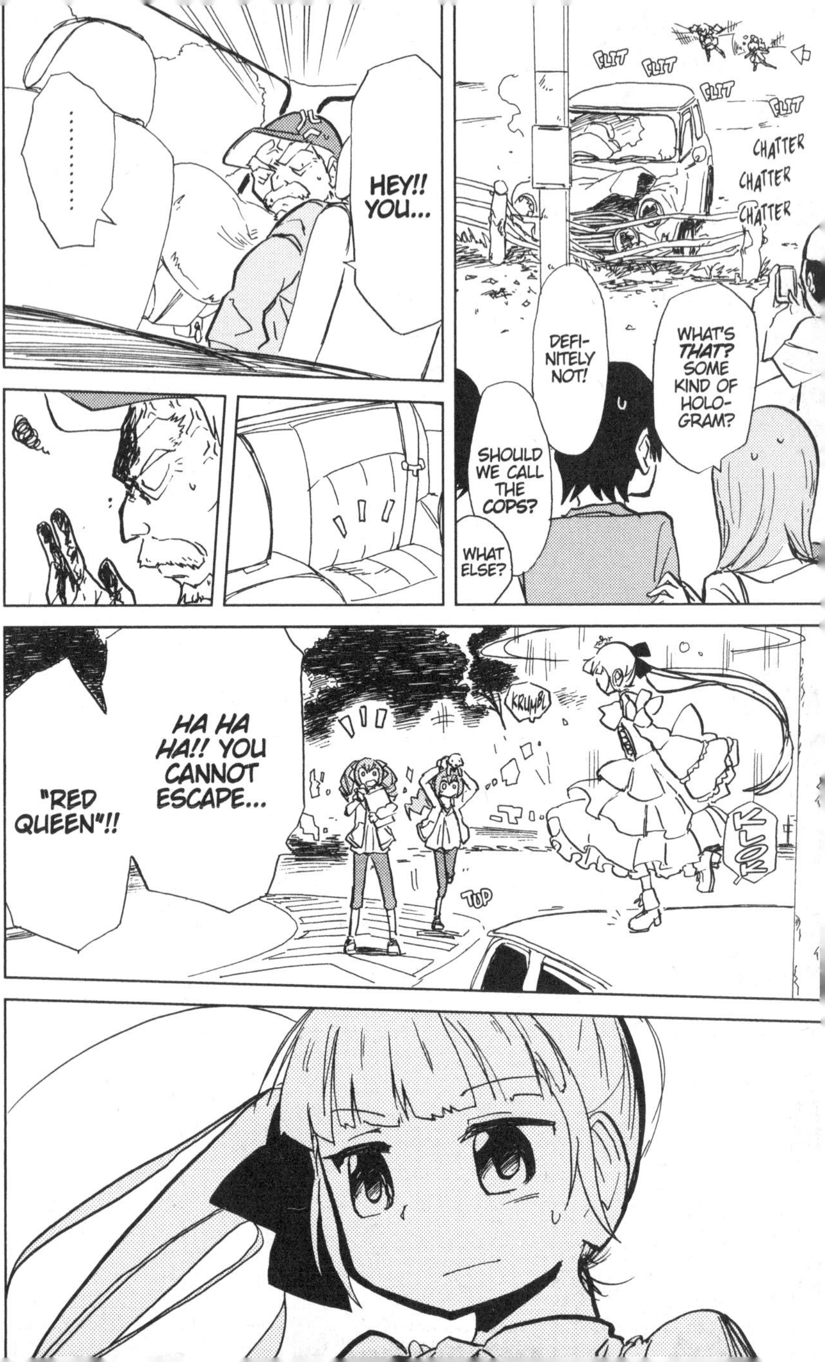
FLIT
FLIT
FLIT
FLIT
CHATTER
CHATTER
CHATTER
WHAT'S THAT? SOME KIND OF HOLOGRAM?
DEFINITELY NOT!
SHOULD WE CALL THE COPS?
WHAT ELSE?
HEY!! YOU...
......
KRUMBL
FWOOM
HA HA HA!! YOU CANNOT ESCAPE...
"RED QUEEN"!!
TOP

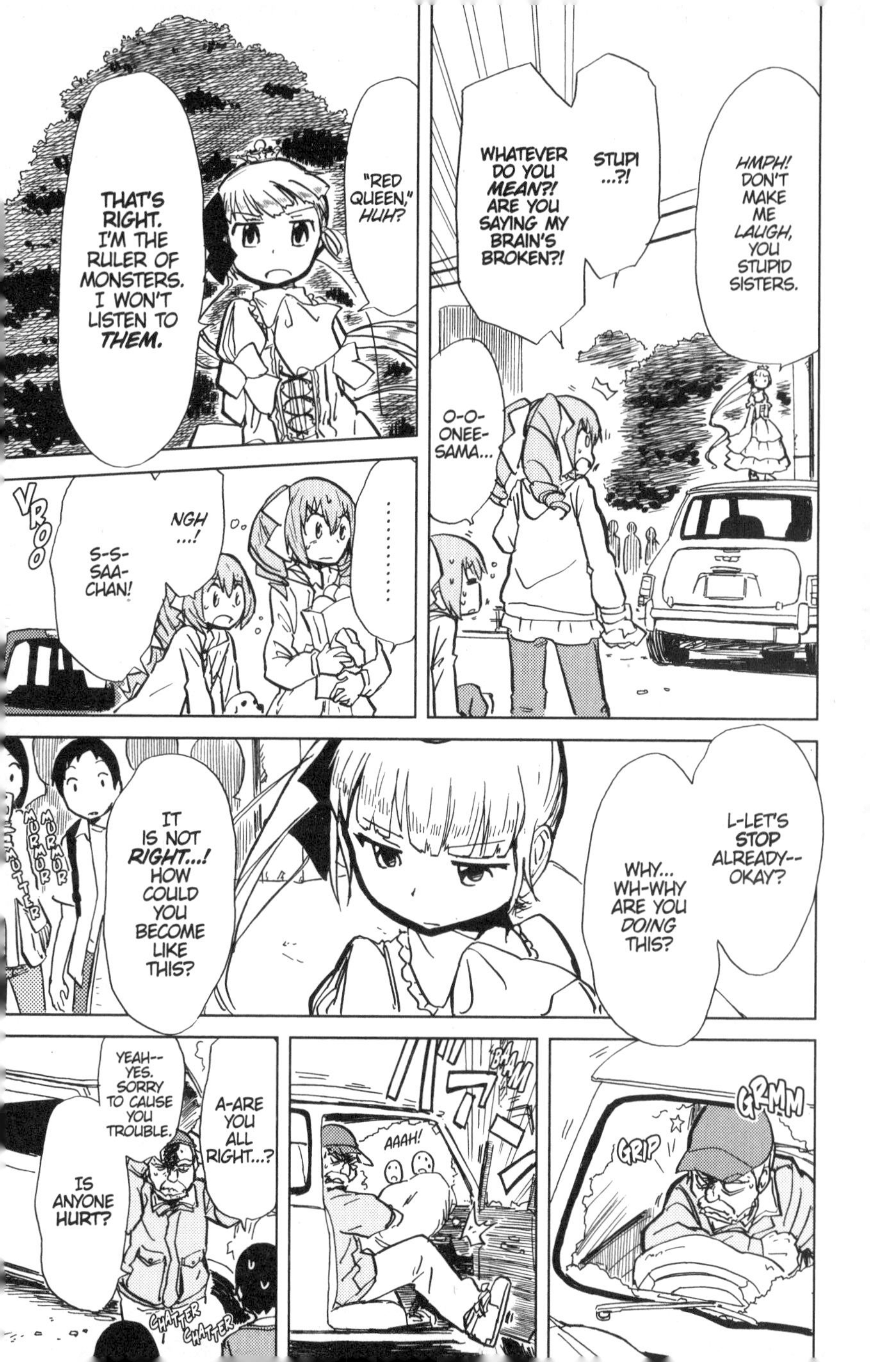
HMPH! DON'T MAKE ME LAUGH, YOU STUPID SISTERS.
STUPI ...?!
WHATEVER DO YOU MEAN?! ARE YOU SAYING MY BRAIN'S BROKEN?!
O-O-ONEE-SAMA...
"RED QUEEN," HUH?
THAT'S RIGHT. I'M THE RULER OF MONSTERS. I WON'T LISTEN TO THEM.
......
NGH ...!
S-S-SAA-CHAN!
VROOO
L-LET'S STOP ALREADY--OKAY?
WHY... WH-WHY ARE YOU DOING THIS?
IT IS NOT RIGHT...! HOW COULD YOU BECOME LIKE THIS?
MURMUR MURMUR
MUTTER
GRMM
GRIP
BLAM
AAAH!
A-ARE YOU ALL RIGHT...?
YEAH-- YES. SORRY TO CAUSE YOU TROUBLE.
IS ANYONE HURT?
CHATTER CHATTER

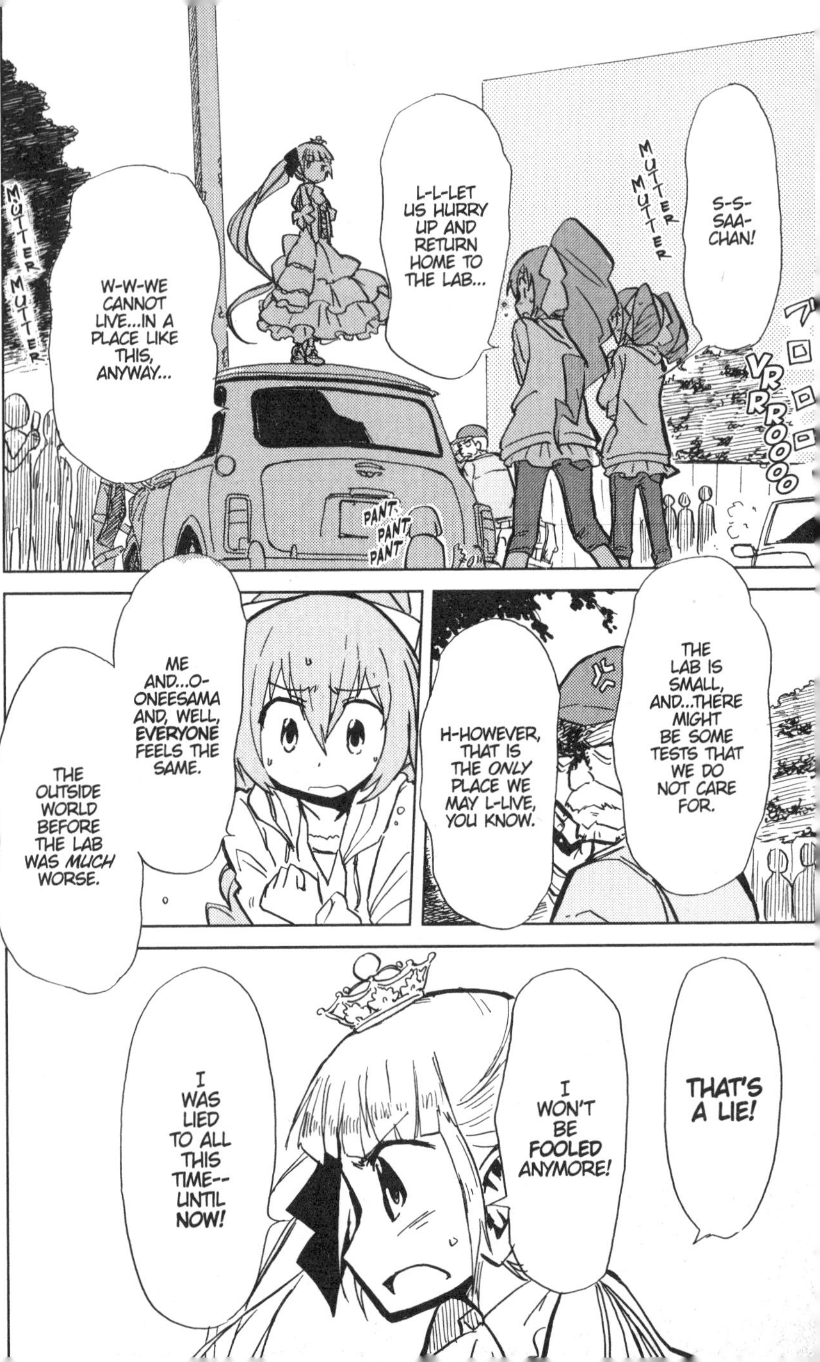

S-S-SAA-CHAN!
ブロロロ
VRROOOO
MUTTER MUTTER
L-L-LET US HURRY UP AND RETURN HOME TO THE LAB...
W-W-WE CANNOT LIVE...IN A PLACE LIKE THIS, ANYWAY...
MUTTER MUTTER
PANT PANT PANT
THE LAB IS SMALL, AND...THERE MIGHT BE SOME TESTS THAT WE DO NOT CARE FOR.
H-HOWEVER, THAT IS THE *ONLY* PLACE WE MAY L-LIVE, YOU KNOW.
ME AND...O-ONEESAMA AND, WELL, **EVERYONE** FEELS THE SAME.
THE OUTSIDE WORLD BEFORE THE LAB WAS *MUCH* WORSE.
THAT'S A LIE!
I WON'T BE FOOLED ANYMORE!
I WAS LIED TO ALL THIS TIME--UNTIL NOW!

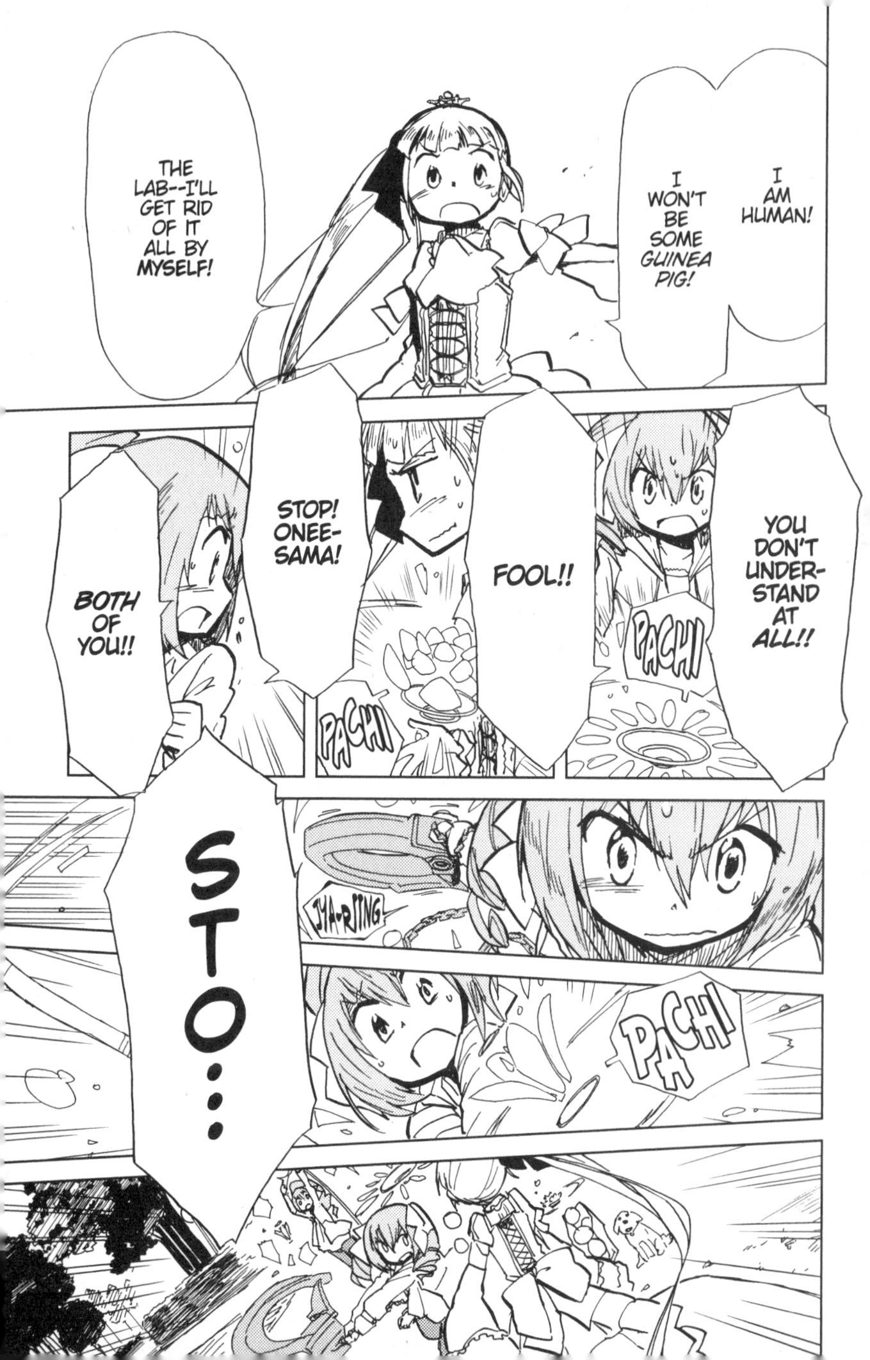
I AM HUMAN!
I WON'T BE SOME GUINEA PIG!
THE LAB--I'LL GET RID OF IT ALL BY MYSELF!
YOU DON'T UNDER-STAND AT ALL!!
PACHI
FOOL!!
STOP! ONEE-SAMA!
PACHI
BOTH OF YOU!!
JYA-RING
PACHI
STO...

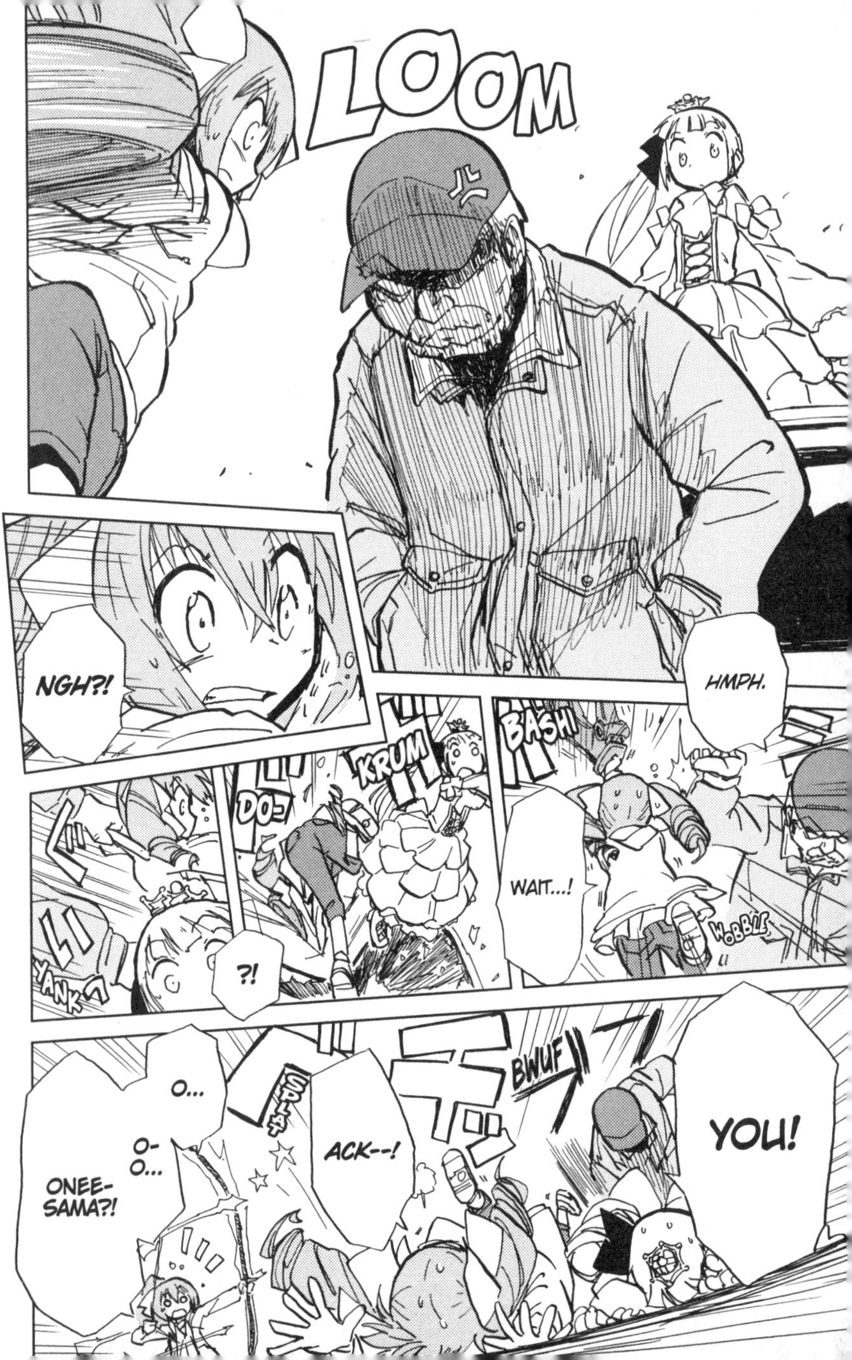
LOOM
HMPH.
NGH?!
BASH
WAIT...!
WOBBLE
KRUM
?!
YANK
BWUF
YOU!
ACK--!
O...
O-
O...
ONEE-
SAMA?!

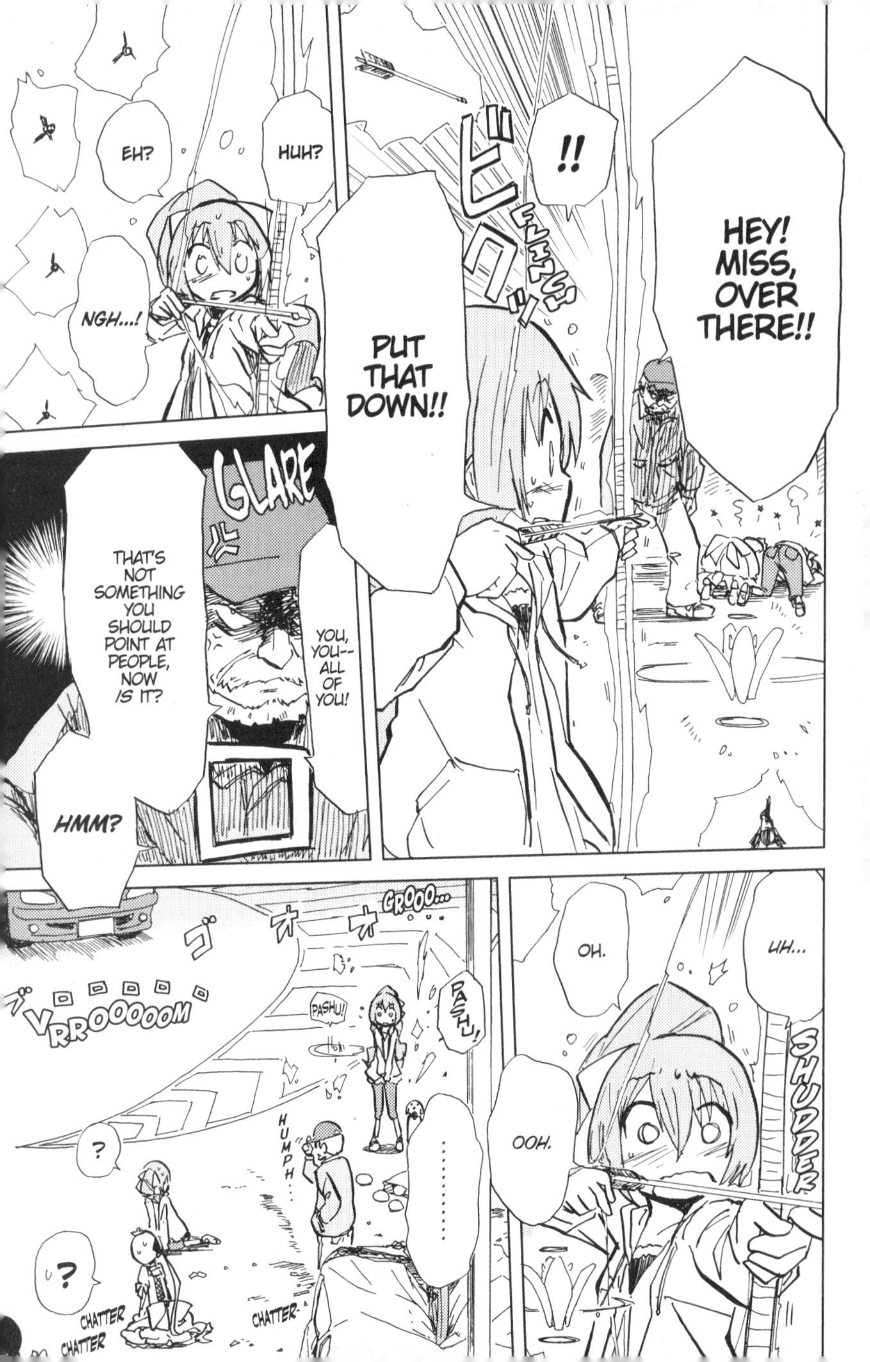
HEY! MISS, OVER THERE!!
!!
FWING!
PUT THAT DOWN!!
HUH?
EH?
NGH...!
GLARE
YOU, YOU-- ALL OF YOU!
THAT'S NOT SOMETHING YOU SHOULD POINT AT PEOPLE, NOW IS IT?
HMM?
UH...
OH.
SHUDDER
OOH.
GROOO...
VRROOOOOOM
PASHU!
PASHU!
......
HUMPH...
?
?
CHATTER
CHATTER
CHATTER

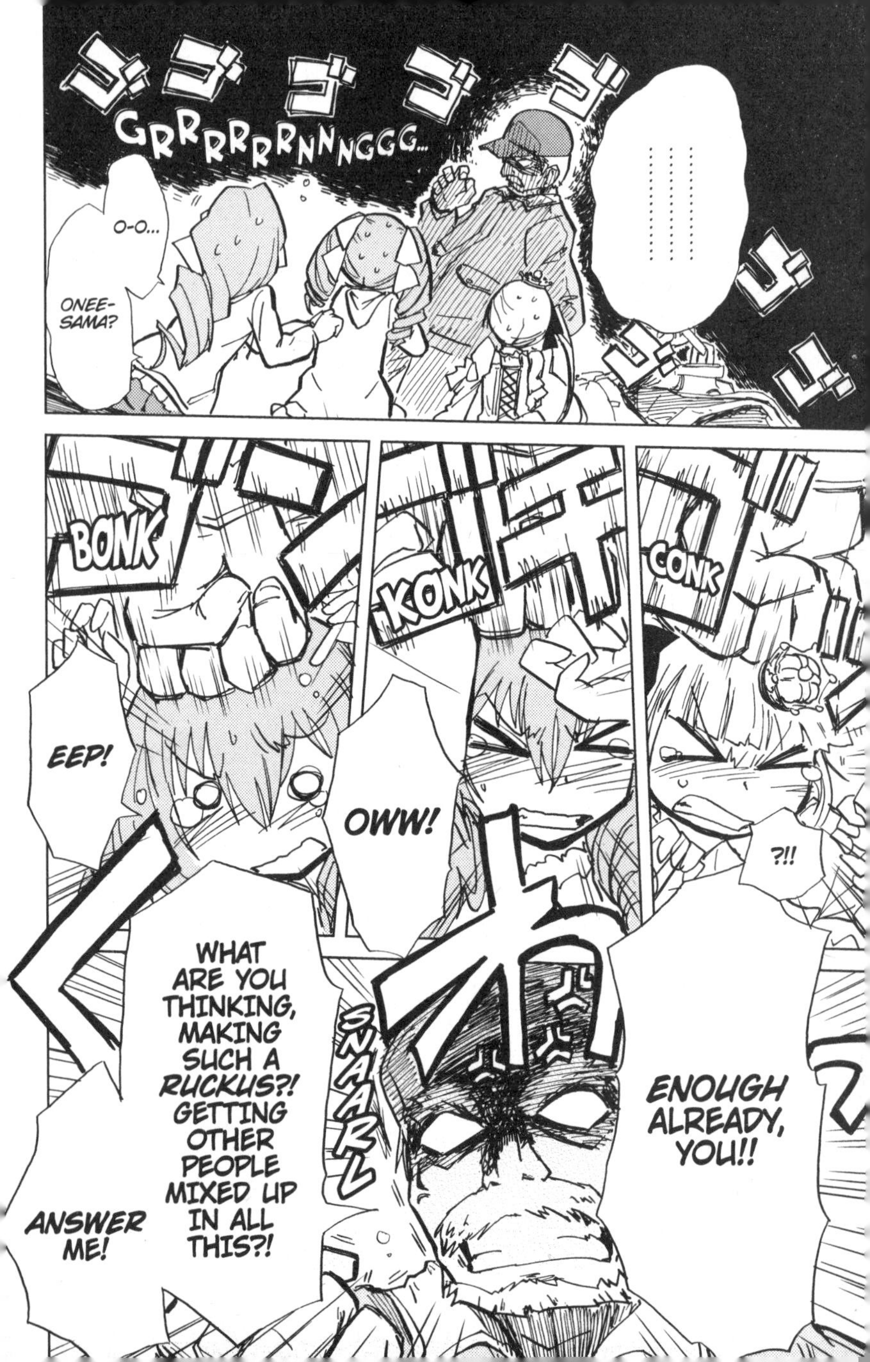
......
GRRRRRRNNNGGG...
O-O... ONEE-SAMA?
CONK
?!!
KONK
OWW!
BONK
EEP!
ENOUGH ALREADY, YOU!!
SNAARL
WHAT ARE YOU THINKING, MAKING SUCH A RUCKUS?! GETTING OTHER PEOPLE MIXED UP IN ALL THIS?!
ANSWER ME!

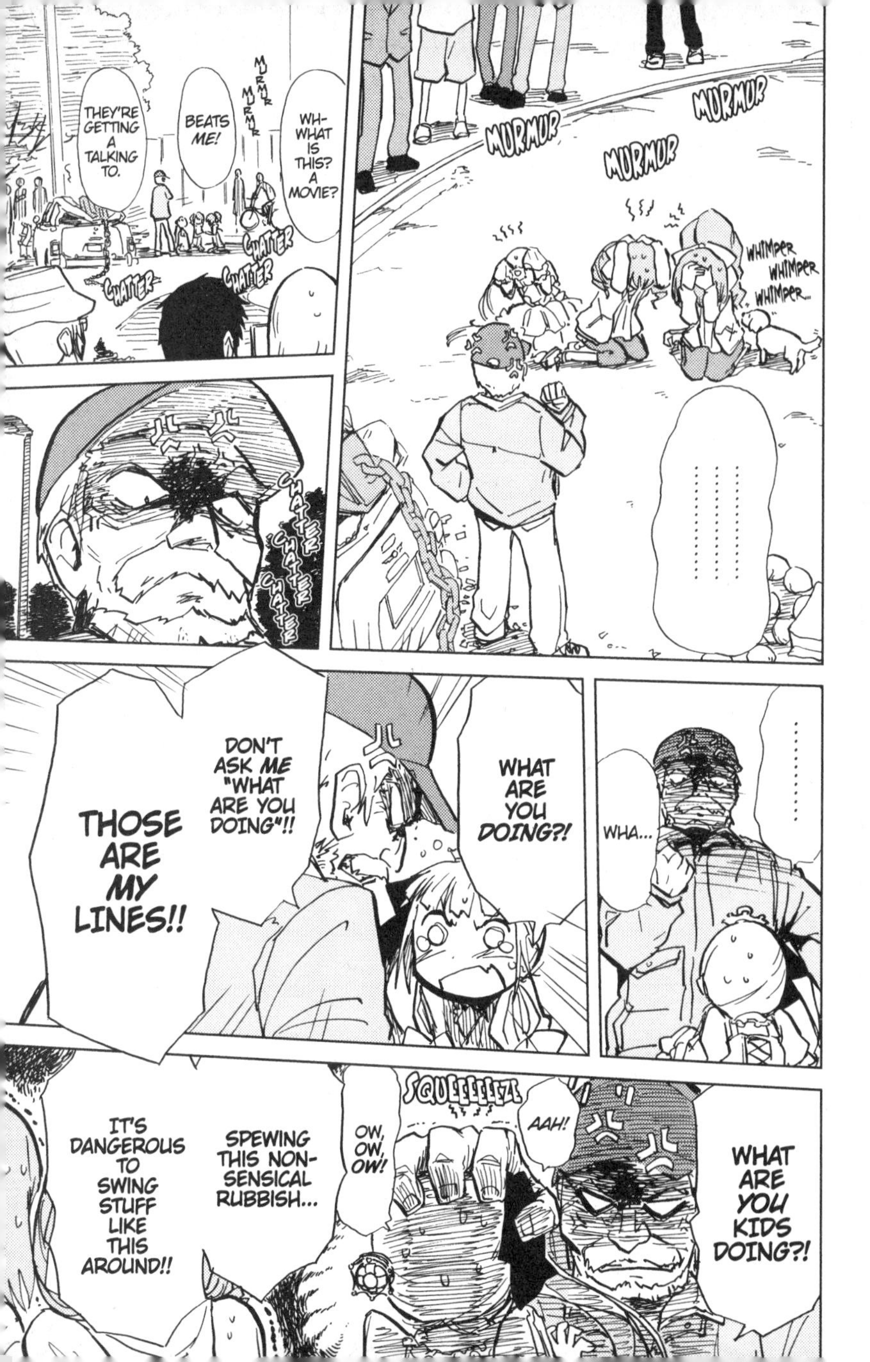
MURMUR
MURMUR
MURMUR
WHIMPER
WHIMPER
WHIMPER...
......
WH-WHAT IS THIS? A MOVIE?
MURMUR MURMUR
BEATS ME!
THEY'RE GETTING A TALKING TO.
CHATTER
CHATTER
CHATTER
CHATTER
CHATTER
CHATTER
......
WHA...
WHAT ARE YOU DOING?!
DON'T ASK ME "WHAT ARE YOU DOING"!!
THOSE ARE MY LINES!!
WHAT ARE YOU KIDS DOING?!
AAH!
SQUEEEEEEZE
OW, OW, OW!
SPEWING THIS NON-SENSICAL RUBBISH...
IT'S DANGEROUS TO SWING STUFF LIKE THIS AROUND!!

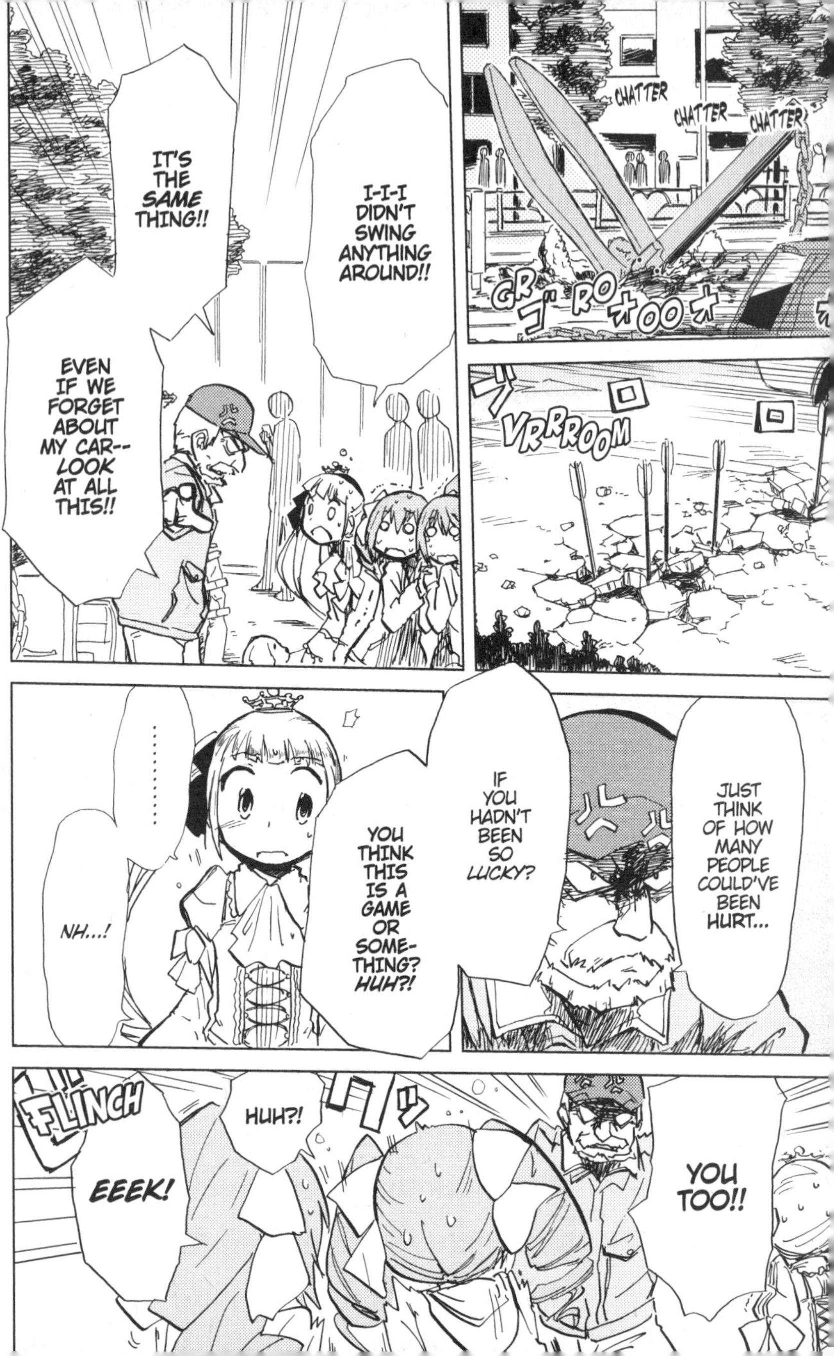
CHATTER
CHATTER
CHATTER
GR RO OO
VRRROOM
I-I-I DIDN'T SWING ANYTHING AROUND!!
IT'S THE SAME THING!!
EVEN IF WE FORGET ABOUT MY CAR-- LOOK AT ALL THIS!!
JUST THINK OF HOW MANY PEOPLE COULD'VE BEEN HURT...
IF YOU HADN'T BEEN SO LUCKY?
YOU THINK THIS IS A GAME OR SOMETHING? HUH?!
......
NH...!
YOU TOO!!
HUH?!
FLINCH
EEEK!

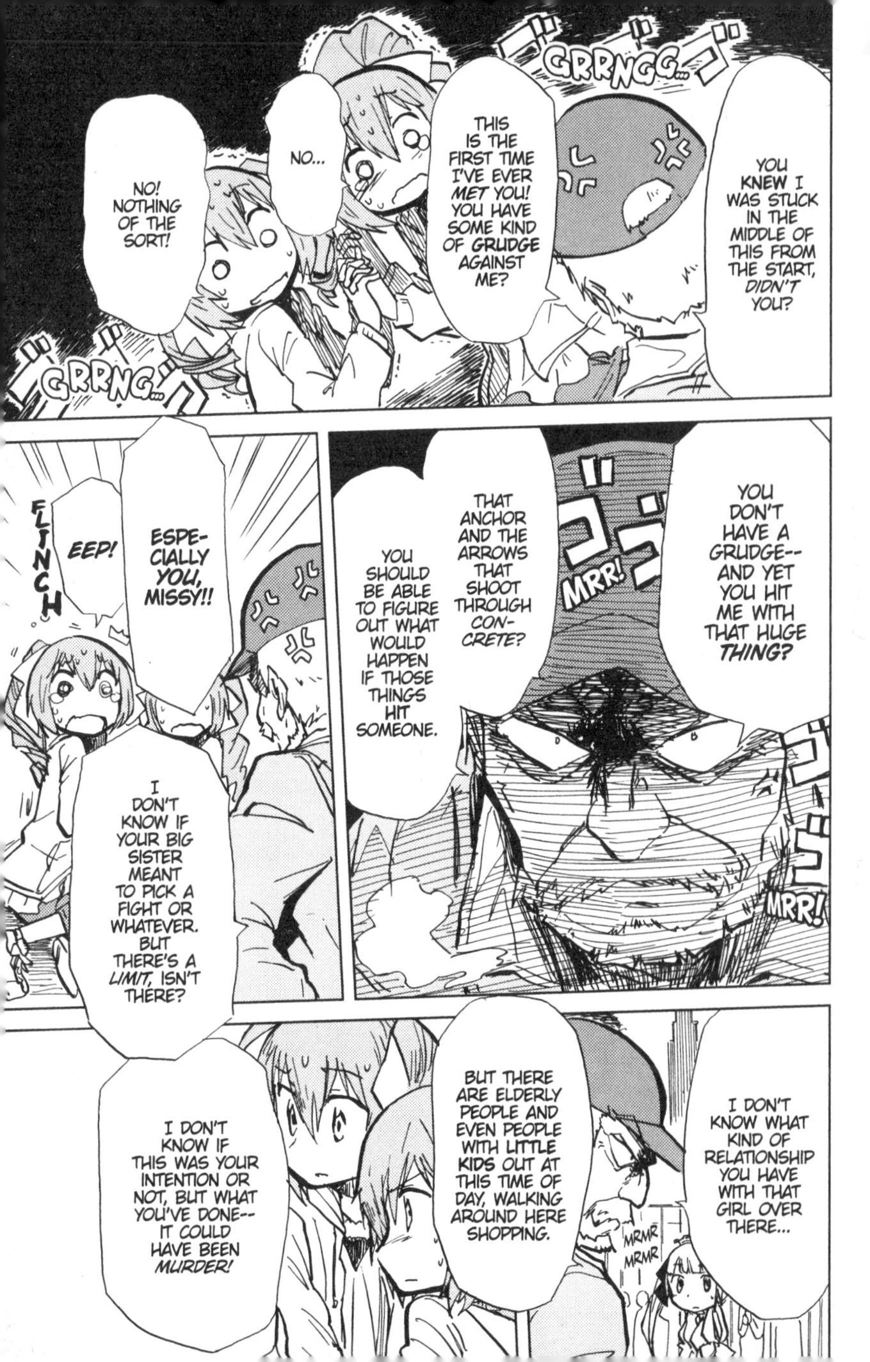
YOU KNEW I WAS STUCK IN THE MIDDLE OF THIS FROM THE START, DIDN'T YOU?
GRRNGG...
THIS IS THE FIRST TIME I'VE EVER MET YOU! YOU HAVE SOME KIND OF GRUDGE AGAINST ME?
NO...
NO! NOTHING OF THE SORT!
GRRNG...
YOU DON'T HAVE A GRUDGE-- AND YET YOU HIT ME WITH THAT HUGE THING?
MRR!
MRR!
THAT ANCHOR AND THE ARROWS THAT SHOOT THROUGH CON-CRETE?
YOU SHOULD BE ABLE TO FIGURE OUT WHAT WOULD HAPPEN IF THOSE THINGS HIT SOMEONE.
ESPE-CIALLY YOU, MISSY!!
EEP!
FLINCH
I DON'T KNOW IF YOUR BIG SISTER MEANT TO PICK A FIGHT OR WHATEVER. BUT THERE'S A LIMIT, ISN'T THERE?
I DON'T KNOW WHAT KIND OF RELATIONSHIP YOU HAVE WITH THAT GIRL OVER THERE...
MRMR MRMR
BUT THERE ARE ELDERLY PEOPLE AND EVEN PEOPLE WITH LITTLE KIDS OUT AT THIS TIME OF DAY, WALKING AROUND HERE SHOPPING.
I DON'T KNOW IF THIS WAS YOUR INTENTION OR NOT, BUT WHAT YOU'VE DONE-- IT COULD HAVE BEEN MURDER!

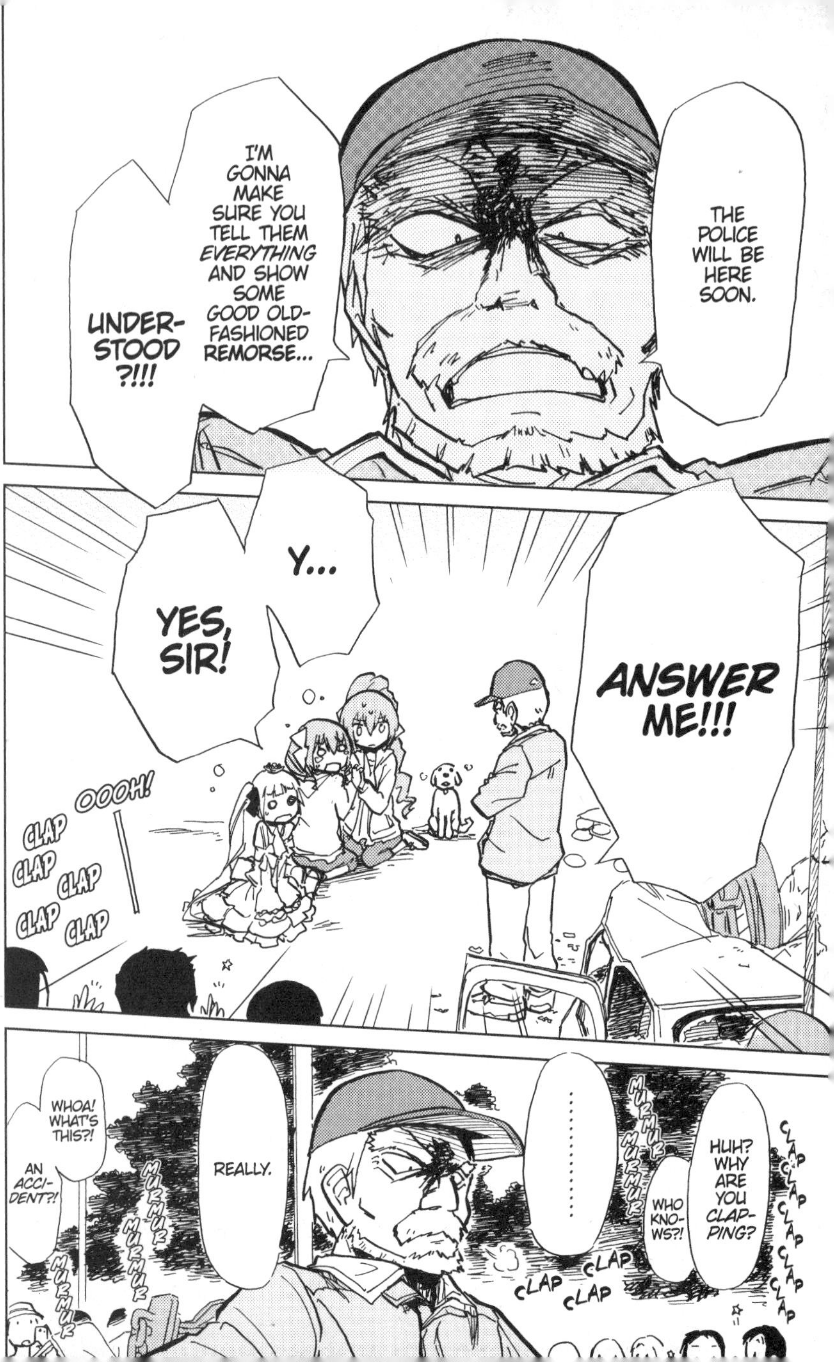
THE POLICE WILL BE HERE SOON.
I'M GONNA MAKE SURE YOU TELL THEM *EVERYTHING* AND SHOW SOME GOOD OLD-FASHIONED REMORSE...
UNDER-STOOD ?!!!
ANSWER ME!!!
Y...
YES, SIR!
OOOH!
CLAP CLAP CLAP CLAP CLAP
CLAP CLAP CLAP CLAP CLAP CLAP
HUH? WHY ARE YOU CLAP-PING?
WHO KNOWS?!
MURMUR MURMUR
......
CLAP CLAP CLAP CLAP
REALLY.
MURMUR MURMUR
WHOA! WHAT'S THIS?!
AN ACCI-DENT?!
MURMUR

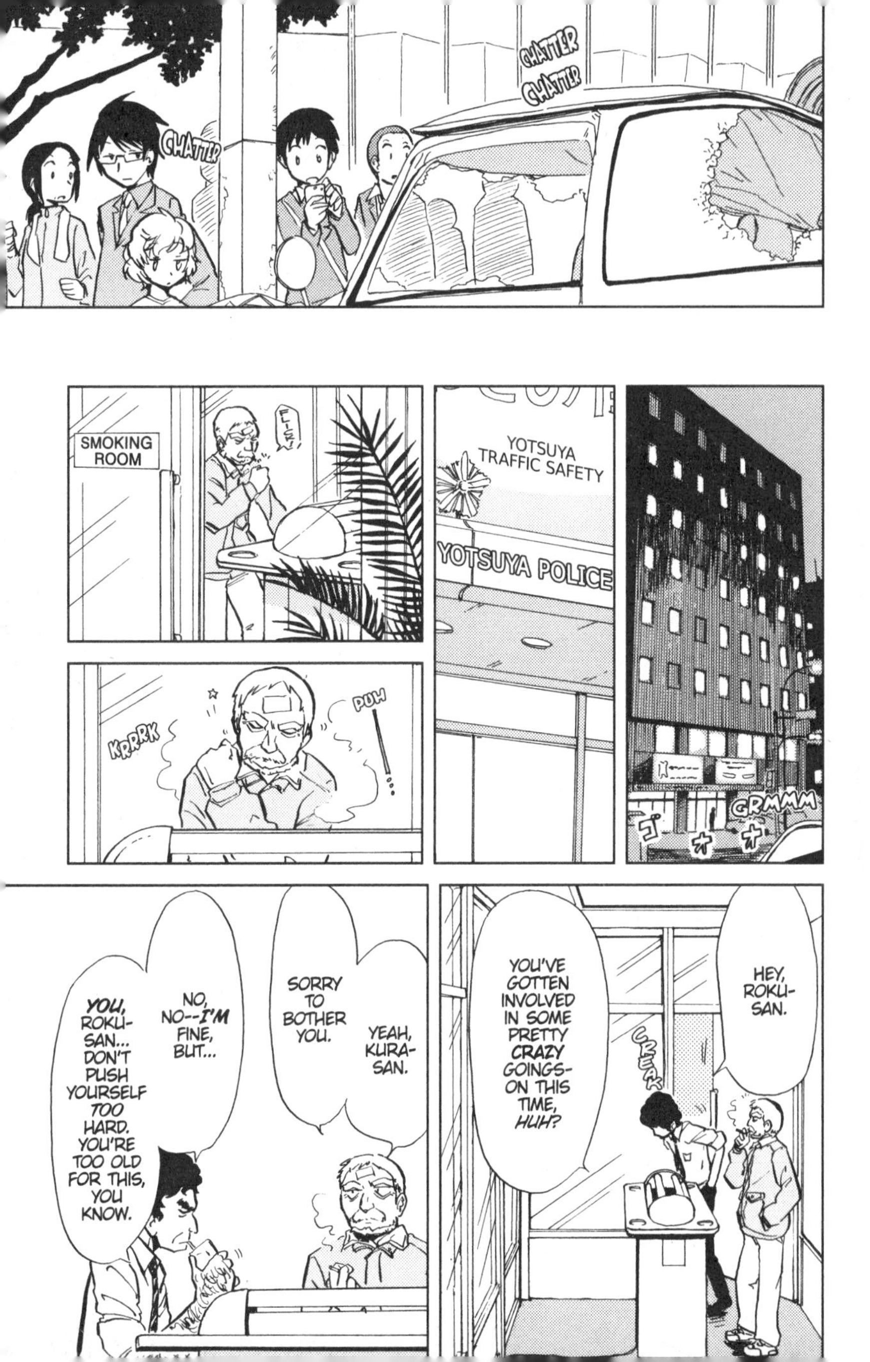
CHATTER
CHATTER
CHATTER
GRMMM
ゴオオ
YOTSUYA TRAFFIC SAFETY
YOTSUYA POLICE
SMOKING ROOM
FLICK!
PUH
KRRRK
HEY, ROKU-SAN.
CREAK
YOU'VE GOTTEN INVOLVED IN SOME PRETTY CRAZY GOINGS-ON THIS TIME, HUH?
YEAH, KURA-SAN.
SORRY TO BOTHER YOU.
NO, NO--I'M FINE, BUT...
YOU, ROKU-SAN... DON'T PUSH YOURSELF TOO HARD. YOU'RE TOO OLD FOR THIS, YOU KNOW.

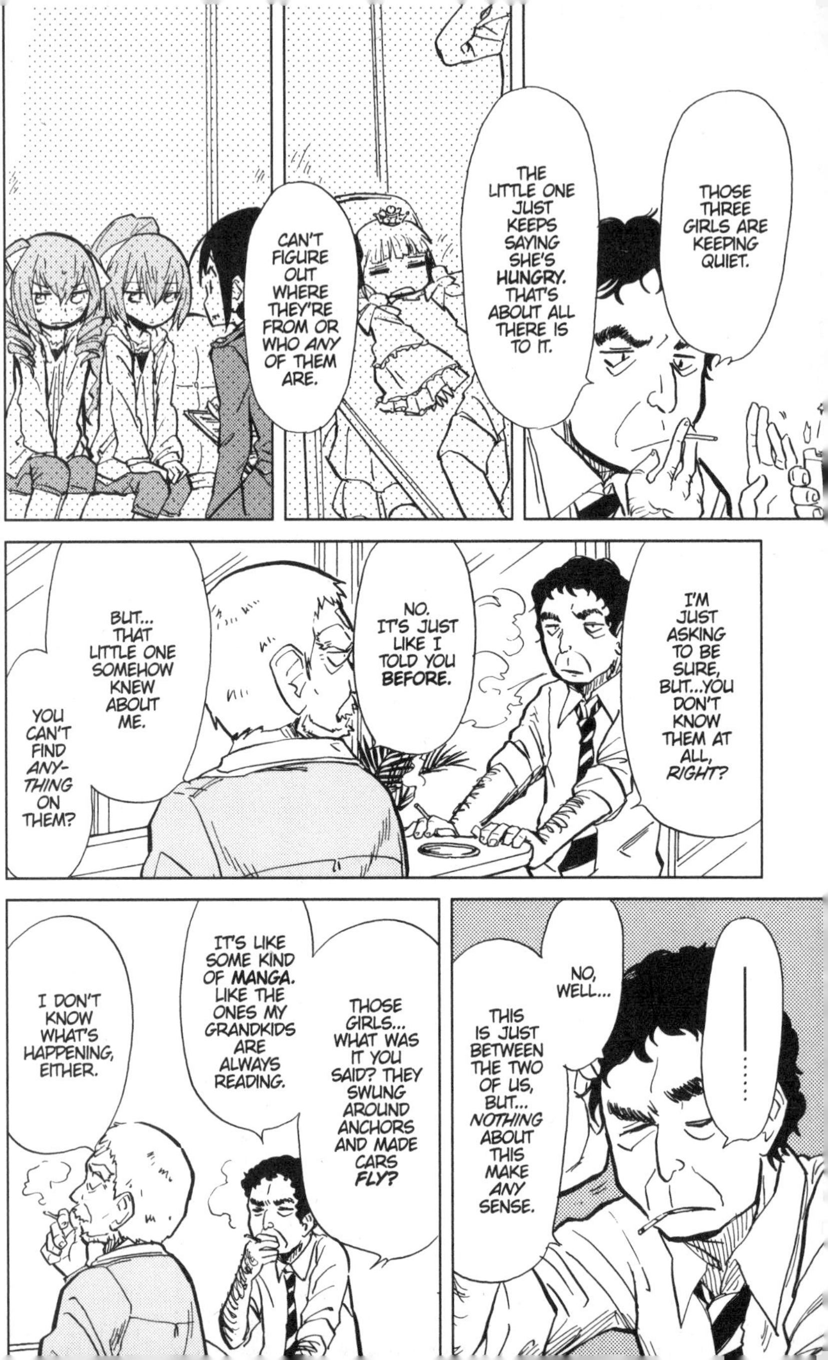
THOSE THREE GIRLS ARE KEEPING QUIET.
THE LITTLE ONE JUST KEEPS SAYING SHE'S HUNGRY. THAT'S ABOUT ALL THERE IS TO IT.
CAN'T FIGURE OUT WHERE THEY'RE FROM OR WHO ANY OF THEM ARE.
I'M JUST ASKING TO BE SURE, BUT...YOU DON'T KNOW THEM AT ALL, RIGHT?
NO. IT'S JUST LIKE I TOLD YOU BEFORE.
BUT... THAT LITTLE ONE SOMEHOW KNEW ABOUT ME.
YOU CAN'T FIND ANYTHING ON THEM?
......
NO, WELL...
THIS IS JUST BETWEEN THE TWO OF US, BUT... NOTHING ABOUT THIS MAKE ANY SENSE.
THOSE GIRLS... WHAT WAS IT YOU SAID? THEY SWUNG AROUND ANCHORS AND MADE CARS FLY?
IT'S LIKE SOME KIND OF MANGA. LIKE THE ONES MY GRANDKIDS ARE ALWAYS READING.
I DON'T KNOW WHAT'S HAPPENING, EITHER.

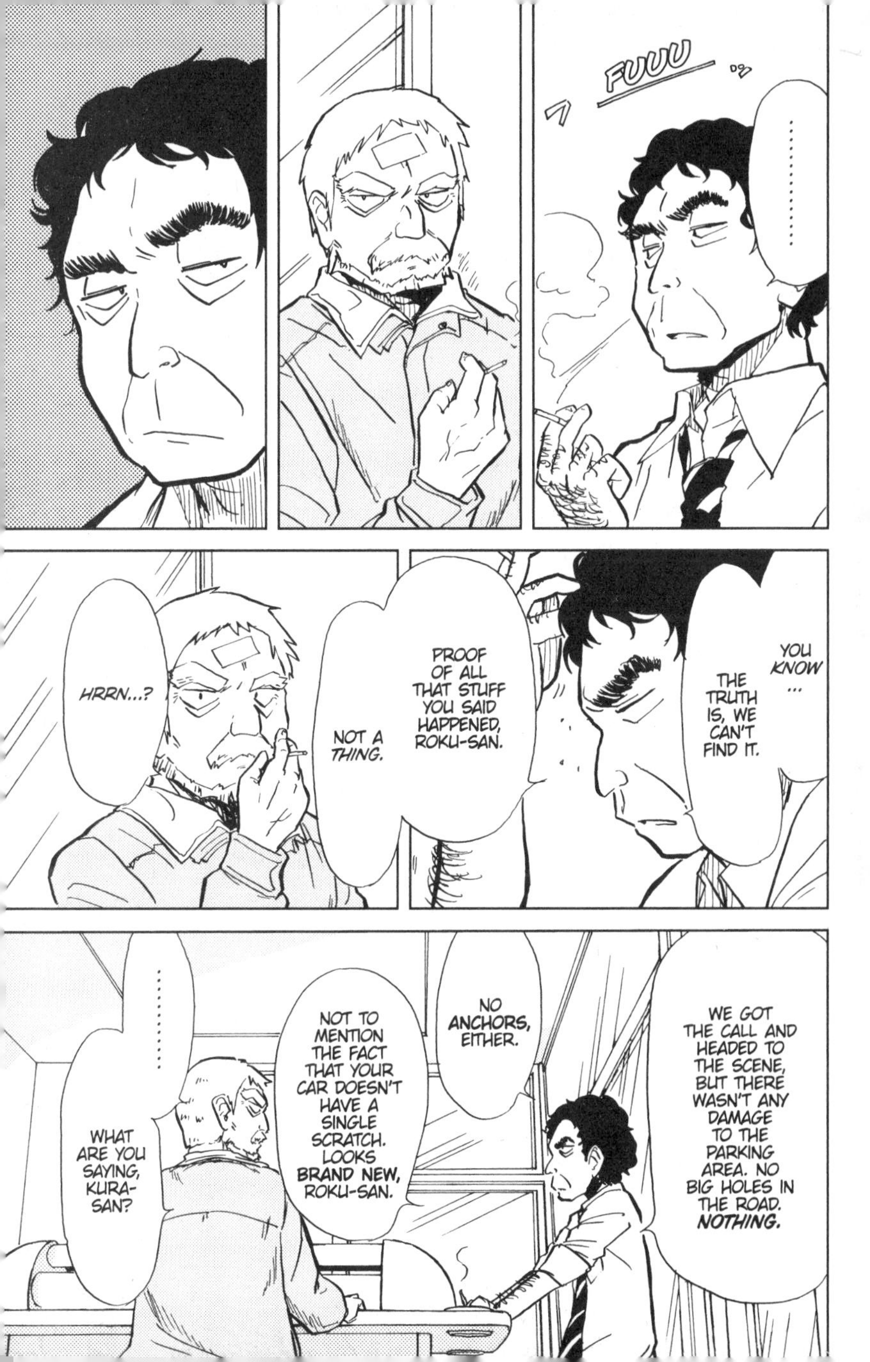
......
FUUU
YOU KNOW...
THE TRUTH IS, WE CAN'T FIND IT.
PROOF OF ALL THAT STUFF YOU SAID HAPPENED, ROKU-SAN.
NOT A THING.
HRRN...?
WE GOT THE CALL AND HEADED TO THE SCENE, BUT THERE WASN'T ANY DAMAGE TO THE PARKING AREA. NO BIG HOLES IN THE ROAD. NOTHING.
NO ANCHORS, EITHER.
NOT TO MENTION THE FACT THAT YOUR CAR DOESN'T HAVE A SINGLE SCRATCH. LOOKS BRAND NEW, ROKU-SAN.
......
WHAT ARE YOU SAYING, KURA-SAN?

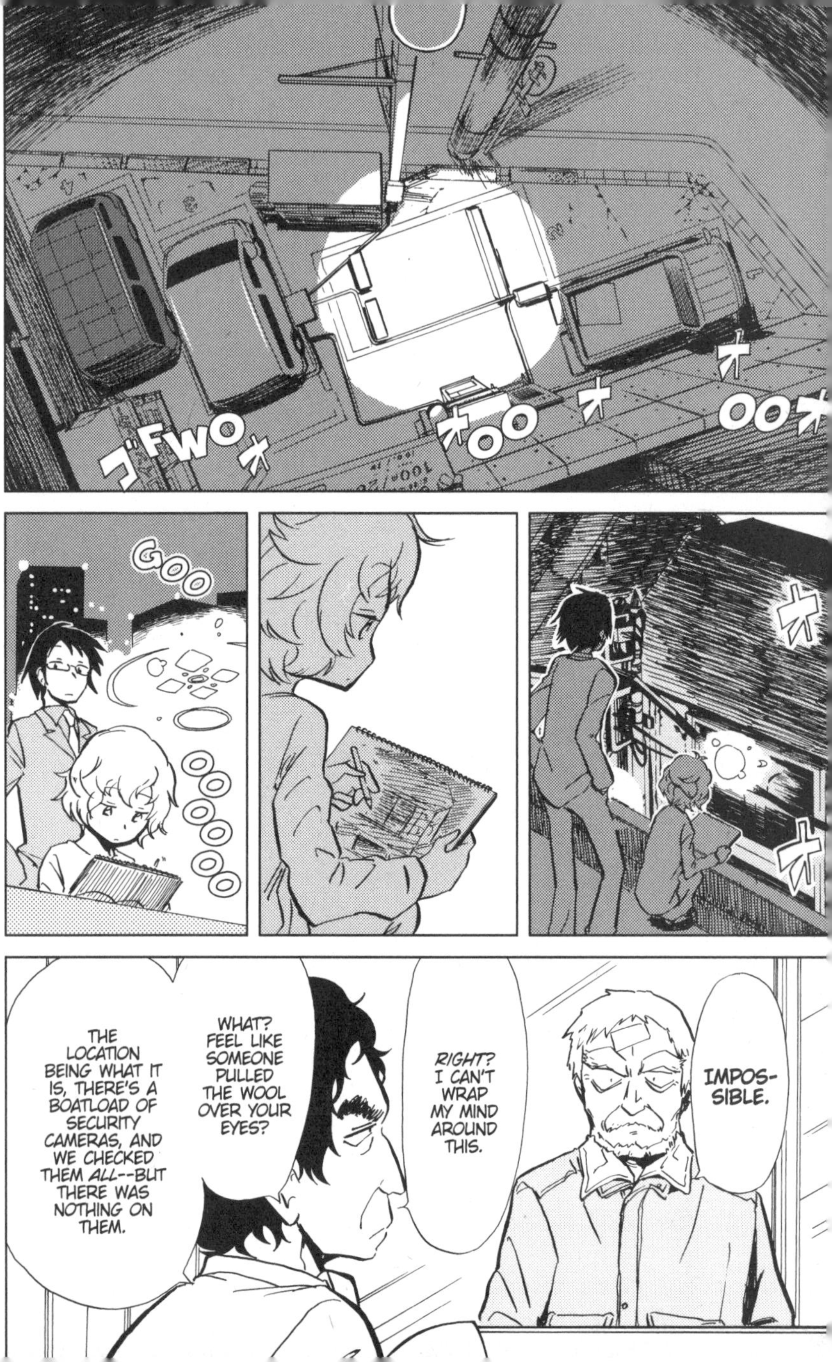

ゴFWOオ オOO オ オ OOオ
オ
オ
GOO
OOOOOO
IMPOS-SIBLE.
RIGHT? I CAN'T WRAP MY MIND AROUND THIS.
WHAT? FEEL LIKE SOMEONE PULLED THE WOOL OVER YOUR EYES?
THE LOCATION BEING WHAT IT IS, THERE'S A BOATLOAD OF SECURITY CAMERAS, AND WE CHECKED THEM *ALL*--BUT THERE WAS NOTHING ON THEM.

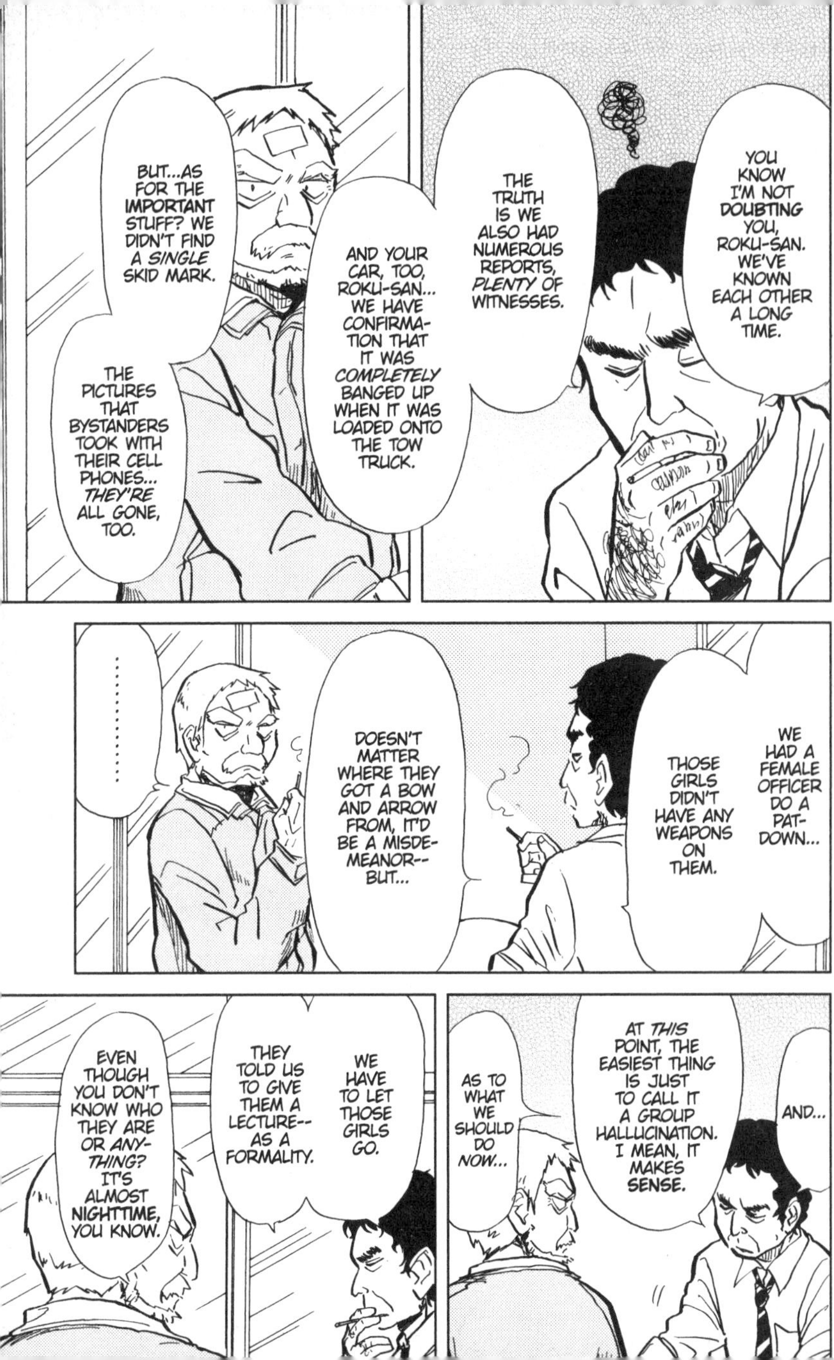
YOU KNOW I'M NOT DOUBTING YOU, ROKU-SAN. WE'VE KNOWN EACH OTHER A LONG TIME.
THE TRUTH IS WE ALSO HAD NUMEROUS REPORTS, *PLENTY* OF WITNESSES.
AND YOUR CAR, TOO, ROKU-SAN... WE HAVE CONFIRMATION THAT IT WAS *COMPLETELY* BANGED UP WHEN IT WAS LOADED ONTO THE TOW TRUCK.
BUT...AS FOR THE IMPORTANT STUFF? WE DIDN'T FIND A *SINGLE* SKID MARK.
THE PICTURES THAT BYSTANDERS TOOK WITH THEIR CELL PHONES... *THEY'RE* ALL GONE, TOO.
WE HAD A FEMALE OFFICER DO A PAT-DOWN...
THOSE GIRLS DIDN'T HAVE ANY WEAPONS ON THEM.
DOESN'T MATTER WHERE THEY GOT A BOW AND ARROW FROM, IT'D BE A MISDEMEANOR--BUT...
......
AND...
AT *THIS* POINT, THE EASIEST THING IS JUST TO CALL IT A GROUP HALLUCINATION. I MEAN, IT MAKES SENSE.
AS TO WHAT WE SHOULD DO *NOW*...
WE HAVE TO LET THOSE GIRLS GO.
THEY TOLD US TO GIVE THEM A LECTURE--AS A FORMALITY.
EVEN THOUGH YOU DON'T KNOW WHO THEY ARE OR *ANYTHING?* IT'S ALMOST NIGHTTIME, YOU KNOW.

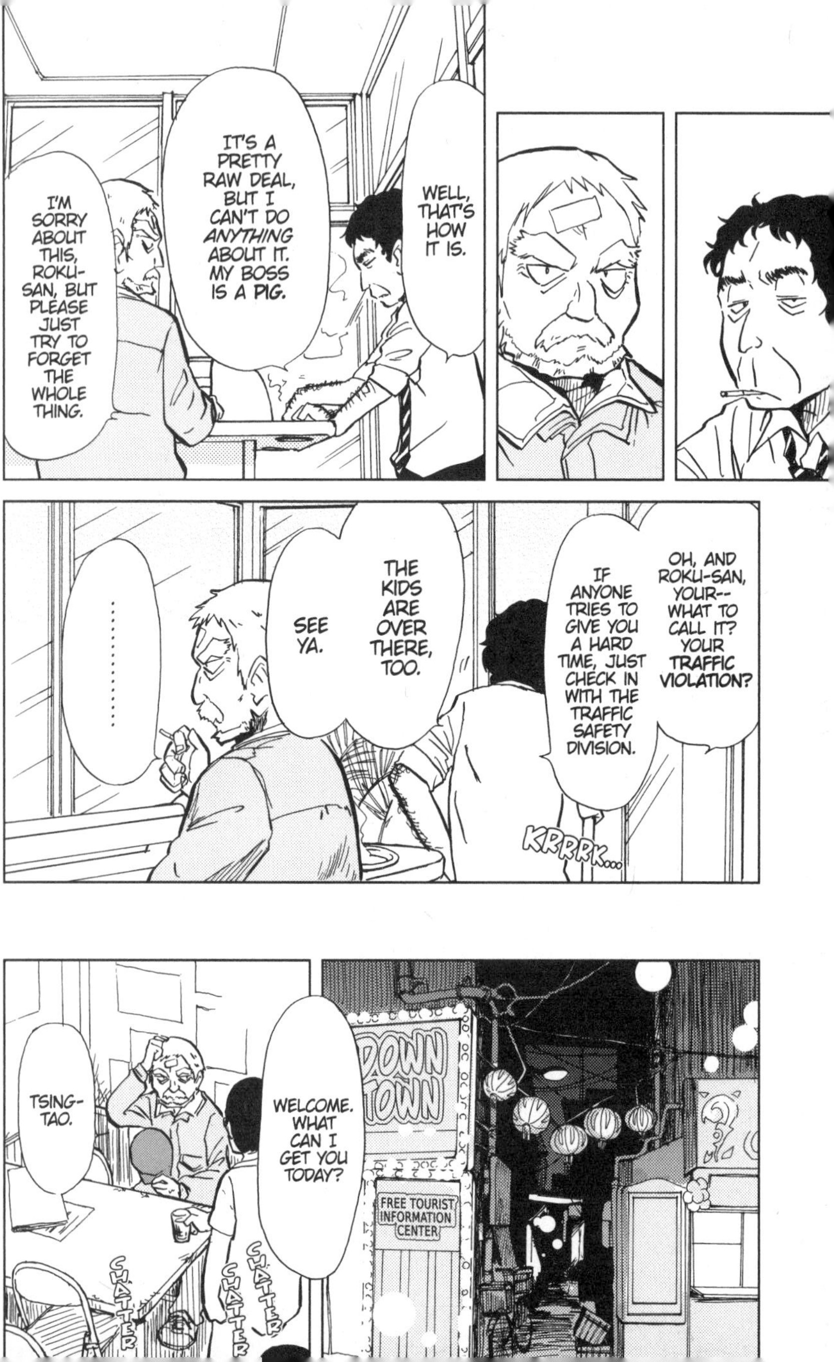
WELL, THAT'S HOW IT IS.
IT'S A PRETTY RAW DEAL, BUT I CAN'T DO *ANYTHING* ABOUT IT. MY BOSS IS A PIG.
I'M SORRY ABOUT THIS, ROKU-SAN, BUT PLEASE JUST TRY TO FORGET THE WHOLE THING.
OH, AND ROKU-SAN, YOUR-- WHAT TO CALL IT? YOUR TRAFFIC VIOLATION?
IF ANYONE TRIES TO GIVE YOU A HARD TIME, JUST CHECK IN WITH THE TRAFFIC SAFETY DIVISION.
KRRRK...
THE KIDS ARE OVER THERE, TOO.
SEE YA.
......
DOWN TOWN
FREE TOURIST INFORMATION CENTER
WELCOME. WHAT CAN I GET YOU TODAY?
TSING-TAO.
CHATTER
CHATTER
CHATTER

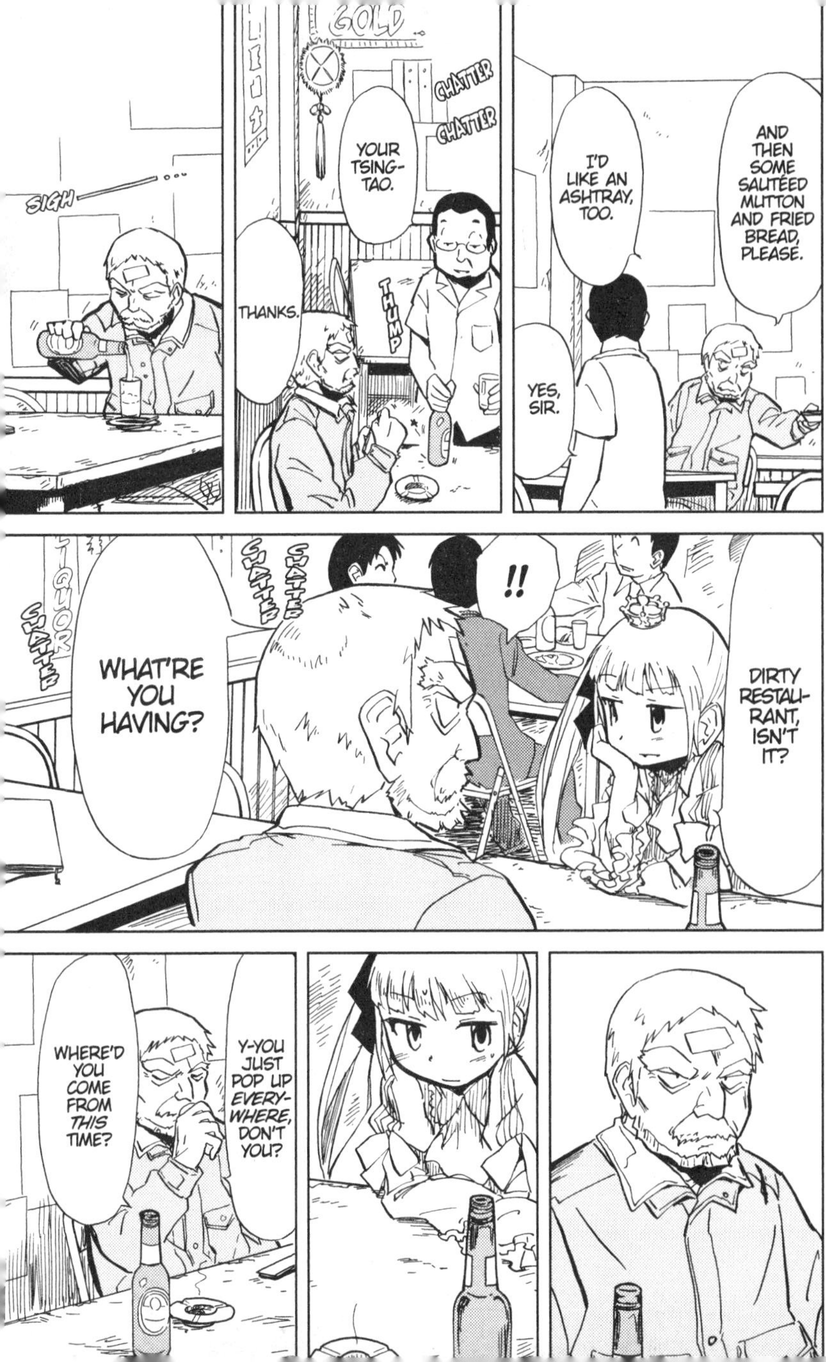
AND THEN SOME SAUTÉED MUTTON AND FRIED BREAD, PLEASE.
I'D LIKE AN ASHTRAY, TOO.
YES, SIR.
GOLD
CHATTER
CHATTER
YOUR TSING-TAO.
THUMP
THANKS.
SIGH.........
DIRTY RESTAURANT, ISN'T IT?
!!
CHATTER
CHATTER
WHAT'RE YOU HAVING?
LIQUOR
CHATTER
Y-YOU JUST POP UP *EVERYWHERE*, DON'T YOU?
WHERE'D YOU COME FROM *THIS* TIME?

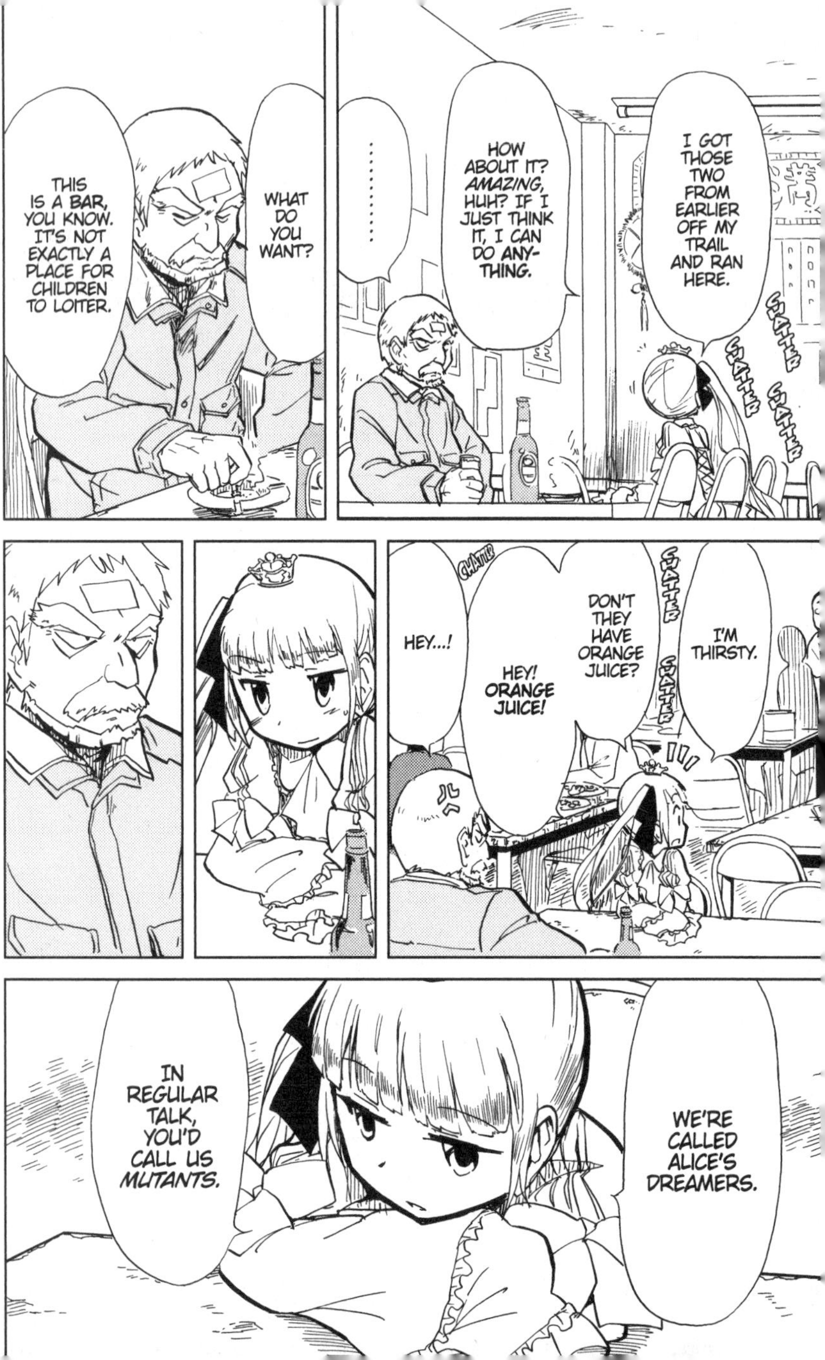
I GOT THOSE TWO FROM EARLIER OFF MY TRAIL AND RAN HERE.
CHATTER
CHATTER
CHATTER
CHATTER
HOW ABOUT IT? *AMAZING*, HUH? IF I JUST THINK IT, I CAN DO **ANYTHING**.
....
WHAT DO YOU WANT?
THIS IS A BAR, YOU KNOW. IT'S NOT EXACTLY A PLACE FOR CHILDREN TO LOITER.
I'M THIRSTY.
CHATTER
CHATTER
DON'T THEY HAVE ORANGE JUICE?
HEY! ORANGE JUICE!
CHATTER
HEY...!
WE'RE CALLED ALICE'S DREAMERS.
IN REGULAR TALK, YOU'D CALL US *MUTANTS*.

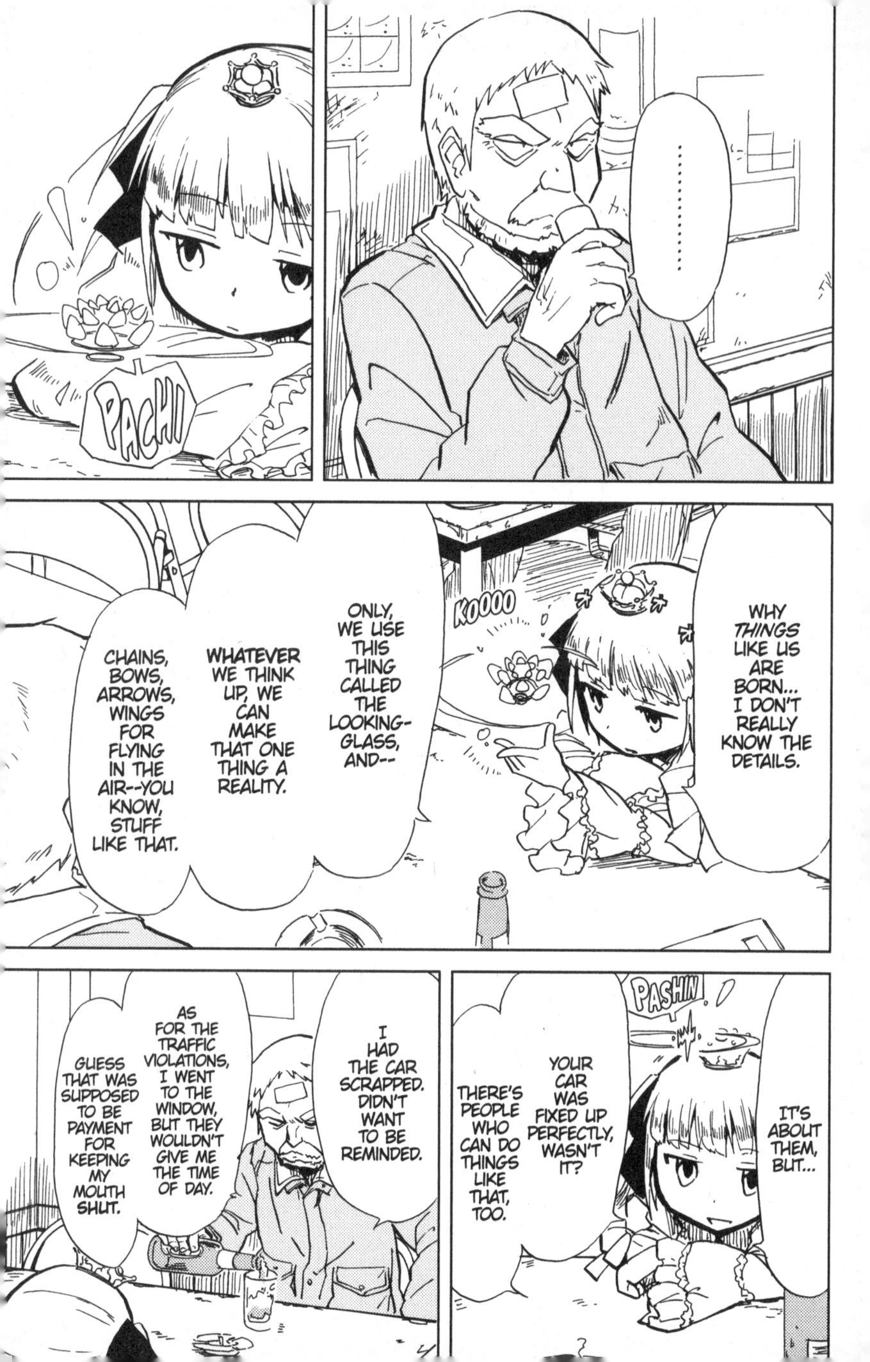
......
PACHI
WHY *THINGS* LIKE US ARE BORN... I DON'T REALLY KNOW THE DETAILS.
KOOOO
ONLY, WE USE THIS THING CALLED THE LOOKING-GLASS, AND--
WHATEVER WE THINK UP, WE CAN MAKE THAT ONE THING A REALITY.
CHAINS, BOWS, ARROWS, WINGS FOR FLYING IN THE AIR--YOU KNOW, STUFF LIKE THAT.
PASHIN
IT'S ABOUT THEM, BUT...
YOUR CAR WAS FIXED UP PERFECTLY, WASN'T IT?
THERE'S PEOPLE WHO CAN DO THINGS LIKE THAT, TOO.
I HAD THE CAR SCRAPPED. DIDN'T WANT TO BE REMINDED.
AS FOR THE TRAFFIC VIOLATIONS, I WENT TO THE WINDOW, BUT THEY WOULDN'T GIVE ME THE TIME OF DAY.
GUESS THAT WAS SUPPOSED TO BE PAYMENT FOR KEEPING MY MOUTH SHUT.

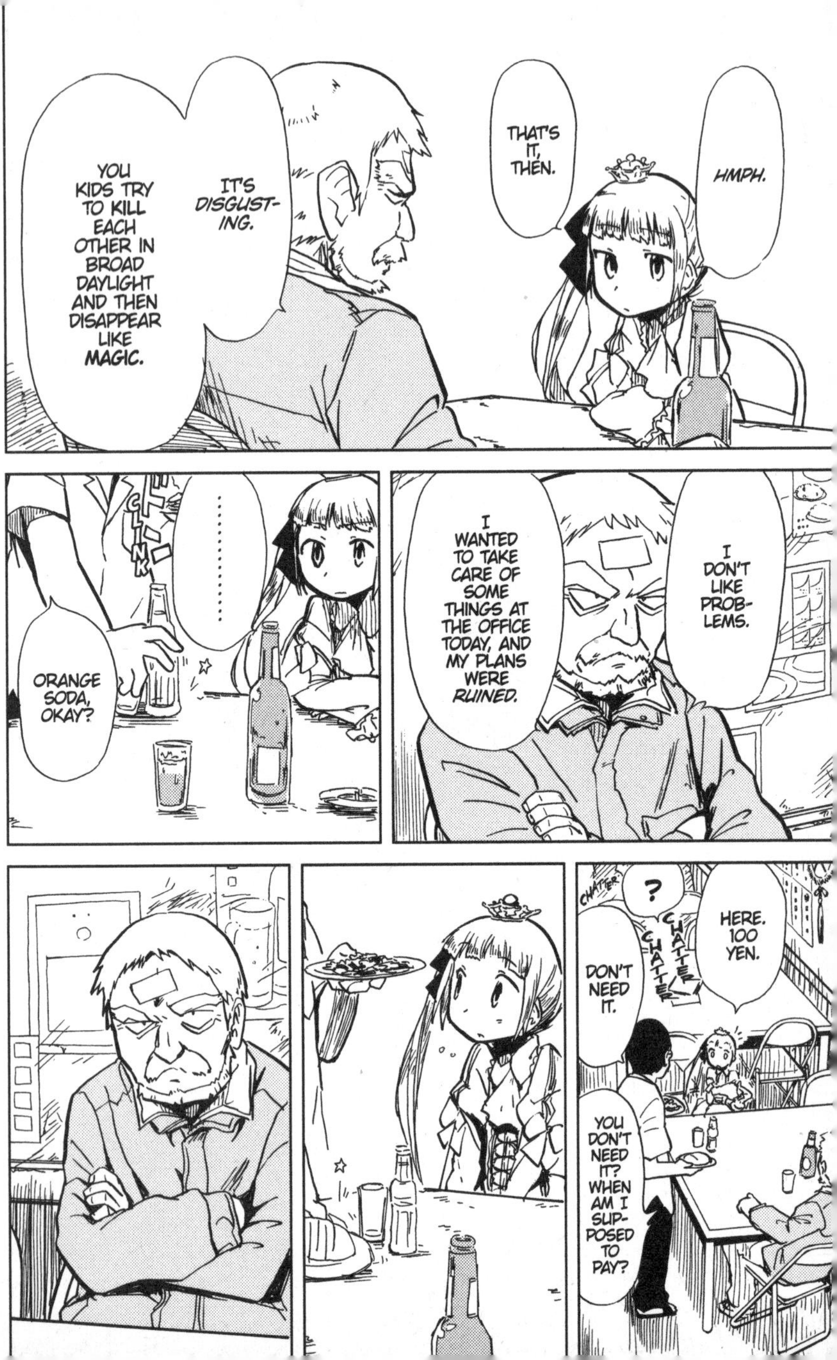
HMPH.
THAT'S IT, THEN.
IT'S DISGUSTING.
YOU KIDS TRY TO KILL EACH OTHER IN BROAD DAYLIGHT AND THEN DISAPPEAR LIKE MAGIC.
I DON'T LIKE PROBLEMS.
I WANTED TO TAKE CARE OF SOME THINGS AT THE OFFICE TODAY, AND MY PLANS WERE RUINED.
......
CLINK
ORANGE SODA, OKAY?
HERE. 100 YEN.
?
CHATTER CHATTER
CHATTER
DON'T NEED IT.
YOU DON'T NEED IT? WHEN AM I SUPPOSED TO PAY?

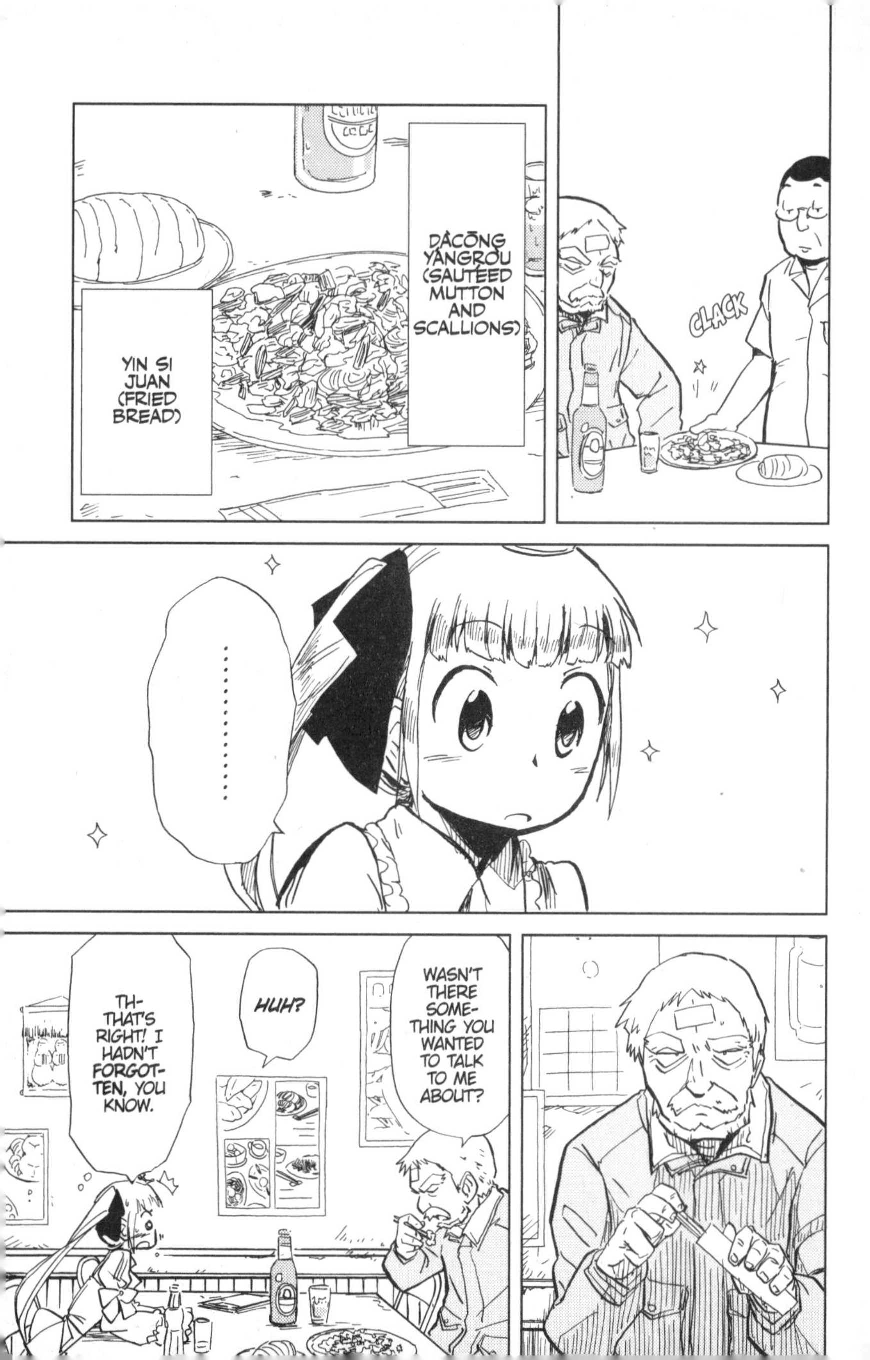
CLACK
DÀCŌNG YÁNGRÒU (SAUTÉED MUTTON AND SCALLIONS)
YIN SI JUAN (FRIED BREAD)
......
WASN'T THERE SOME-THING YOU WANTED TO TALK TO ME ABOUT?
HUH?
TH-THAT'S RIGHT! I HADN'T FORGOT-TEN, YOU KNOW.

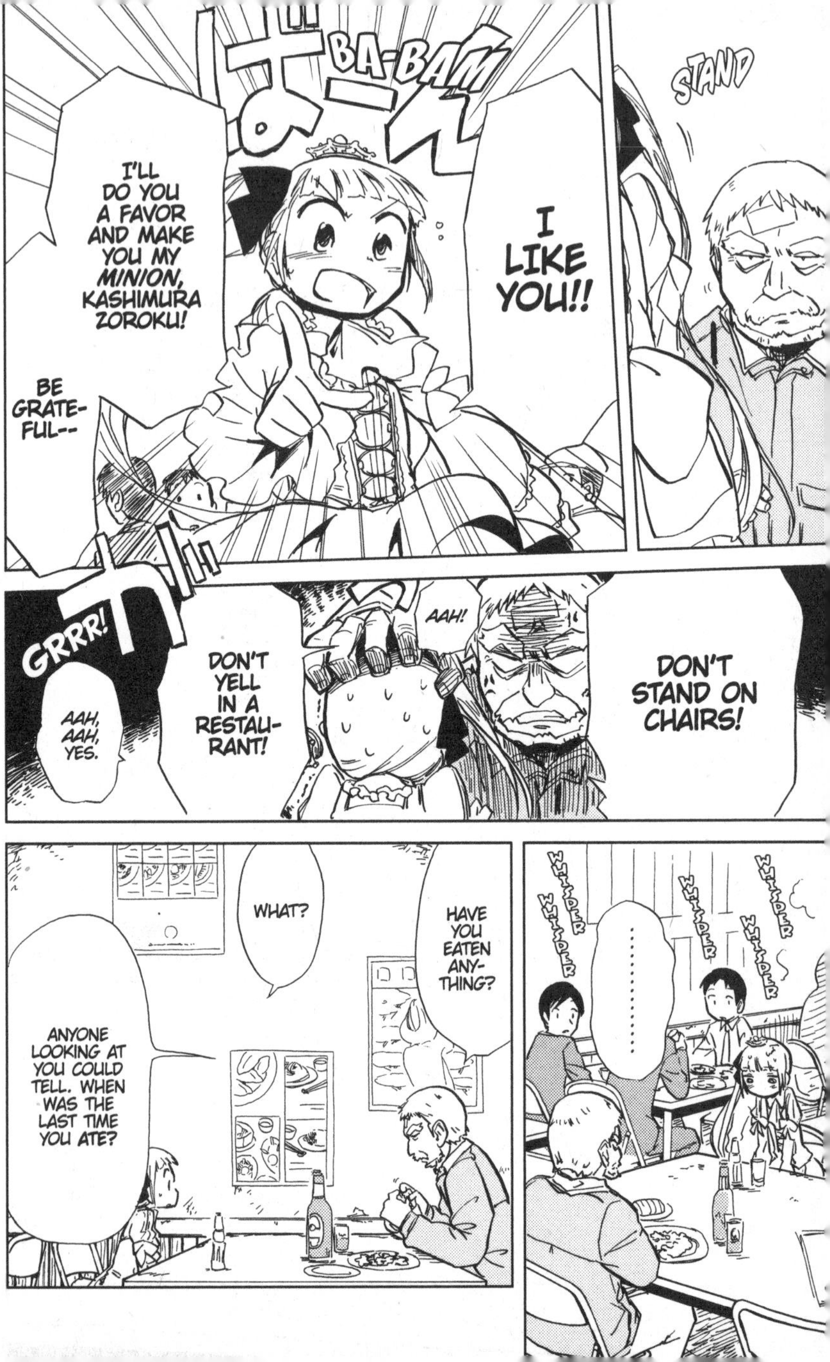
STAND
BA-BAM
I LIKE YOU!!
I'LL DO YOU A FAVOR AND MAKE YOU MY *MINION*, KASHIMURA ZOROKU!
BE GRATEFUL--
DON'T STAND ON CHAIRS!
AAH!
DON'T YELL IN A RESTAURANT!
GRRR!
AAH, AAH, YES.
WHISPER WHISPER
WHISPER WHISPER
WHISPER WHISPER
......
HAVE YOU EATEN ANYTHING?
WHAT?
ANYONE LOOKING AT YOU COULD TELL. WHEN WAS THE LAST TIME YOU ATE?

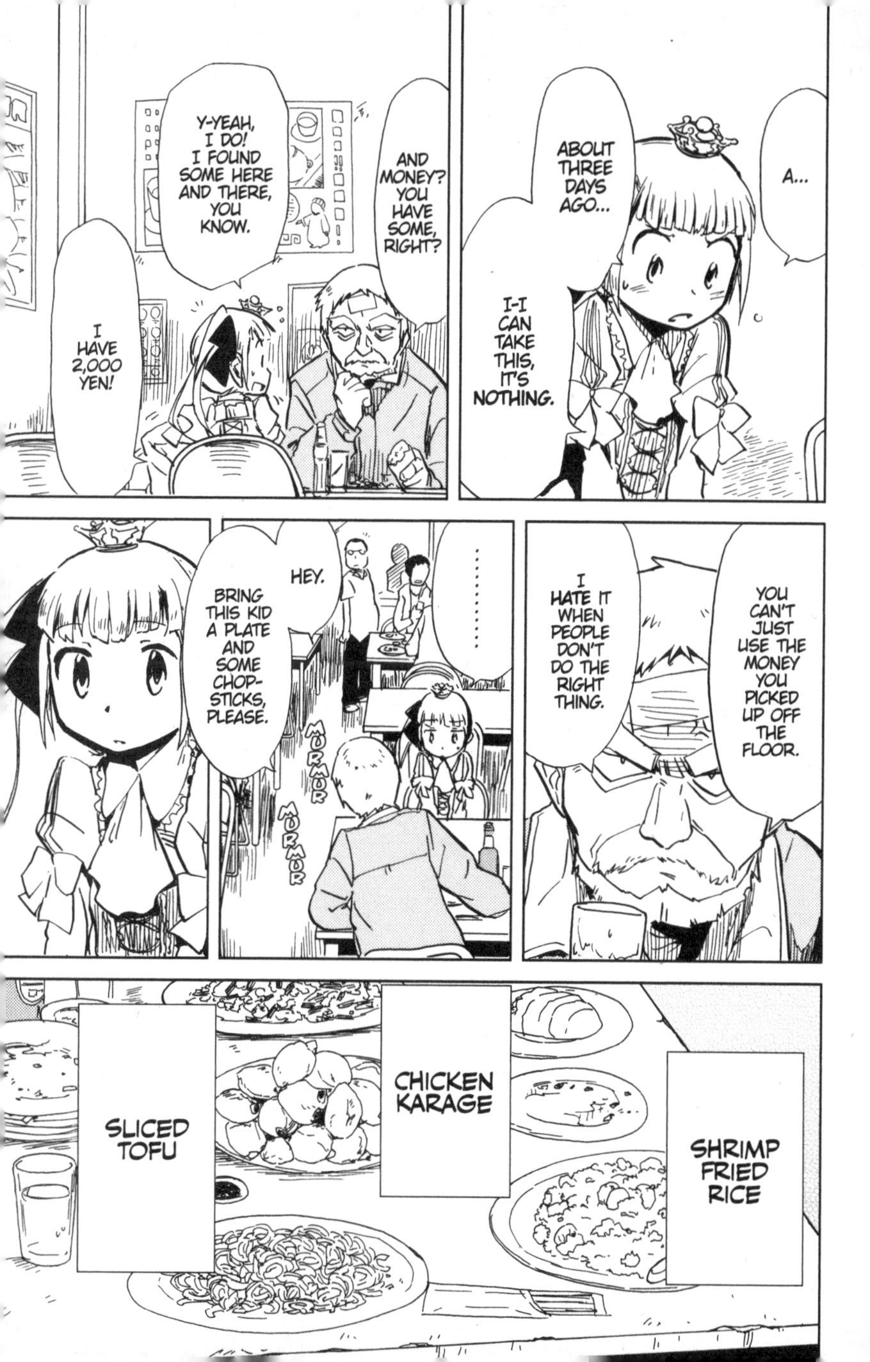
A...
ABOUT THREE DAYS AGO...
I-I CAN TAKE THIS, IT'S NOTHING.
AND MONEY? YOU HAVE SOME, RIGHT?
Y-YEAH, I DO! I FOUND SOME HERE AND THERE, YOU KNOW.
I HAVE 2,000 YEN!
YOU CAN'T JUST USE THE MONEY YOU PICKED UP OFF THE FLOOR.
I HATE IT WHEN PEOPLE DON'T DO THE RIGHT THING.
......
HEY.
BRING THIS KID A PLATE AND SOME CHOP-STICKS, PLEASE.
MURMUR
MURMUR
SHRIMP FRIED RICE
CHICKEN KARAGE
SLICED TOFU

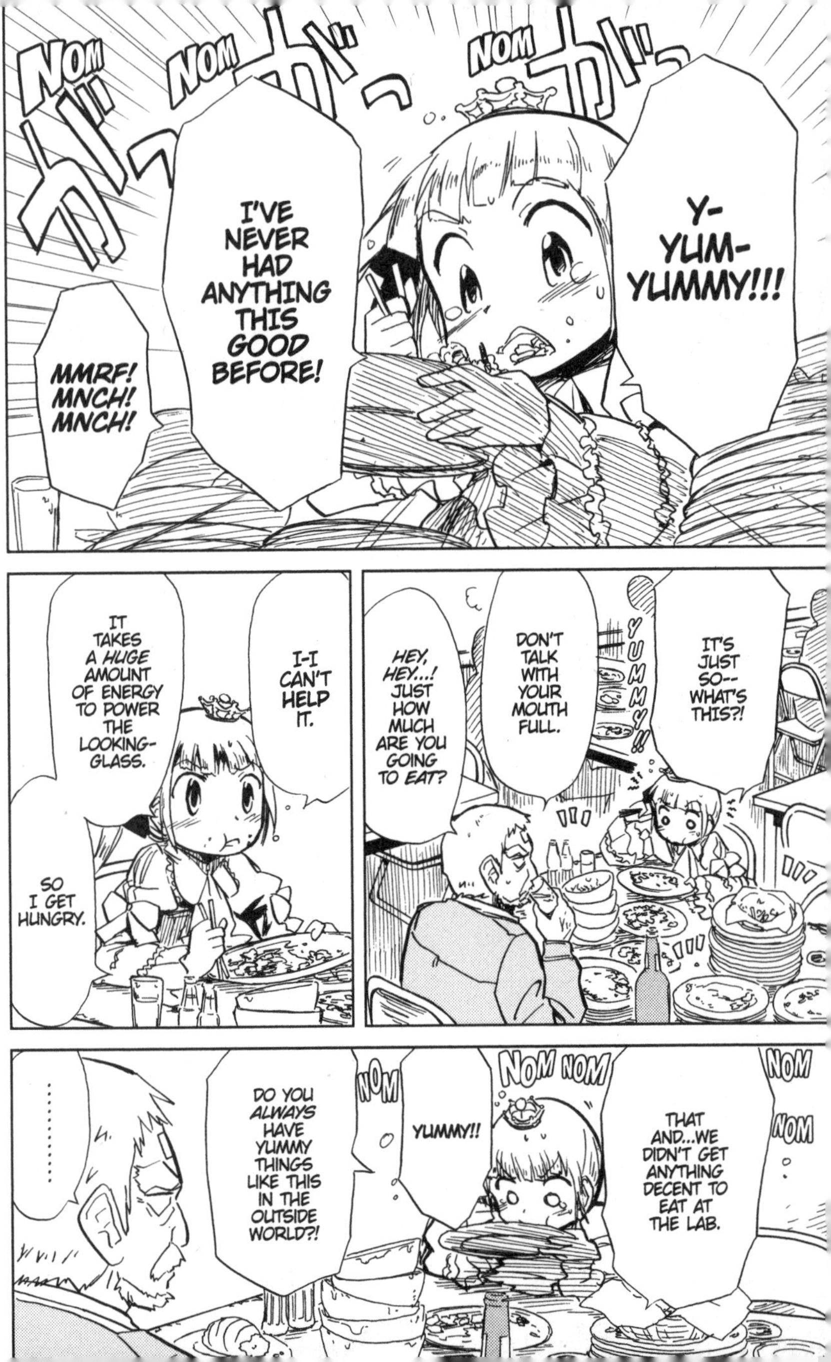
NOM
Y-YUM-YUMMY!!!
NOM
I'VE NEVER HAD ANYTHING THIS GOOD BEFORE!
NOM
MMRF! MNCH! MNCH!
IT'S JUST SO-- WHAT'S THIS?!
YUMMY!!
DON'T TALK WITH YOUR MOUTH FULL.
HEY, HEY...! JUST HOW MUCH ARE YOU GOING TO EAT?
I-I CAN'T HELP IT.
IT TAKES A HUGE AMOUNT OF ENERGY TO POWER THE LOOKING-GLASS.
SO I GET HUNGRY.
NOM NOM
THAT AND...WE DIDN'T GET ANYTHING DECENT TO EAT AT THE LAB.
NOM NOM
YUMMY!!
NOM
DO YOU ALWAYS HAVE YUMMY THINGS LIKE THIS IN THE OUTSIDE WORLD?!
....

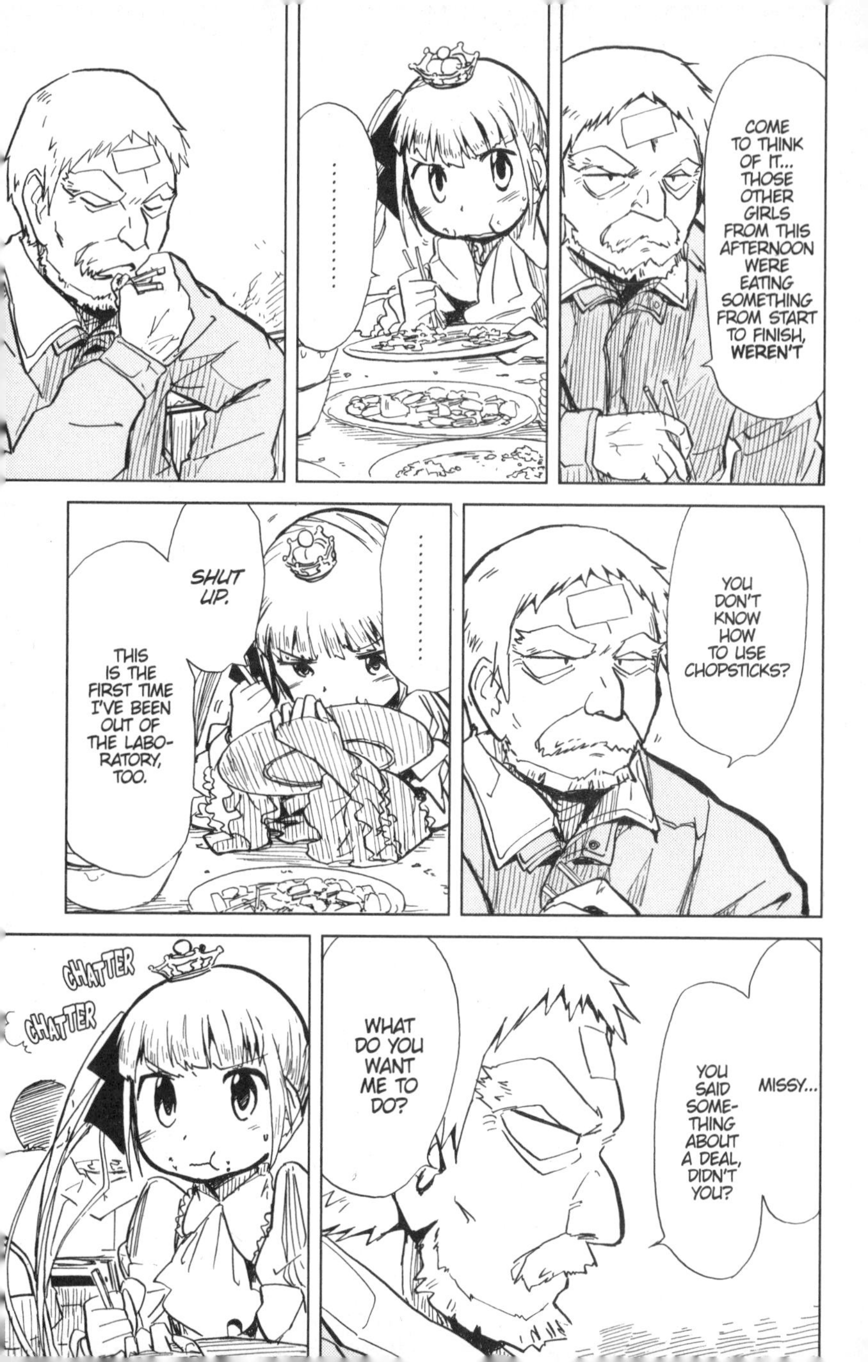
COME TO THINK OF IT... THOSE OTHER GIRLS FROM THIS AFTERNOON WERE EATING SOMETHING FROM START TO FINISH, WEREN'T
......
YOU DON'T KNOW HOW TO USE CHOPSTICKS?
......
SHUT UP.
THIS IS THE FIRST TIME I'VE BEEN OUT OF THE LABO-RATORY, TOO.
MISSY...
YOU SAID SOME-THING ABOUT A DEAL, DIDN'T YOU?
WHAT DO YOU WANT ME TO DO?
CHATTER
CHATTER

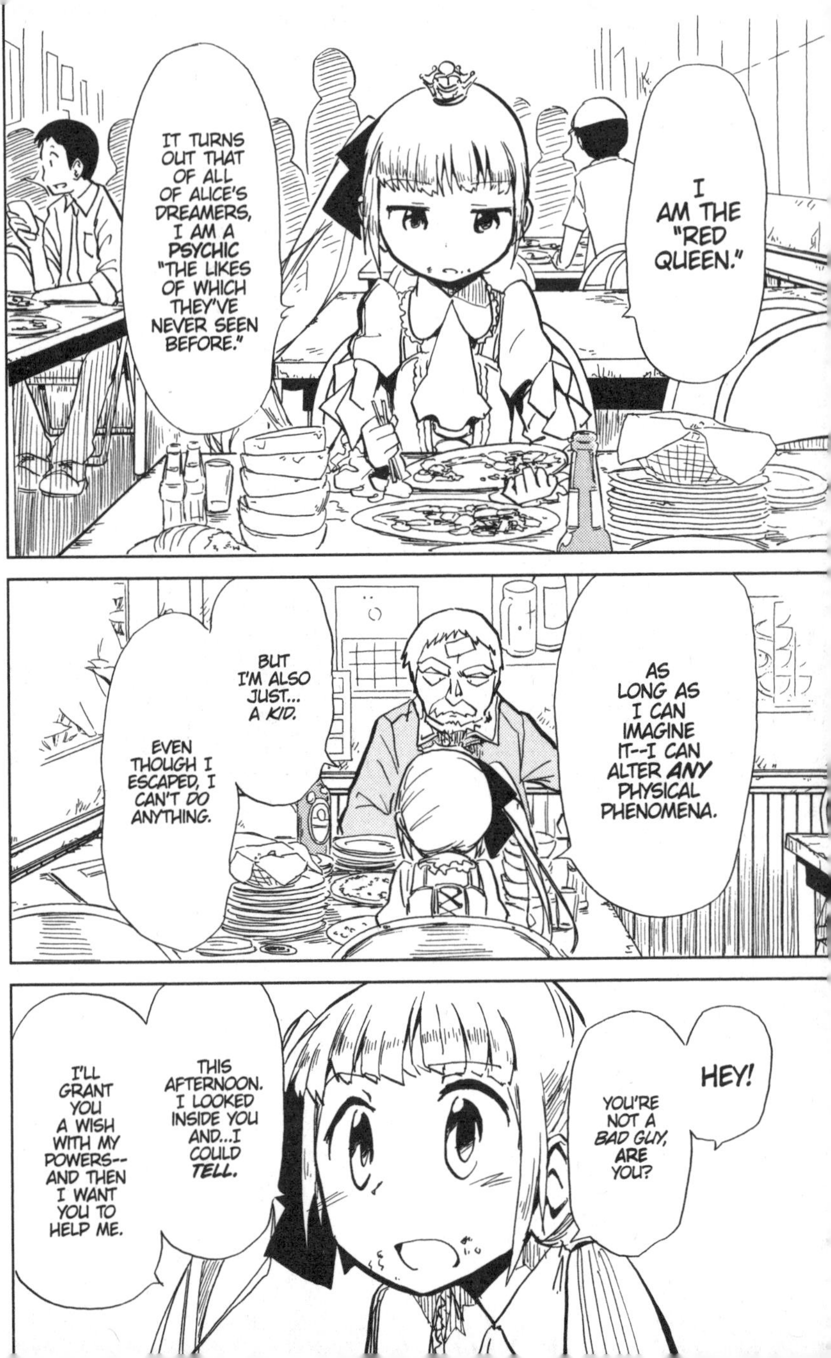
I AM THE "RED QUEEN."
IT TURNS OUT THAT OF ALL OF ALICE'S DREAMERS, I AM A **PSYCHIC** "THE LIKES OF WHICH THEY'VE NEVER SEEN BEFORE."
AS LONG AS I CAN IMAGINE IT--I CAN ALTER ***ANY*** PHYSICAL PHENOMENA.
BUT I'M ALSO JUST... A *KID*.
EVEN THOUGH I ESCAPED, I CAN'T *DO* ANYTHING.
HEY!
YOU'RE NOT A *BAD GUY*, ARE YOU?
THIS AFTERNOON. I LOOKED INSIDE YOU AND...I COULD ***TELL.***
I'LL GRANT YOU A WISH WITH MY POWERS--AND THEN I WANT YOU TO HELP ME.

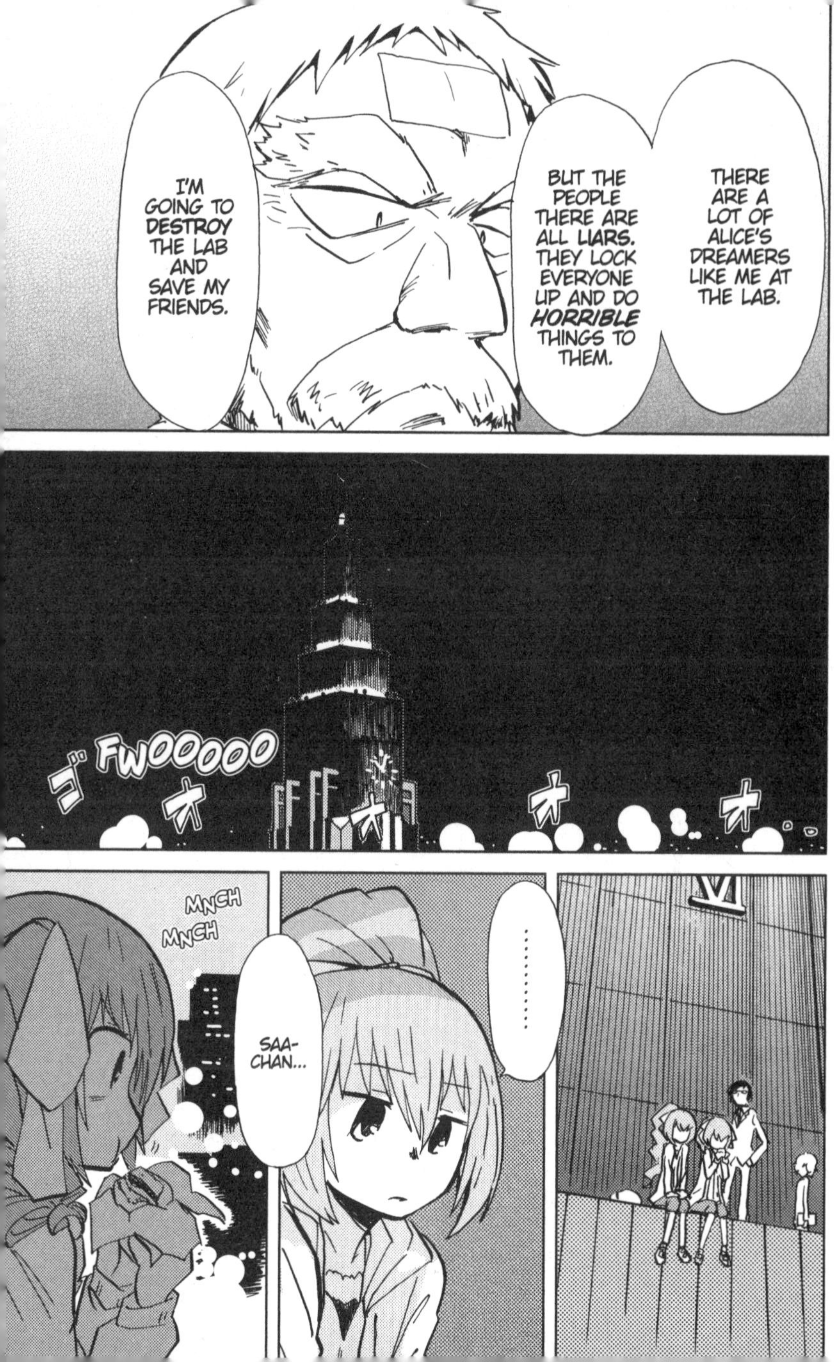
THERE ARE A LOT OF ALICE'S DREAMERS LIKE ME AT THE LAB.
BUT THE PEOPLE THERE ARE ALL LIARS. THEY LOCK EVERYONE UP AND DO HORRIBLE THINGS TO THEM.
I'M GOING TO DESTROY THE LAB AND SAVE MY FRIENDS.
FWOOOOOO
....
SAA-CHAN...
MNCH
MNCH

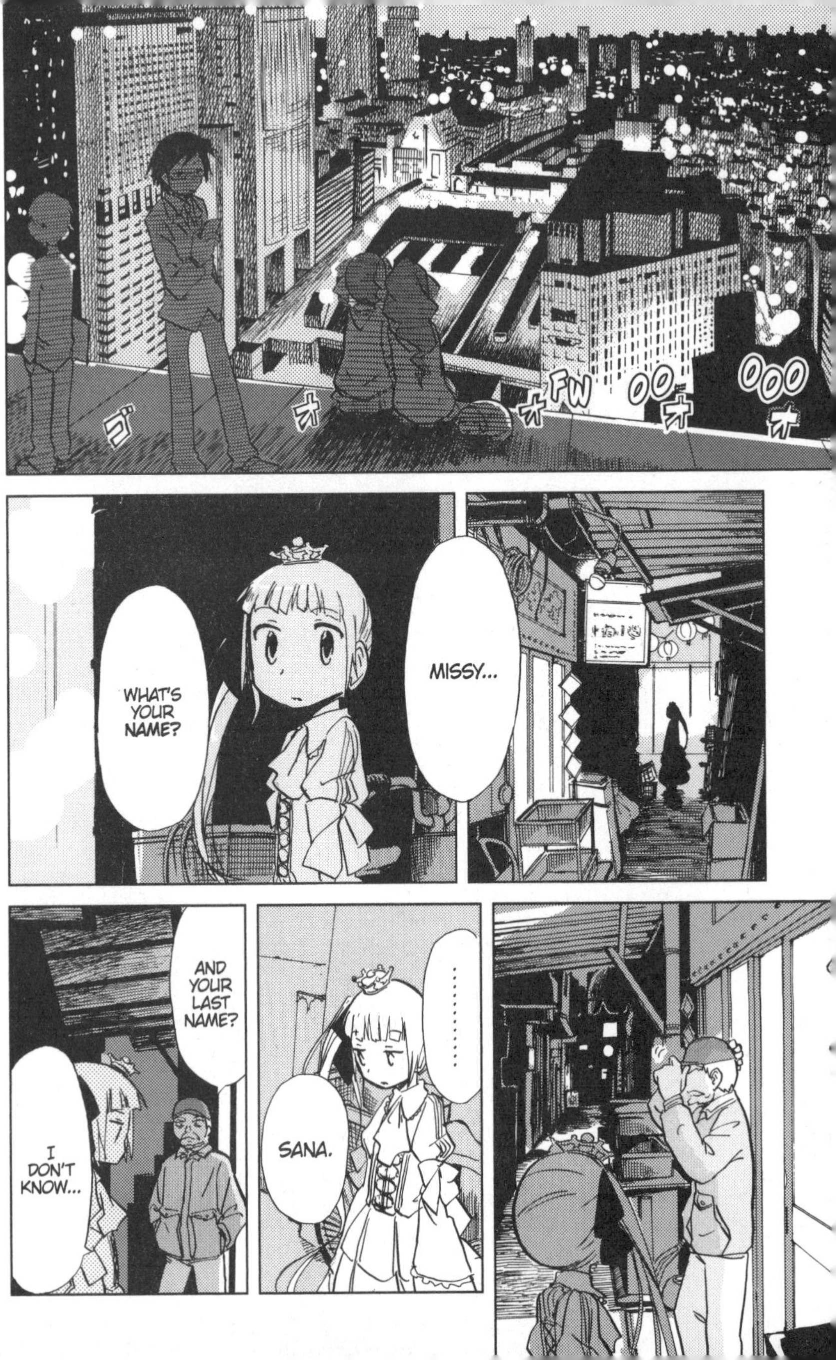
ゴオ
FW
OO
OOO
オオオ
MISSY...
WHAT'S YOUR NAME?
......
SANA.
AND YOUR LAST NAME?
I DON'T KNOW...

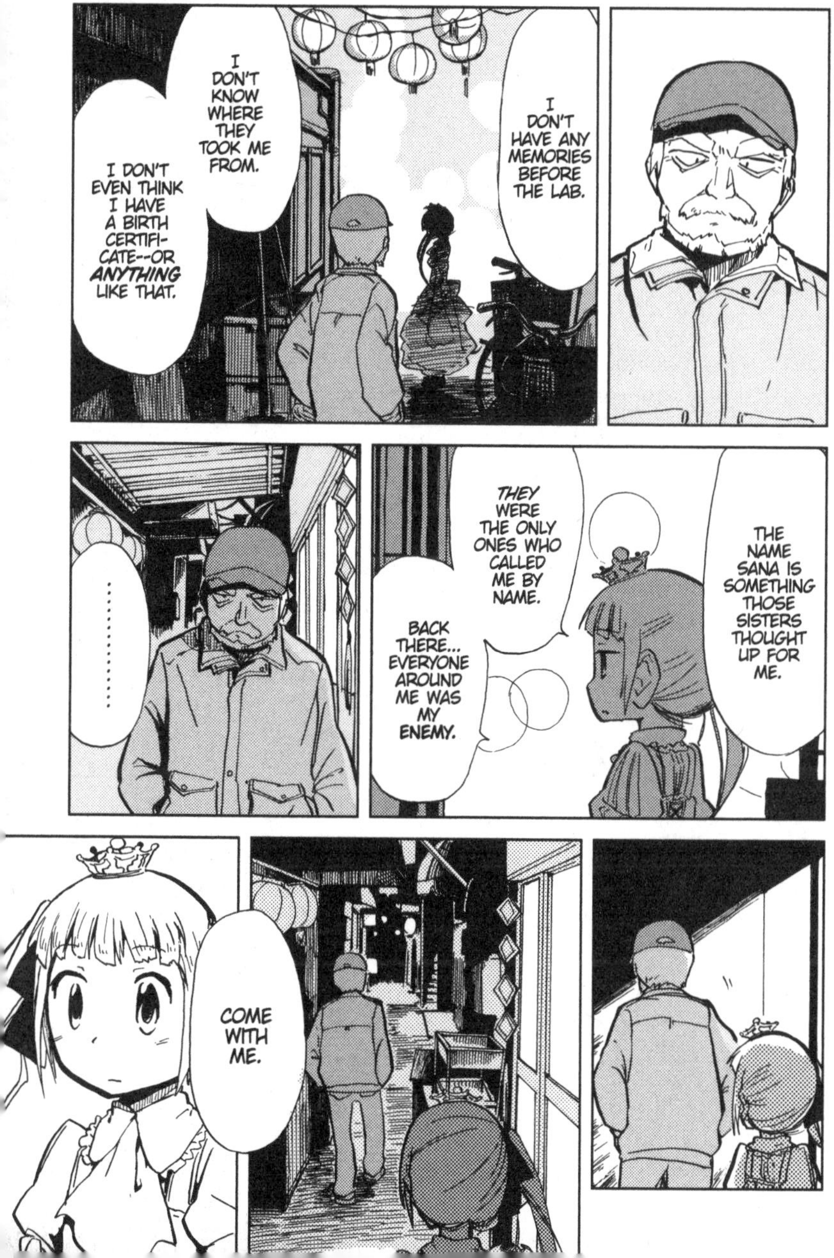
I DON'T HAVE ANY MEMORIES BEFORE THE LAB.
I DON'T KNOW WHERE THEY TOOK ME FROM.
I DON'T EVEN THINK I HAVE A BIRTH CERTIFI-CATE--OR *ANYTHING* LIKE THAT.
THE NAME SANA IS SOMETHING THOSE SISTERS THOUGHT UP FOR ME.
THEY WERE THE ONLY ONES WHO CALLED ME BY NAME.
BACK THERE... EVERYONE AROUND ME WAS MY **ENEMY.**
......
COME WITH ME.

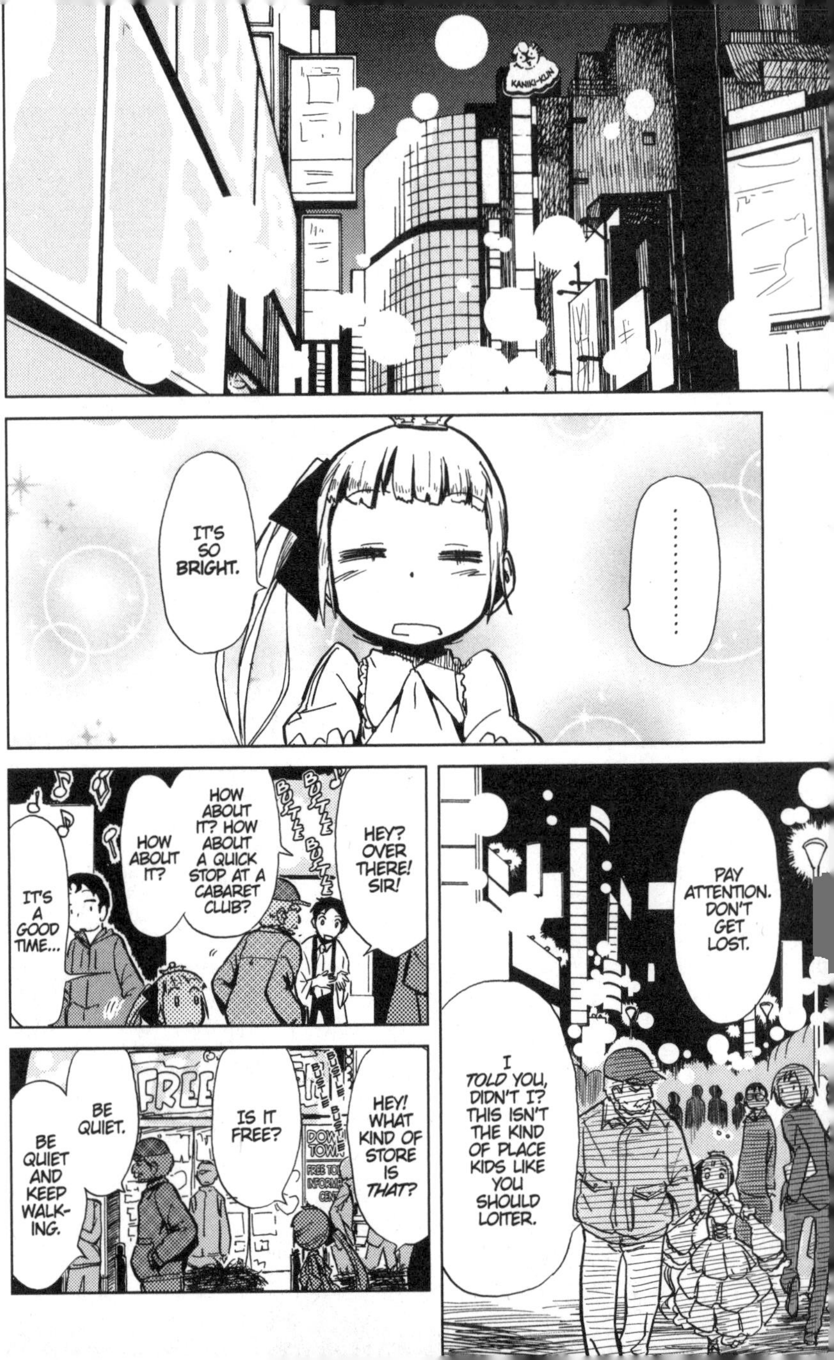
KANIKI-KUN
......
IT'S SO BRIGHT.
PAY ATTENTION. DON'T GET LOST.
I *TOLD* YOU, DIDN'T I? THIS ISN'T THE KIND OF PLACE KIDS LIKE YOU SHOULD LOITER.
HEY? OVER THERE! SIR!
BUSTLE BUSTLE BUSTLE
HOW ABOUT IT? HOW ABOUT A QUICK STOP AT A CABARET CLUB?
HOW ABOUT IT?
IT'S A GOOD TIME...
HEY! WHAT KIND OF STORE IS *THAT*?
BUSTLE BUSTLE
IS IT FREE?
BE QUIET.
BE QUIET AND KEEP WALKING.

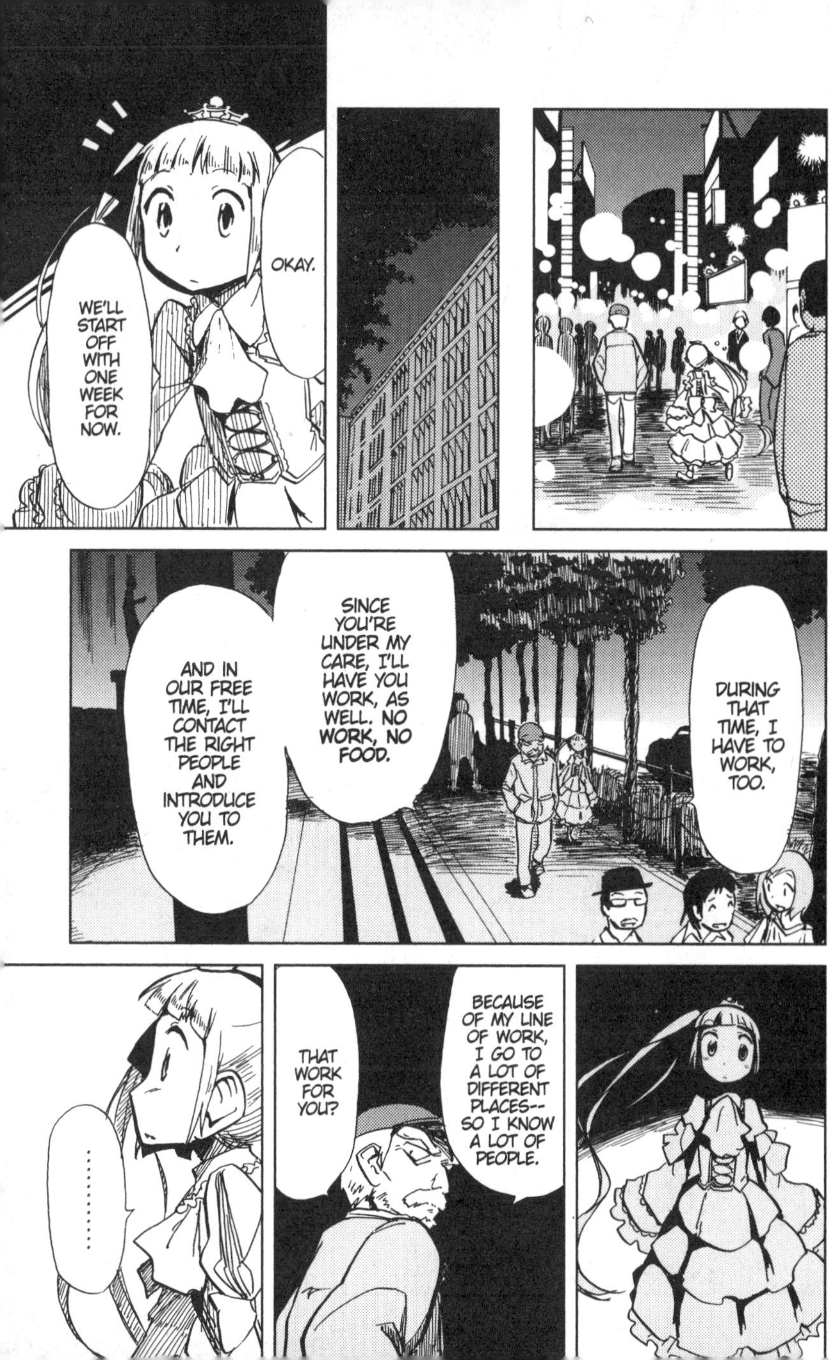
WE'LL START OFF WITH ONE WEEK FOR NOW.
OKAY.
DURING THAT TIME, I HAVE TO WORK, TOO.
SINCE YOU'RE UNDER MY CARE, I'LL HAVE YOU WORK, AS WELL. NO WORK, NO FOOD.
AND IN OUR FREE TIME, I'LL CONTACT THE RIGHT PEOPLE AND INTRODUCE YOU TO THEM.
BECAUSE OF MY LINE OF WORK, I GO TO A LOT OF DIFFERENT PLACES-- SO I KNOW A LOT OF PEOPLE.
THAT WORK FOR YOU?
....

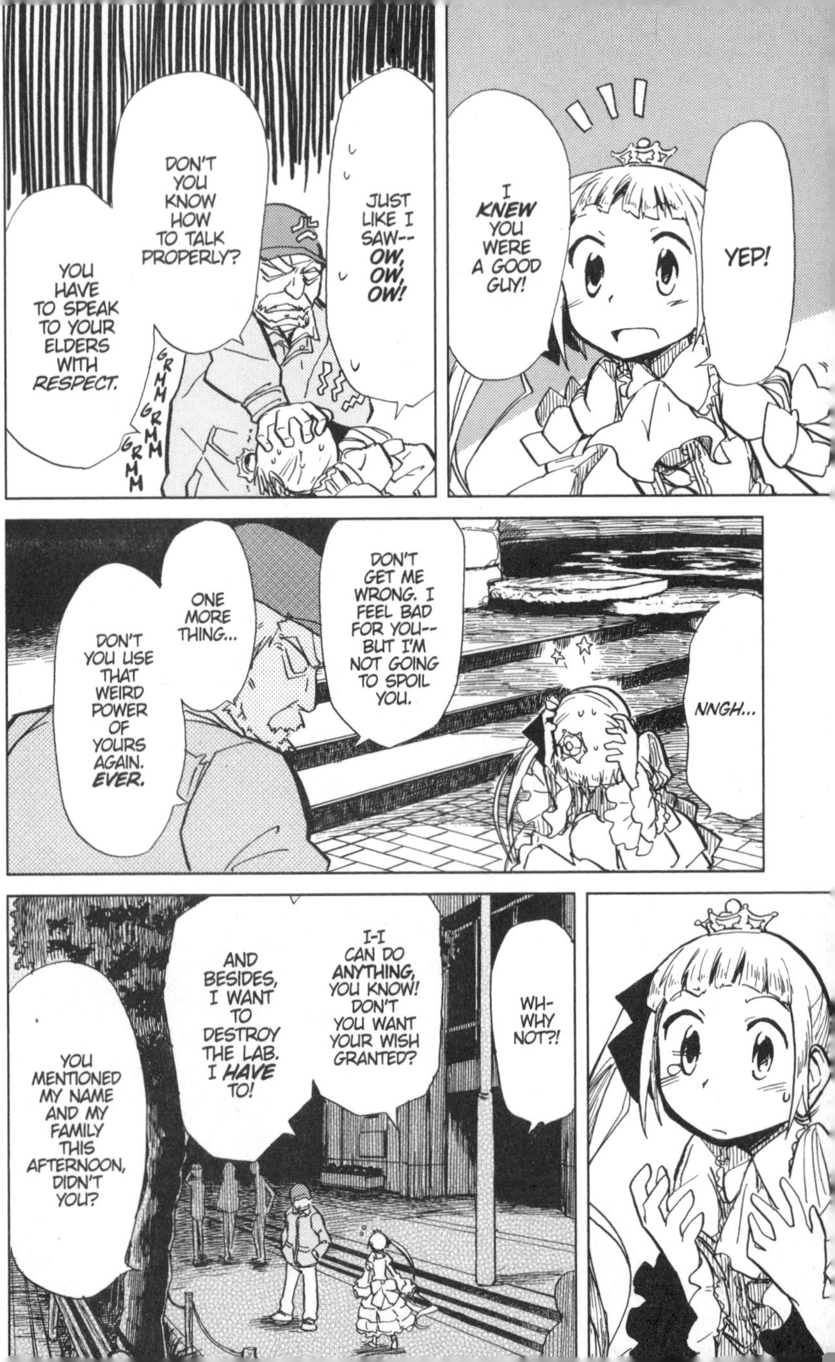
YEP!
I KNEW YOU WERE A GOOD GUY!
JUST LIKE I SAW-- OW, OW, OW!
DON'T YOU KNOW HOW TO TALK PROPERLY?
YOU HAVE TO SPEAK TO YOUR ELDERS WITH RESPECT.
GRMM GRMM GRMM
NNGH...
DON'T GET ME WRONG. I FEEL BAD FOR YOU-- BUT I'M NOT GOING TO SPOIL YOU.
ONE MORE THING...
DON'T YOU USE THAT WEIRD POWER OF YOURS AGAIN. EVER.
WH-WHY NOT?!
I-I CAN DO ANYTHING, YOU KNOW! DON'T YOU WANT YOUR WISH GRANTED?
AND BESIDES, I WANT TO DESTROY THE LAB. I HAVE TO!
YOU MENTIONED MY NAME AND MY FAMILY THIS AFTERNOON, DIDN'T YOU?

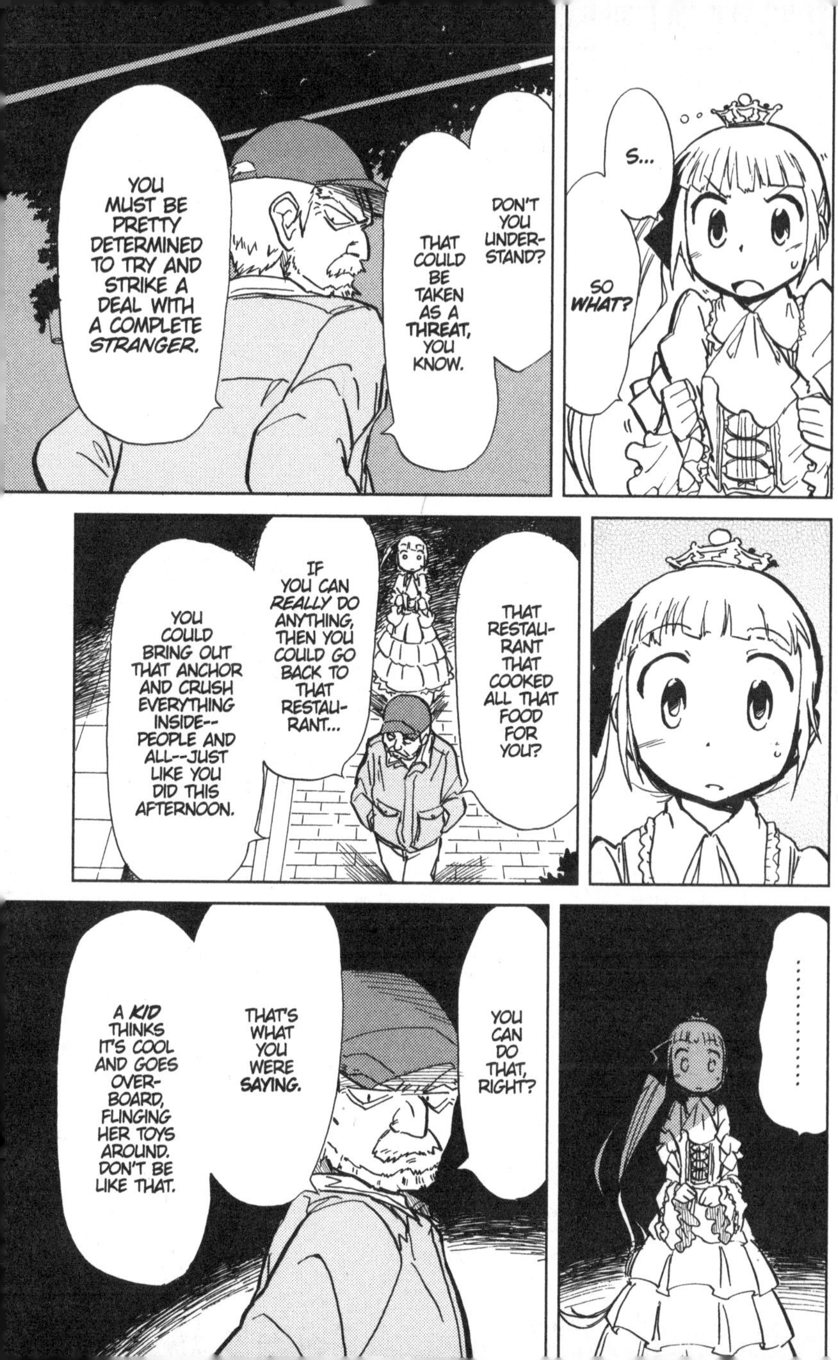
S...
SO WHAT?
DON'T YOU UNDERSTAND?
THAT COULD BE TAKEN AS A THREAT, YOU KNOW.
YOU MUST BE PRETTY DETERMINED TO TRY AND STRIKE A DEAL WITH A COMPLETE STRANGER.
THAT RESTAURANT THAT COOKED ALL THAT FOOD FOR YOU?
IF YOU CAN REALLY DO ANYTHING, THEN YOU COULD GO BACK TO THAT RESTAURANT...
YOU COULD BRING OUT THAT ANCHOR AND CRUSH EVERYTHING INSIDE-- PEOPLE AND ALL--JUST LIKE YOU DID THIS AFTERNOON.
......
YOU CAN DO THAT, RIGHT?
THAT'S WHAT YOU WERE SAYING.
A KID THINKS IT'S COOL AND GOES OVERBOARD, FLINGING HER TOYS AROUND. DON'T BE LIKE THAT.

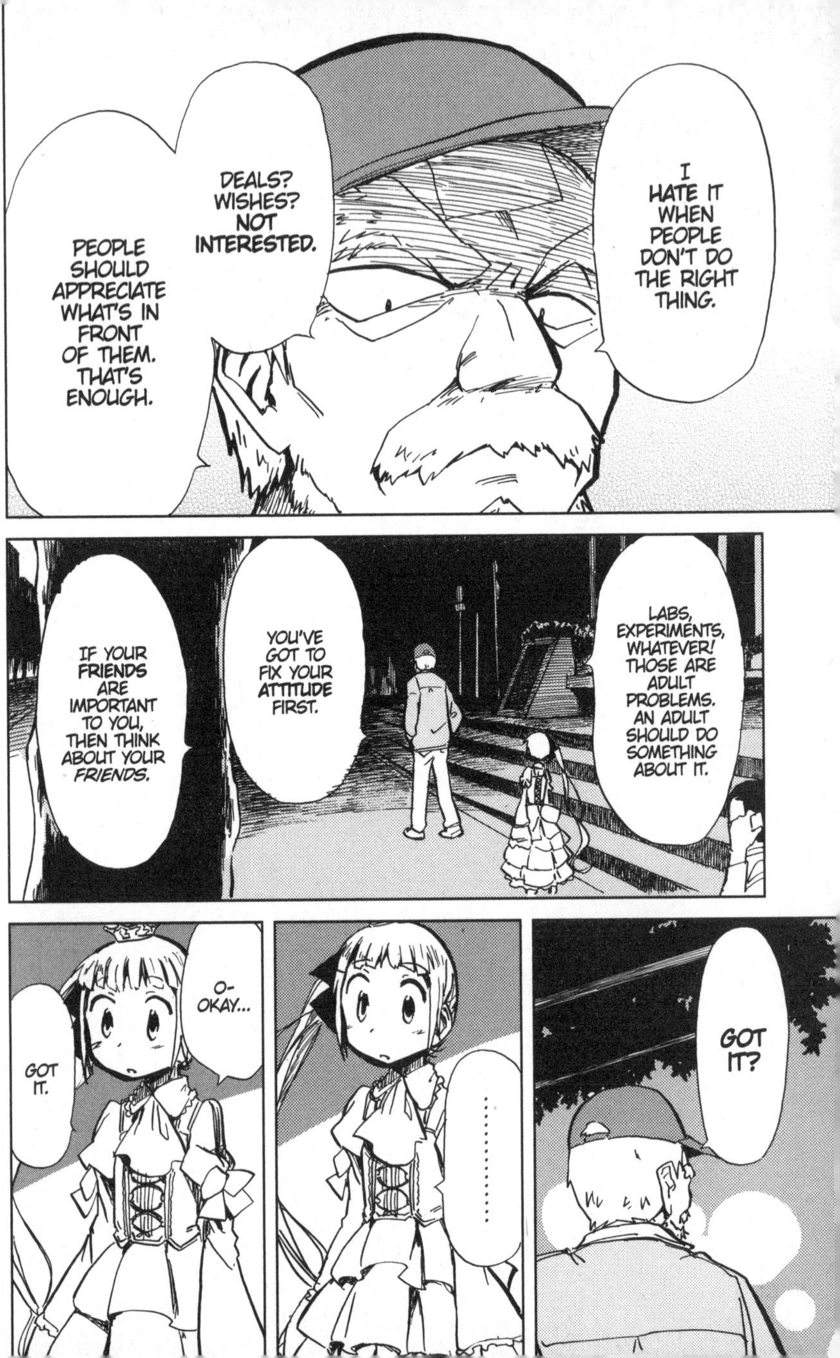
I HATE IT WHEN PEOPLE DON'T DO THE RIGHT THING.
DEALS? WISHES? NOT INTERESTED.
PEOPLE SHOULD APPRECIATE WHAT'S IN FRONT OF THEM. THAT'S ENOUGH.
LABS, EXPERIMENTS, WHATEVER! THOSE ARE ADULT PROBLEMS. AN ADULT SHOULD DO SOMETHING ABOUT IT.
YOU'VE GOT TO FIX YOUR ATTITUDE FIRST.
IF YOUR FRIENDS ARE IMPORTANT TO YOU, THEN THINK ABOUT YOUR *FRIENDS.*
GOT IT?
......
O-OKAY...
GOT IT.

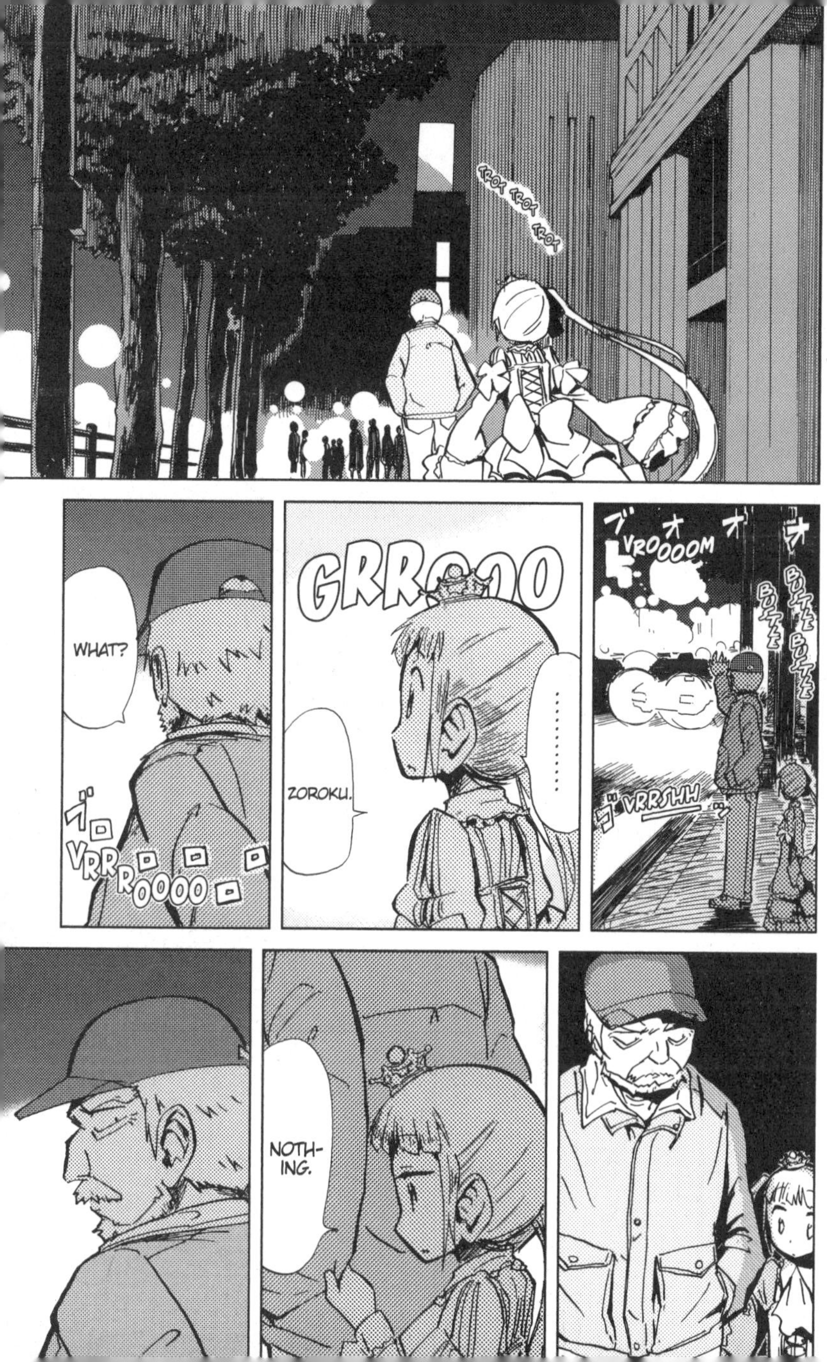
TROT TROT TROT
ブオオオ
VROOOOM
BUSTLE BUSTLE
BUSTLE
ゴ
VRRSHH
GRROOO
......
ZOROKU.
WHAT?
ブロロロ
VRRROOOO
NOTH-ING.

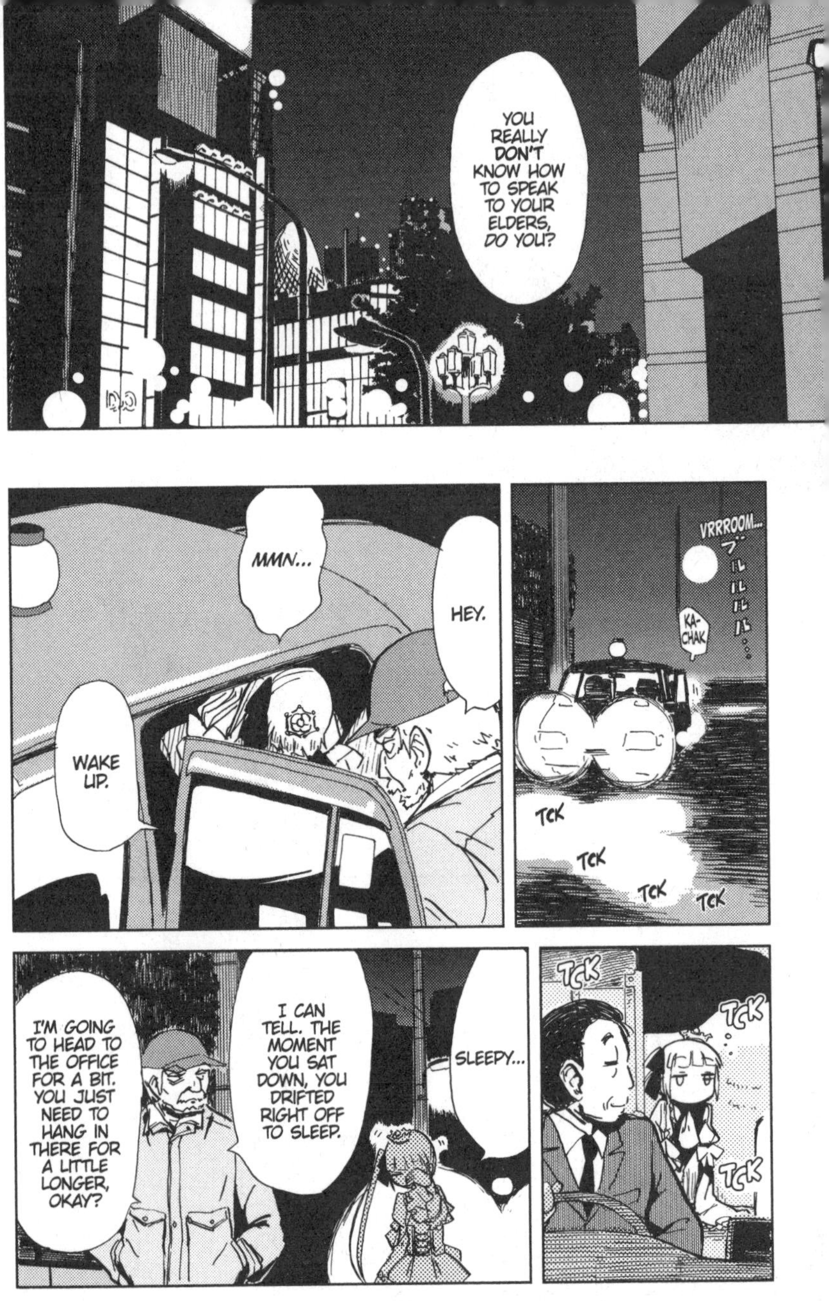
YOU REALLY DON'T KNOW HOW TO SPEAK TO YOUR ELDERS, DO YOU?
VRRROOM...
ブルルル...
KA-CHAK
TCK
TCK
TCK
TCK
HEY.
MMN...
WAKE UP.
TCK
TCK
TCK
SLEEPY...
I CAN TELL. THE MOMENT YOU SAT DOWN, YOU DRIFTED RIGHT OFF TO SLEEP.
I'M GOING TO HEAD TO THE OFFICE FOR A BIT. YOU JUST NEED TO HANG IN THERE FOR A LITTLE LONGER, OKAY?

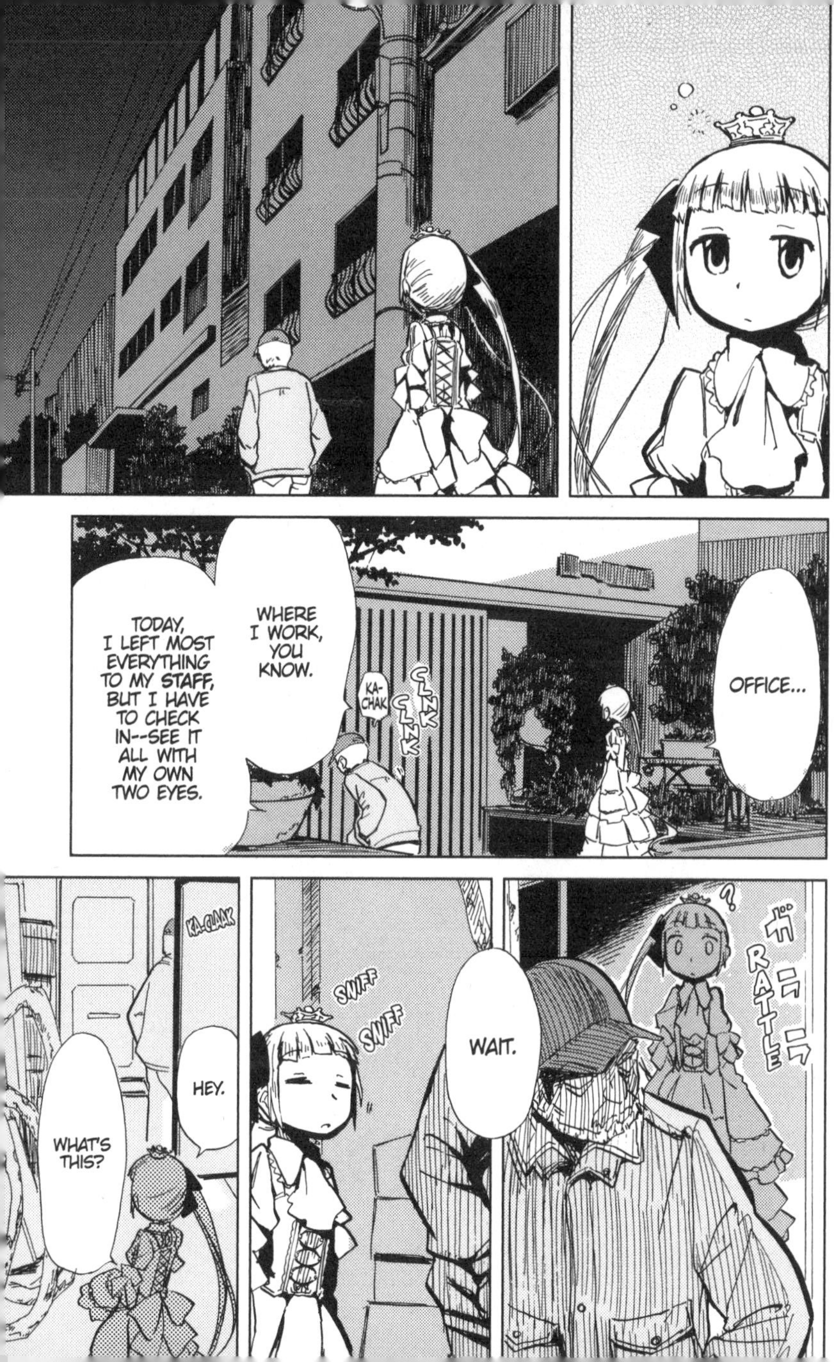
OFFICE...
CLNK CLNK
KA-CHAK
WHERE I WORK, YOU KNOW.
TODAY, I LEFT MOST EVERYTHING TO MY STAFF, BUT I HAVE TO CHECK IN--SEE IT ALL WITH MY OWN TWO EYES.
RATTLE
WAIT.
SNIFF SNIFF
KA-CLAAK
HEY.
WHAT'S THIS?

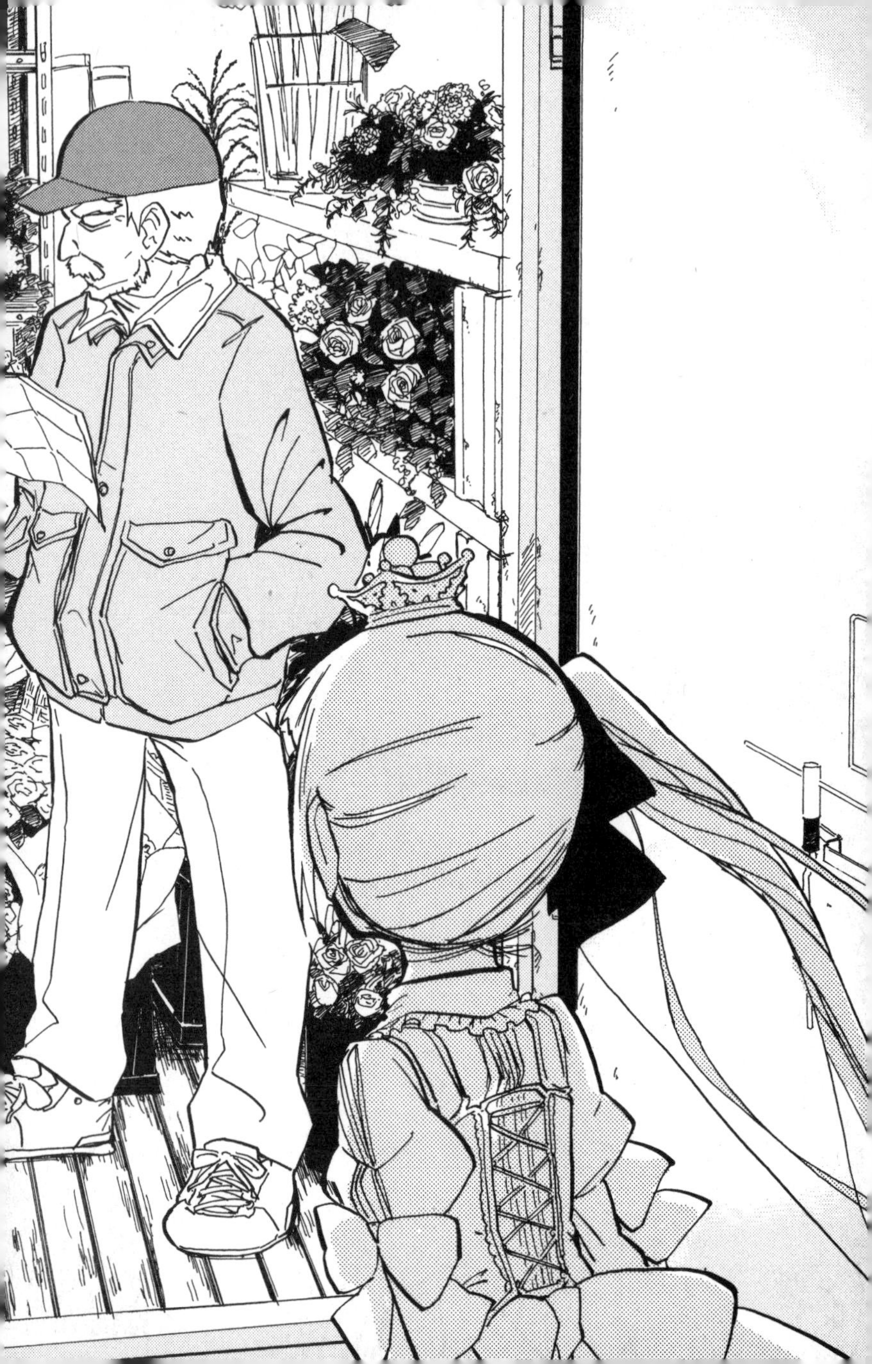

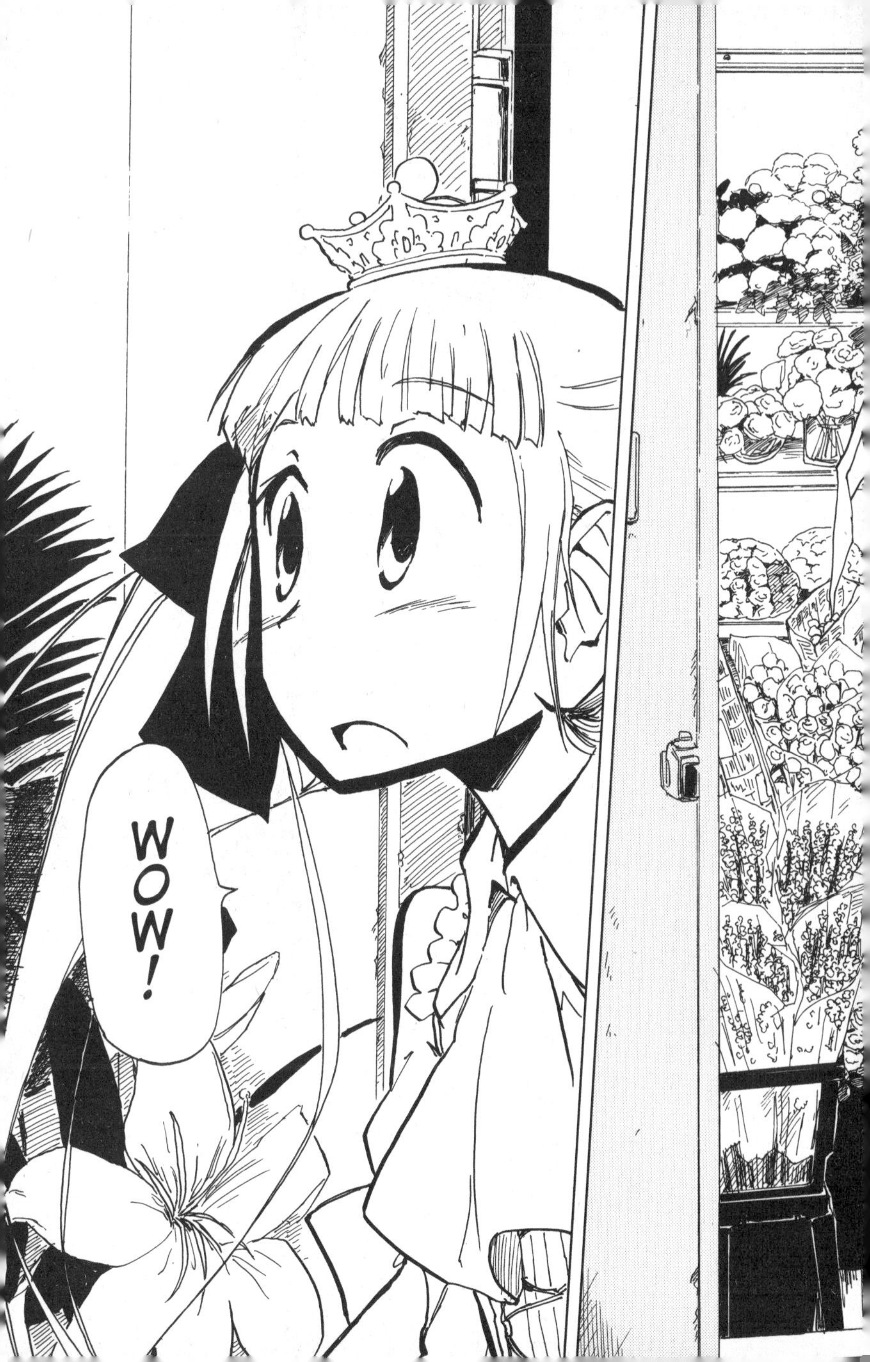
WOW!

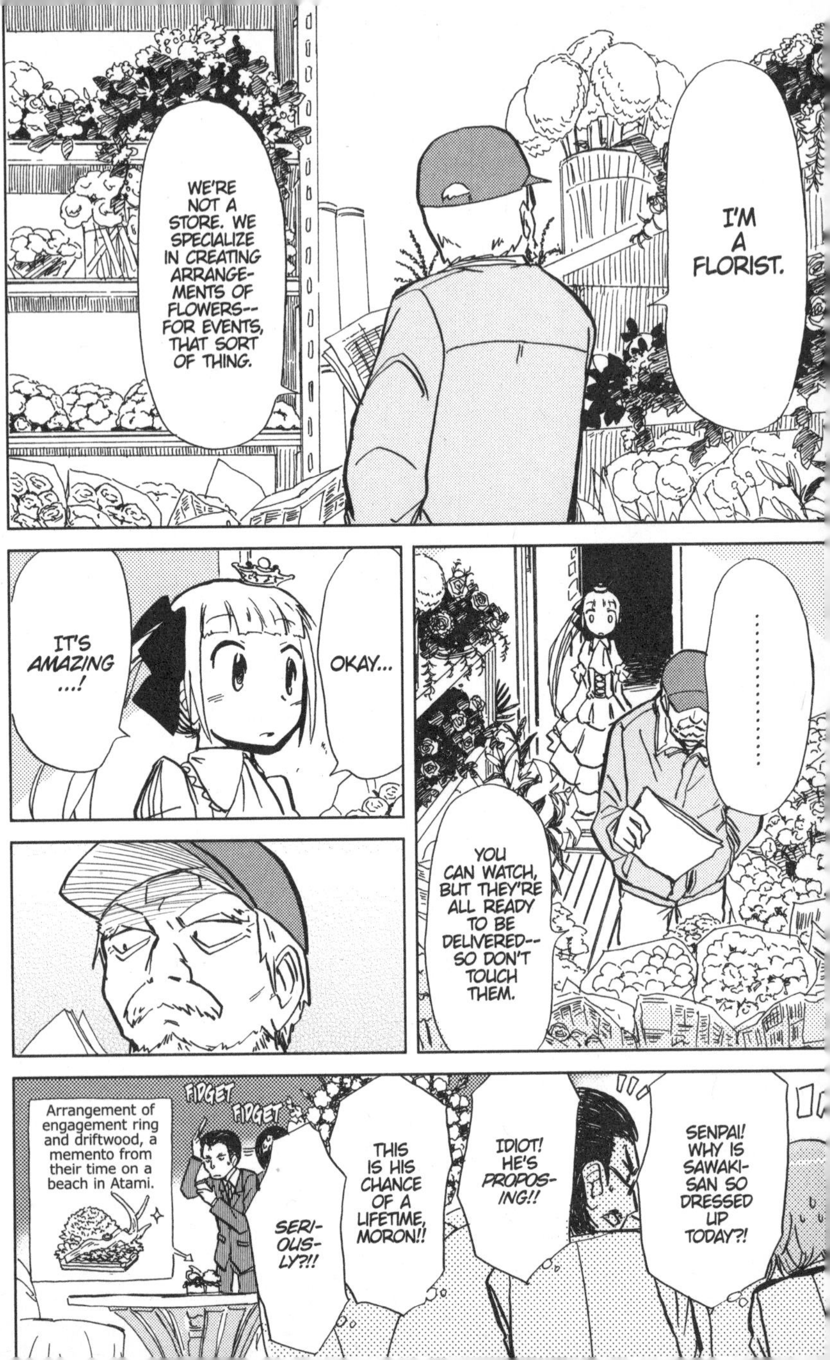
I'M A FLORIST.
WE'RE NOT A STORE. WE SPECIALIZE IN CREATING ARRANGE-MENTS OF FLOWERS--FOR EVENTS, THAT SORT OF THING.
......
YOU CAN WATCH, BUT THEY'RE ALL READY TO BE DELIVERED--SO DON'T TOUCH THEM.
OKAY...
IT'S AMAZING ...!
SENPAI! WHY IS SAWAKI-SAN SO DRESSED UP TODAY?!
IDIOT! HE'S PROPOS-ING!!
THIS IS HIS CHANCE OF A LIFETIME, MORON!!
SERI-OUS-LY?!!
FIDGET
FIDGET
Arrangement of engagement ring and driftwood, a memento from their time on a beach in Atami.

Alice & Zoroku

❖

"That depends
a good deal on where you want to get to,"
said the Cat.

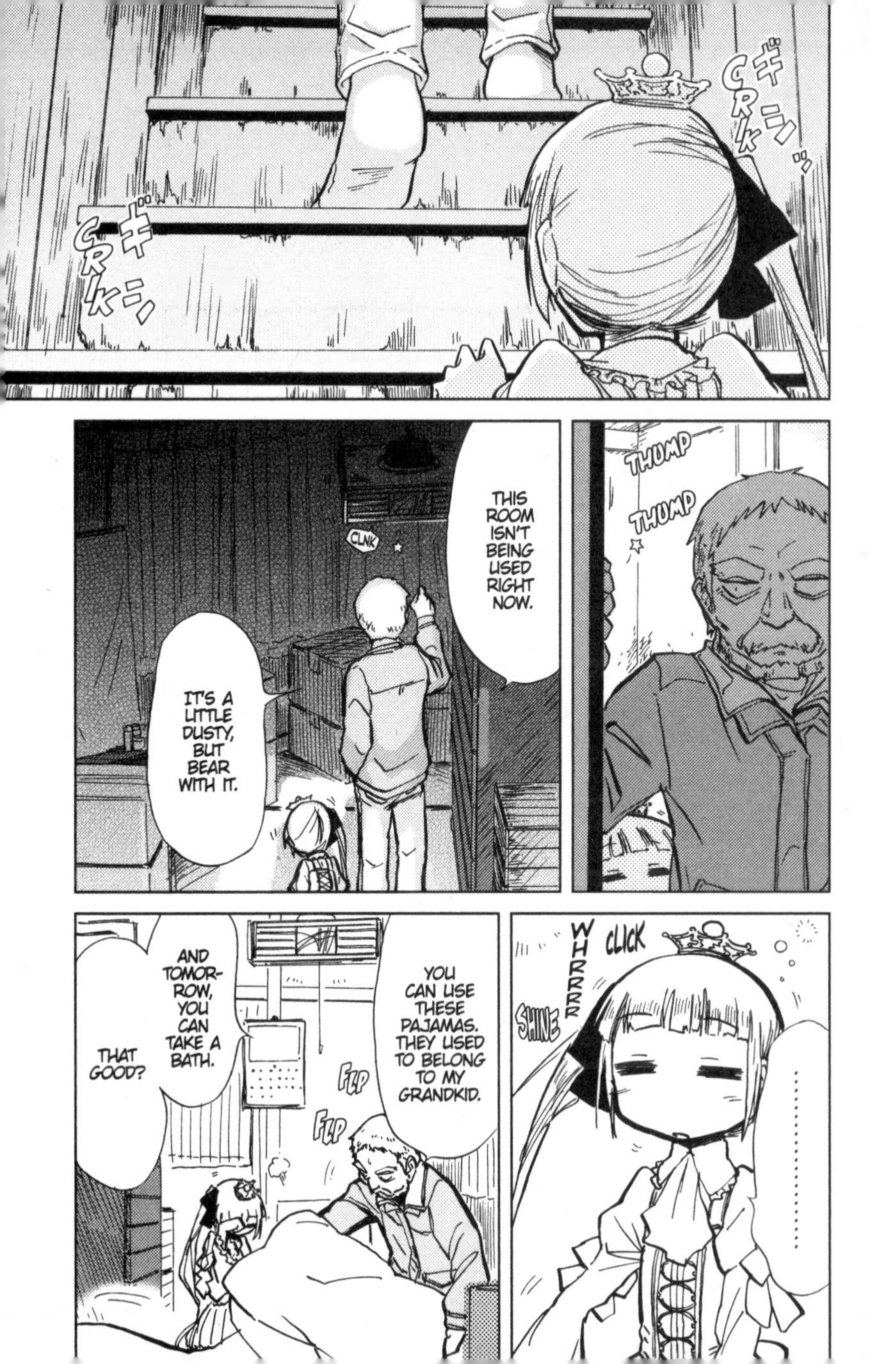
CRIK
CRIK
THUMP
THUMP
CLNK
THIS ROOM ISN'T BEING USED RIGHT NOW.
IT'S A LITTLE DUSTY, BUT BEAR WITH IT.
CLICK
WHRRRR
SHINE
......
YOU CAN USE THESE PAJAMAS. THEY USED TO BELONG TO MY GRANDKID.
FLP
FLP
AND TOMORROW, YOU CAN TAKE A BATH.
THAT GOOD?

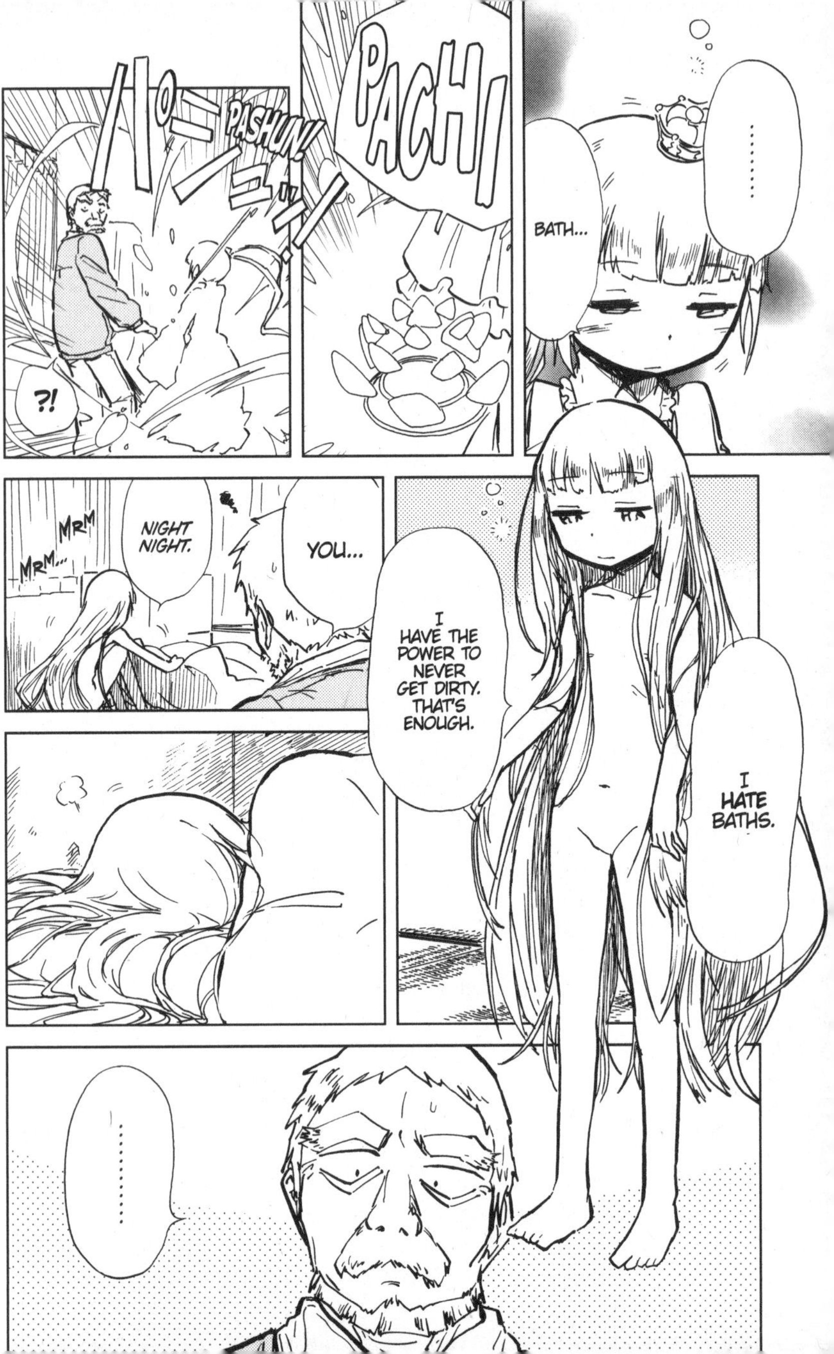
......
BATH...
PACHI
PASHUN!
?!
I HAVE THE POWER TO NEVER GET DIRTY. THAT'S ENOUGH.
I HATE BATHS.
YOU...
NIGHT NIGHT.
MRM MRM...
......

Chapter.2
Dream of the Triangular Room

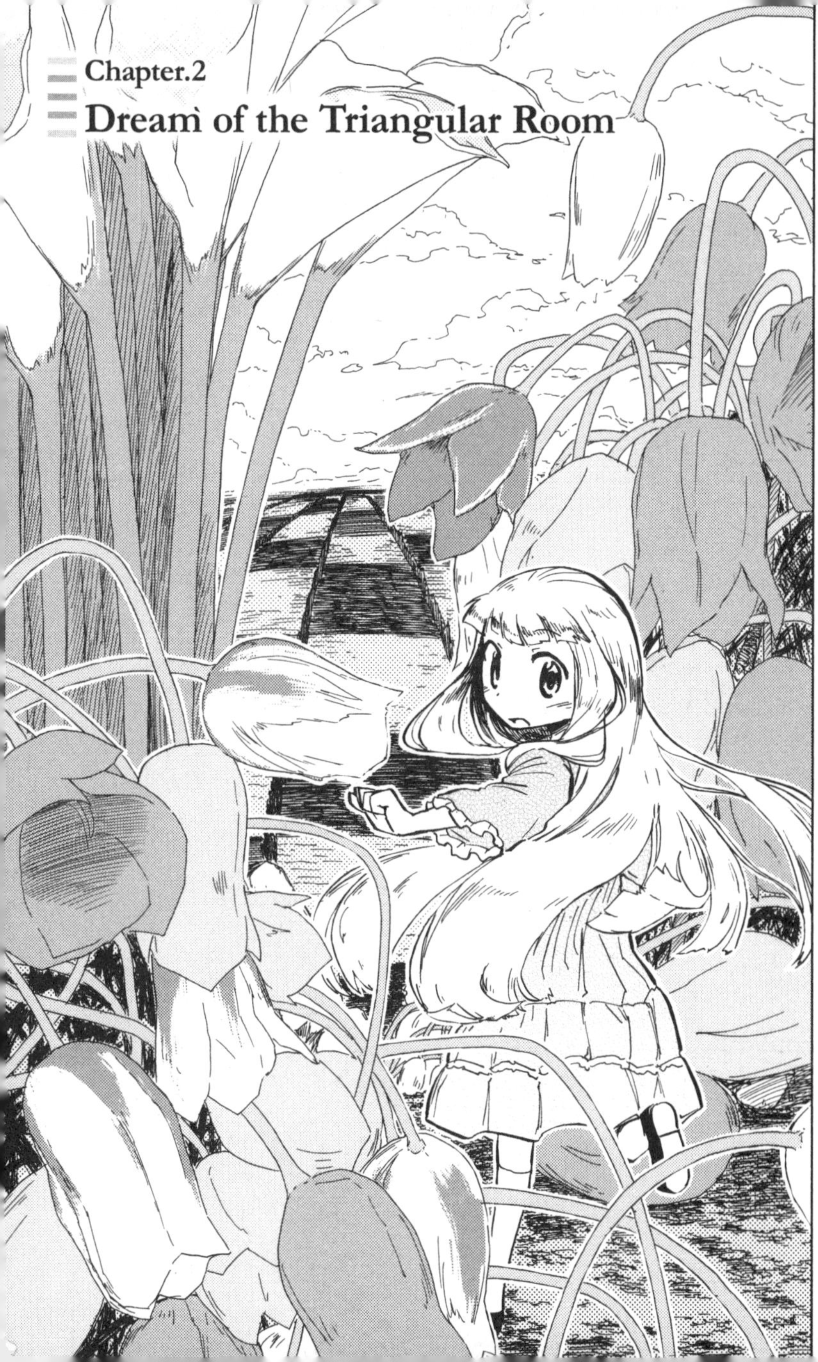

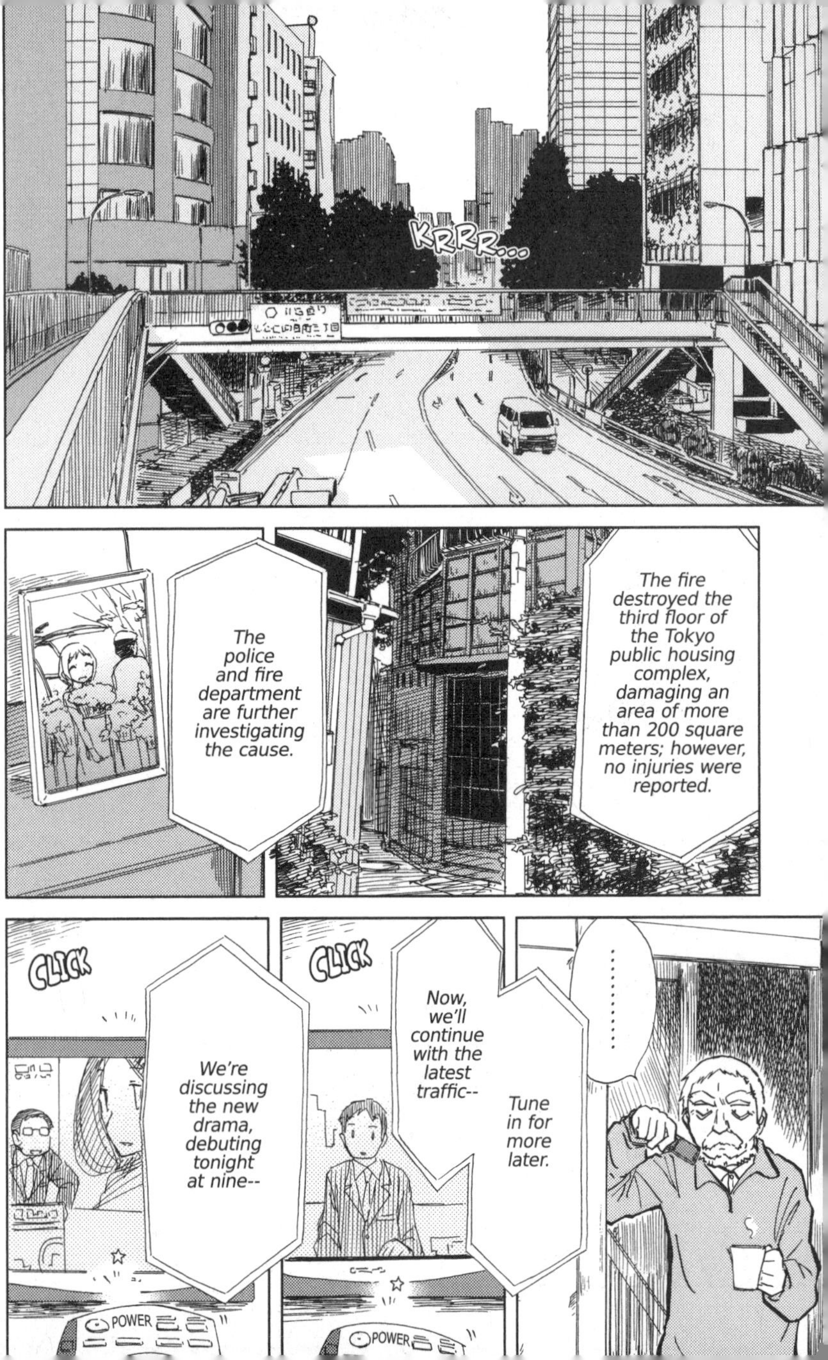
KRRR...
The fire destroyed the third floor of the Tokyo public housing complex, damaging an area of more than 200 square meters; however, no injuries were reported.
The police and fire department are further investigating the cause.
......
Now, we'll continue with the latest traffic--
Tune in for more later.
CLICK
POWER
CLICK
We're discussing the new drama, debuting tonight at nine--
POWER

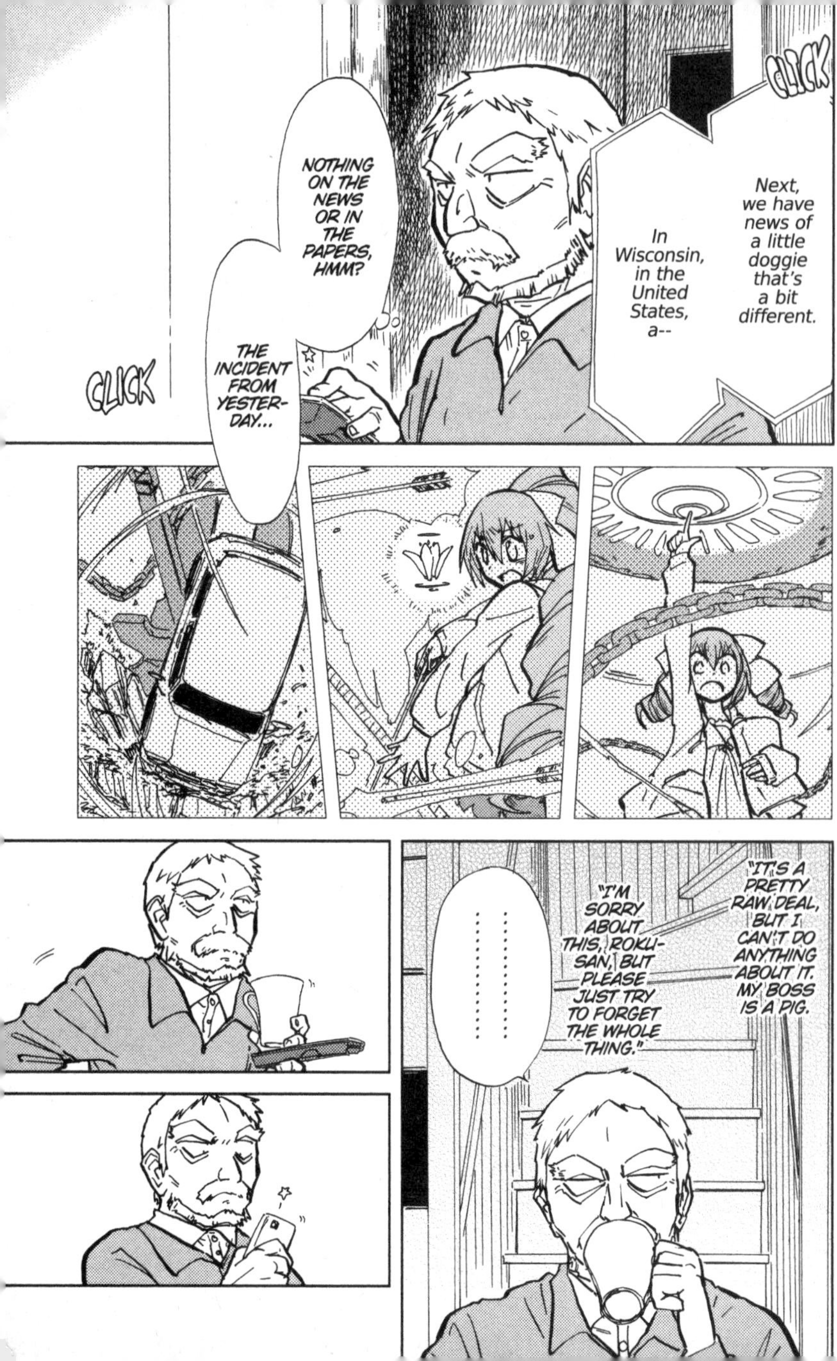
CLICK
Next, we have news of a little doggie that's a bit different.
In Wisconsin, in the United States, a--
NOTHING ON THE NEWS OR IN THE PAPERS, HMM?
THE INCIDENT FROM YESTERDAY...
CLICK
"IT'S A PRETTY RAW DEAL, BUT I CAN'T DO ANYTHING ABOUT IT. MY BOSS IS A PIG.
"I'M SORRY ABOUT THIS, ROKU-SAN, BUT PLEASE JUST TRY TO FORGET THE WHOLE THING."
......

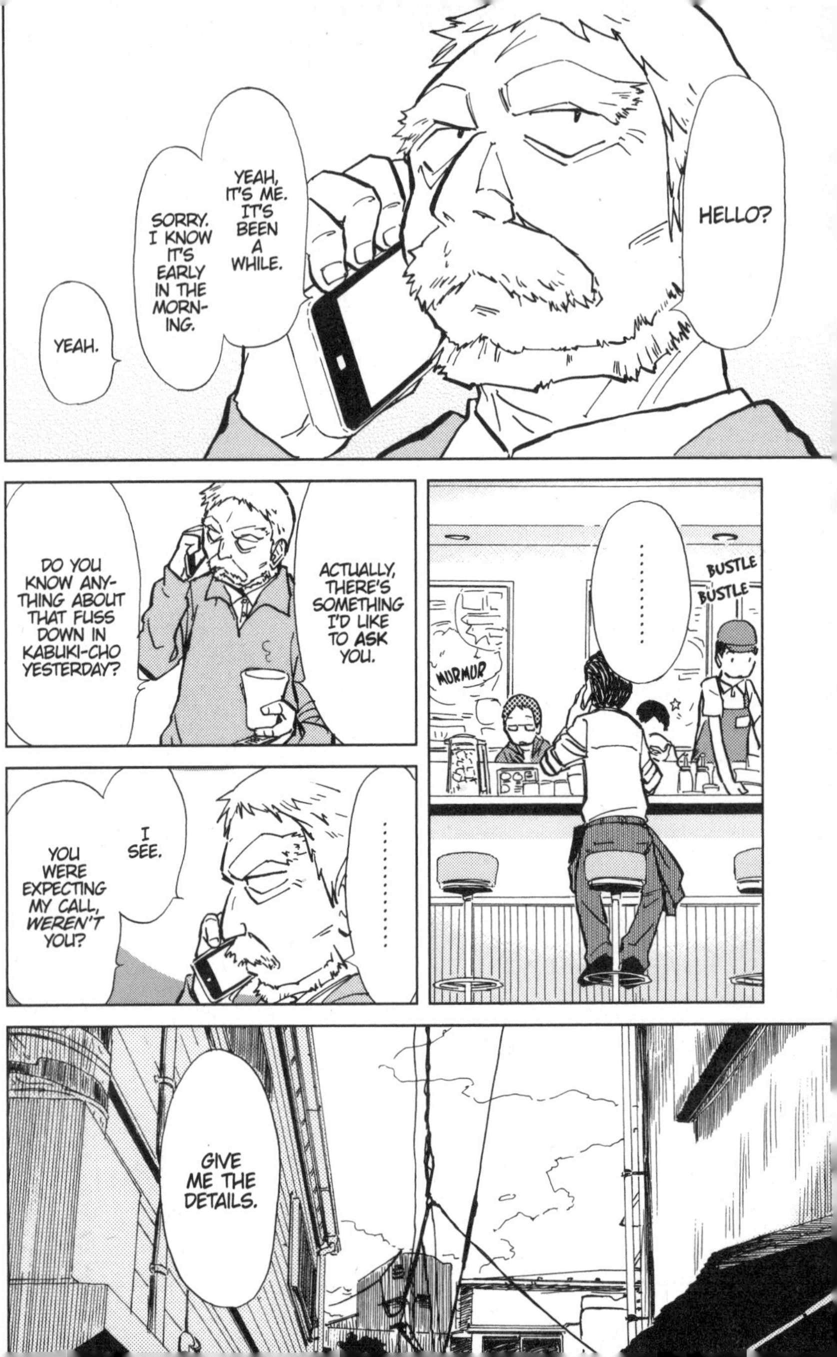
HELLO?
YEAH, IT'S ME. IT'S BEEN A WHILE.
SORRY. I KNOW IT'S EARLY IN THE MORNING.
YEAH.
......
BUSTLE
BUSTLE
MURMUR
ACTUALLY, THERE'S SOMETHING I'D LIKE TO ASK YOU.
DO YOU KNOW ANYTHING ABOUT THAT FUSS DOWN IN KABUKI-CHO YESTERDAY?
......
I SEE.
YOU WERE EXPECTING MY CALL, WEREN'T YOU?
GIVE ME THE DETAILS.

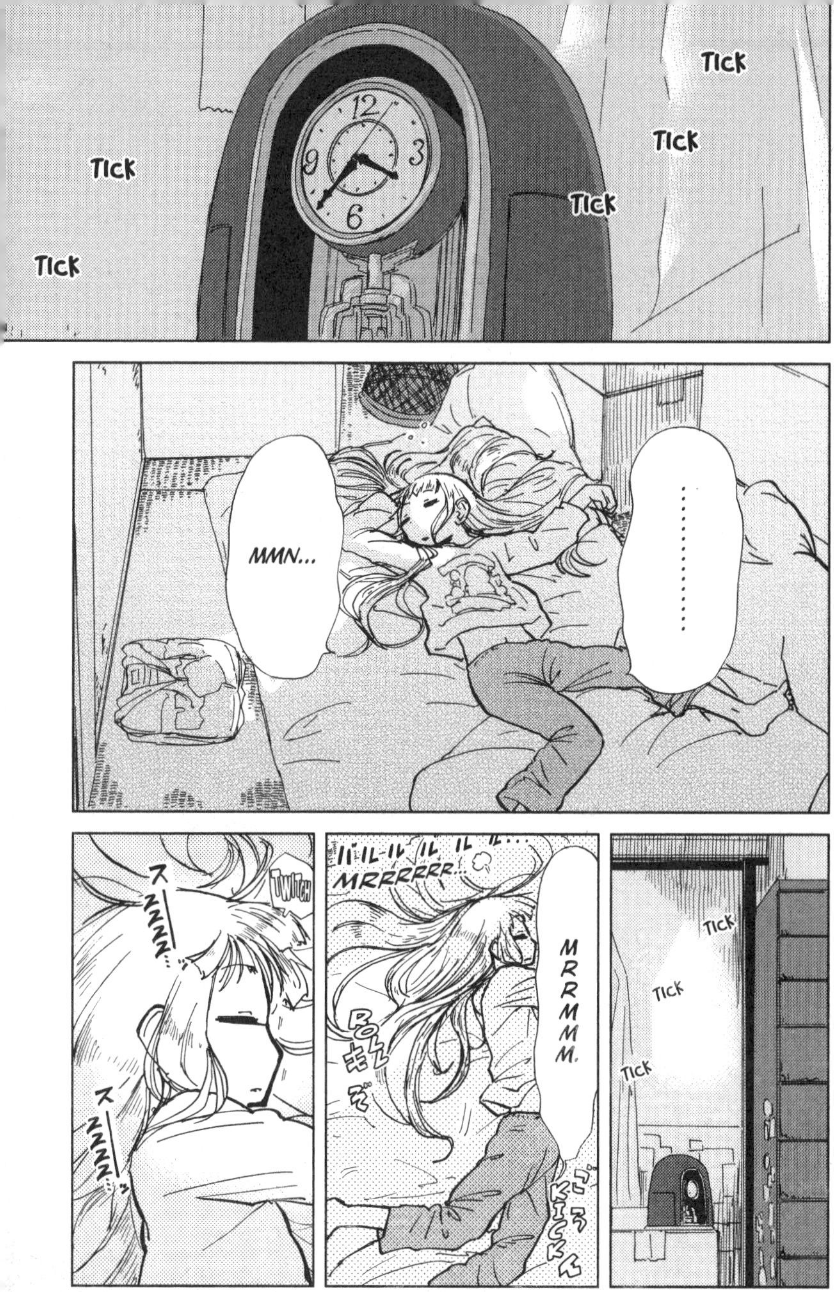
TICK
TICK
TICK
TICK
TICK
MMN...
TICK
TICK
TICK
バルルルル...
MRRRRRR...
MRRMMM.
もぞ
ROLL
ごろん
KICK
TWITCH
ス—ZZZZ...ッ
ス—ZZZZ...ッ

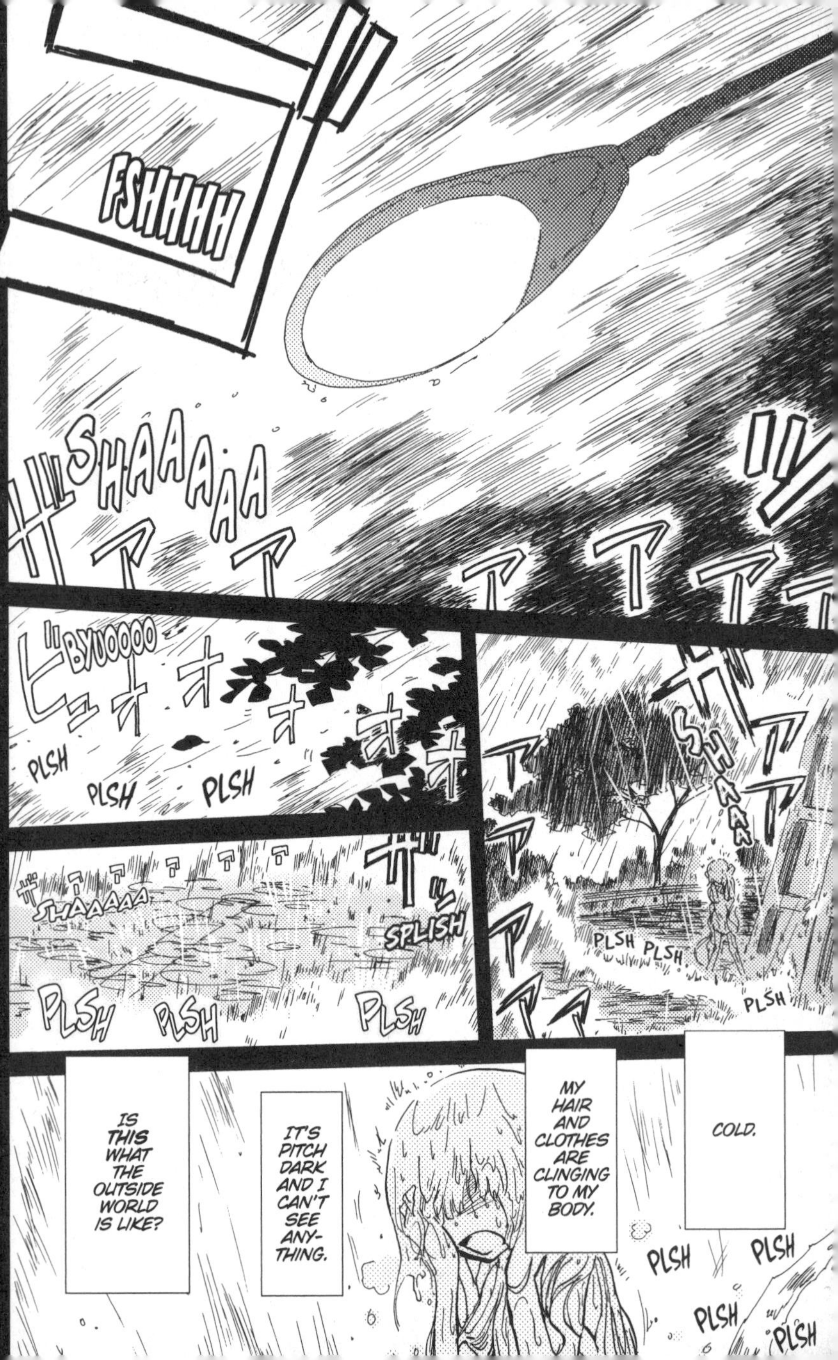
FSHHHH
SHAAAAAA
SHAAAA
PLSH PLSH
PLSH
BYUOOOO
PLSH
PLSH
PLSH
SHAAAAA
SPLISH
PLSH
PLSH
PLSH
COLD.
MY HAIR AND CLOTHES ARE CLINGING TO MY BODY.
IT'S PITCH DARK AND I CAN'T SEE ANYTHING.
IS THIS WHAT THE OUTSIDE WORLD IS LIKE?
PLSH
PLSH
PLSH
PLSH

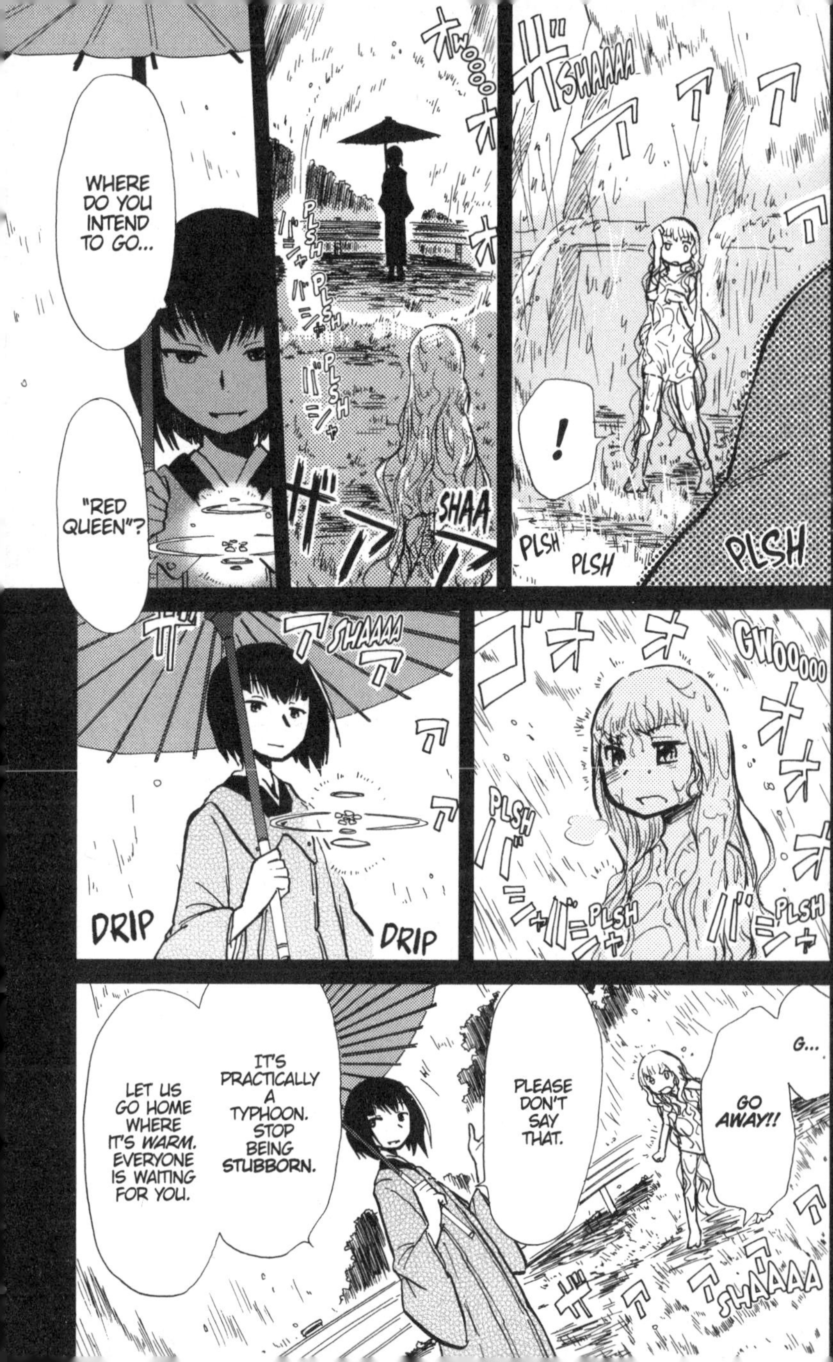
SHAAAAA
!
PLSH
PLSH
PLSH
OWOOOO
PLSH
PLSH
PLSH
SHAA
WHERE DO YOU INTEND TO GO...
"RED QUEEN"?
GWOOOOOO
PLSH
PLSH
PLSH
SHAAAA
DRIP
DRIP
G...
GO AWAY!!
PLEASE DON'T SAY THAT.
IT'S PRACTICALLY A TYPHOON. STOP BEING STUBBORN.
LET US GO HOME WHERE IT'S *WARM*. EVERYONE IS WAITING FOR YOU.
SHAAAAA

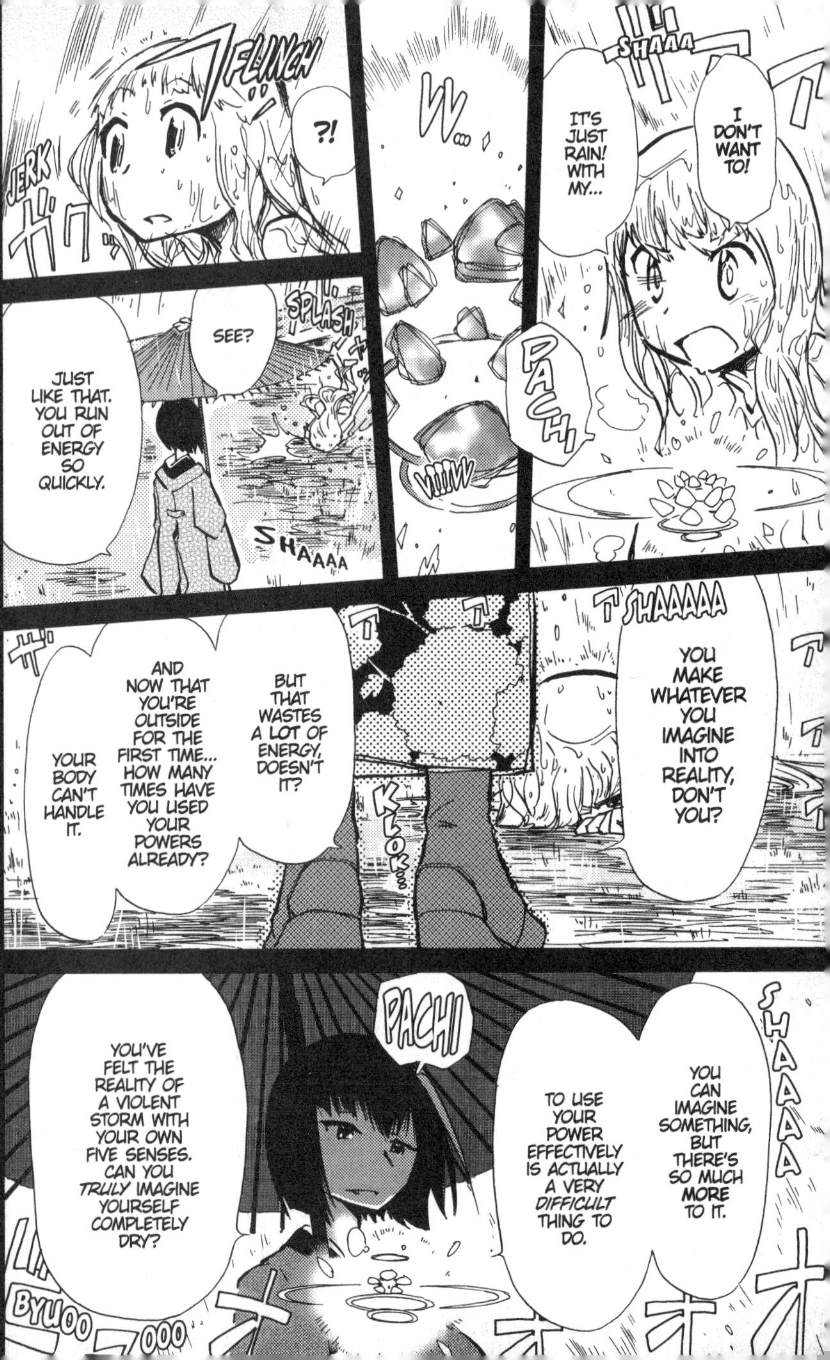
SHAAA
I DON'T WANT TO!
IT'S JUST RAIN! WITH MY...
PACHI
JERK
FLINCH
?!
SPLASH
SEE?
JUST LIKE THAT. YOU RUN OUT OF ENERGY SO QUICKLY.
SHAAAAA
SHAAAAAA
YOU MAKE WHATEVER YOU IMAGINE INTO REALITY, DON'T YOU?
BUT THAT WASTES A LOT OF ENERGY, DOESN'T IT?
AND NOW THAT YOU'RE OUTSIDE FOR THE FIRST TIME... HOW MANY TIMES HAVE YOU USED YOUR POWERS ALREADY?
YOUR BODY CAN'T HANDLE IT.
KLOK...
SHAAAAA
YOU CAN IMAGINE SOMETHING, BUT THERE'S SO MUCH MORE TO IT.
TO USE YOUR POWER EFFECTIVELY IS ACTUALLY A VERY *DIFFICULT* THING TO DO.
PACHI
YOU'VE FELT THE REALITY OF A VIOLENT STORM WITH YOUR OWN FIVE SENSES. CAN YOU *TRULY* IMAGINE YOURSELF COMPLETELY DRY?
BYUOO
OOO

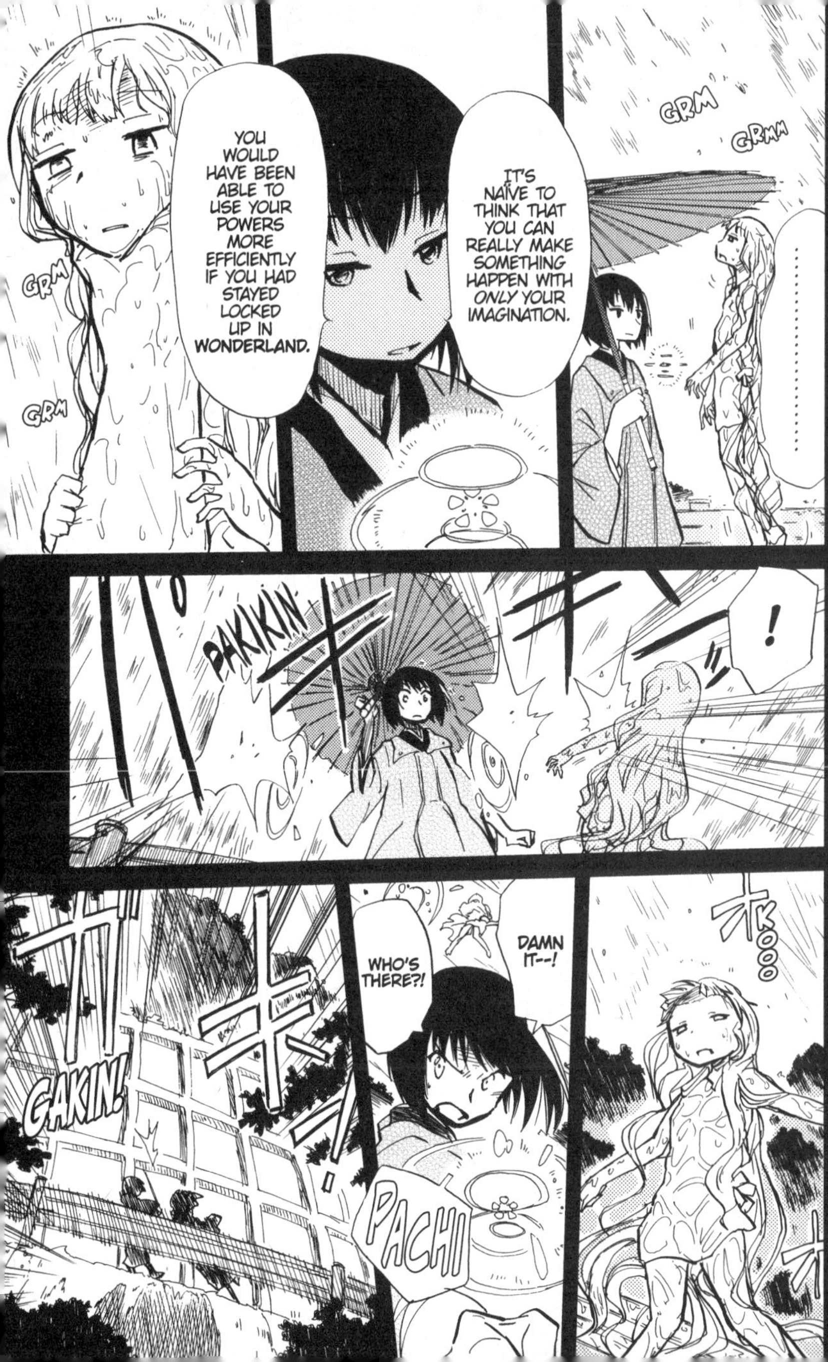
GRM
GRMM
IT'S NAÏVE TO THINK THAT YOU CAN REALLY MAKE SOMETHING HAPPEN WITH *ONLY* YOUR IMAGINATION.
YOU WOULD HAVE BEEN ABLE TO USE YOUR POWERS MORE EFFICIENTLY IF YOU HAD STAYED LOCKED UP IN WONDERLAND.
GRM
GRM
!
PAKIKIN
KOOO
DAMN IT--!
WHO'S THERE?!
PACHI
GAKIN!

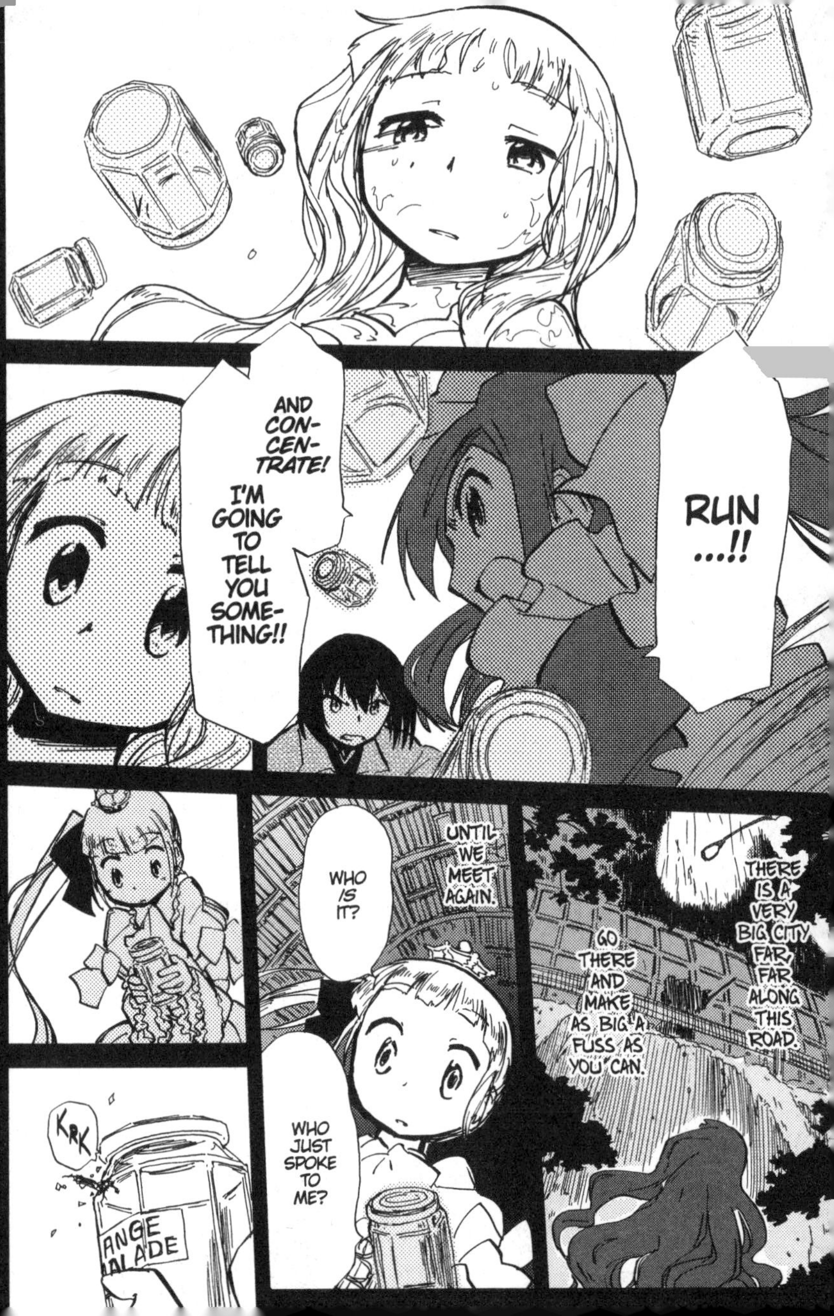
RUN ...!!
AND CON-CEN-TRATE!
I'M GOING TO TELL YOU SOME-THING!!
THERE IS A VERY BIG CITY FAR, FAR ALONG THIS ROAD.
GO THERE AND MAKE AS BIG A FUSS AS YOU CAN.
UNTIL WE MEET AGAIN.
WHO IS IT?
WHO JUST SPOKE TO ME?
KRK
ANGE
ALADE

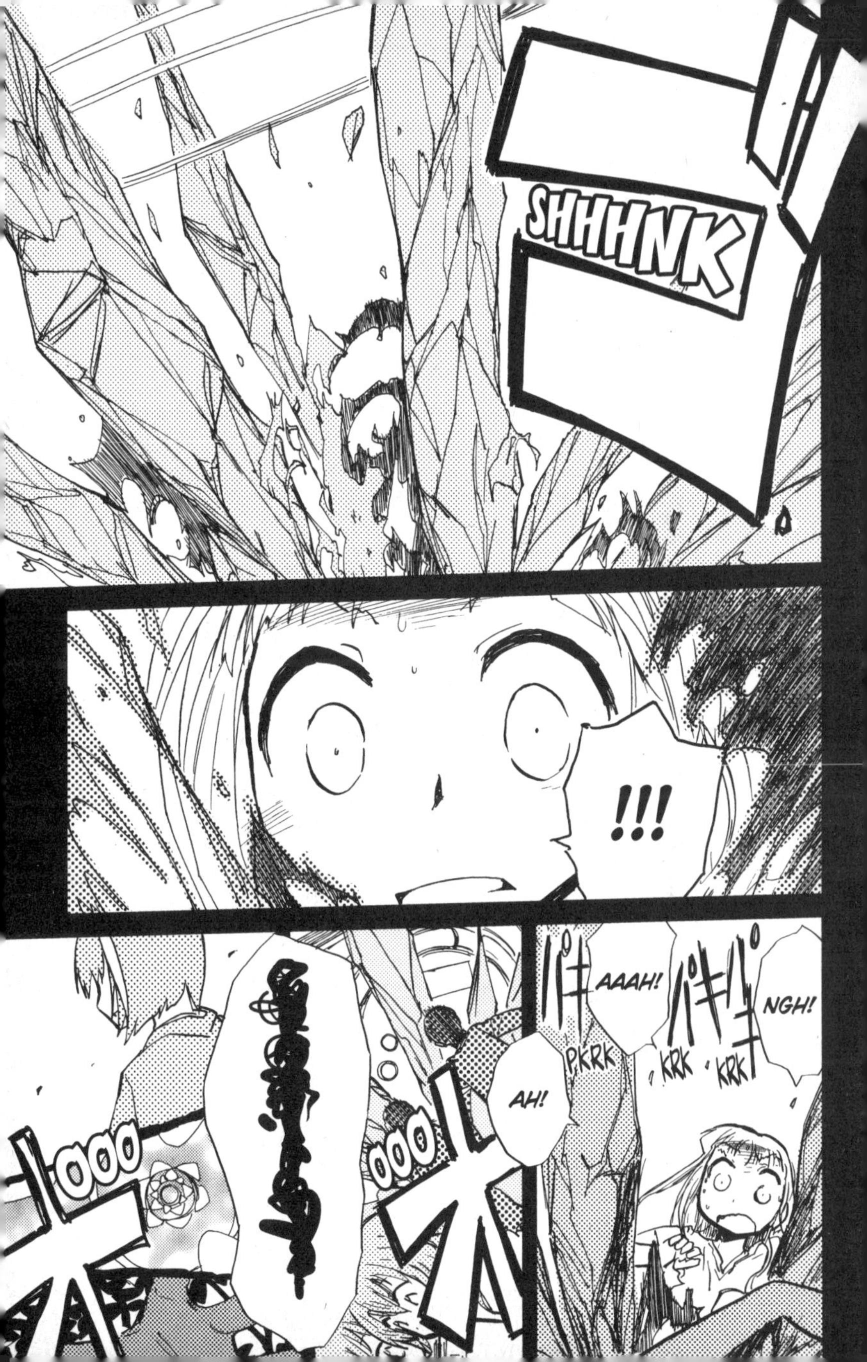
SHHHNK
!!!
NGH!
パキパキ
KRK
KRK
AAAH!
パキ
P,KRK
AH!

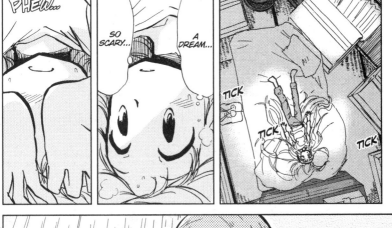

PHEW...

SO SCARY...

A DREAM...

TICK

TICK

TICK

GROGGY

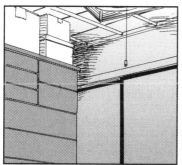

WHIRRRR...

I RAN AWAY FROM THE LAB AND CAME TO ZOROKU'S HOUSE.

THAT'S RIGHT...

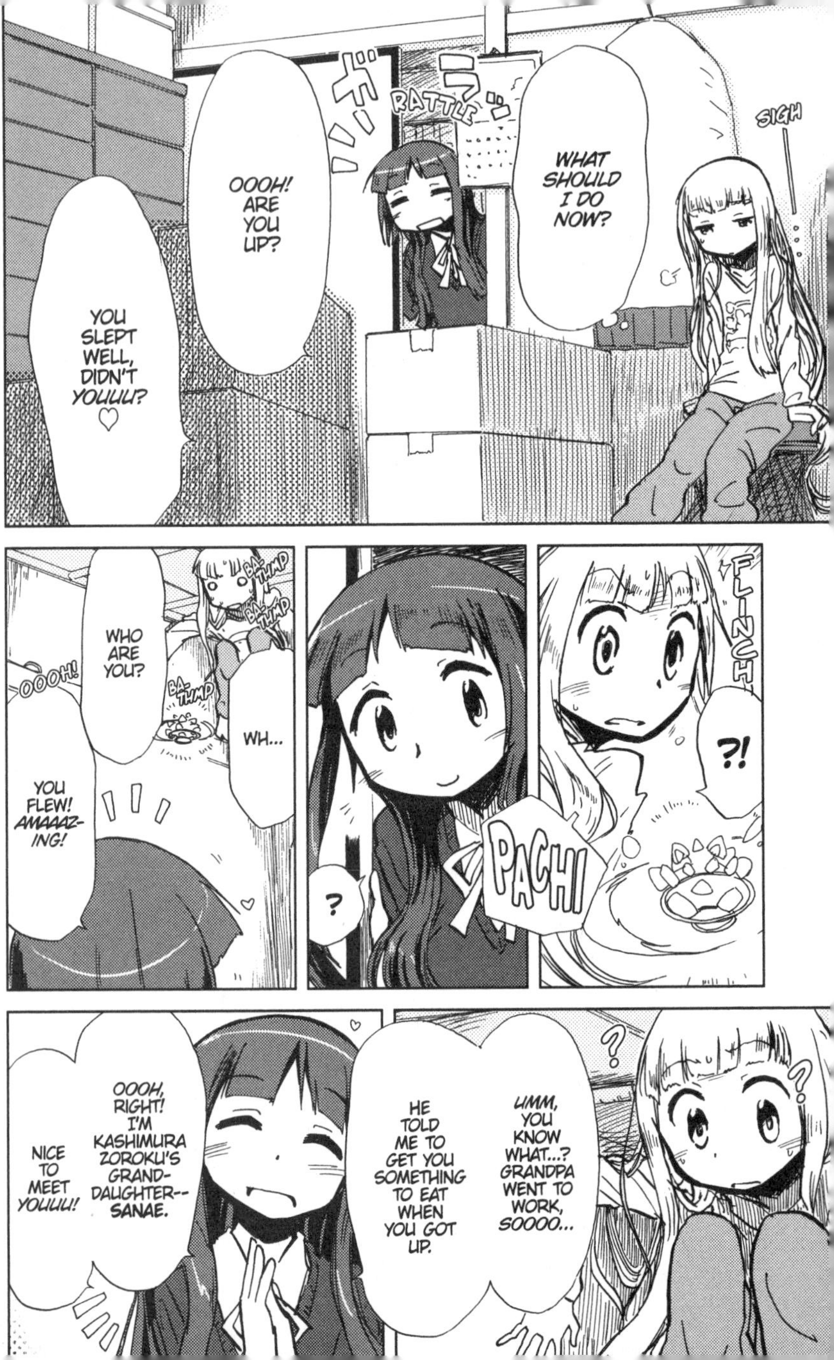
SIGH
WHAT SHOULD I DO NOW?
RATTLE
OOOH! ARE YOU UP?
YOU SLEPT WELL, DIDN'T YOUUU? ♡
FLINCH
?!
PACHI
?
BA-THUMP BA-THUMP
WH...
WHO ARE YOU?
BA-THUMP
OOOH!
YOU FLEW! AMAAAZING!
UMM, YOU KNOW WHAT...? GRANDPA WENT TO WORK, SOOOO...
HE TOLD ME TO GET YOU SOMETHING TO EAT WHEN YOU GOT UP.
OOOH, RIGHT! I'M KASHIMURA ZOROKU'S GRAND-DAUGHTER--SANAE.
NICE TO MEET YOUUU!

Alice & Zoroku

• ◆ •

"The Queen of Hearts, she made some tarts,
All on a summer day:
The Knave of Hearts, he stole those tarts,
And took them quite away!"

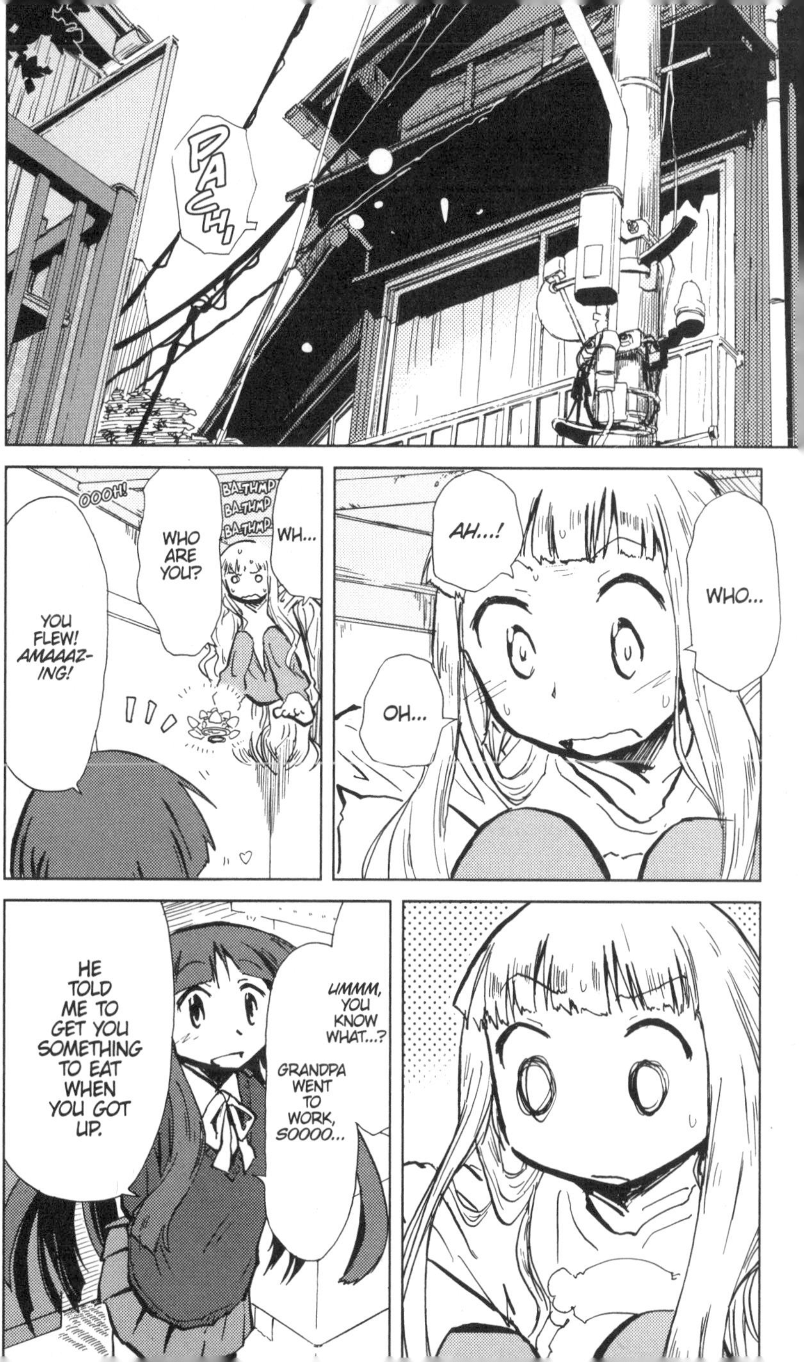
PACHI
AH...!
WHO...
OH...
WH...
BA-THMP BA-THMP BA-THMP
WHO ARE YOU?
OOOH!
YOU FLEW! AMAAAZ-ING!
UMMM, YOU KNOW WHAT...?
GRANDPA WENT TO WORK, SOOOO...
HE TOLD ME TO GET YOU SOMETHING TO EAT WHEN YOU GOT UP.

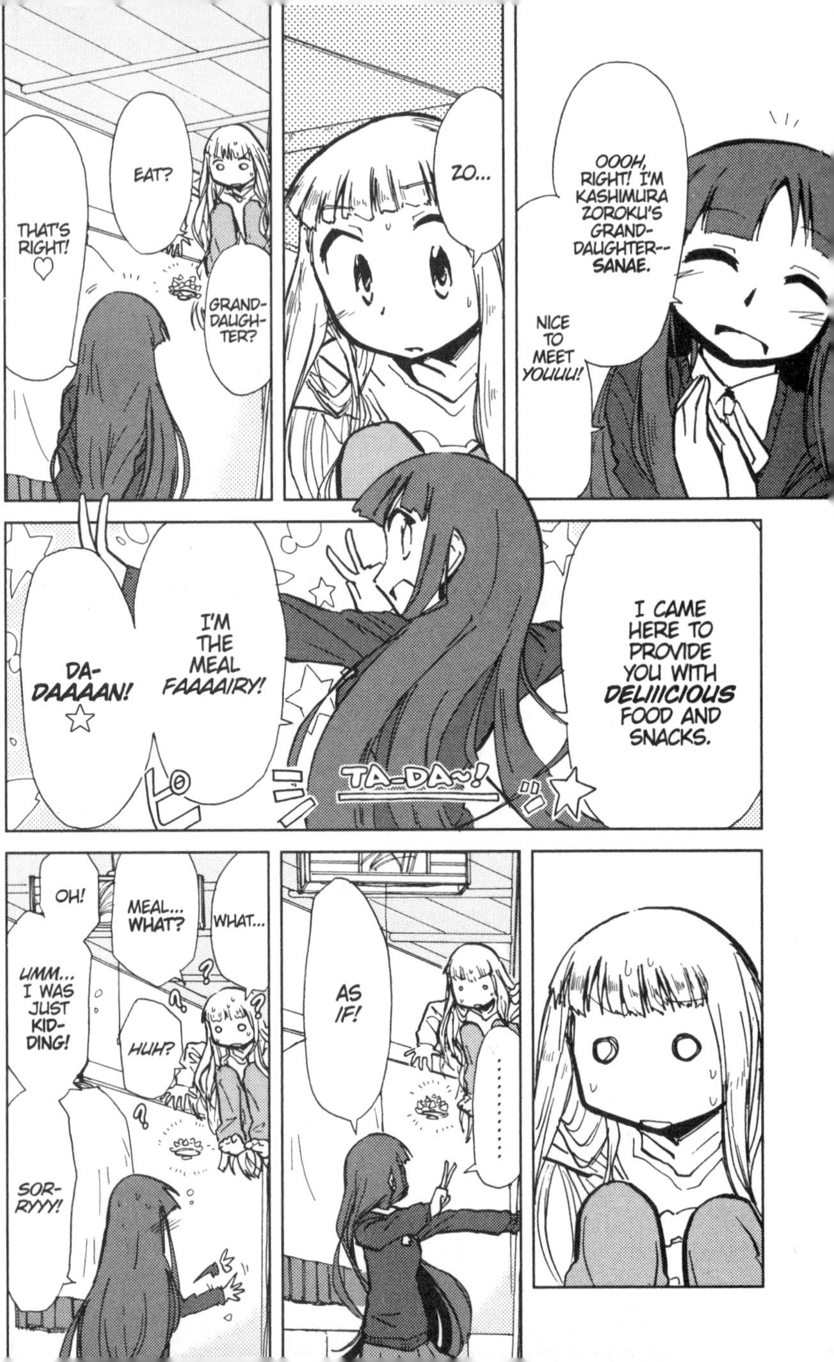
OOOH, RIGHT! I'M KASHIMURA ZOROKU'S GRAND-DAUGHTER--SANAE.
NICE TO MEET YOUUU!
ZO...
EAT?
GRAND-DAUGHTER?
THAT'S RIGHT! ♡
I CAME HERE TO PROVIDE YOU WITH DELIIICIOUS FOOD AND SNACKS.
TA-DA~!
I'M THE MEAL FAAAAIRY!
DA-DAAAAN! ☆
......
AS IF!
WHAT...
MEAL... WHAT?
OH!
HUH?
UMM... I WAS JUST KID-DING!
SOR-RYYY!

Chapter.3

The Meal Fairy Appears

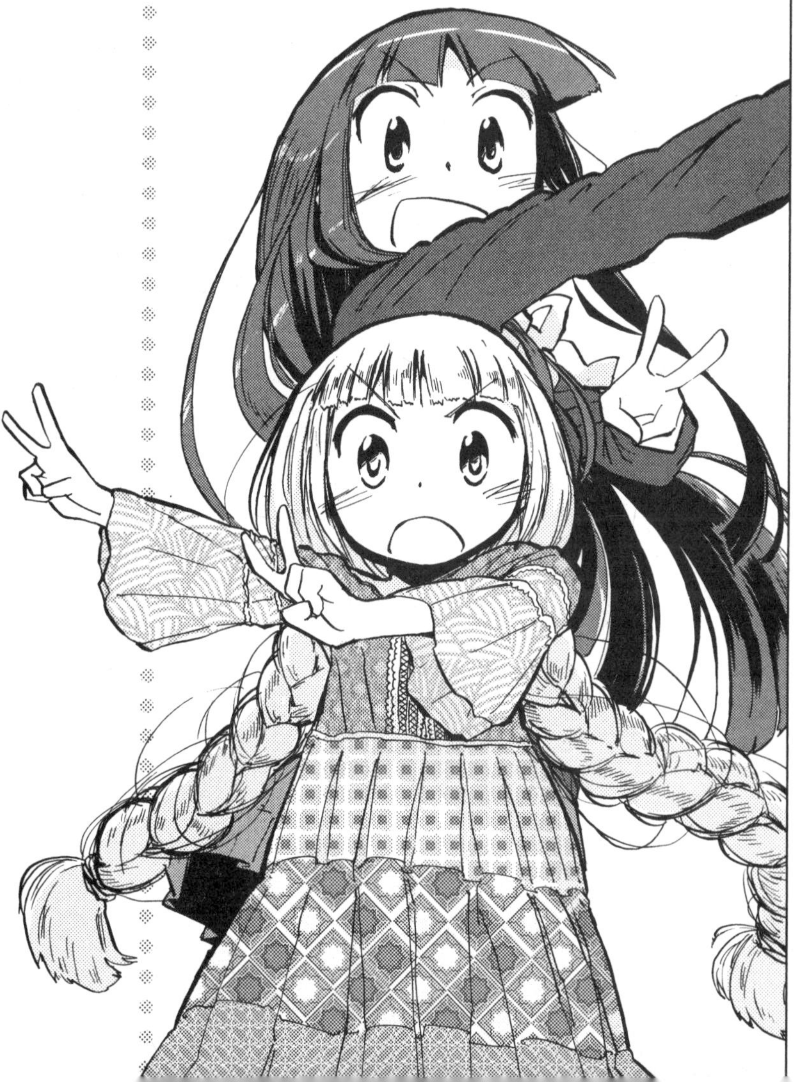

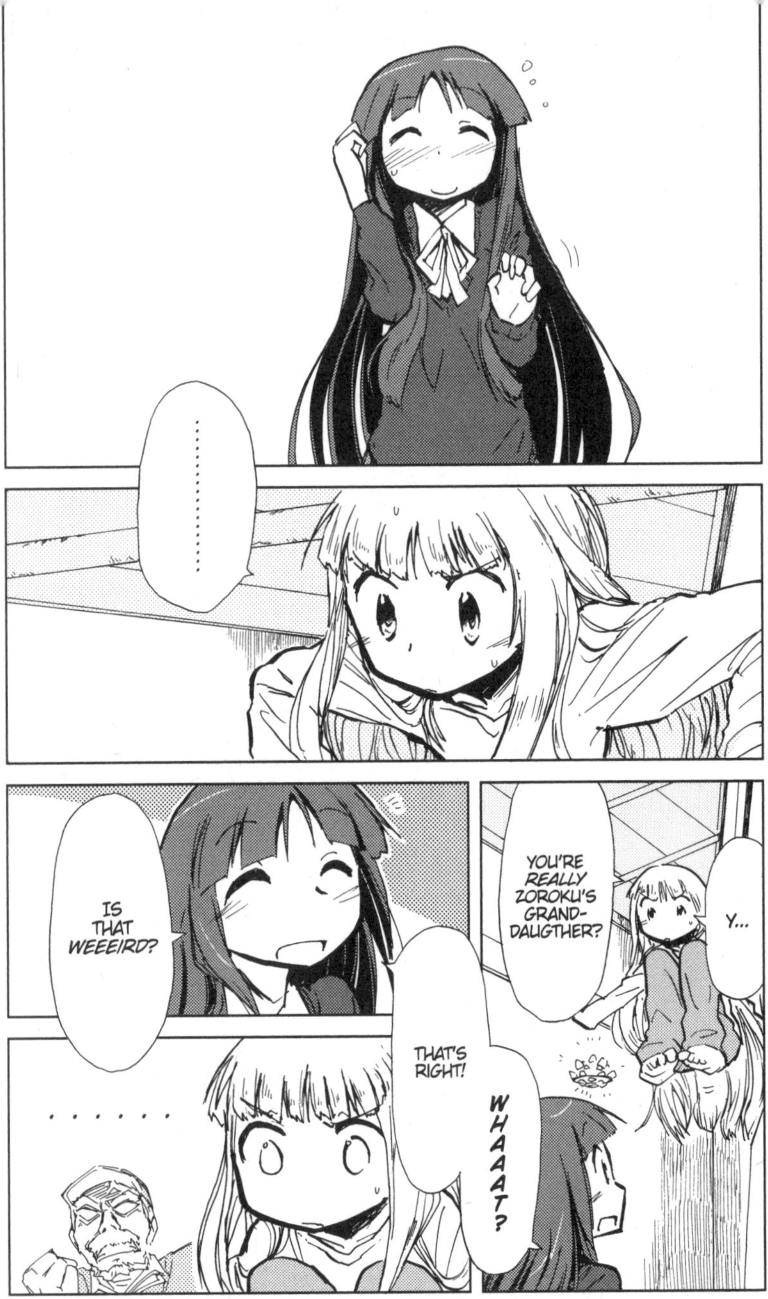
......
YOU'RE REALLY ZOROKU'S GRAND-DAUGTHER?
Y...
IS THAT WEEEIRD?
THAT'S RIGHT!
WHAAAAT?
. . . . . .

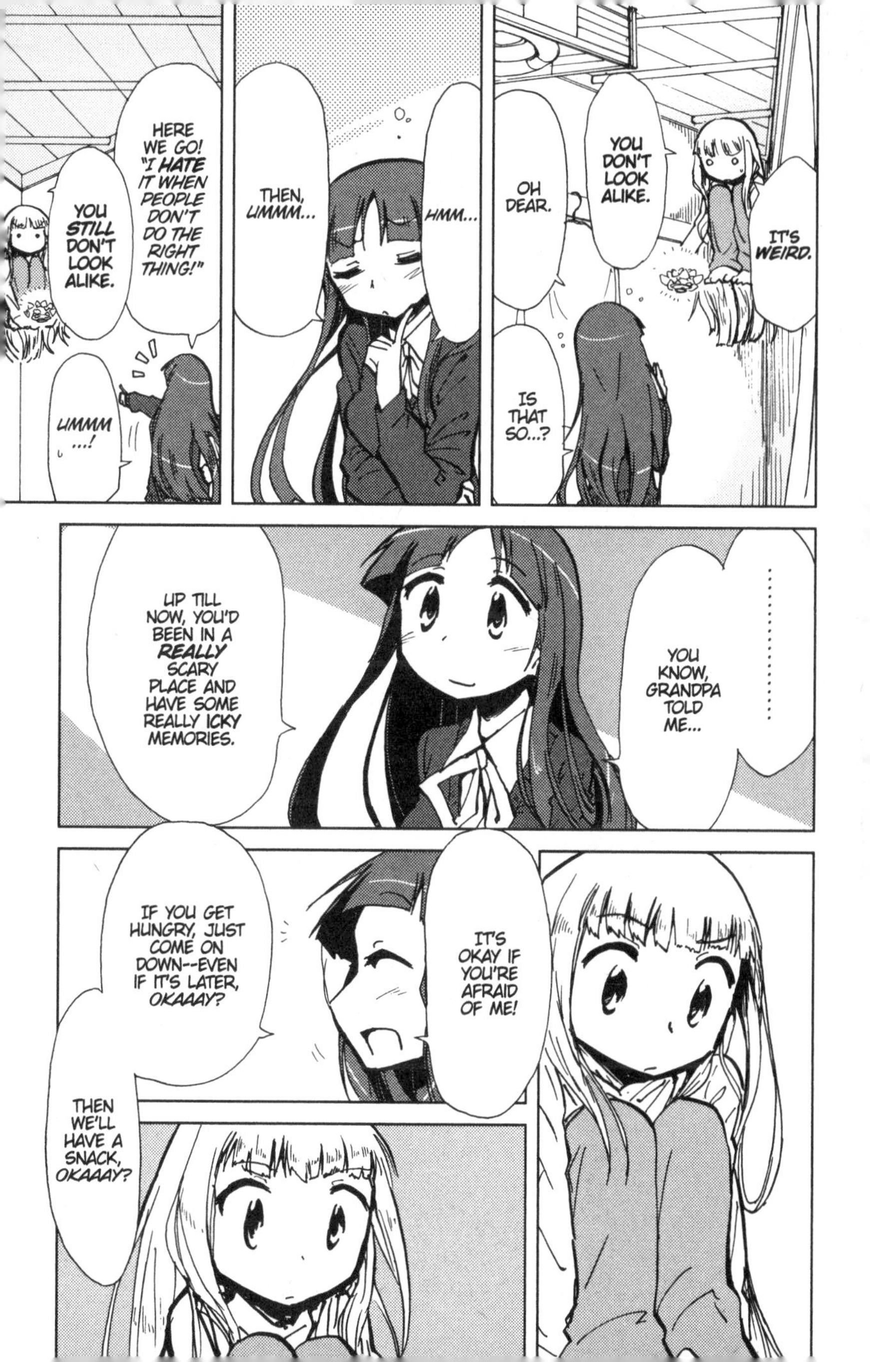
YOU DON'T LOOK ALIKE.
IT'S *WEIRD.*
OH DEAR.
IS THAT SO...?
HMM...
THEN, UMMM...
HERE WE GO! "I ***HATE*** IT WHEN PEOPLE DON'T DO THE RIGHT THING!"
YOU ***STILL*** DON'T LOOK ALIKE.
UMMM ...!
....
YOU KNOW, GRANDPA TOLD ME...
UP TILL NOW, YOU'D BEEN IN A ***REALLY*** SCARY PLACE AND HAVE SOME REALLY ICKY MEMORIES.
IT'S OKAY IF YOU'RE AFRAID OF ME!
IF YOU GET HUNGRY, JUST COME ON DOWN--EVEN IF IT'S LATER, *OKAAAY?*
THEN WE'LL HAVE A SNACK, *OKAAAY?*

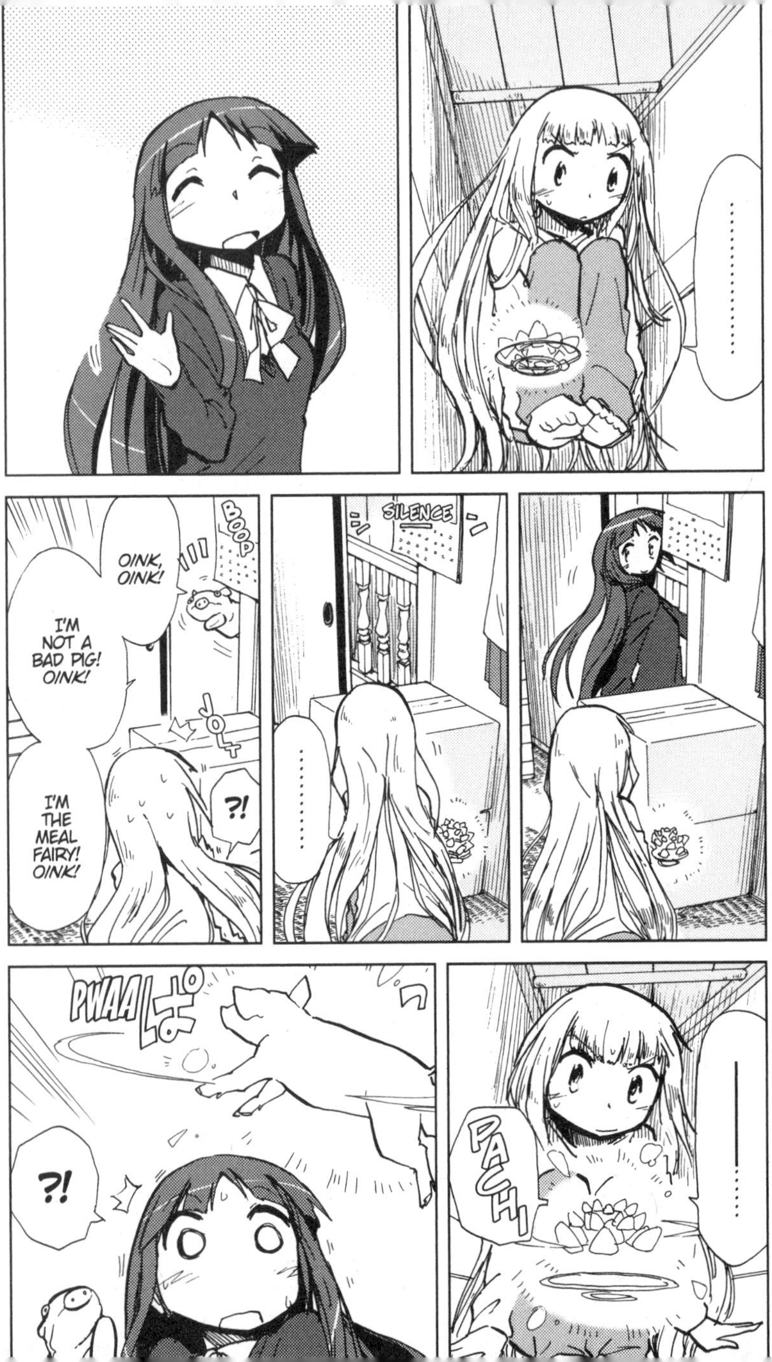
……
SILENCE
……
BOOP
OINK, OINK!
I'M NOT A BAD PIG! OINK!
JOLT
?!
I'M THE MEAL FAIRY! OINK!
……
PACHI
PWAA
ぱ
?!

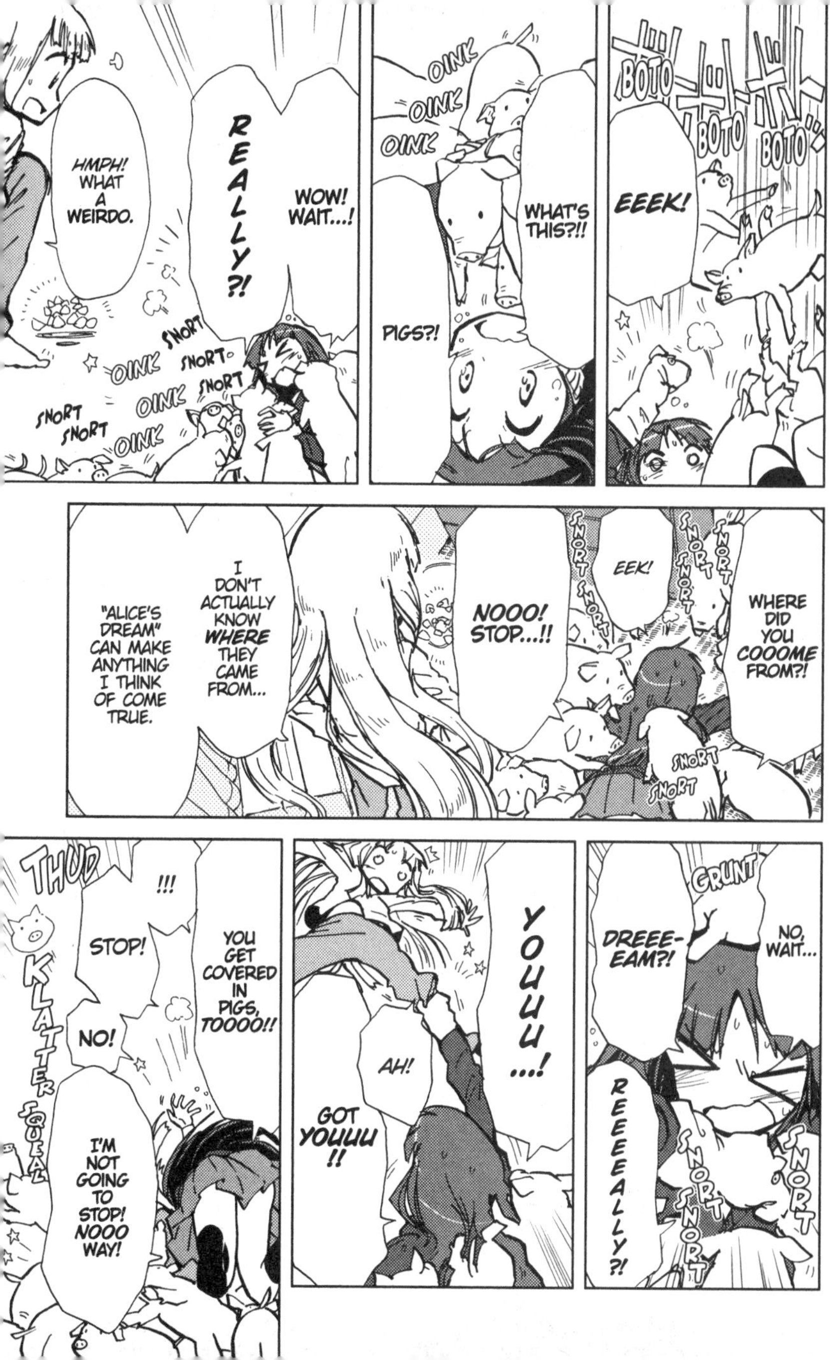
BOTO
BOTO
BOTO
EEEK!
OINK
OINK
OINK
WHAT'S THIS?!!
PIGS?!
WOW! WAIT...!
REALLY?!
HMPH! WHAT A WEIRDO.
SNORT
SNORT
OINK
SNORT
OINK
SNORT SNORT
OINK
SNORT
SNORT
WHERE DID YOU COOOME FROM?!
EEK!
SNORT SNORT
NOOO! STOP...!!
I DON'T ACTUALLY KNOW WHERE THEY CAME FROM...
"ALICE'S DREAM" CAN MAKE ANYTHING I THINK OF COME TRUE.
SNORT
SNORT
GRUNT
NO, WAIT...
DREEE-EAM?!
REEEEALLY?!
SNORT
SNORT SNORT
YOUUU...!
AH!
GOT YOUUU!!
!!!
YOU GET COVERED IN PIGS, TOOOO!!
STOP!
NO!
I'M NOT GOING TO STOP! NOOO WAY!
THUD
KLATTER
SQUEAL

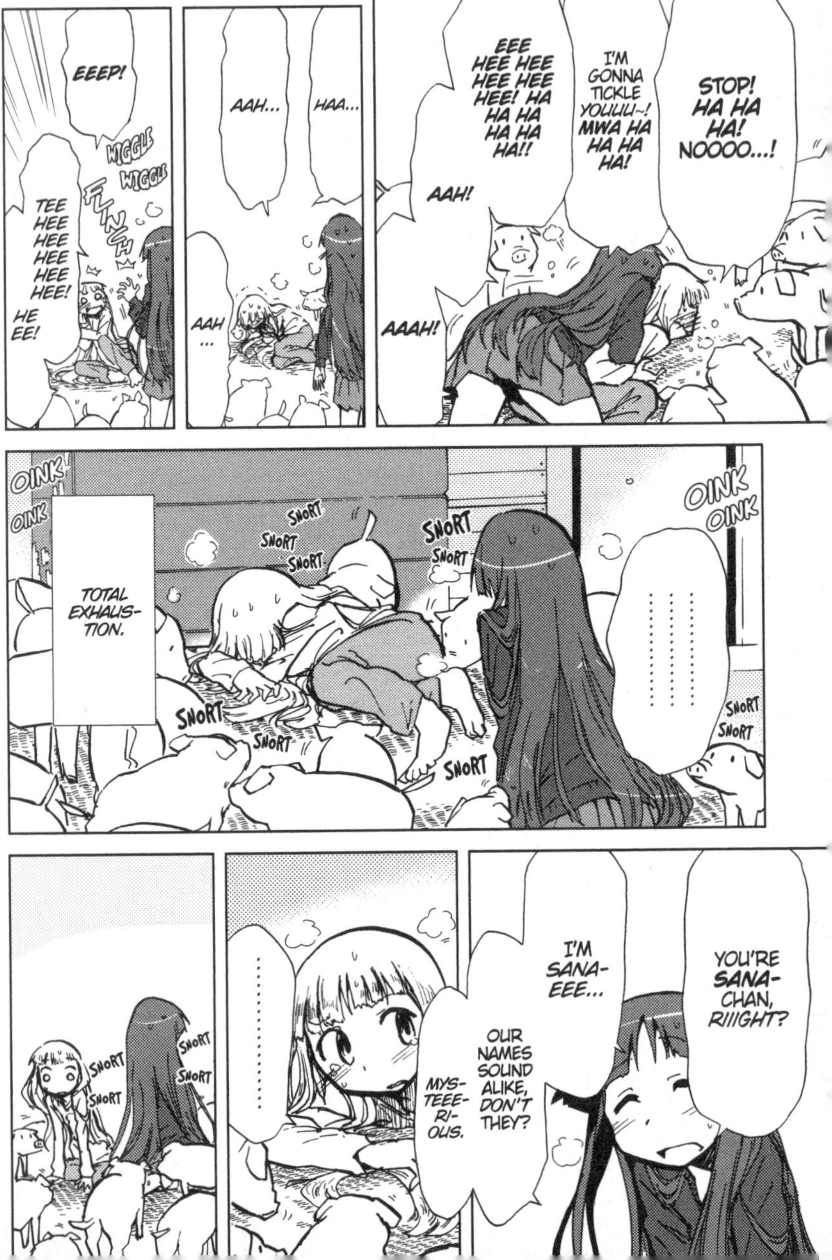
STOP! HA HA HA! NOOOO...!
I'M GONNA TICKLE YOUUU~! MWA HA HA HA HA!
EEE HEE HEE HEE HEE HEE! HA HA HA HA HA HA!!
AAH!
AAAH!
HAA...
AAH...
AAH ...
EEEP!
WIGGLE WIGGLE
FLINCH
TEE HEE HEE HEE HEE HEE!
HE EE!
OINK OINK
......
SNORT SNORT
SNORT SNORT
SNORT SNORT SNORT
TOTAL EXHAUSTION.
OINK OINK
SNORT
SNORT
SNORT
YOU'RE SANA-CHAN, RIIIGHT?
I'M SANA-EEE...
OUR NAMES SOUND ALIKE, DON'T THEY?
MYS-TEEE-RI-OUS.
......
SNORT SNORT
SNORT SNORT

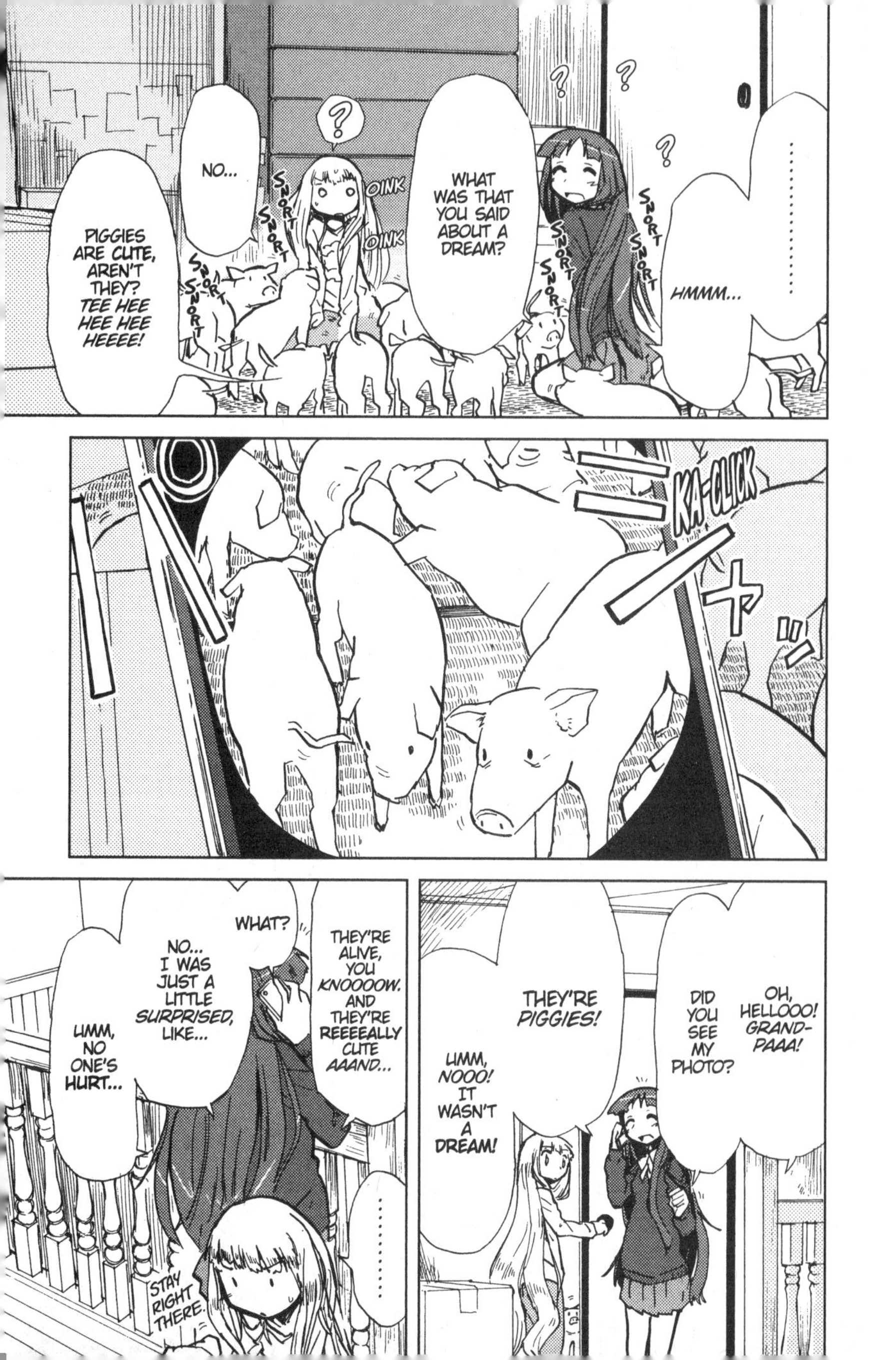
......
HMMM...
SNORT SNORT
WHAT WAS THAT YOU SAID ABOUT A DREAM?
SNORT SNORT
?
?
?
OINK OINK
NO...
SNORT SNORT
PIGGIES ARE CUTE, AREN'T THEY? TEE HEE HEE HEE HEEEE!
SNORT SNORT
KA-CLICK
OH, HELLOOO! GRANDPAAA!
DID YOU SEE MY PHOTO?
THEY'RE PIGGIES!
UMM, NOOO! IT WASN'T A DREAM!
THEY'RE ALIVE, YOU KNOOOOW. AND THEY'RE REEEEALLY CUTE AAAND...
WHAT?
NO... I WAS JUST A LITTLE SURPRISED, LIKE...
UMM, NO ONE'S HURT...
......
STAY RIGHT THERE.

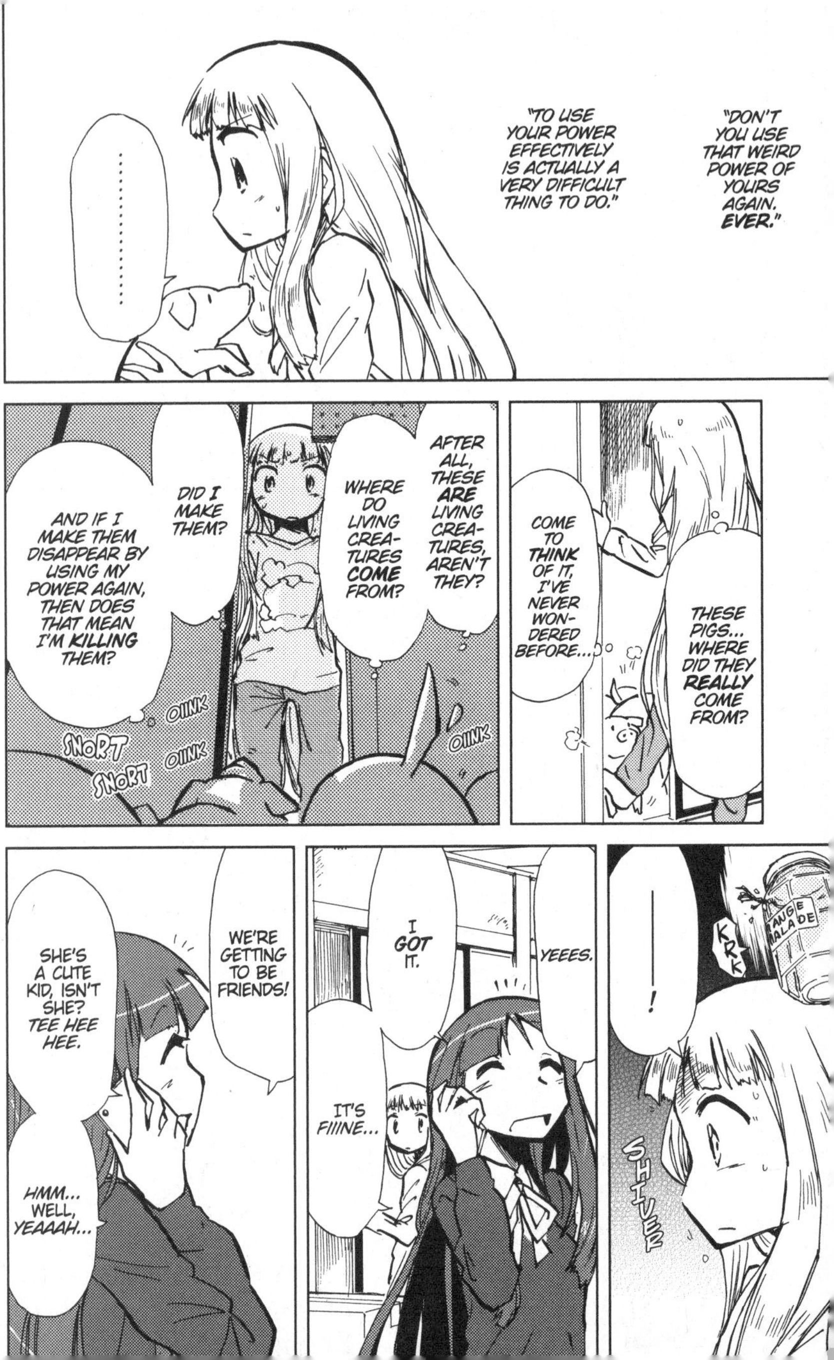
"DON'T YOU USE THAT WEIRD POWER OF YOURS AGAIN. **EVER.**"
"TO USE YOUR POWER EFFECTIVELY IS ACTUALLY A VERY DIFFICULT THING TO DO."
......
COME TO **THINK** OF IT, I'VE NEVER WONDERED BEFORE...
THESE PIGS... WHERE DID THEY **REALLY** COME FROM?
AFTER ALL, THESE **ARE** LIVING CREATURES, AREN'T THEY?
WHERE DO LIVING CREATURES **COME** FROM?
DID **I** MAKE THEM?
AND IF I MAKE THEM DISAPPEAR BY USING MY POWER AGAIN, THEN DOES THAT MEAN I'M **KILLING** THEM?
OIINK
OIINK
OIINK
SNORT
SNORT
KRK
!
SHIVER
YEEES.
I **GOT** IT.
IT'S FIIINE...
WE'RE GETTING TO BE FRIENDS!
SHE'S A CUTE KID, ISN'T SHE? TEE HEE HEE.
HMM... WELL, YEAAAH...

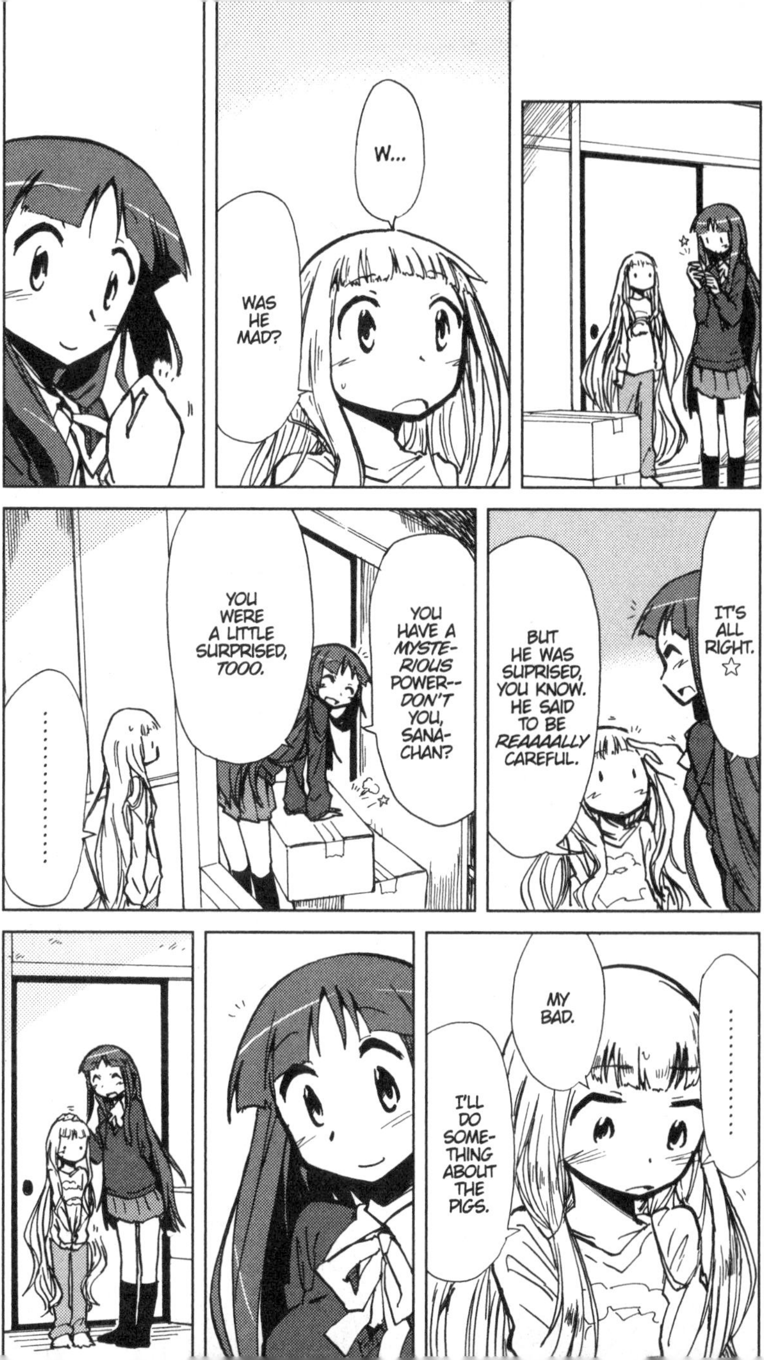
W...
WAS HE MAD?
IT'S ALL RIGHT. ☆
BUT HE WAS SUPRISED, YOU KNOW. HE SAID TO BE *REAAAALLY* CAREFUL.
YOU HAVE A *MYSTERIOUS* POWER-- *DON'T* YOU, SANA-CHAN?
YOU WERE A LITTLE SURPRISED, *TOOO.*
....
....
MY BAD.
I'LL DO SOMETHING ABOUT THE PIGS.

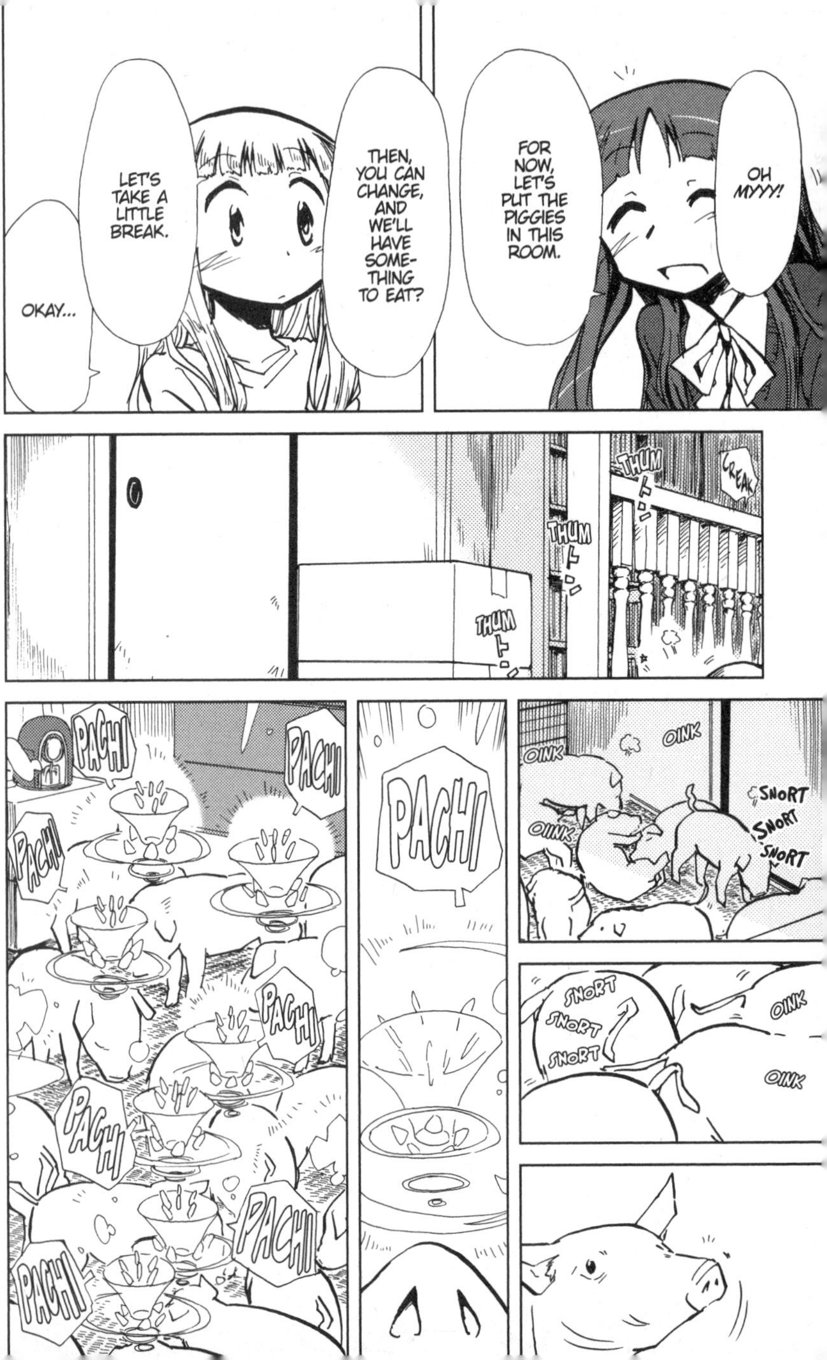
OH MYYY!
FOR NOW, LET'S PUT THE PIGGIES IN THIS ROOM.
THEN, YOU CAN CHANGE, AND WE'LL HAVE SOME-THING TO EAT?
LET'S TAKE A LITTLE BREAK.
OKAY...
CREAK
THUM
THUM
THUM
OINK
OINK
OIINK
SNORT
SNORT
SNORT
OINK
SNORT
SNORT
SNORT
OINK
PACHI
PACHI
PACHI
PACHI
PACHI
PACHI
PACHI
PACHI

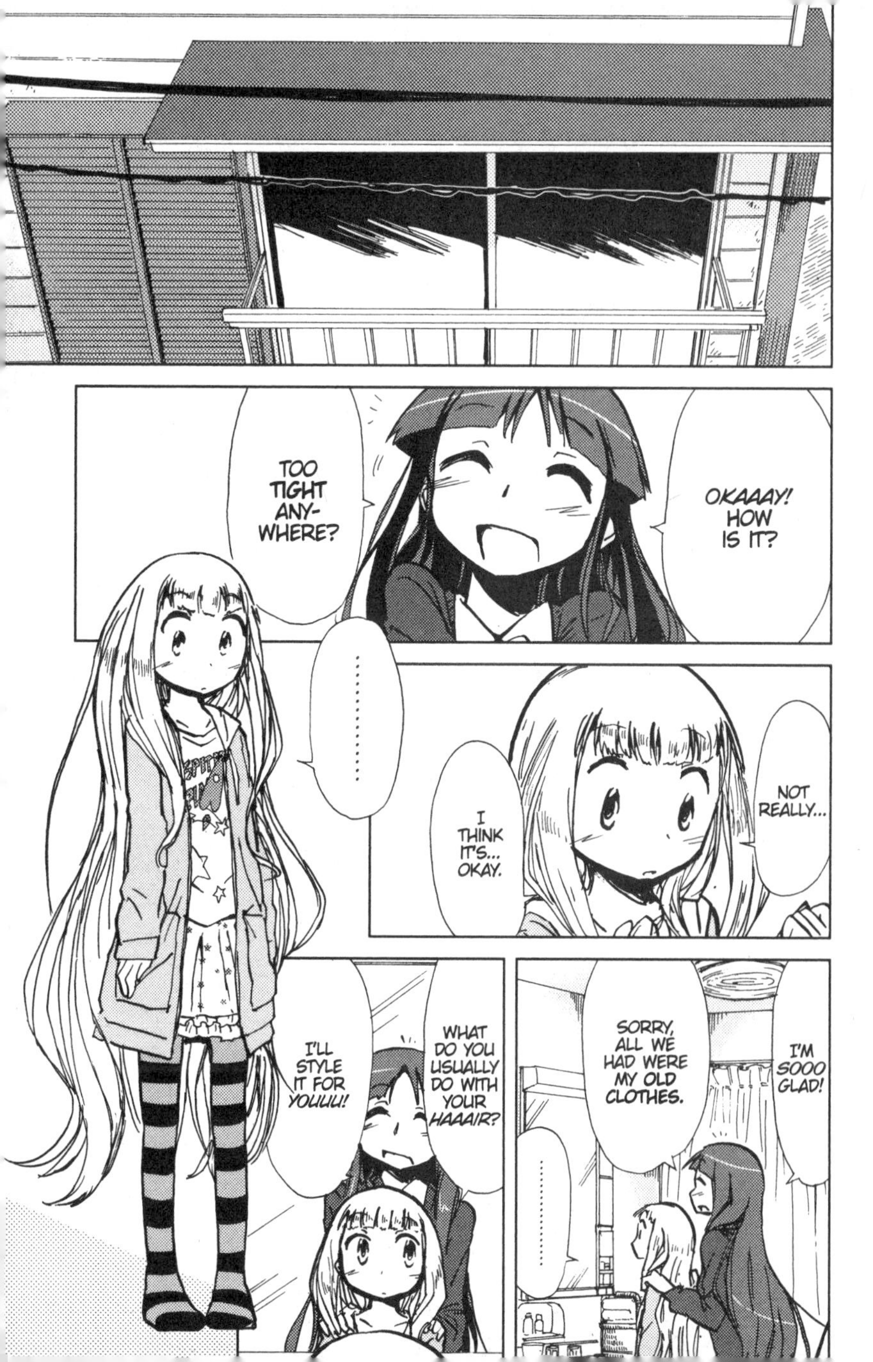
OKAAAY! HOW IS IT?
TOO TIGHT ANY-WHERE?
......
NOT REALLY...
I THINK IT'S... OKAY.
I'M SOOO GLAD!
SORRY, ALL WE HAD WERE MY OLD CLOTHES.
......
WHAT DO YOU USUALLY DO WITH YOUR HAAAIR?
I'LL STYLE IT FOR YOUUU!

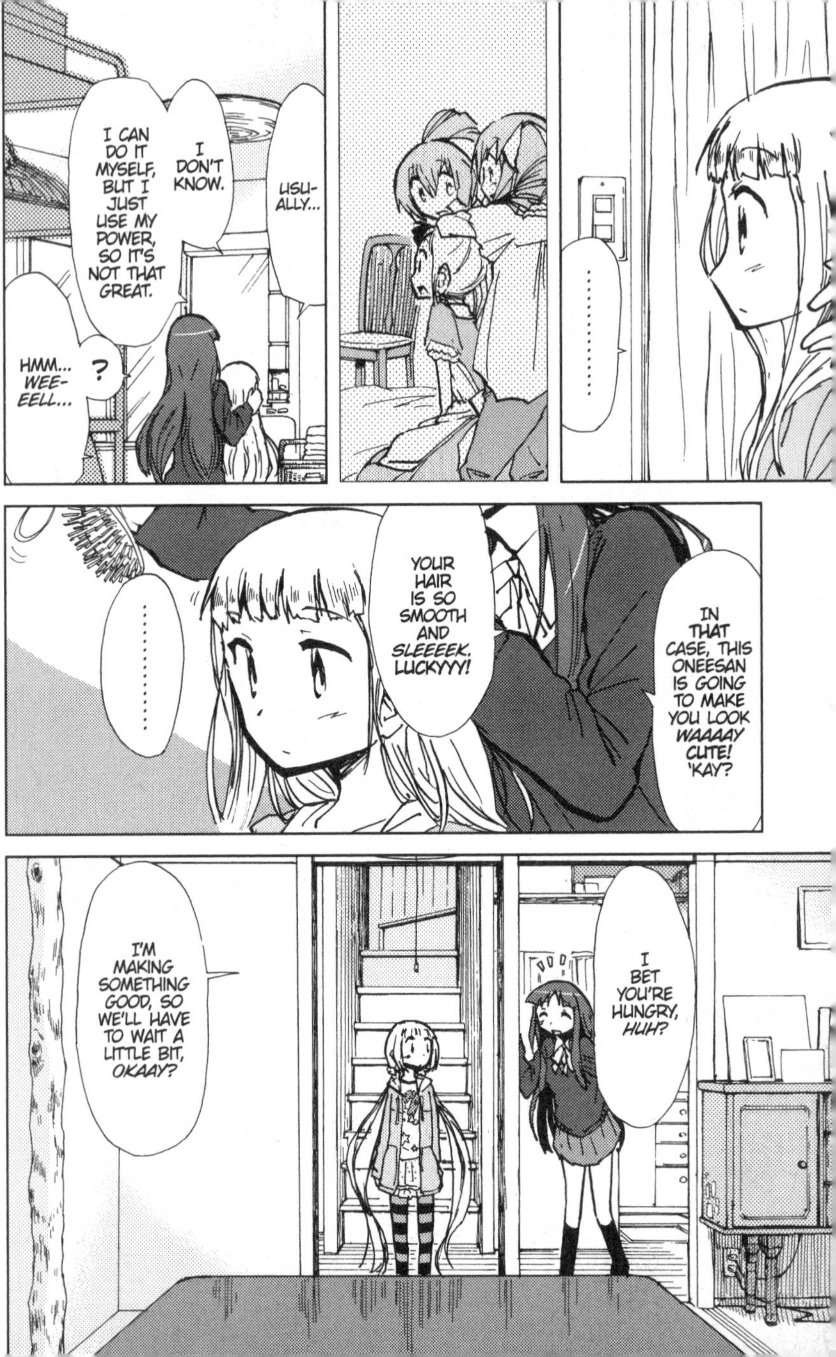
....
USUALLY...
I DON'T KNOW.
I CAN DO IT MYSELF, BUT I JUST USE MY POWER, SO IT'S NOT THAT GREAT.
?
HMM... WEE-EELL...
IN THAT CASE, THIS ONEESAN IS GOING TO MAKE YOU LOOK *WAAAAY* CUTE! 'KAY?
YOUR HAIR IS SO SMOOTH AND *SLEEEEK.* LUCKYYY!
....
I BET YOU'RE HUNGRY, *HUH?*
I'M MAKING SOMETHING GOOD, SO WE'LL HAVE TO WAIT A LITTLE BIT, *OKAAY?*

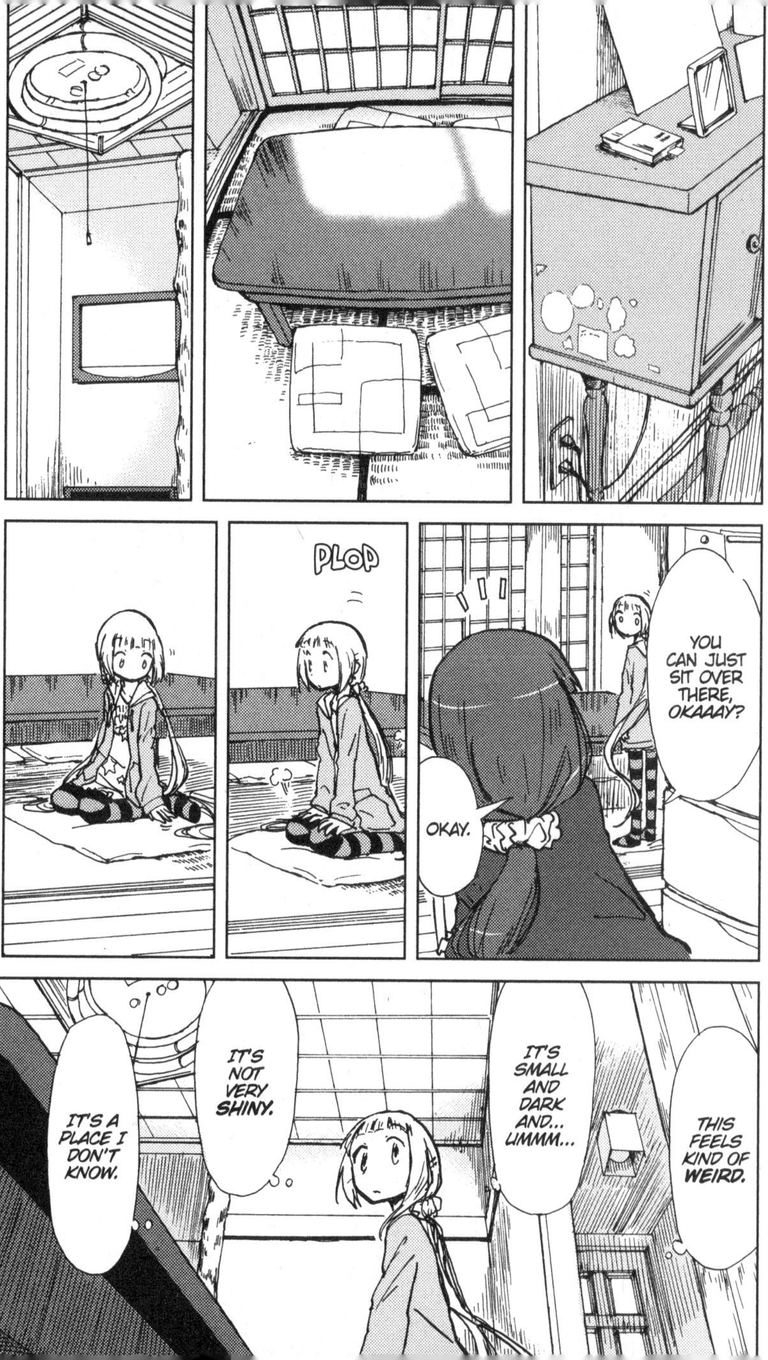
YOU CAN JUST SIT OVER THERE, OKAAAY?
OKAY.
PLOP
THIS FEELS KIND OF WEIRD.
IT'S SMALL AND DARK AND... UMMM...
IT'S NOT VERY SHINY.
IT'S A PLACE I DON'T KNOW.

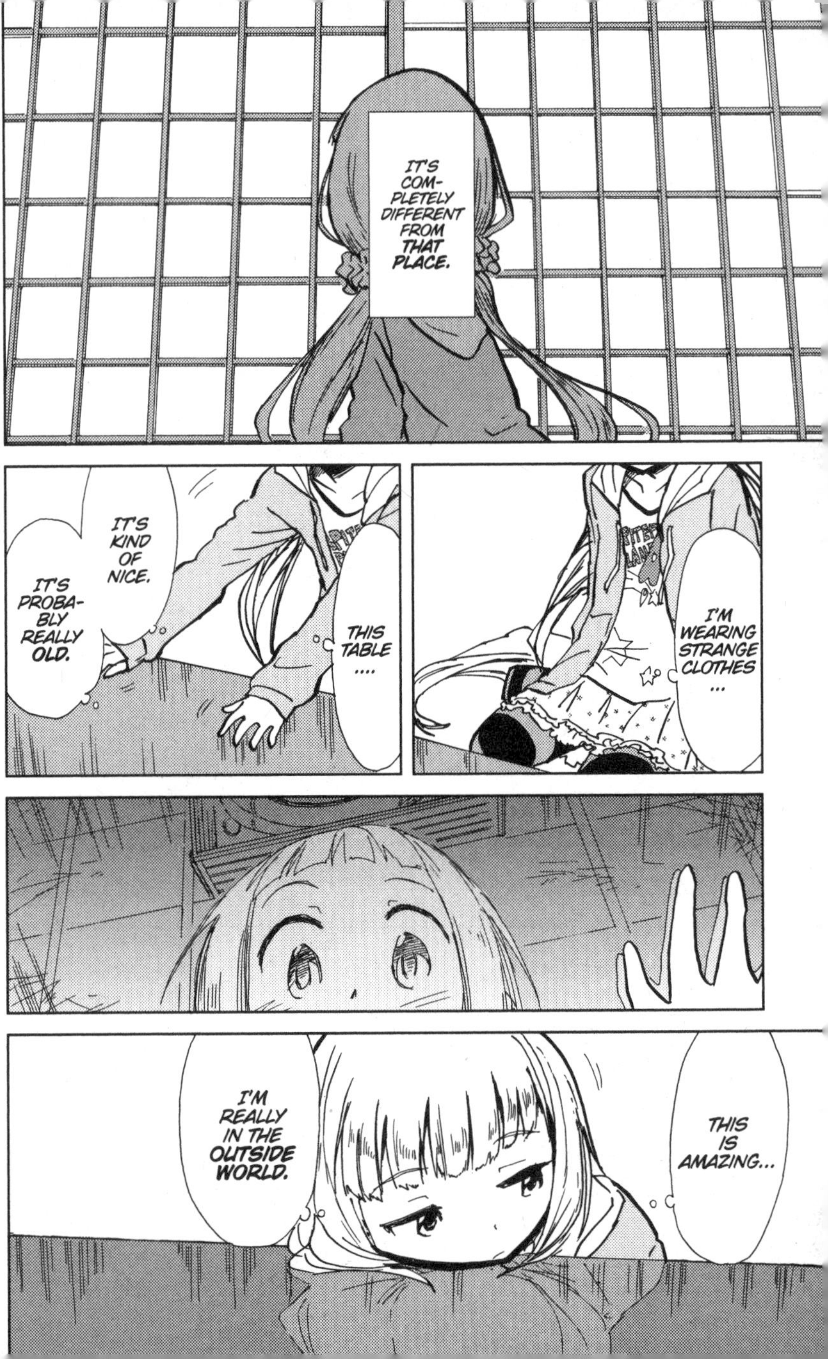
IT'S COMPLETELY DIFFERENT FROM THAT PLACE.
I'M WEARING STRANGE CLOTHES...
THIS TABLE....
IT'S KIND OF NICE.
IT'S PROBABLY REALLY OLD.
THIS IS AMAZING...
I'M REALLY IN THE OUTSIDE WORLD.

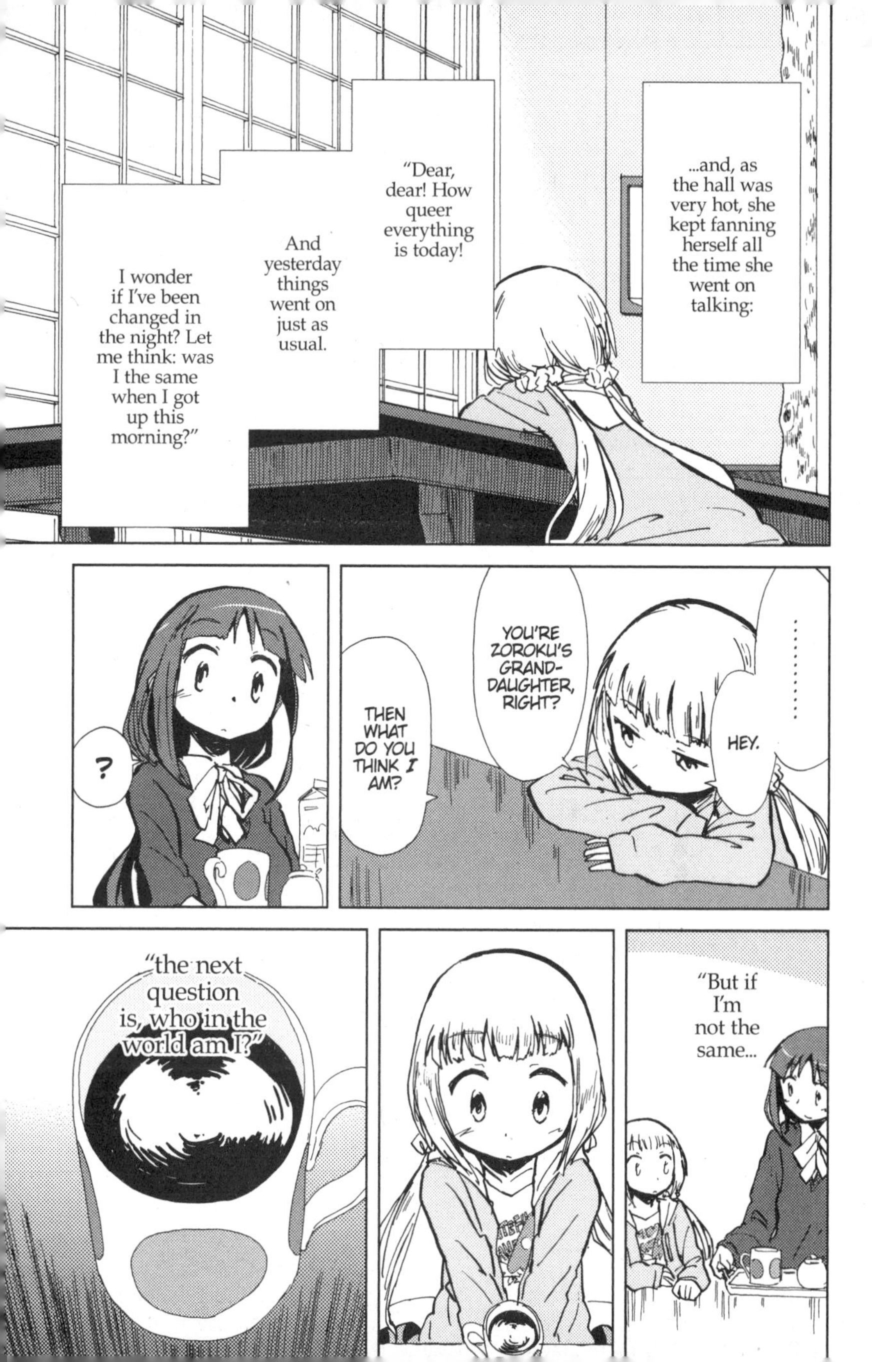
...and, as the hall was very hot, she kept fanning herself all the time she went on talking:
"Dear, dear! How queer everything is today!
And yesterday things went on just as usual.
I wonder if I've been changed in the night? Let me think: was I the same when I got up this morning?"
......
HEY.
YOU'RE ZOROKU'S GRAND-DAUGHTER, RIGHT?
THEN WHAT DO YOU THINK *I* AM?
?
"But if I'm not the same...
"the next question is, who in the world am I?"

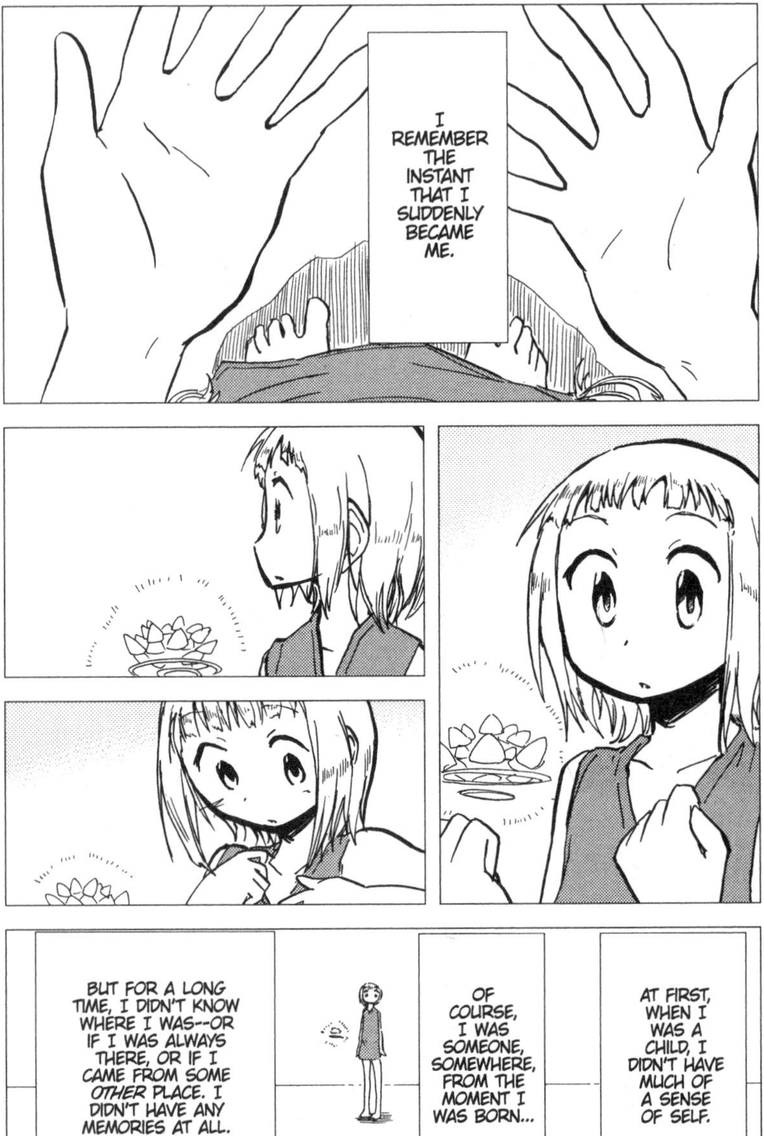
I REMEMBER THE INSTANT THAT I SUDDENLY BECAME ME.
AT FIRST, WHEN I WAS A CHILD, I DIDN'T HAVE MUCH OF A SENSE OF SELF.
OF COURSE, I WAS SOMEONE, SOMEWHERE, FROM THE MOMENT I WAS BORN...
BUT FOR A LONG TIME, I DIDN'T KNOW WHERE I WAS--OR IF I WAS ALWAYS THERE, OR IF I CAME FROM SOME *OTHER* PLACE. I DIDN'T HAVE ANY MEMORIES AT ALL.

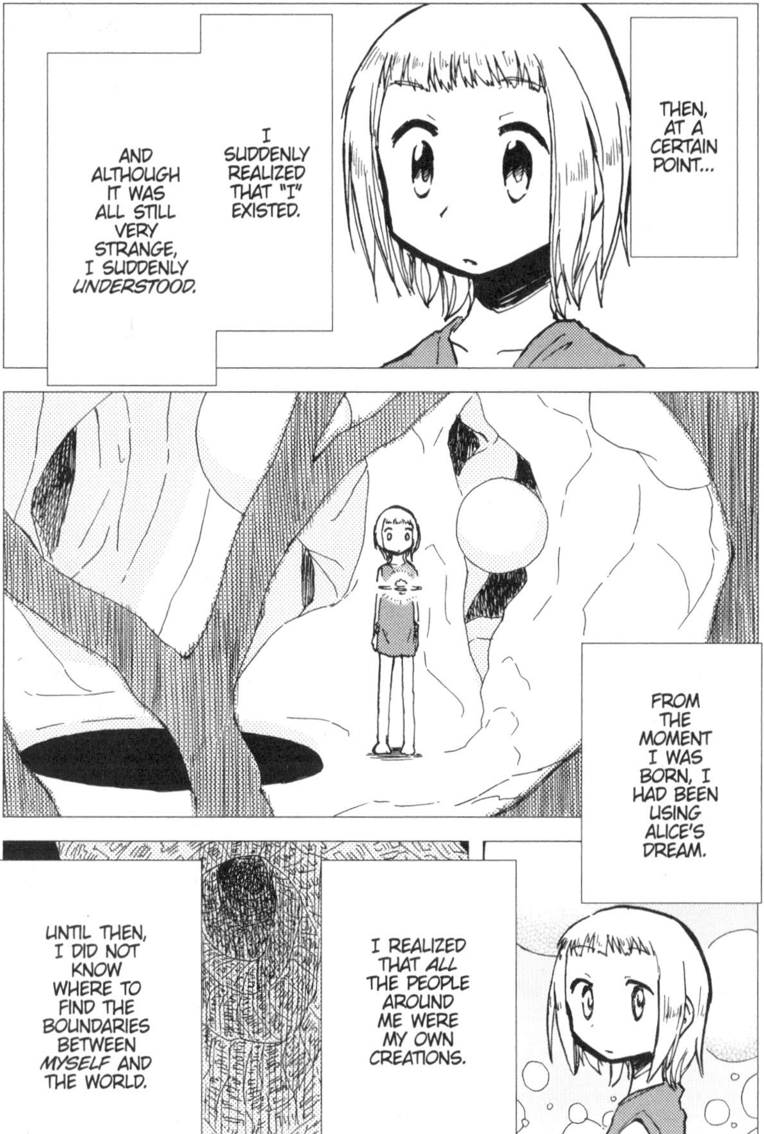
THEN, AT A CERTAIN POINT...
I SUDDENLY REALIZED THAT "I" EXISTED.
AND ALTHOUGH IT WAS ALL STILL VERY STRANGE, I SUDDENLY *UNDERSTOOD.*
FROM THE MOMENT I WAS BORN, I HAD BEEN USING ALICE'S DREAM.
I REALIZED THAT *ALL* THE PEOPLE AROUND ME WERE MY OWN CREATIONS.
UNTIL THEN, I DID NOT KNOW WHERE TO FIND THE BOUNDARIES BETWEEN *MYSELF* AND THE WORLD.

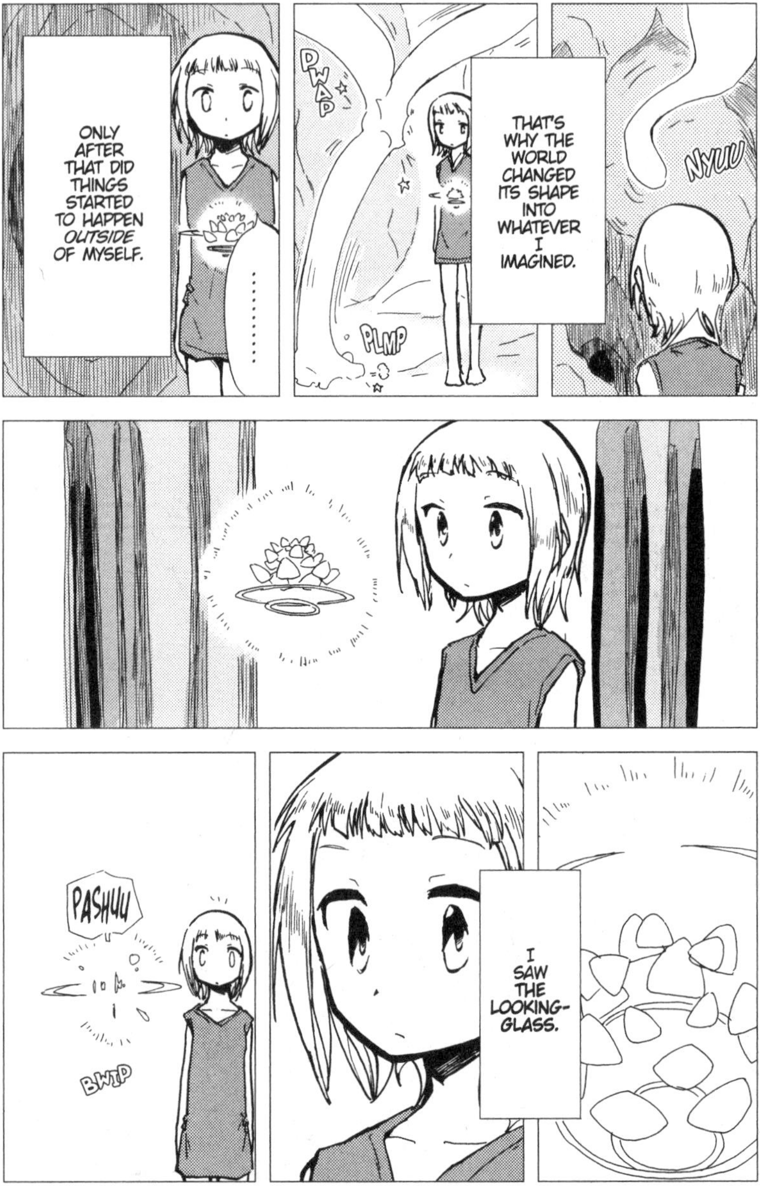
NYUU
THAT'S WHY THE WORLD CHANGED ITS SHAPE INTO WHATEVER I IMAGINED.
PWAP
PLMP
ONLY AFTER THAT DID THINGS STARTED TO HAPPEN *OUTSIDE* OF MYSELF.
I SAW THE LOOKING-GLASS.
PASHUU
BWIP

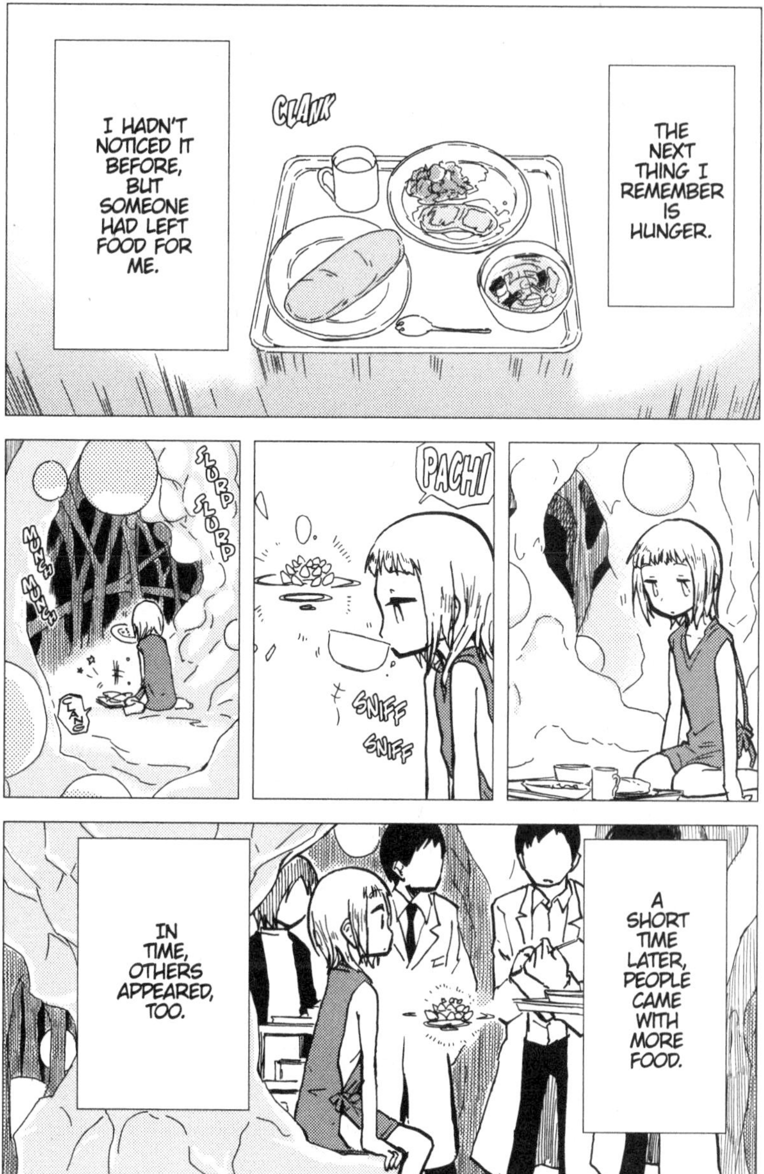
THE NEXT THING I REMEMBER IS HUNGER.
CLANK
I HADN'T NOTICED IT BEFORE, BUT SOMEONE HAD LEFT FOOD FOR ME.
PACHI
SNIFF
SNIFF
SLURP
SLURP
MUNCH
MUNCH
CLANG
A SHORT TIME LATER, PEOPLE CAME WITH MORE FOOD.
IN TIME, OTHERS APPEARED, TOO.

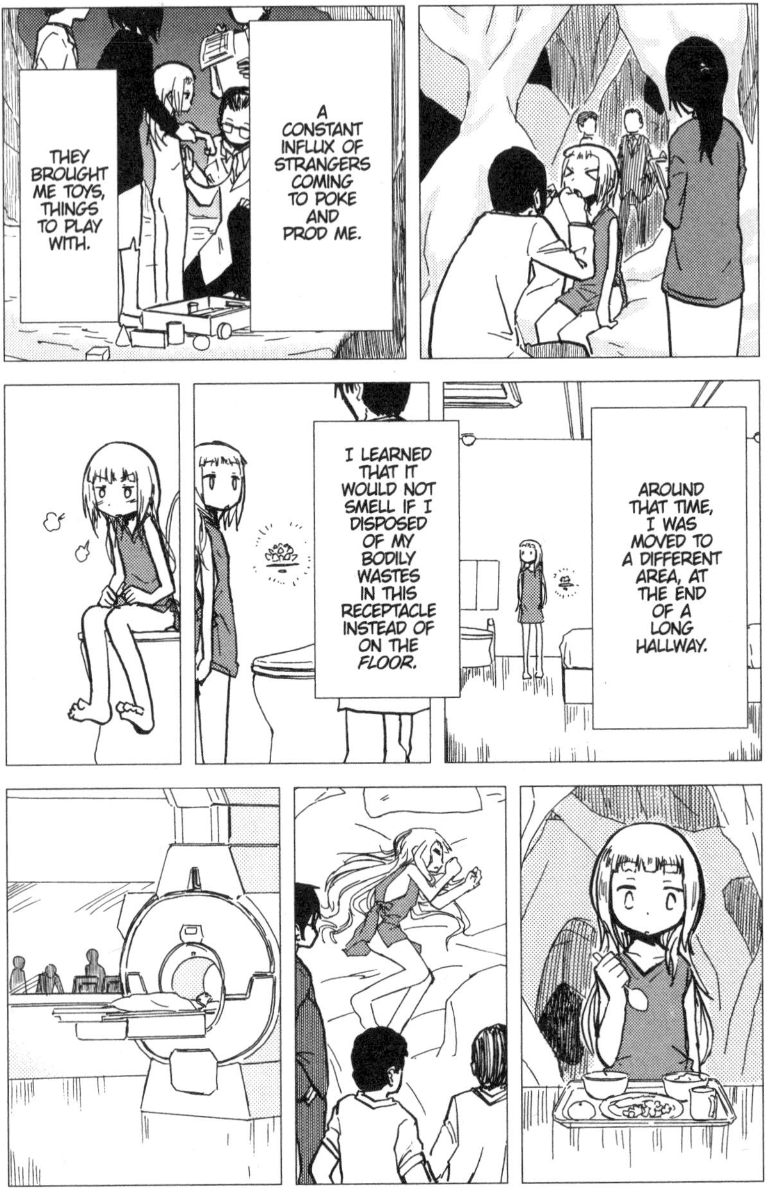
A CONSTANT INFLUX OF STRANGERS COMING TO POKE AND PROD ME.
THEY BROUGHT ME TOYS, THINGS TO PLAY WITH.
AROUND THAT TIME, I WAS MOVED TO A DIFFERENT AREA, AT THE END OF A LONG HALLWAY.
I LEARNED THAT IT WOULD NOT SMELL IF I DISPOSED OF MY BODILY WASTES IN THIS RECEPTACLE INSTEAD OF ON THE *FLOOR.*

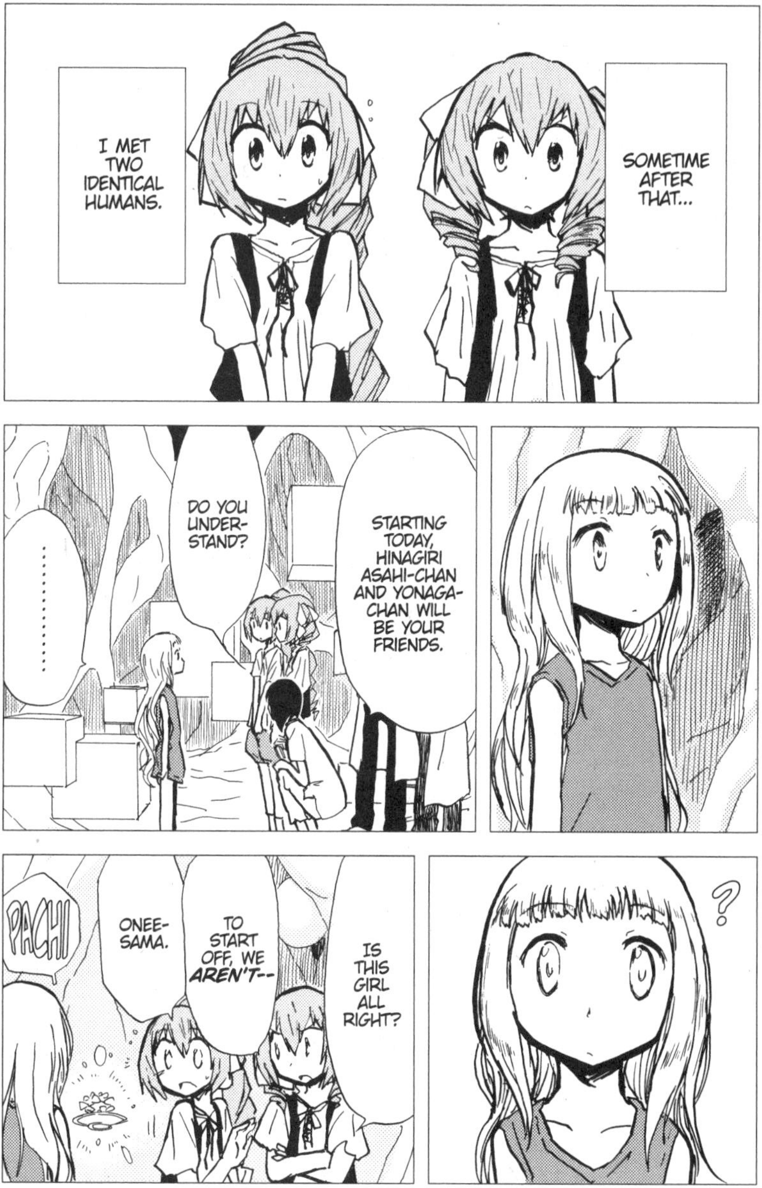
SOMETIME AFTER THAT...
I MET TWO IDENTICAL HUMANS.
STARTING TODAY, HINAGIRI ASAHI-CHAN AND YONAGA-CHAN WILL BE YOUR FRIENDS.
DO YOU UNDER-STAND?
......
?
IS THIS GIRL ALL RIGHT?
TO START OFF, WE AREN'T--
ONEE-SAMA.
PACHI

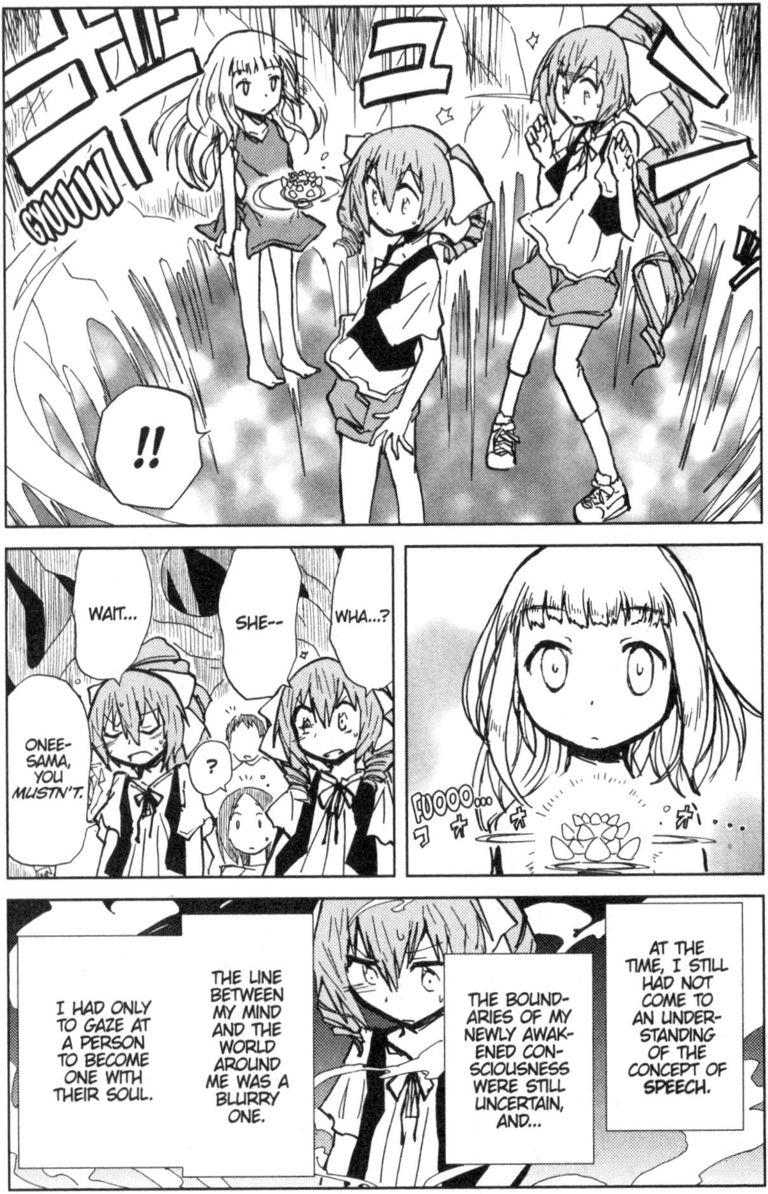
GYUUUN
!!
FUOOO...
WHA...?
SHE--
WAIT...
?
ONEE-SAMA, YOU MUSTN'T.
AT THE TIME, I STILL HAD NOT COME TO AN UNDERSTANDING OF THE CONCEPT OF SPEECH.
THE BOUNDARIES OF MY NEWLY AWAKENED CONSCIOUSNESS WERE STILL UNCERTAIN, AND...
THE LINE BETWEEN MY MIND AND THE WORLD AROUND ME WAS A BLURRY ONE.
I HAD ONLY TO GAZE AT A PERSON TO BECOME ONE WITH THEIR SOUL.

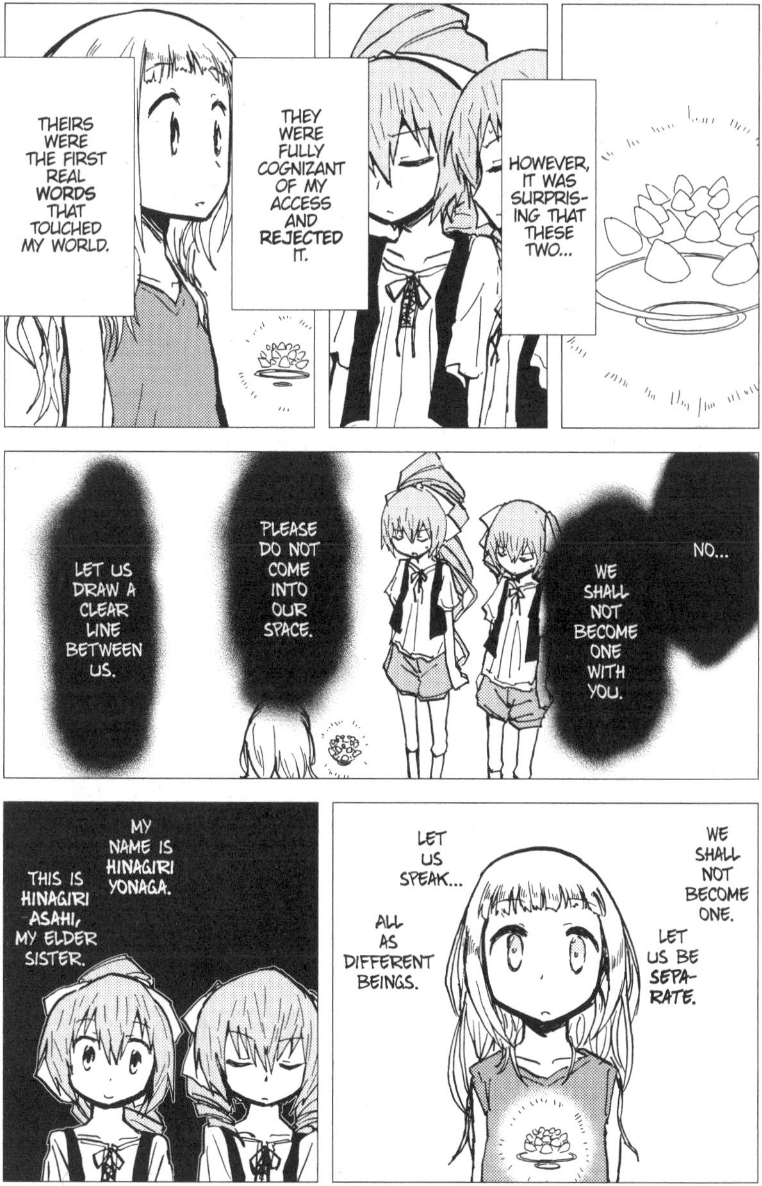
HOWEVER, IT WAS SURPRISING THAT THESE TWO...
THEY WERE FULLY COGNIZANT OF MY ACCESS AND REJECTED IT.
THEIRS WERE THE FIRST REAL WORDS THAT TOUCHED MY WORLD.
NO...
WE SHALL NOT BECOME ONE WITH YOU.
PLEASE DO NOT COME INTO OUR SPACE.
LET US DRAW A CLEAR LINE BETWEEN US.
WE SHALL NOT BECOME ONE.
LET US SPEAK...
LET US BE SEPARATE.
ALL AS DIFFERENT BEINGS.
MY NAME IS HINAGIRI YONAGA.
THIS IS HINAGIRI ASAHI, MY ELDER SISTER.

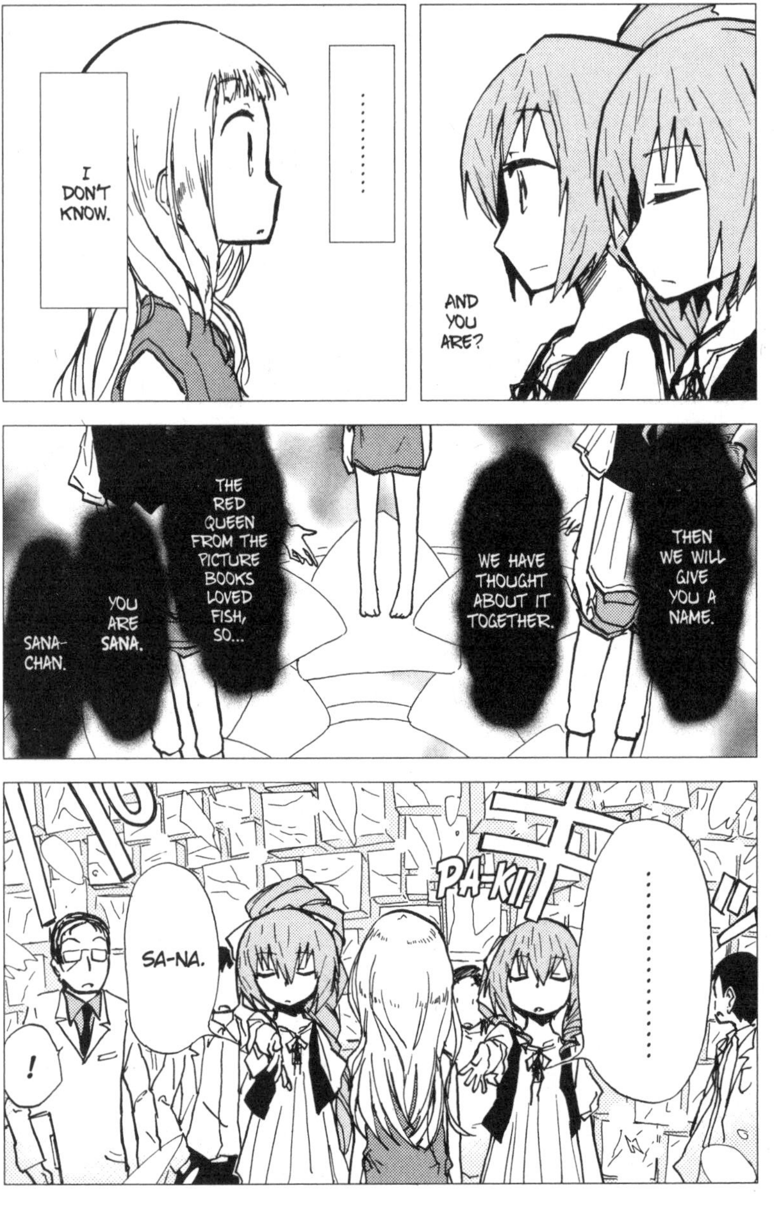
AND YOU ARE?
......
I DON'T KNOW.
THEN WE WILL GIVE YOU A NAME.
WE HAVE THOUGHT ABOUT IT TOGETHER.
THE RED QUEEN FROM THE PICTURE BOOKS LOVED FISH, SO...
YOU ARE SANA.
SANA-CHAN.
PA-KII
......
SA-NA.
!

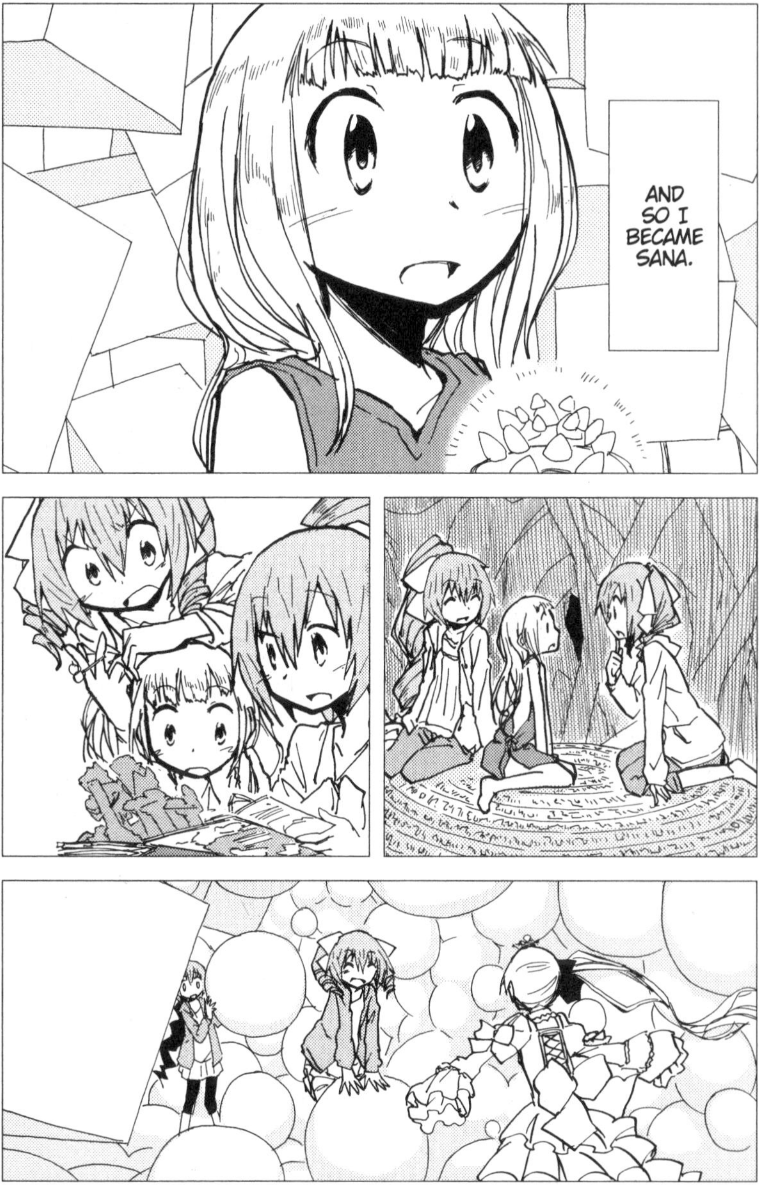
AND SO I BECAME SANA.

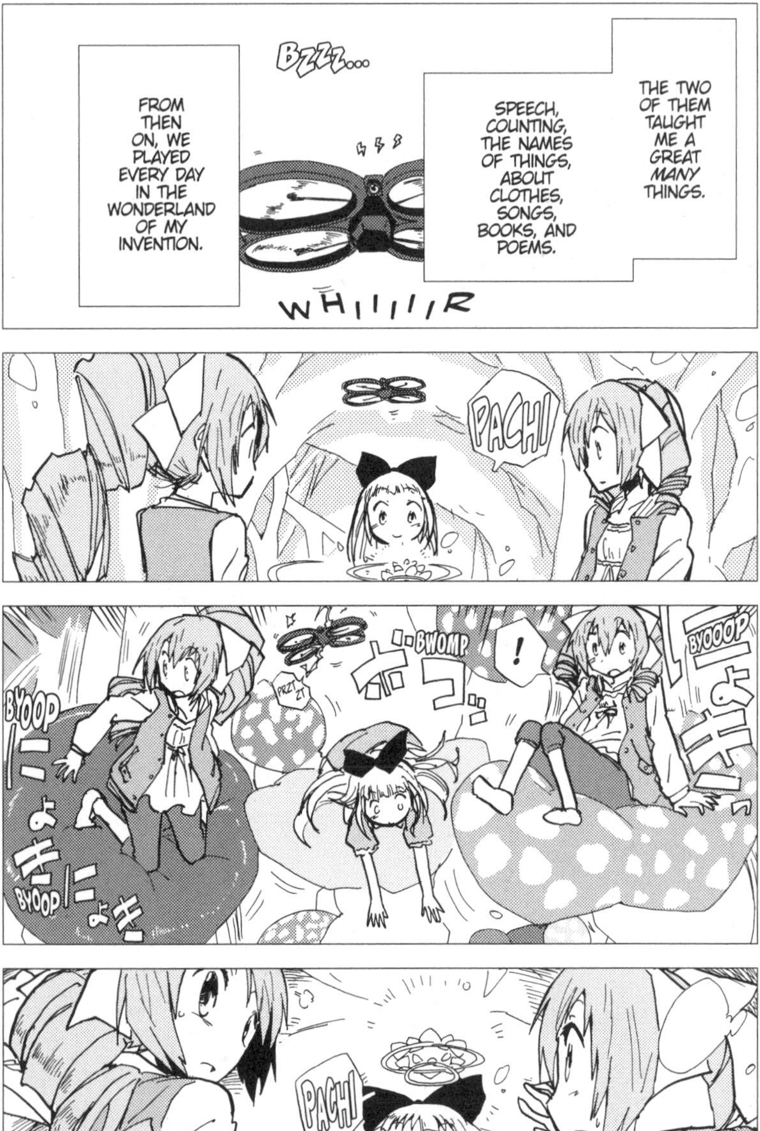
THE TWO OF THEM TAUGHT ME A GREAT MANY THINGS.
SPEECH, COUNTING, THE NAMES OF THINGS, ABOUT CLOTHES, SONGS, BOOKS, AND POEMS.
BZZZ...
FROM THEN ON, WE PLAYED EVERY DAY IN THE WONDERLAND OF MY INVENTION.
WHIIIIIR
PACHI
BYOOOP
!
BWOMP
PRZT ZT
BYOOP
BYOOP
PACHI

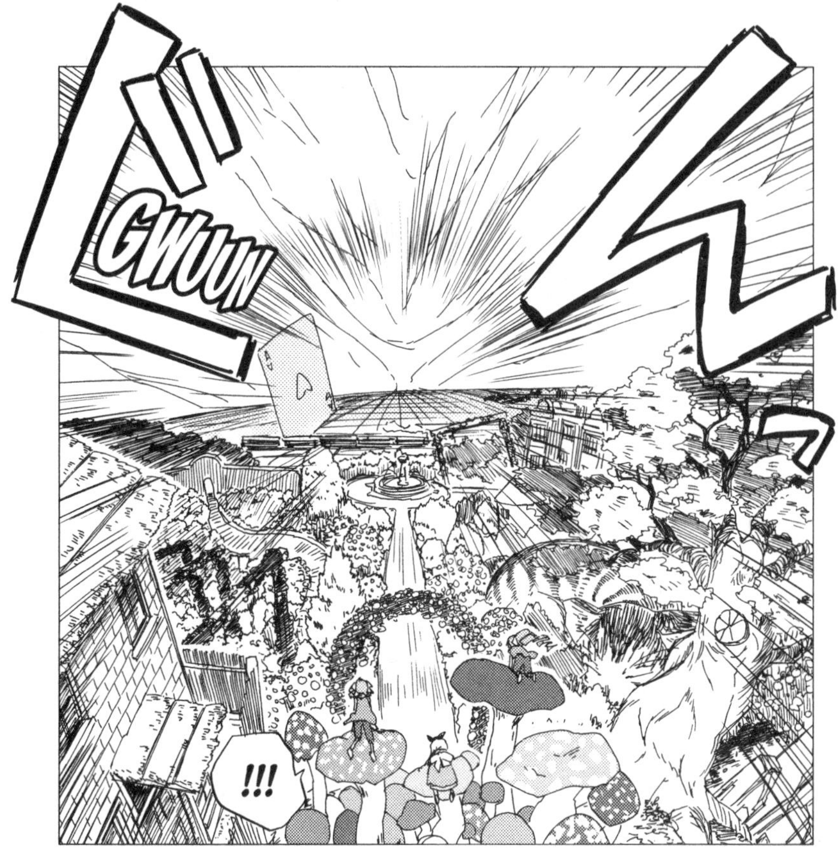
GWUUN
!!!

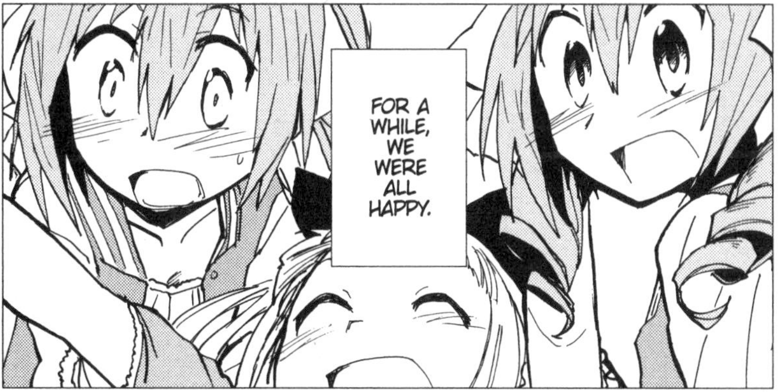
FOR A WHILE, WE WERE ALL HAPPY.

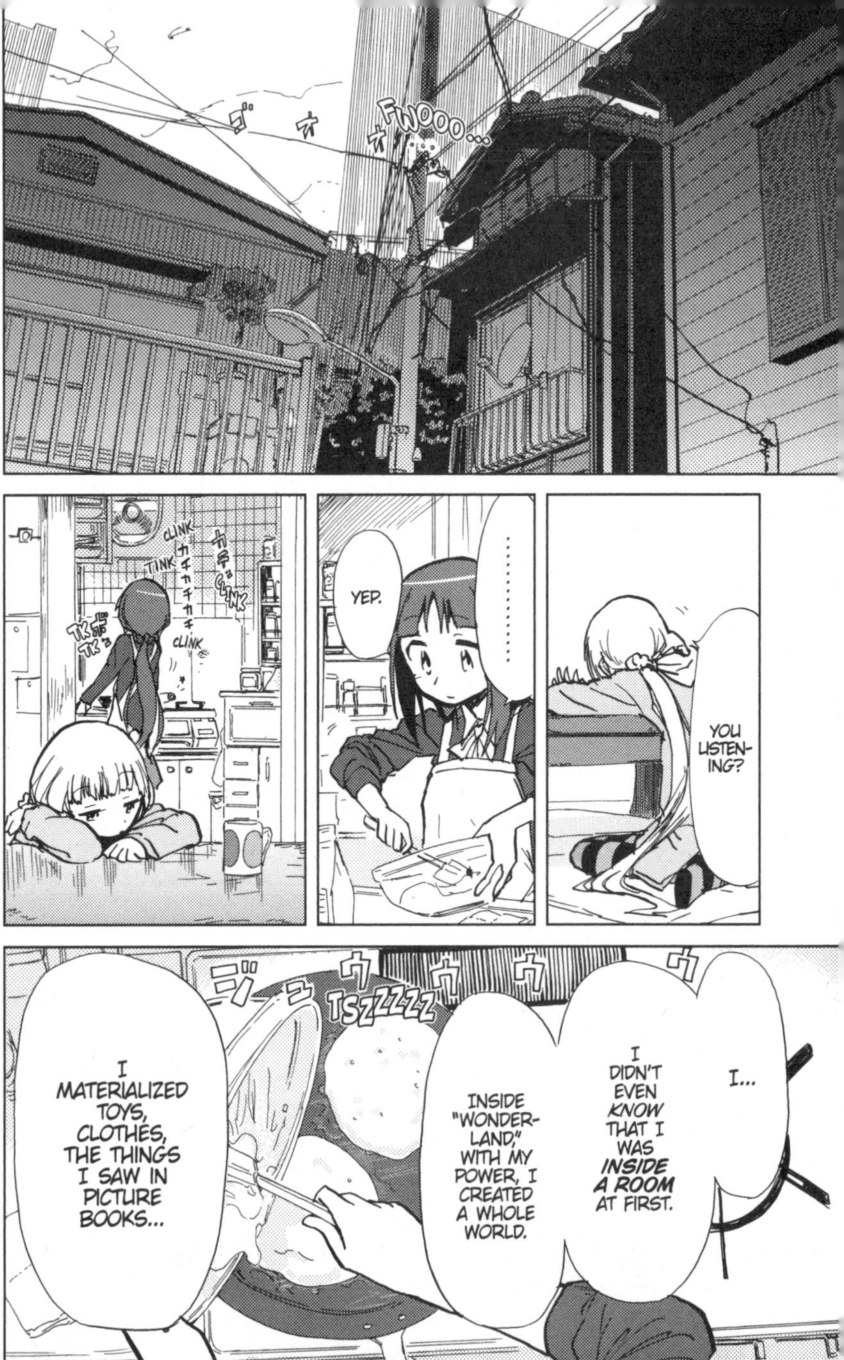

FWOOO...
YOU LISTEN-ING?
......
YEP.
CLINK
TINK
CLINK
CLINK
TK TK
I...
I DIDN'T EVEN KNOW THAT I WAS INSIDE A ROOM AT FIRST.
INSIDE "WONDER-LAND," WITH MY POWER, I CREATED A WHOLE WORLD.
TSZZZZZ
I MATERIALIZED TOYS, CLOTHES, THE THINGS I SAW IN PICTURE BOOKS...

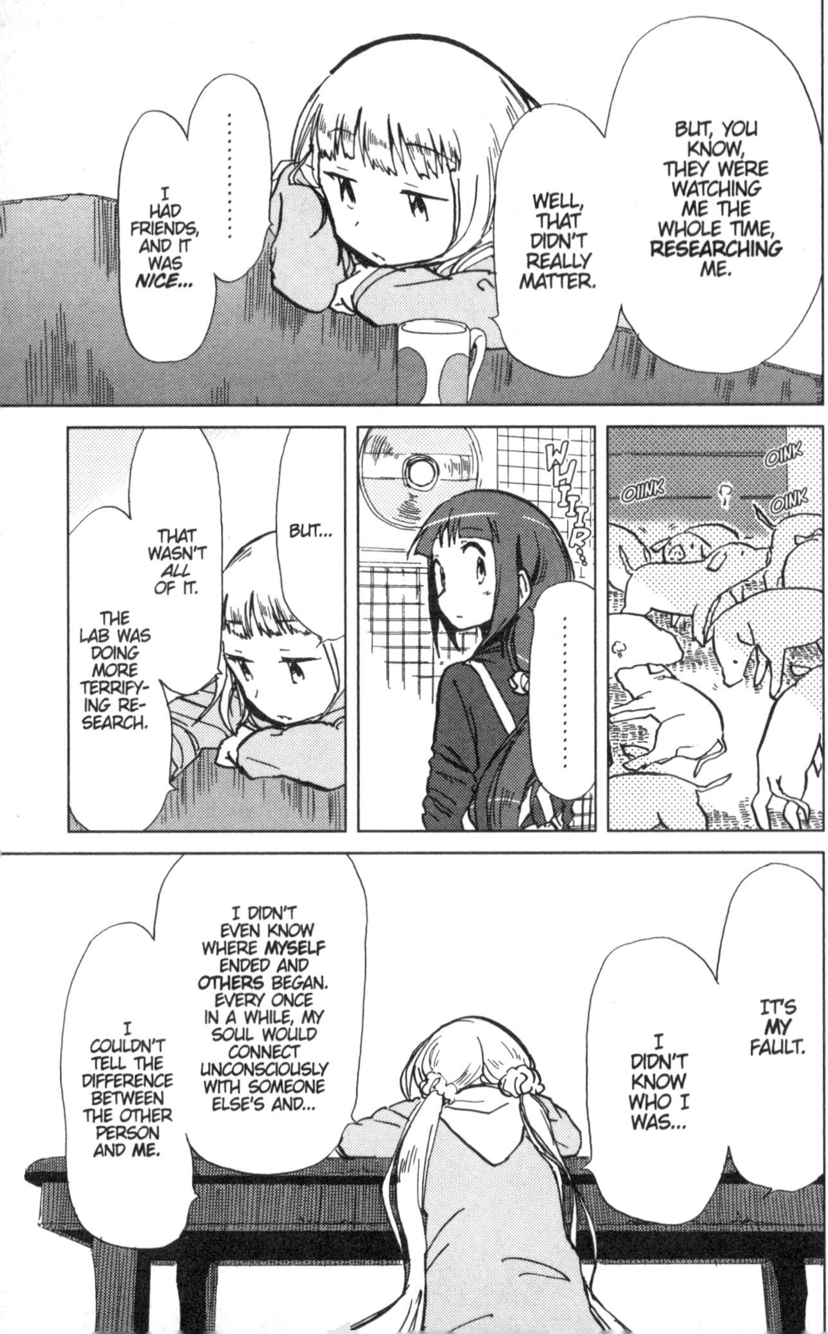
BUT, YOU KNOW, THEY WERE WATCHING ME THE WHOLE TIME, RESEARCHING ME.
WELL, THAT DIDN'T REALLY MATTER.
......
I HAD FRIENDS, AND IT WAS NICE...
OINK
OINK
OINK
WHIIIR...
......
BUT...
THAT WASN'T ALL OF IT.
THE LAB WAS DOING MORE TERRIFYING RESEARCH.
IT'S MY FAULT.
I DIDN'T KNOW WHO I WAS...
I DIDN'T EVEN KNOW WHERE MYSELF ENDED AND OTHERS BEGAN. EVERY ONCE IN A WHILE, MY SOUL WOULD CONNECT UNCONSCIOUSLY WITH SOMEONE ELSE'S AND...
I COULDN'T TELL THE DIFFERENCE BETWEEN THE OTHER PERSON AND ME.

AND SO...

IN THE DEPTHS OF THE LAB, DEEP, *DEEP* DOWN...

MY FRIENDS...

THEY WERE DOING SOMETHING TO THEM AND MAKING THEM... *NOT HUMAN.*

I SAW IT.

SHHHNK

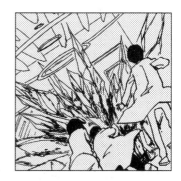

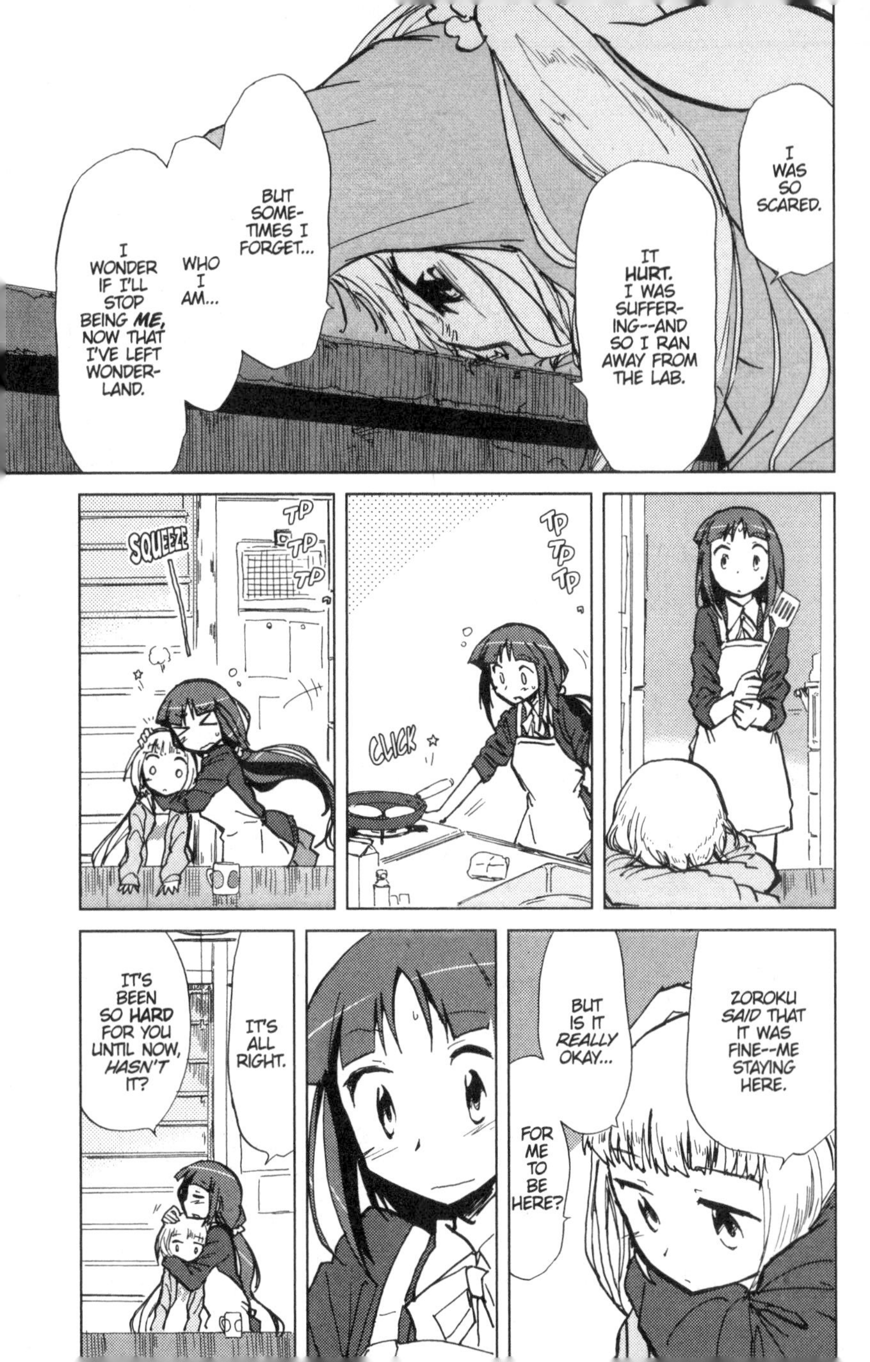
I WAS SO SCARED.
IT HURT. I WAS SUFFERING--AND SO I RAN AWAY FROM THE LAB.
BUT SOMETIMES I FORGET...
WHO I AM...
I WONDER IF I'LL STOP BEING *ME*, NOW THAT I'VE LEFT WONDERLAND.
TP TP TP
CLICK
TP TP TP
SQUEEZE
ZOROKU *SAID* THAT IT WAS FINE--ME STAYING HERE.
BUT IS IT *REALLY* OKAY...
FOR ME TO BE HERE?
IT'S ALL RIGHT.
IT'S BEEN SO **HARD** FOR YOU UNTIL NOW, *HASN'T* IT?

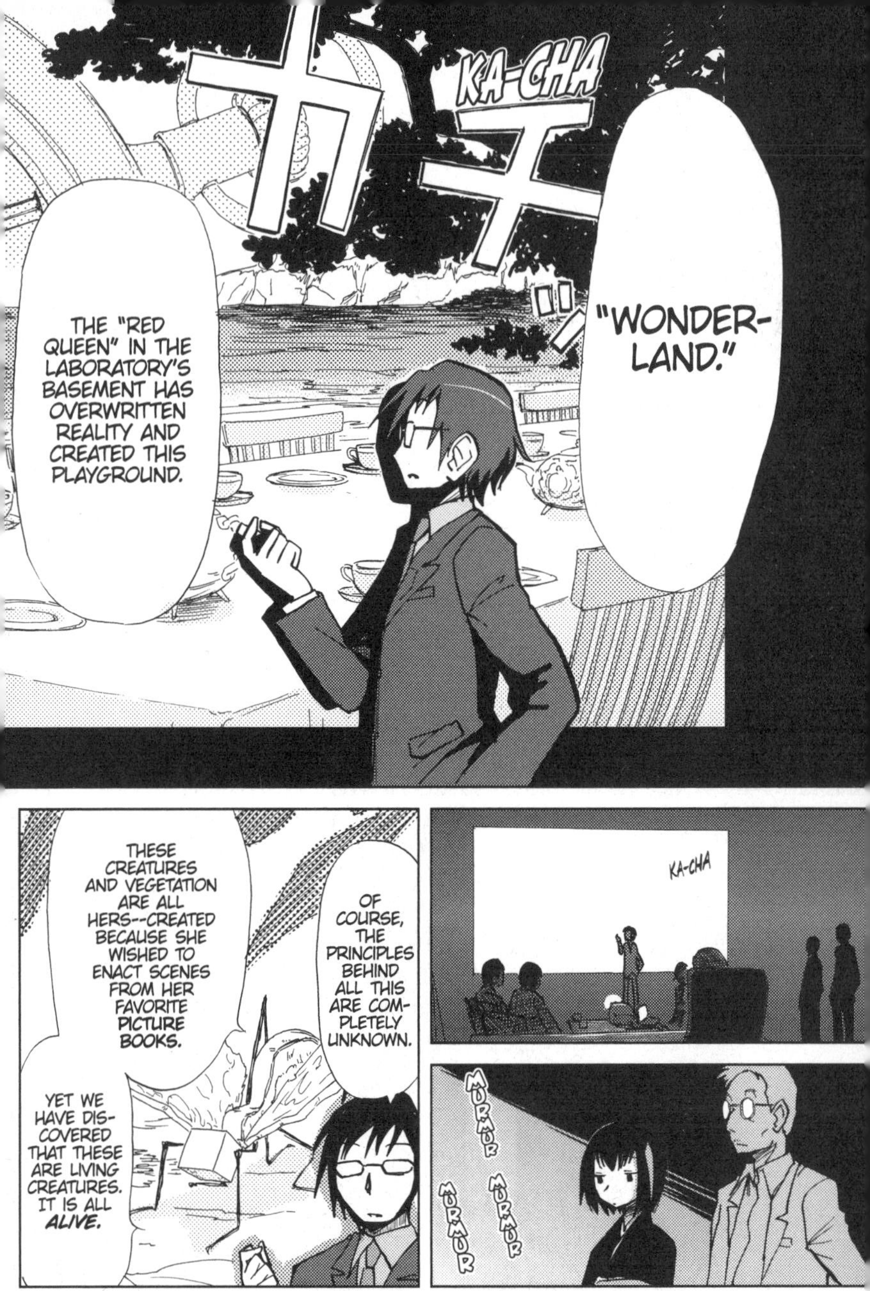
KA-CHA
"WONDER-LAND."
THE "RED QUEEN" IN THE LABORATORY'S BASEMENT HAS OVERWRITTEN REALITY AND CREATED THIS PLAYGROUND.
KA-CHA
MURMUR MURMUR MURMUR
OF COURSE, THE PRINCIPLES BEHIND ALL THIS ARE COMPLETELY UNKNOWN.
THESE CREATURES AND VEGETATION ARE ALL HERS--CREATED BECAUSE SHE WISHED TO ENACT SCENES FROM HER FAVORITE PICTURE BOOKS.
YET WE HAVE DISCOVERED THAT THESE ARE LIVING CREATURES. IT IS ALL ***ALIVE.***

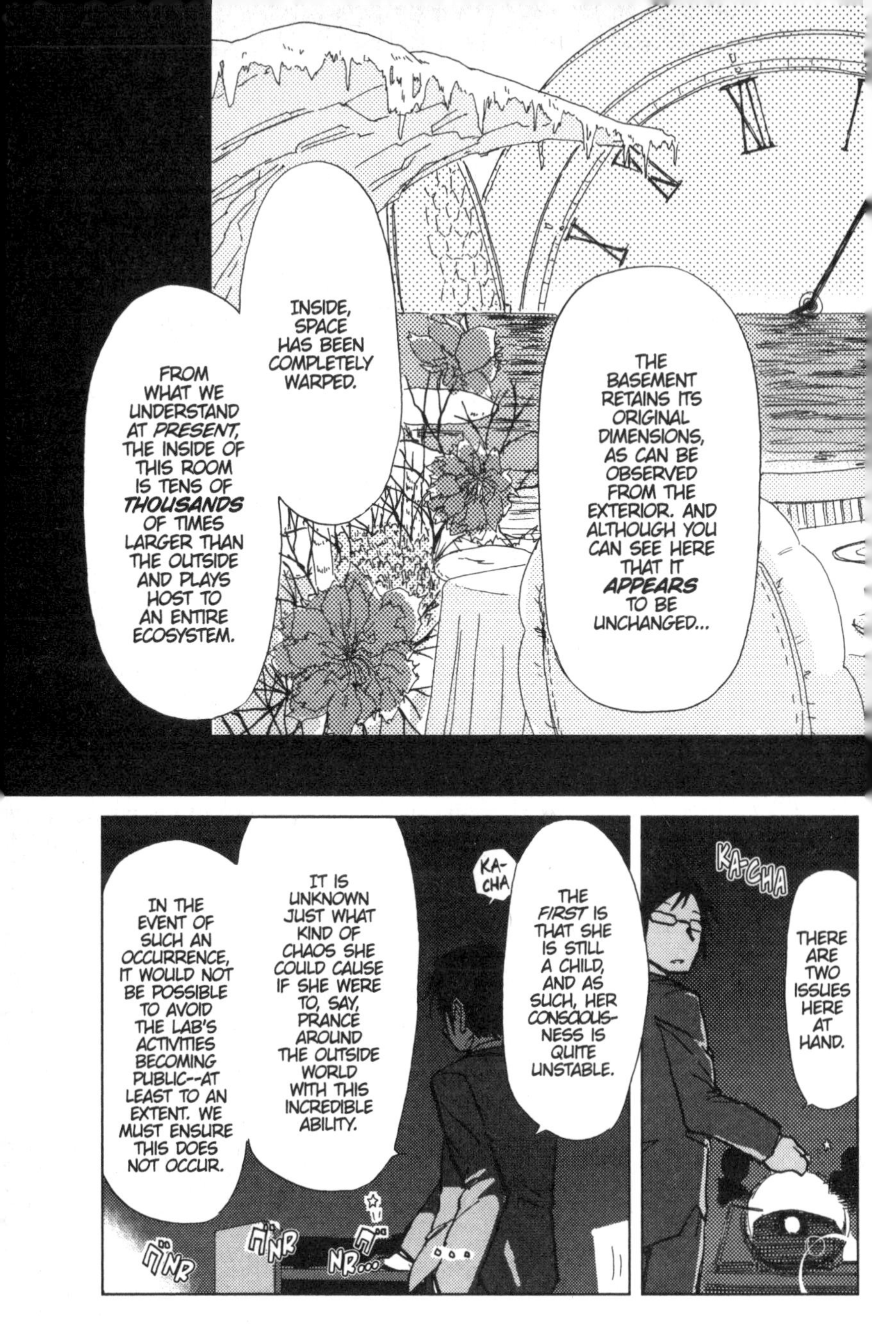
THE BASEMENT RETAINS ITS ORIGINAL DIMENSIONS, AS CAN BE OBSERVED FROM THE EXTERIOR. AND ALTHOUGH YOU CAN SEE HERE THAT IT APPEARS TO BE UNCHANGED...
INSIDE, SPACE HAS BEEN COMPLETELY WARPED.
FROM WHAT WE UNDERSTAND AT PRESENT, THE INSIDE OF THIS ROOM IS TENS OF THOUSANDS OF TIMES LARGER THAN THE OUTSIDE AND PLAYS HOST TO AN ENTIRE ECOSYSTEM.
KA-CHA
THERE ARE TWO ISSUES HERE AT HAND.
KA-CHA
THE FIRST IS THAT SHE IS STILL A CHILD, AND AS SUCH, HER CONSCIOUS-NESS IS QUITE UNSTABLE.
IT IS UNKNOWN JUST WHAT KIND OF CHAOS SHE COULD CAUSE IF SHE WERE TO, SAY, PRANCE AROUND THE OUTSIDE WORLD WITH THIS INCREDIBLE ABILITY.
IN THE EVENT OF SUCH AN OCCURRENCE, IT WOULD NOT BE POSSIBLE TO AVOID THE LAB'S ACTIVITIES BECOMING PUBLIC--AT LEAST TO AN EXTENT. WE MUST ENSURE THIS DOES NOT OCCUR.
NR...

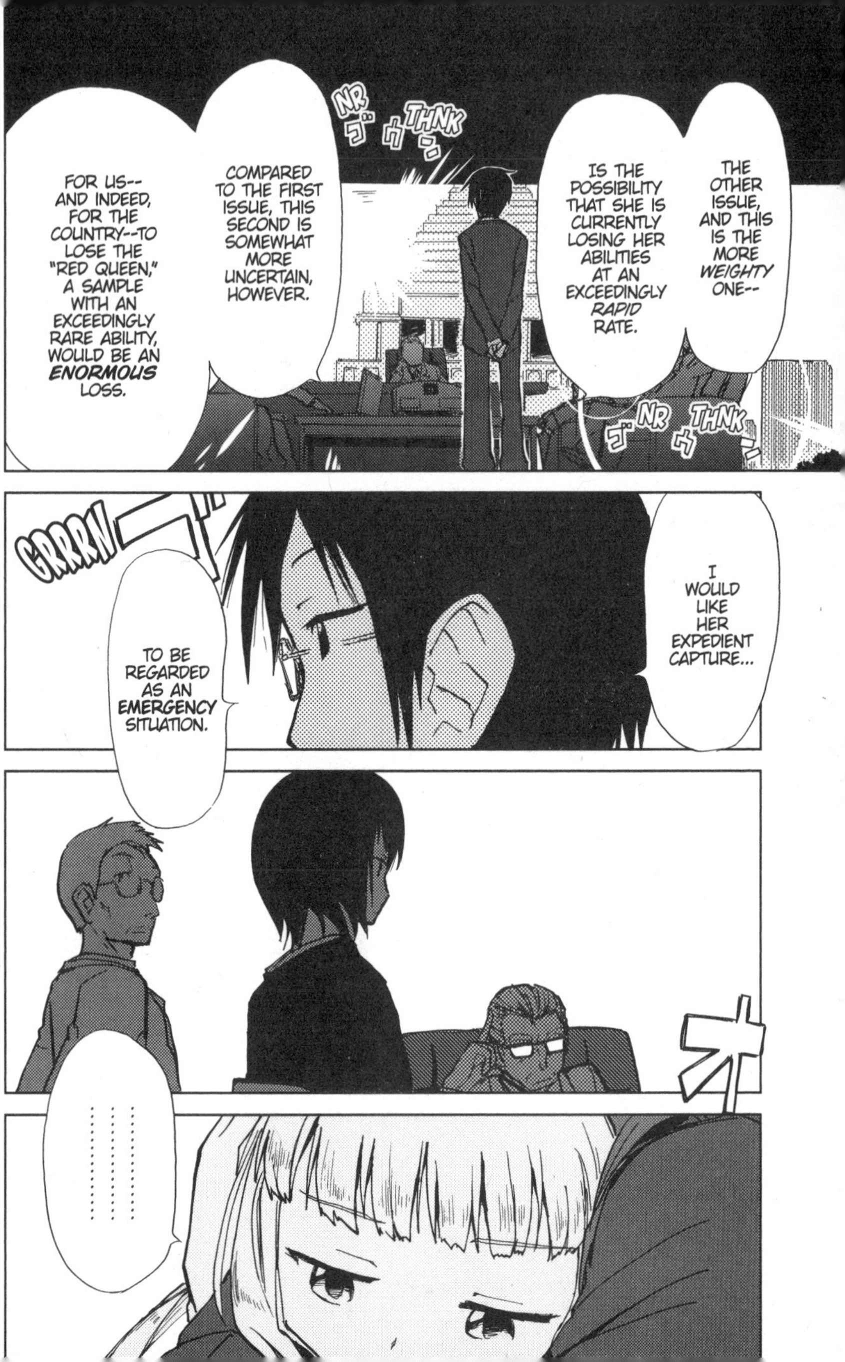
THE OTHER ISSUE, AND THIS IS THE MORE WEIGHTY ONE--
IS THE POSSIBILITY THAT SHE IS CURRENTLY LOSING HER ABILITIES AT AN EXCEEDINGLY RAPID RATE.
NR THNK
NR THNK
COMPARED TO THE FIRST ISSUE, THIS SECOND IS SOMEWHAT MORE UNCERTAIN, HOWEVER.
FOR US--AND INDEED, FOR THE COUNTRY--TO LOSE THE "RED QUEEN," A SAMPLE WITH AN EXCEEDINGLY RARE ABILITY, WOULD BE AN ENORMOUS LOSS.
I WOULD LIKE HER EXPEDIENT CAPTURE...
TO BE REGARDED AS AN EMERGENCY SITUATION.
GRRRN
......

Alice & Zoroku

◆

"If it had grown up," she said to herself,
"it would have made a dreadfully ugly child;
but it makes rather a handsome pig,
I think."

Chapter.4

The Road Home

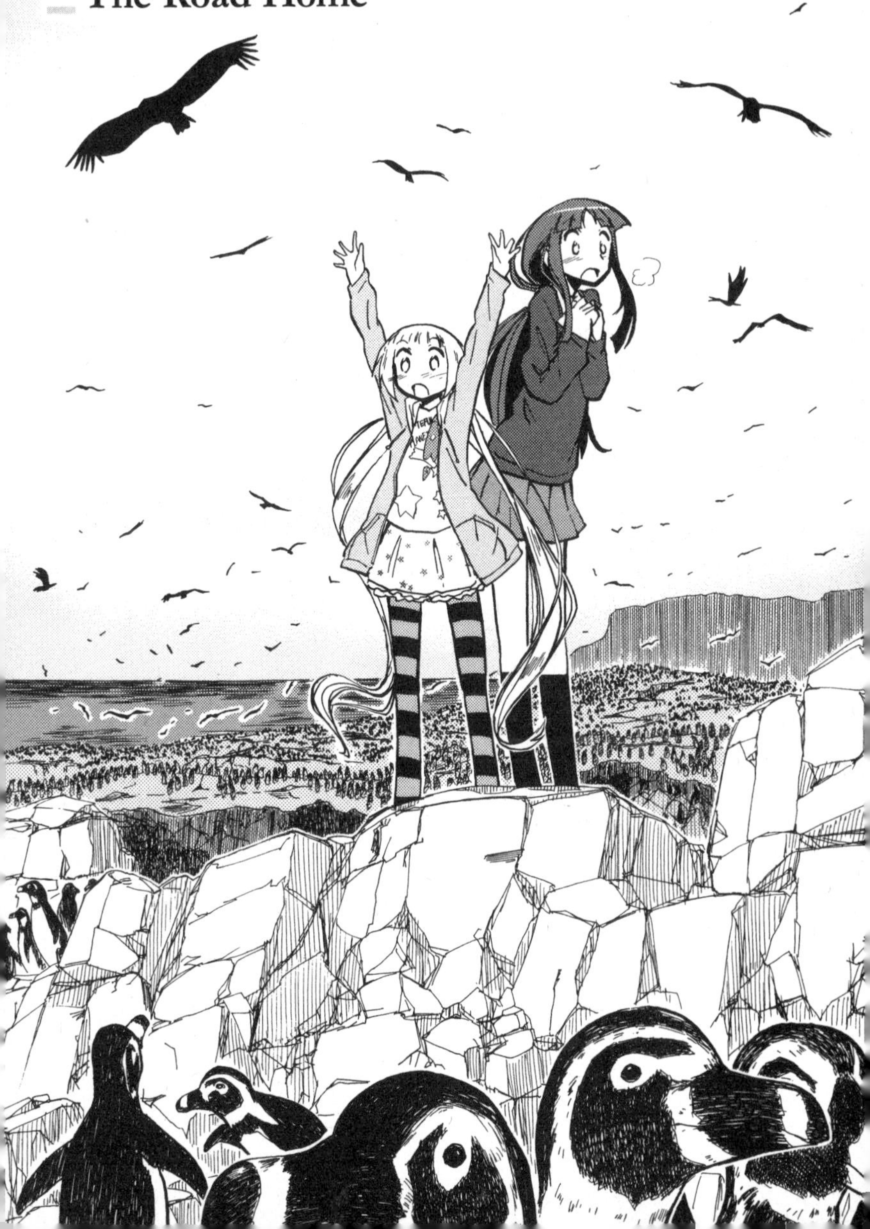

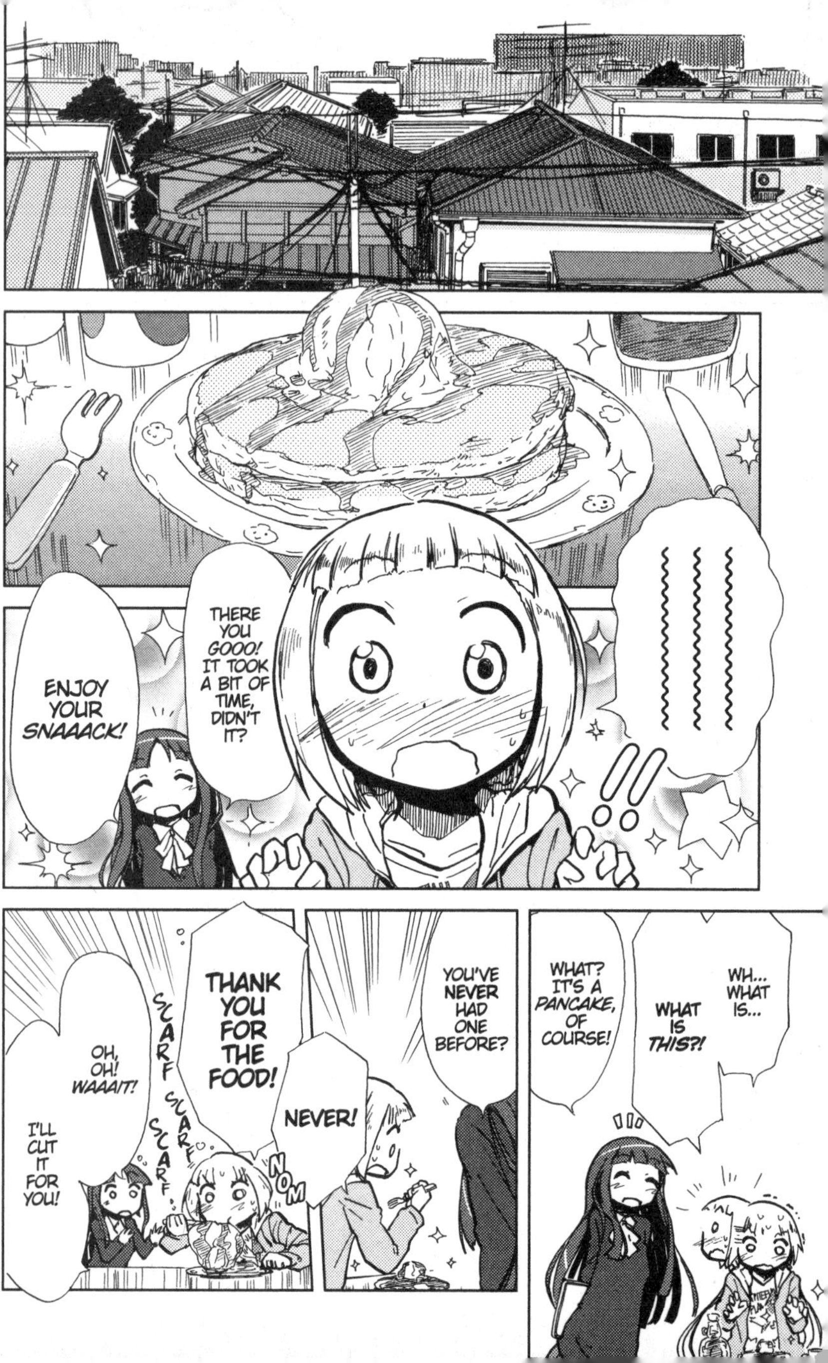
!!
THERE YOU GOOO! IT TOOK A BIT OF TIME, DIDN'T IT?
ENJOY YOUR SNAAACK!
WH... WHAT IS...
WHAT IS THIS?!
WHAT? IT'S A PANCAKE, OF COURSE!
YOU'VE NEVER HAD ONE BEFORE?
NEVER!
NOM
THANK YOU FOR THE FOOD!
SCARF SCARF SCARF
OH, OH! WAAAIT!
I'LL CUT IT FOR YOU!

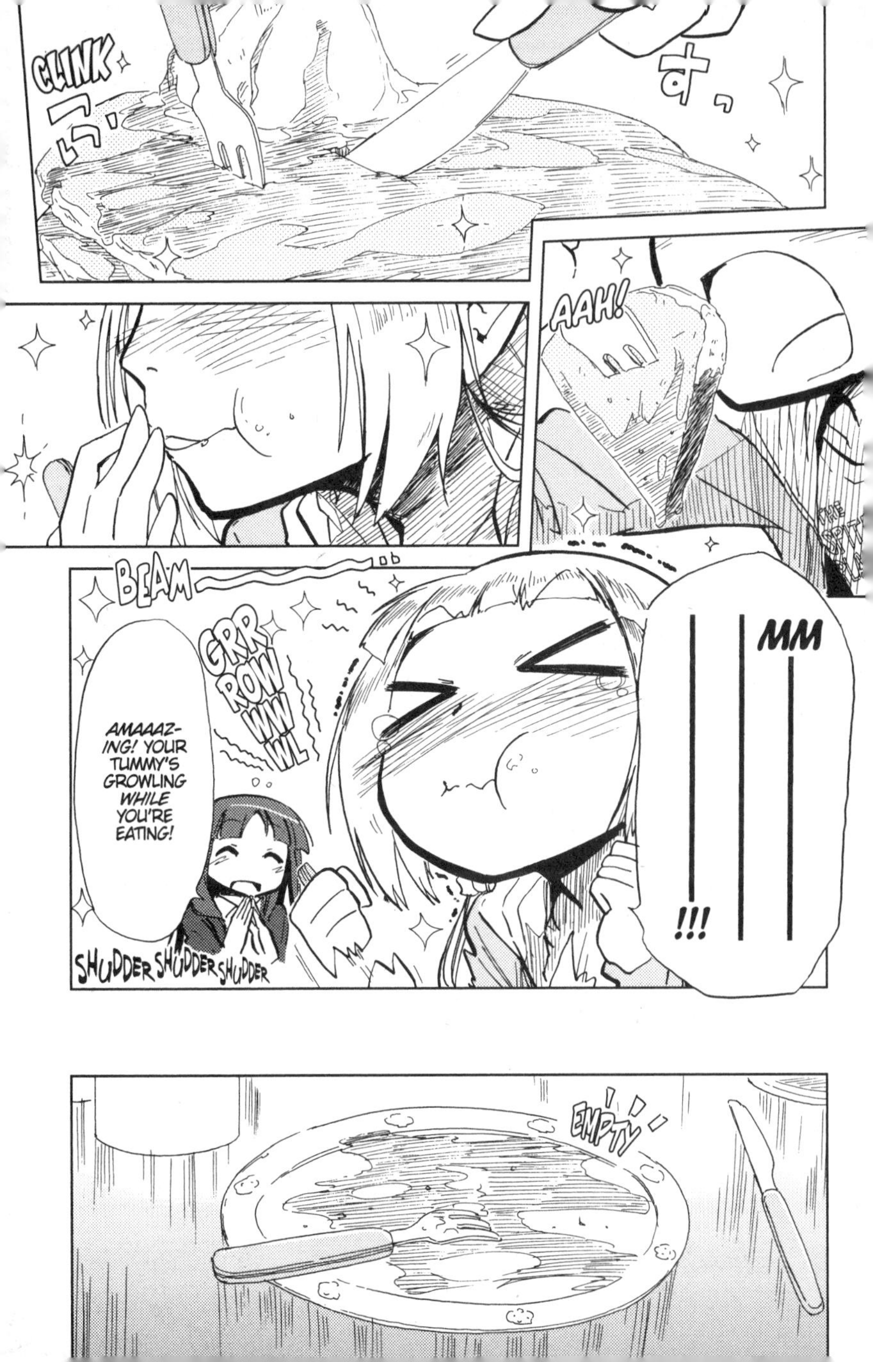
すっ
CLINK
AAH!
MM!!!
GRR ROW WW WL
BEAM
AMAAAZING! YOUR TUMMY'S GROWLING WHILE YOU'RE EATING!
SHUDDER SHUDDER SHUDDER
EMPTY

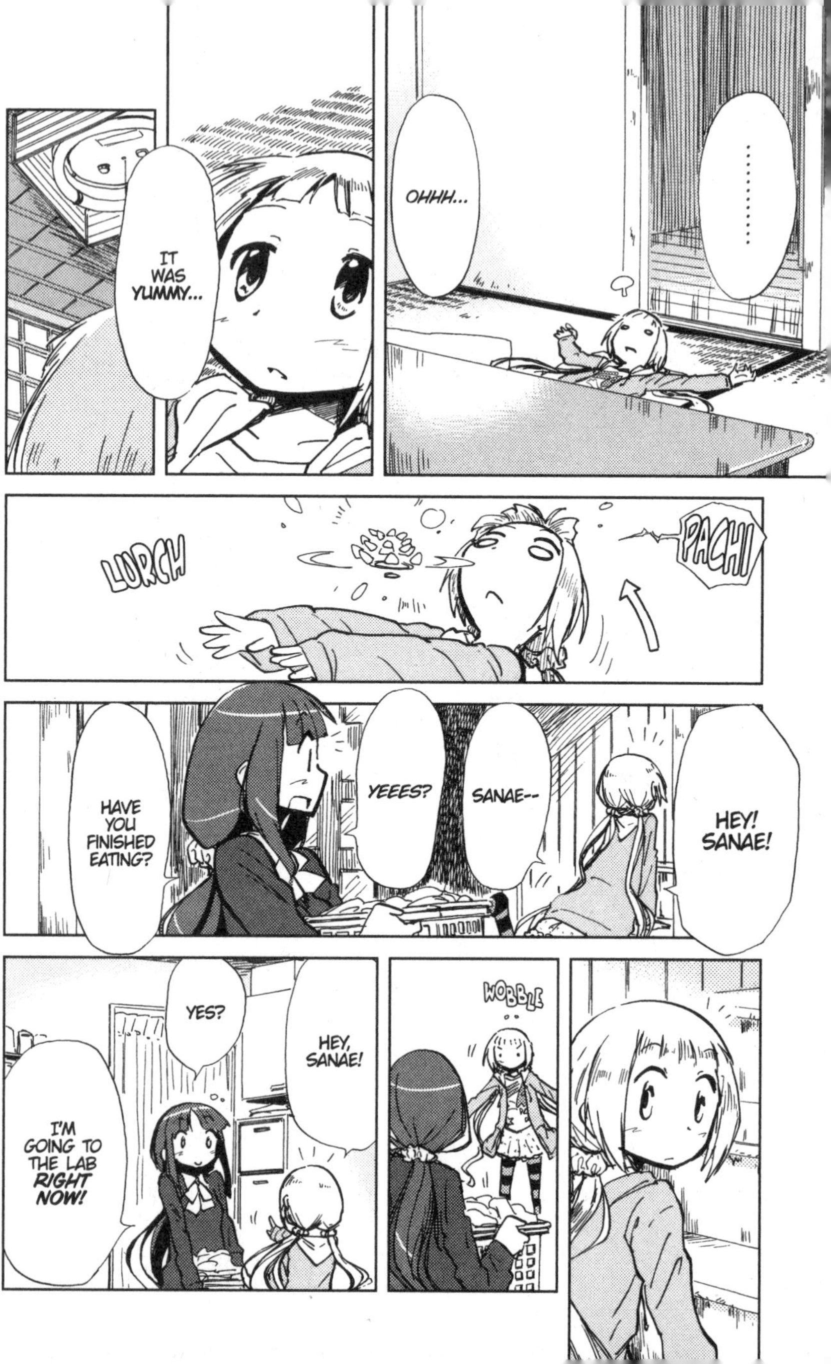
......
OHHH...
IT WAS YUMMY...
PACHI
LURCH
HEY! SANAE!
SANAE--
YEEES?
HAVE YOU FINISHED EATING?
WOBBLE
HEY, SANAE!
YES?
I'M GOING TO THE LAB RIGHT NOW!

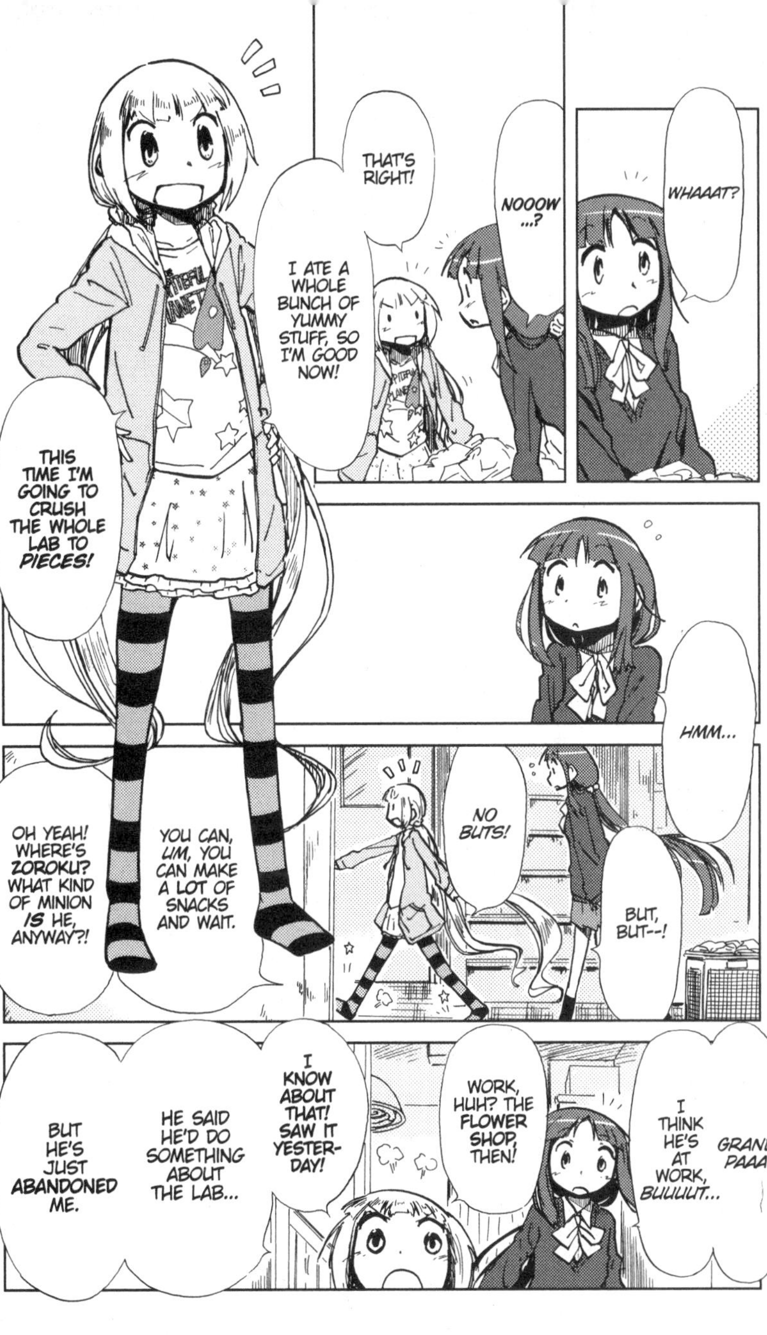
WHAAAT?
NOOOW ...?
THAT'S RIGHT!
I ATE A WHOLE BUNCH OF YUMMY STUFF, SO I'M GOOD NOW!
HMM...
BUT, BUT--!
NO BUTS!
THIS TIME I'M GOING TO CRUSH THE WHOLE LAB TO *PIECES!*
YOU CAN, *UM,* YOU CAN MAKE A LOT OF SNACKS AND WAIT.
OH YEAH! WHERE'S ZOROKU? WHAT KIND OF MINION *IS* HE, ANYWAY?!
GRAND-PAAA?
I THINK HE'S AT WORK, *BUUUUT...*
WORK, HUH? THE FLOWER SHOP, THEN!
I KNOW ABOUT THAT! SAW IT YESTER-DAY!
HE SAID HE'D DO SOMETHING ABOUT THE LAB...
BUT HE'S JUST **ABANDONED** ME.

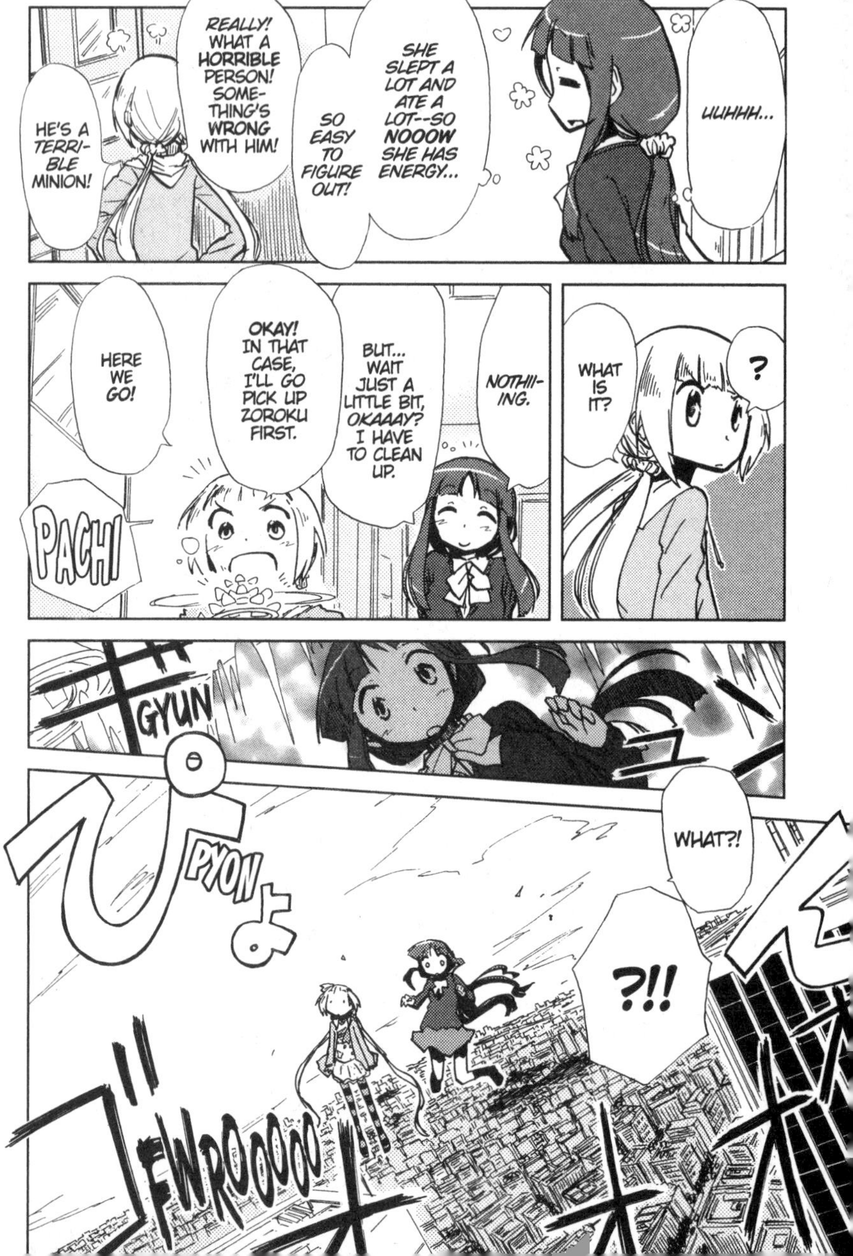
UUHHH...
SHE SLEPT A LOT AND ATE A LOT--SO NOOOW SHE HAS ENERGY...
SO EASY TO FIGURE OUT!
REALLY! WHAT A HORRIBLE PERSON! SOME-THING'S WRONG WITH HIM!
HE'S A TERRI-BLE MINION!
?
WHAT IS IT?
NOTHIII-ING.
BUT... WAIT JUST A LITTLE BIT, OKAAAY? I HAVE TO CLEAN UP.
OKAY! IN THAT CASE, I'LL GO PICK UP ZOROKU FIRST.
HERE WE GO!
PACHI
GYUN
WHAT?!
?!!
PYON
FWROOOOO

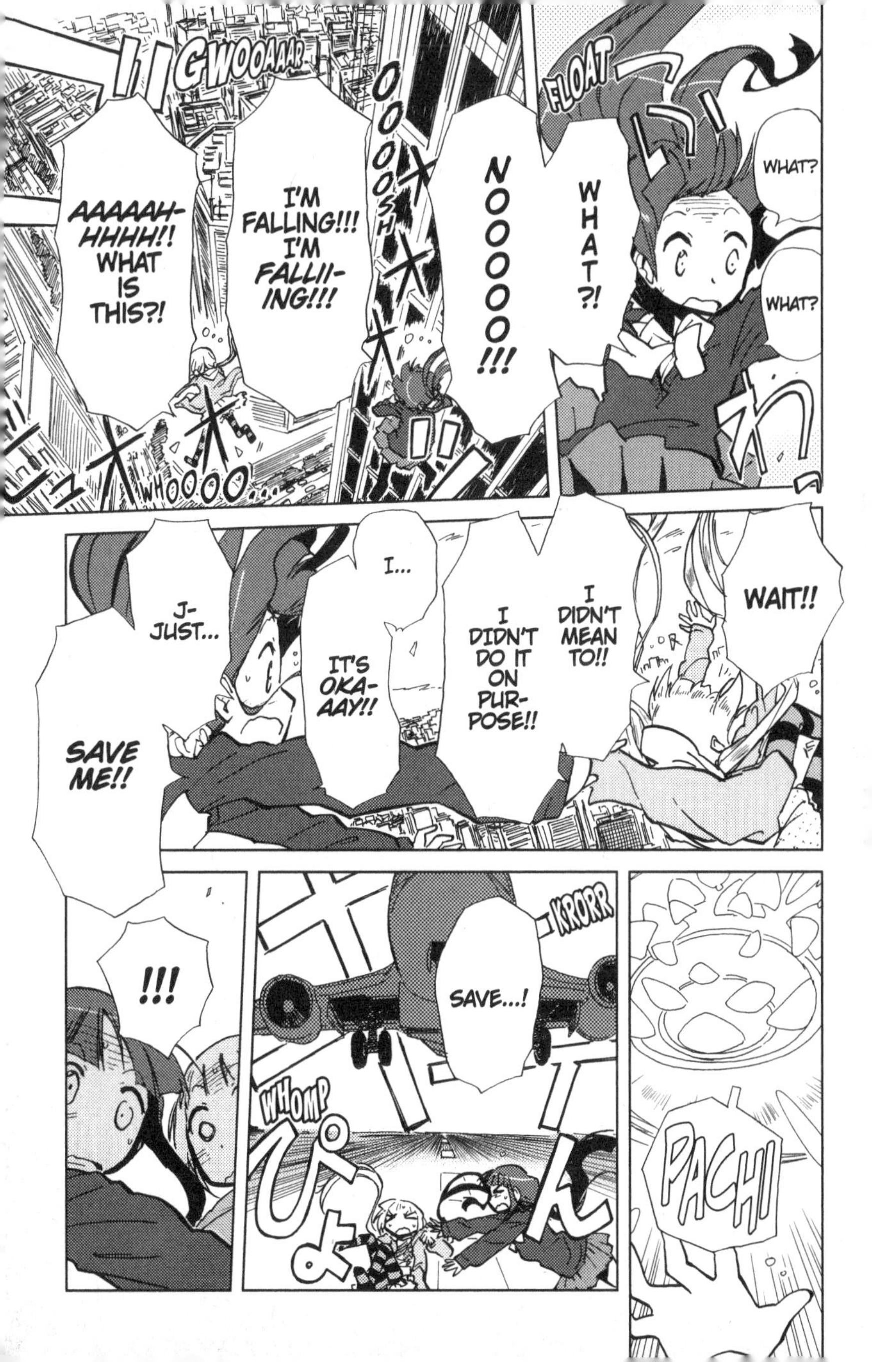
FLOAT
WHAT?
WHAT?
WHAT?!
NOOOOOO!!!
WHOOOSH
I'M FALLING!!! I'M FALLIIING!!!
GWOOAAAR
AAAAAHHHHH!! WHAT IS THIS?!
WHOOOO...
WAIT!!
I DIDN'T MEAN TO!!
I DIDN'T DO IT ON PURPOSE!!
I...
IT'S OKA-AAY!!
J-JUST...
SAVE ME!!
PACHI
KRORR
SAVE...!
WHOMP
ぴょん
!!!

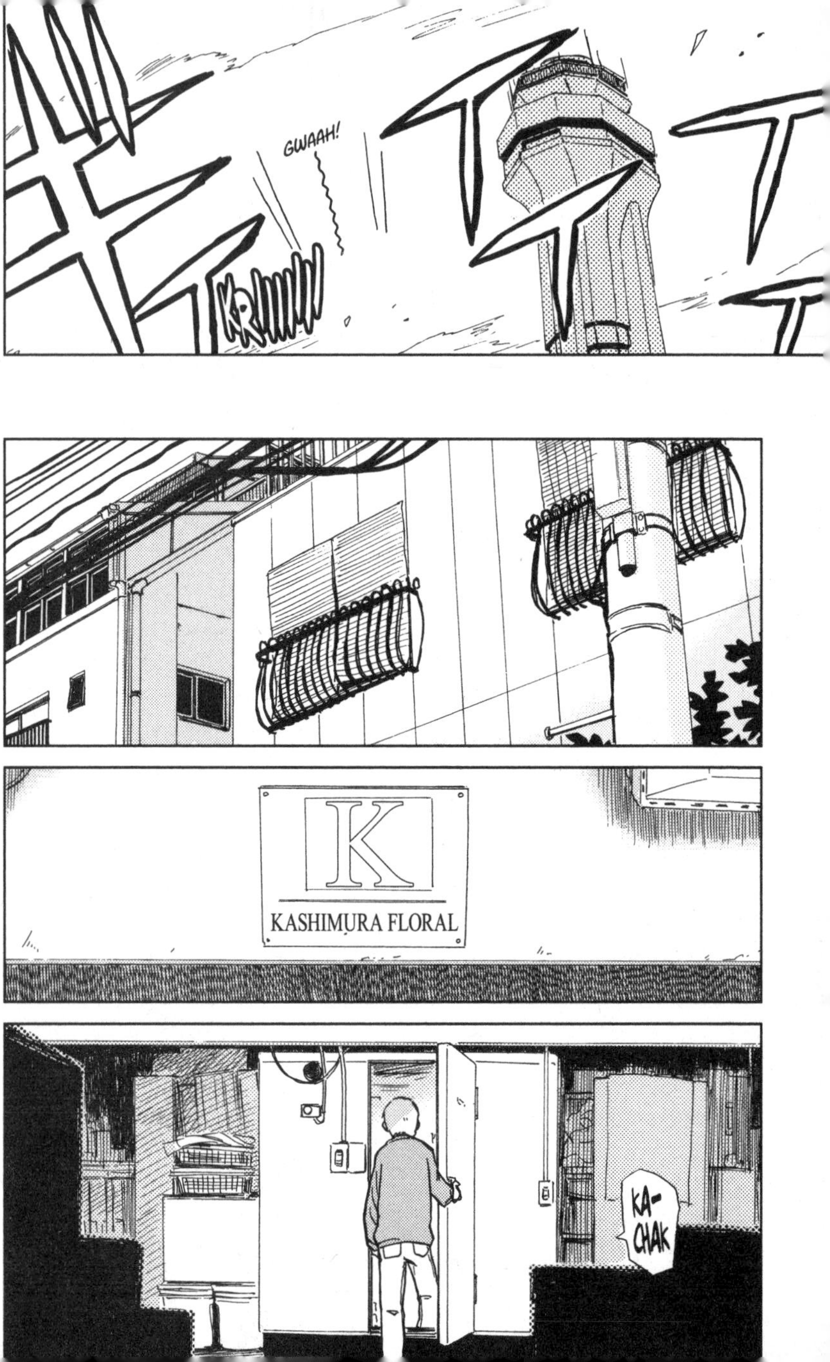
GWAAH!
KRIIIIIN
KASHIMURA FLORAL
KA-CHAK

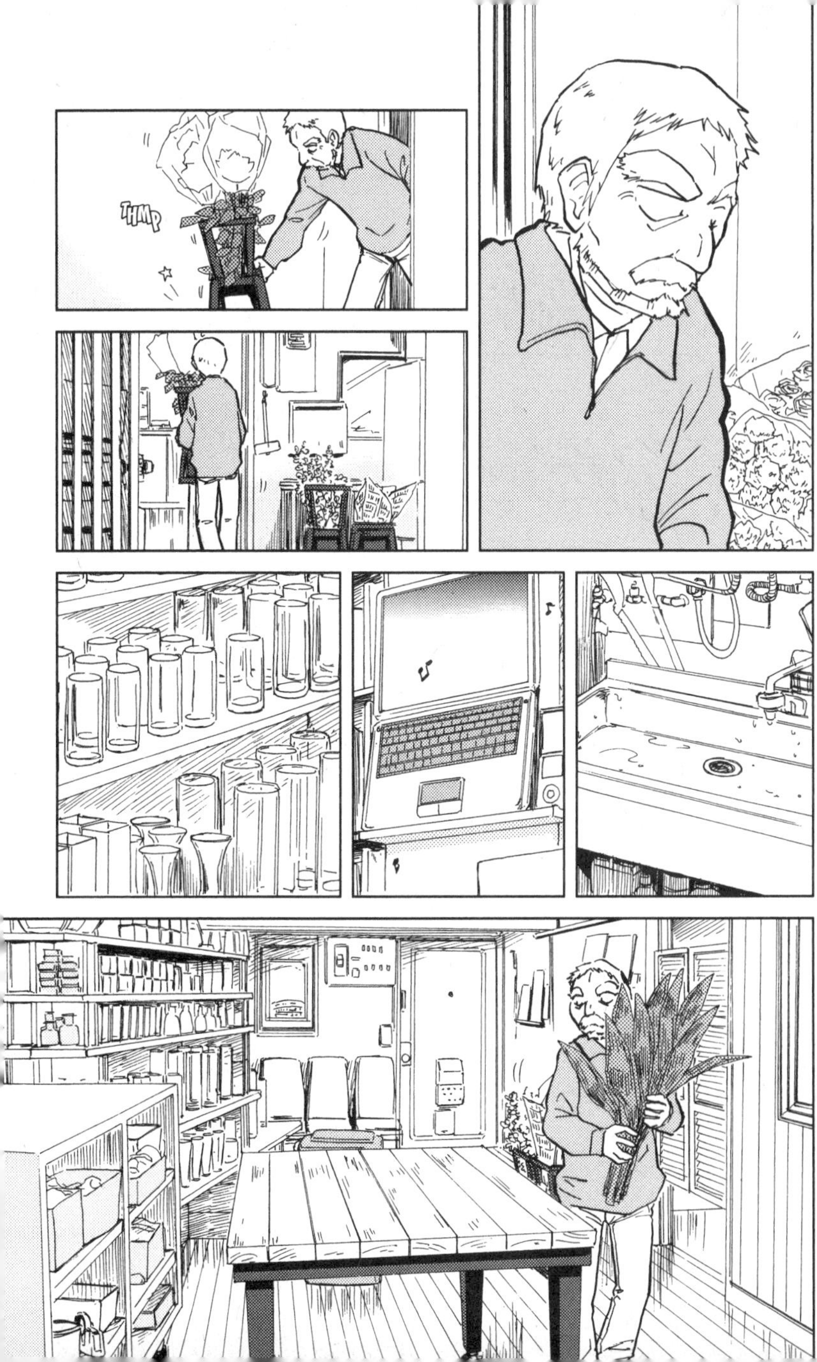
THMP

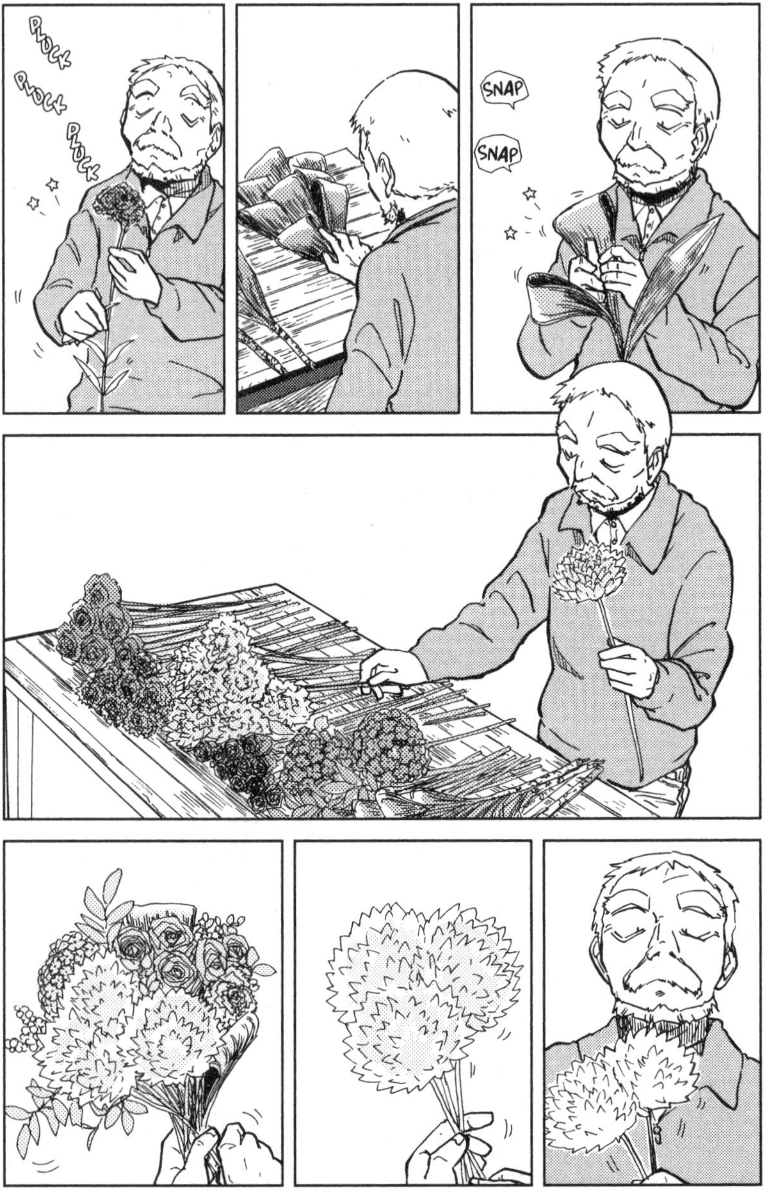
SNAP
SNAP
PLUCK
PLUCK
PLUCK

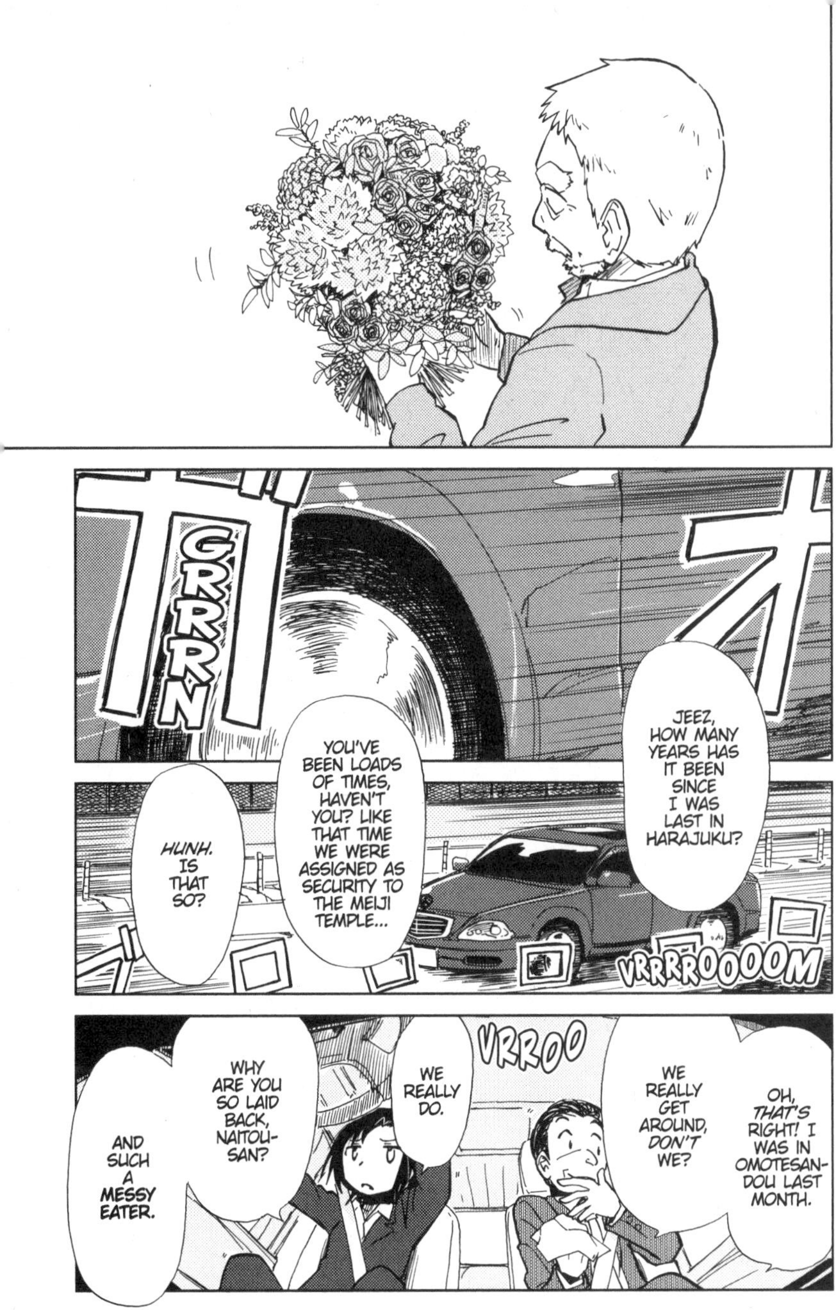
GRRRN
JEEZ, HOW MANY YEARS HAS IT BEEN SINCE I WAS LAST IN HARAJUKU?
YOU'VE BEEN LOADS OF TIMES, HAVEN'T YOU? LIKE THAT TIME WE WERE ASSIGNED AS SECURITY TO THE MEIJI TEMPLE...
HUNH. IS THAT SO?
VRRRROOOOM
VRROO
OH, THAT'S RIGHT! I WAS IN OMOTESAN-DOU LAST MONTH.
WE REALLY GET AROUND, DON'T WE?
WE REALLY DO.
WHY ARE YOU SO LAID BACK, NAITOU-SAN?
AND SUCH A MESSY EATER.

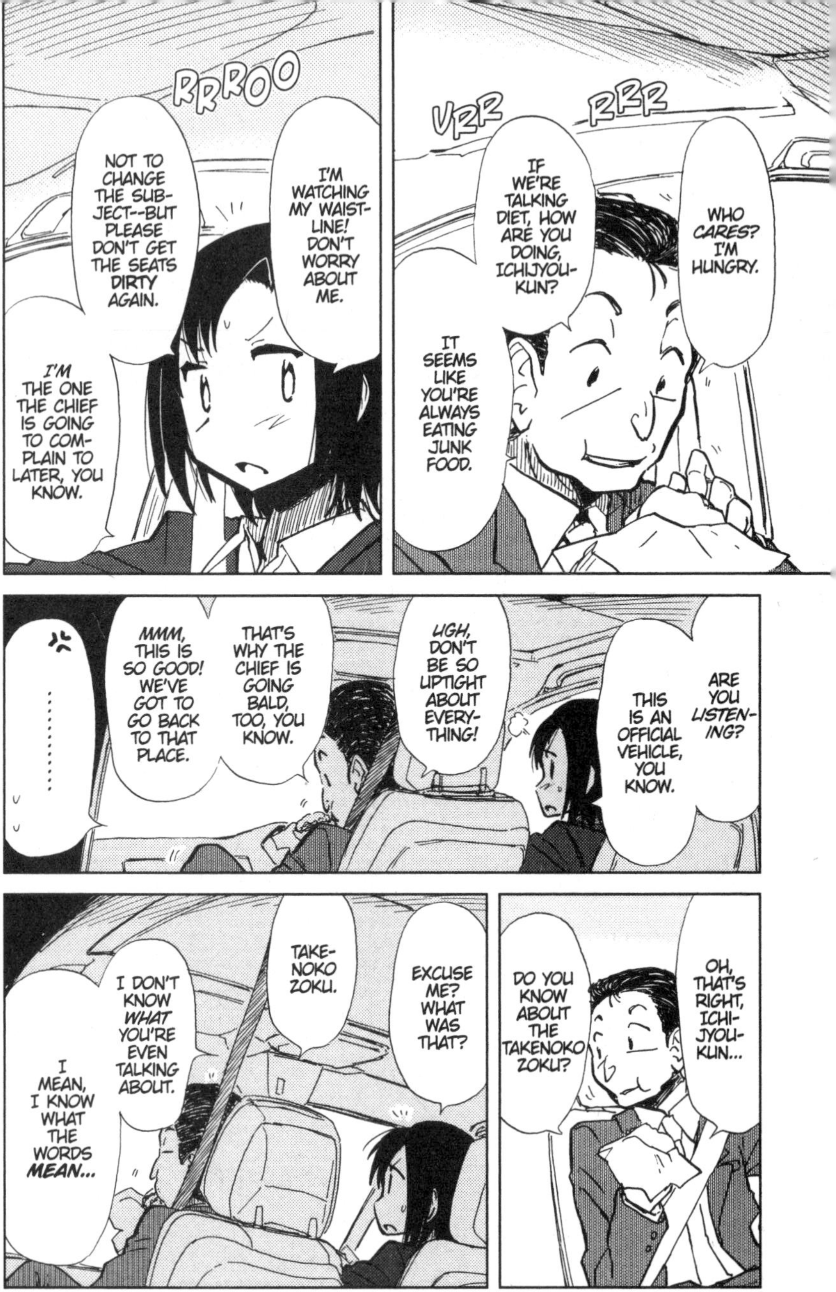
RRR
VRR
WHO CARES? I'M HUNGRY.
IF WE'RE TALKING DIET, HOW ARE YOU DOING, ICHIJYOU-KUN?
IT SEEMS LIKE YOU'RE ALWAYS EATING JUNK FOOD.
RRROO
I'M WATCHING MY WAIST-LINE! DON'T WORRY ABOUT ME.
NOT TO CHANGE THE SUB-JECT--BUT PLEASE DON'T GET THE SEATS *DIRTY* AGAIN.
I'M THE ONE THE CHIEF IS GOING TO COM-PLAIN TO LATER, YOU KNOW.
ARE YOU *LISTEN-ING?*
THIS IS AN OFFICIAL VEHICLE, YOU KNOW.
UGH, DON'T BE SO UPTIGHT ABOUT EVERY-THING!
THAT'S WHY THE CHIEF IS GOING BALD, TOO, YOU KNOW.
MMM, THIS IS SO GOOD! WE'VE GOT TO GO BACK TO THAT PLACE.
....
OH, THAT'S RIGHT, ICHI-JYOU-KUN...
DO YOU KNOW ABOUT THE TAKENOKO ZOKU?
EXCUSE ME? WHAT WAS THAT?
TAKE-NOKO ZOKU.
I DON'T KNOW *WHAT* YOU'RE EVEN TALKING ABOUT.
I MEAN, I KNOW WHAT THE WORDS ***MEAN...***

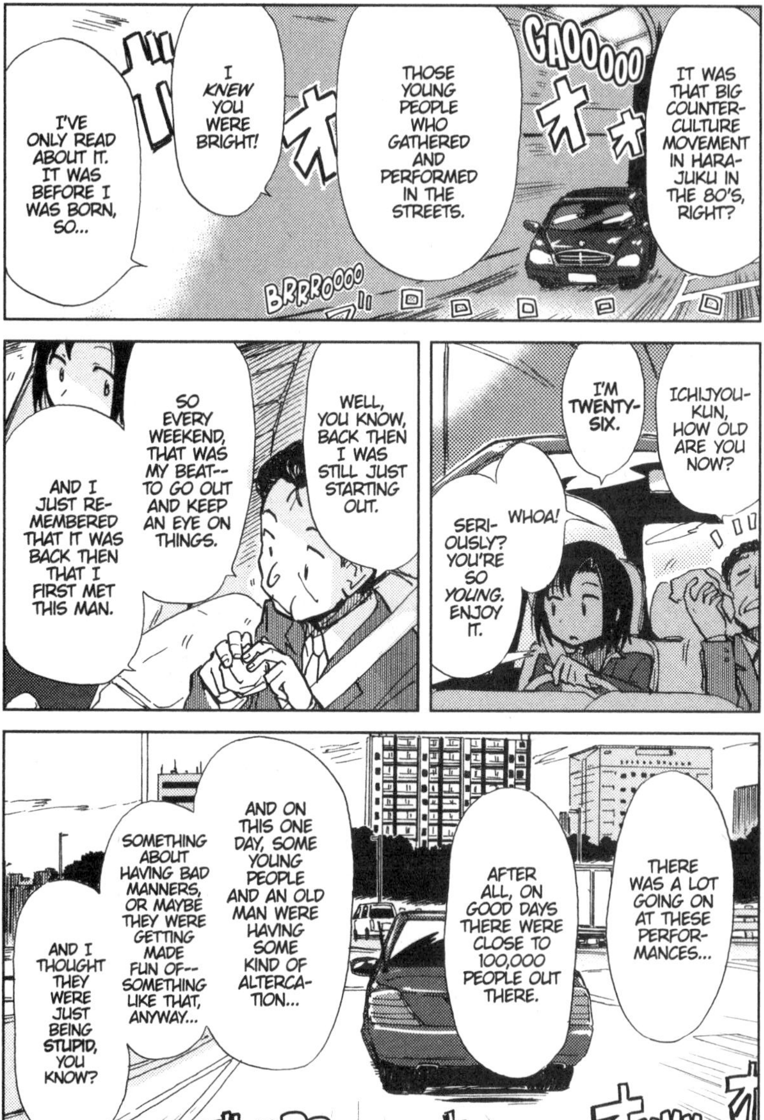
IT WAS THAT BIG COUNTER-CULTURE MOVEMENT IN HARA-JUKU IN THE 80'S, RIGHT?
GAOOOOO
THOSE YOUNG PEOPLE WHO GATHERED AND PERFORMED IN THE STREETS.
I *KNEW* YOU WERE BRIGHT!
I'VE ONLY READ ABOUT IT. IT WAS BEFORE I WAS BORN, SO...
BRRROOOO
ICHIJYOU-KUN, HOW OLD ARE YOU NOW?
I'M TWENTY-SIX.
WHOA!
SERI-OUSLY? YOU'RE SO *YOUNG*. ENJOY IT.
WELL, YOU KNOW, BACK THEN I WAS STILL JUST STARTING OUT.
SO EVERY WEEKEND, THAT WAS MY BEAT--TO GO OUT AND KEEP AN EYE ON THINGS.
AND I JUST RE-MEMBERED THAT IT WAS BACK THEN THAT I FIRST MET THIS MAN.
THERE WAS A LOT GOING ON AT THESE PERFOR-MANCES...
AFTER ALL, ON GOOD DAYS THERE WERE CLOSE TO 100,000 PEOPLE OUT THERE.
AND ON THIS ONE DAY, SOME YOUNG PEOPLE AND AN OLD MAN WERE HAVING SOME KIND OF ALTERCA-TION...
SOMETHING ABOUT HAVING BAD MANNERS, OR MAYBE THEY WERE GETTING MADE FUN OF--SOMETHING LIKE THAT, ANYWAY...
AND I THOUGHT THEY WERE JUST BEING STUPID, YOU KNOW?
MMM
RRM
VRR

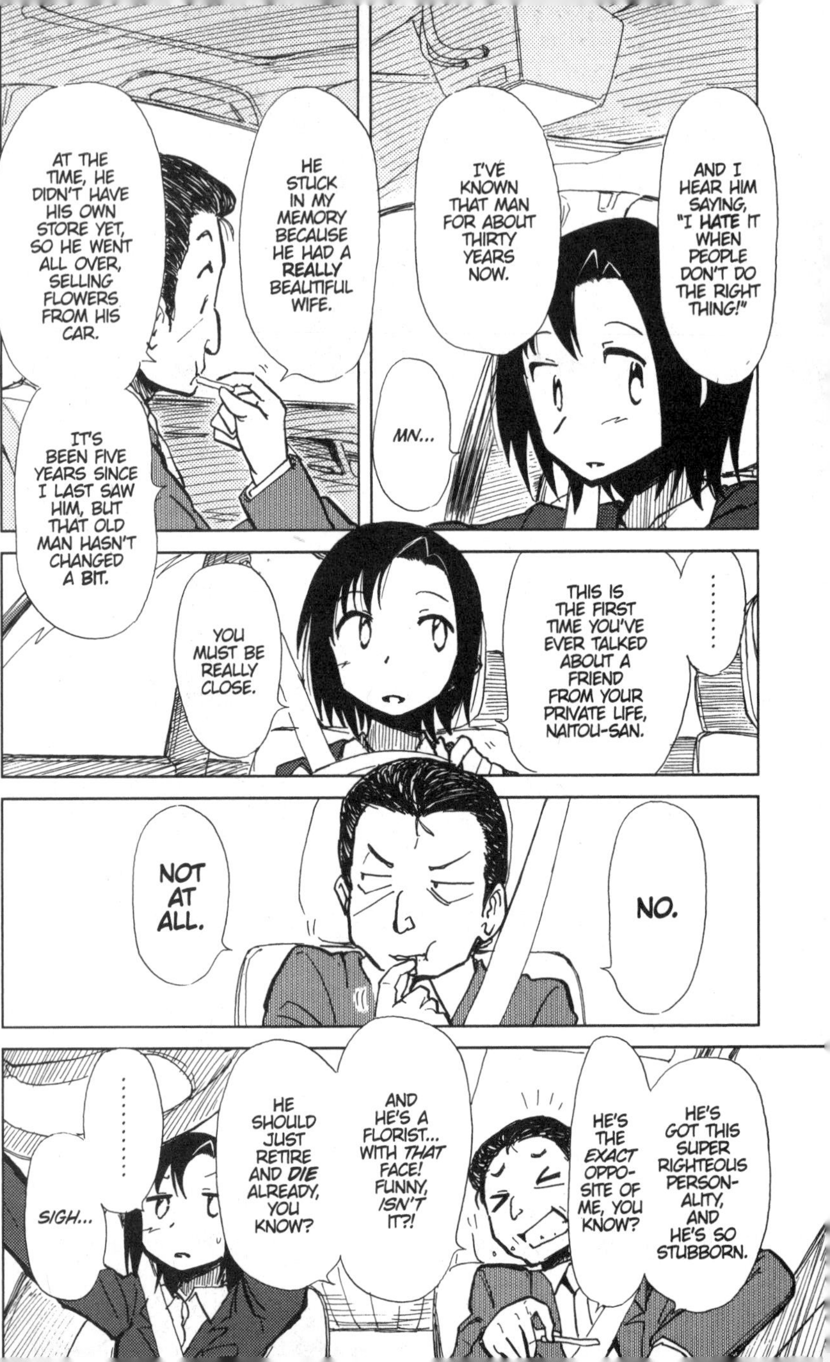
AND I HEAR HIM SAYING, "I HATE IT WHEN PEOPLE DON'T DO THE RIGHT THING!"
I'VE KNOWN THAT MAN FOR ABOUT THIRTY YEARS NOW.
MN...
HE STUCK IN MY MEMORY BECAUSE HE HAD A REALLY BEAUTIFUL WIFE.
AT THE TIME, HE DIDN'T HAVE HIS OWN STORE YET, SO HE WENT ALL OVER, SELLING FLOWERS FROM HIS CAR.
IT'S BEEN FIVE YEARS SINCE I LAST SAW HIM, BUT THAT OLD MAN HASN'T CHANGED A BIT.
......
THIS IS THE FIRST TIME YOU'VE EVER TALKED ABOUT A FRIEND FROM YOUR PRIVATE LIFE, NAITOU-SAN.
YOU MUST BE REALLY CLOSE.
NO.
NOT AT ALL.
HE'S GOT THIS SUPER RIGHTEOUS PERSON-ALITY, AND HE'S SO STUBBORN.
HE'S THE EXACT OPPO-SITE OF ME, YOU KNOW?
AND HE'S A FLORIST... WITH THAT FACE! FUNNY, ISN'T IT?!
HE SHOULD JUST RETIRE AND DIE ALREADY, YOU KNOW?
......
SIGH...

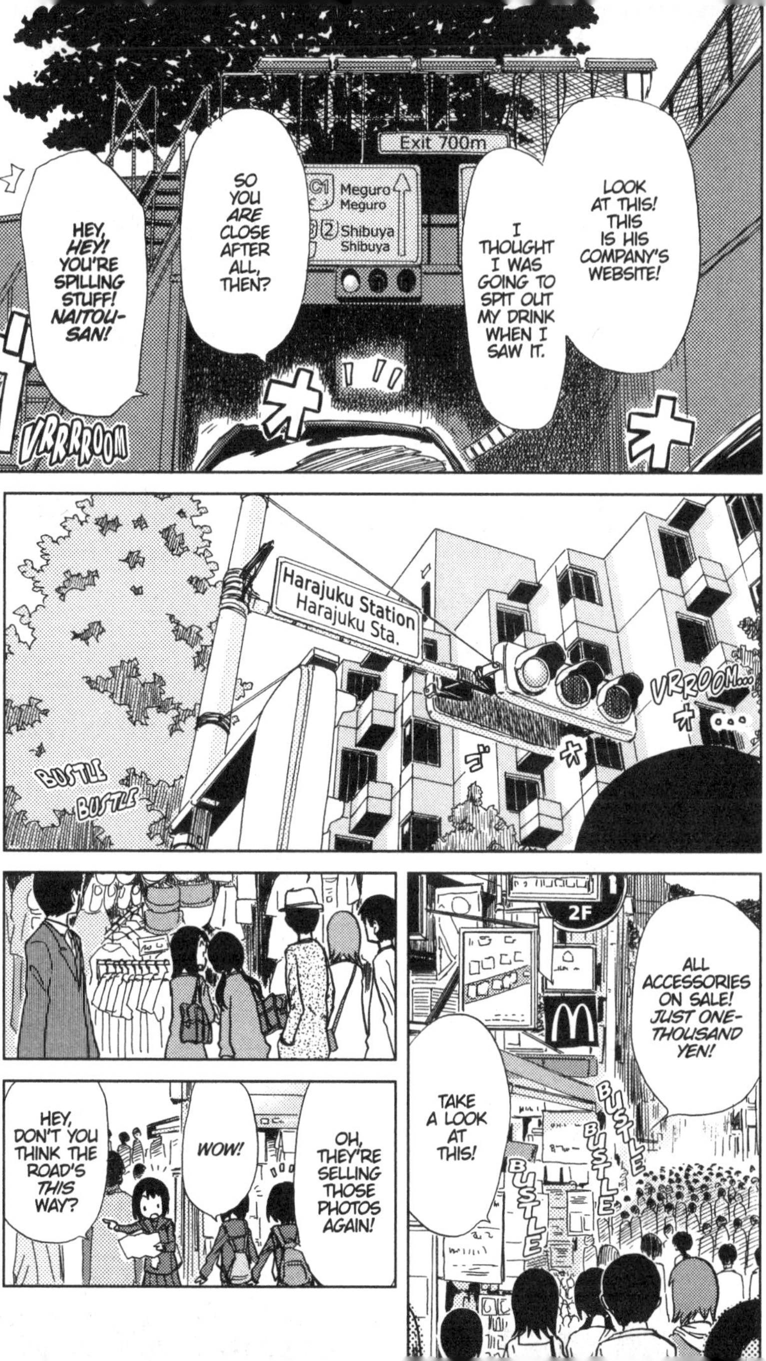
Exit 700m
C1 Meguro
Meguro
2 Shibuya
Shibuya
LOOK AT THIS! THIS IS HIS COMPANY'S WEBSITE!
I THOUGHT I WAS GOING TO SPIT OUT MY DRINK WHEN I SAW IT.
SO YOU ARE CLOSE AFTER ALL, THEN?
HEY, HEY! YOU'RE SPILLING STUFF! NAITOU-SAN!
VRRRROOM
Harajuku Station
Harajuku Sta.
VRROOM...
BUSTLE
BUSTLE
2F
ALL ACCESSORIES ON SALE! JUST ONE-THOUSAND YEN!
TAKE A LOOK AT THIS!
BUSTLE
BUSTLE
BUSTLE
OH, THEY'RE SELLING THOSE PHOTOS AGAIN!
WOW!
HEY, DON'T YOU THINK THE ROAD'S THIS WAY?

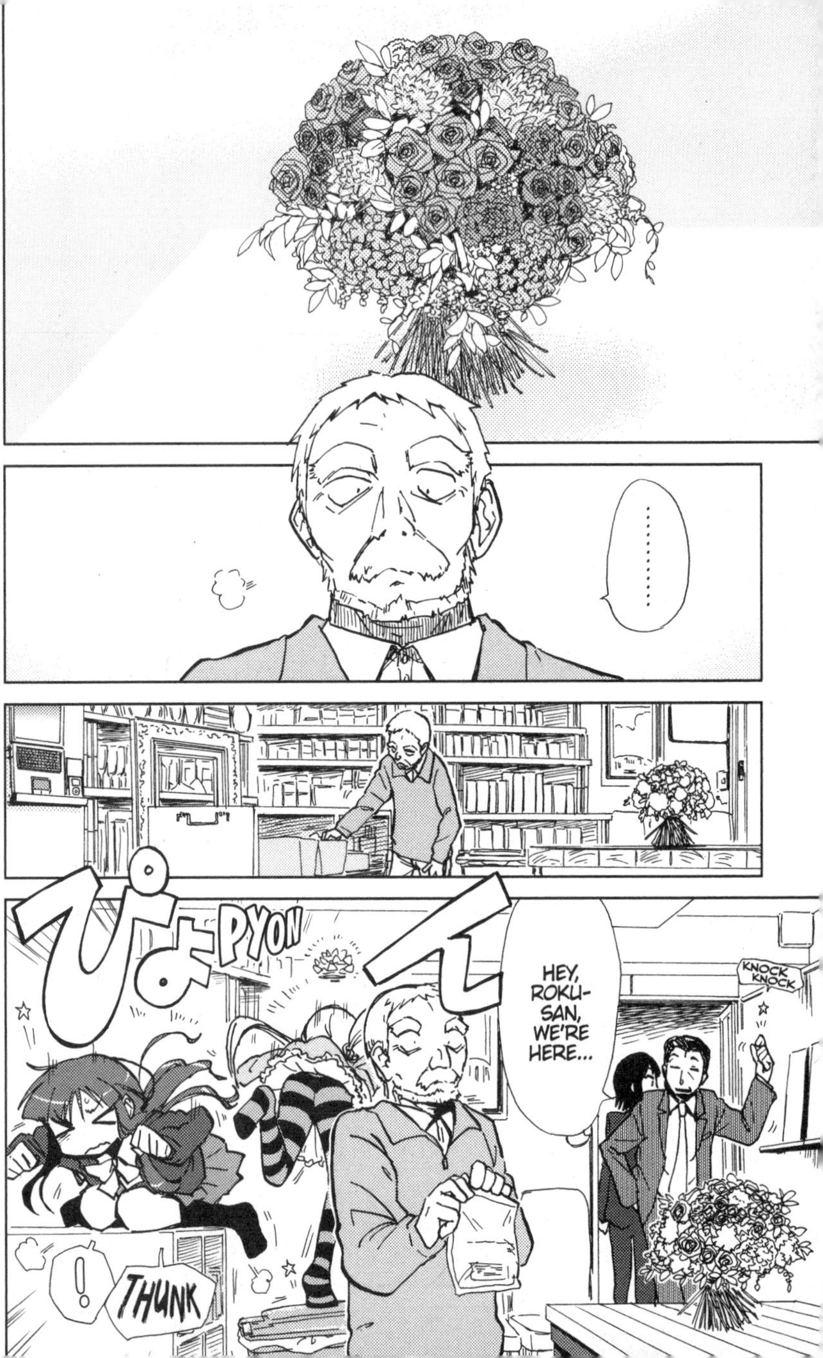
......
KNOCK KNOCK
HEY, ROKU-SAN, WE'RE HERE...
ぴょん
PYON
!
THUNK

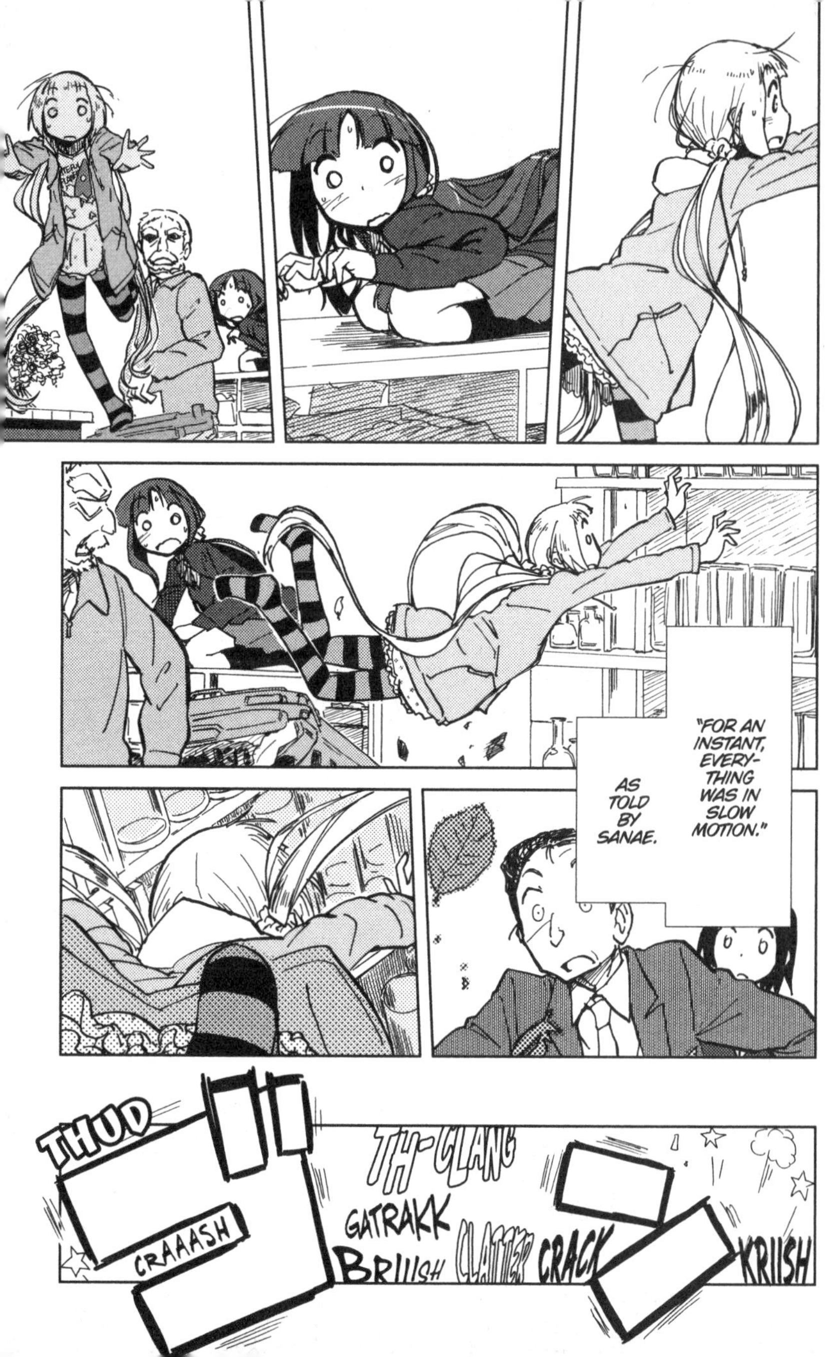
"FOR AN INSTANT, EVERYTHING WAS IN SLOW MOTION."
AS TOLD BY SANAE.
TH-CLANG
KRIISH
CRACK
CLATTER
GATRAKK
BRIIISH
THUD
CRAAASH

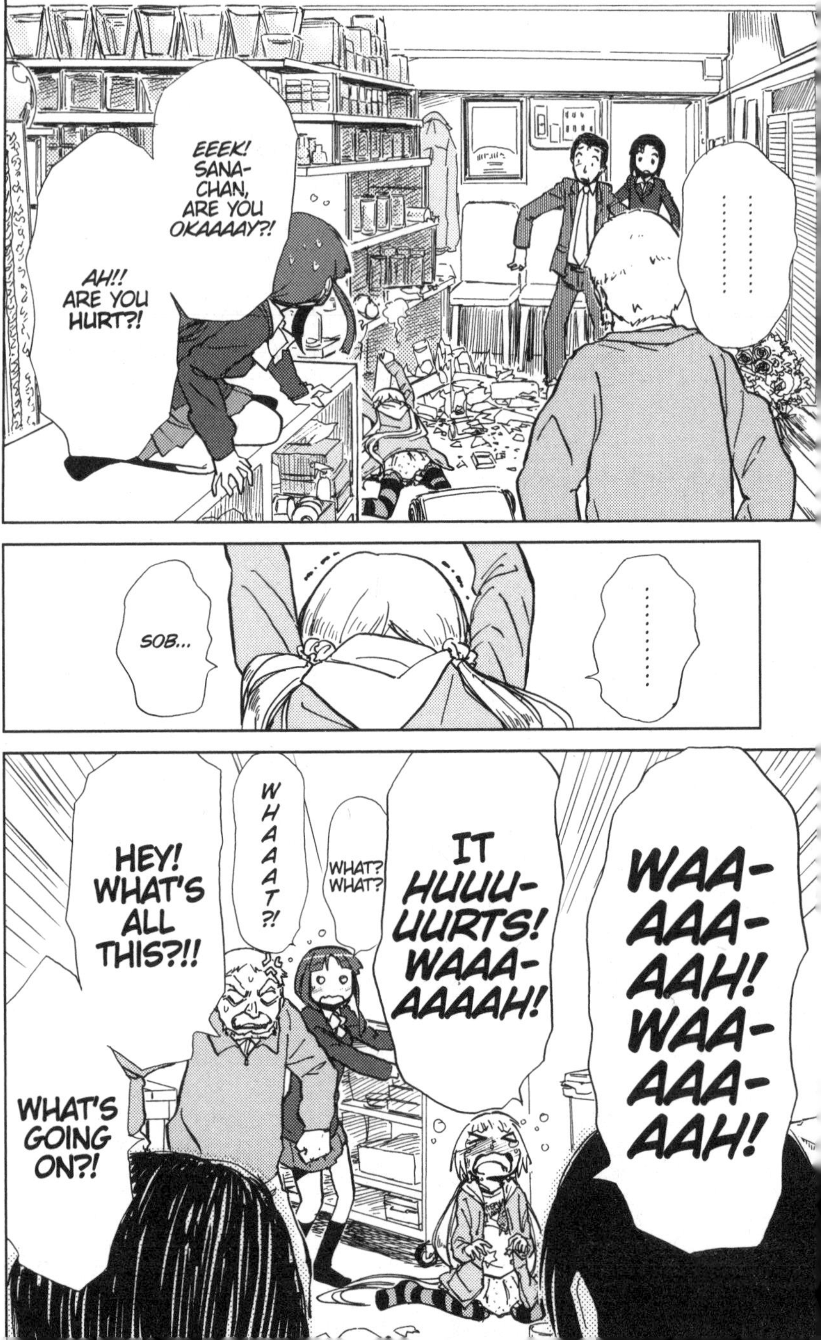
......
EEEK! SANA-CHAN, ARE YOU OKAAAAY?!
AH!! ARE YOU HURT?!
......
SOB...
WAA-AAA-AAH! WAA-AAA-AAA-AAH!
IT HUUUU-UURTS! WAAA-AAAAAH!
WHAT? WHAT?
WHAAAAT?!
HEY! WHAT'S ALL THIS?!!
WHAT'S GOING ON?!

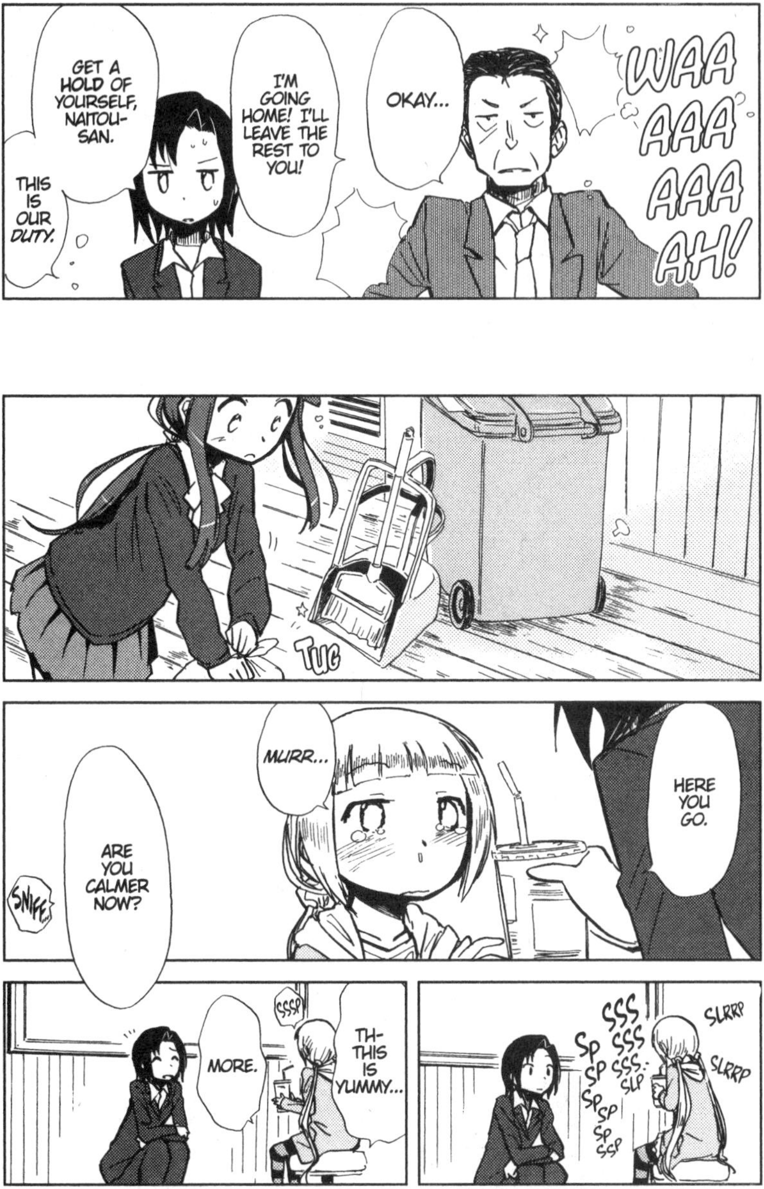
WAAAAAAAAAAH!
OKAY...
I'M GOING HOME! I'LL LEAVE THE REST TO YOU!
GET A HOLD OF YOURSELF, NAITOU-SAN.
THIS IS OUR DUTY.
TUG
HERE YOU GO.
MURR...
ARE YOU CALMER NOW?
SNIFF
SLRRP
SLRRP
SSS SSS SSS SLP
SP SP SP SP SP SSP
TH-THIS IS YUMMY...
SSSP
MORE.

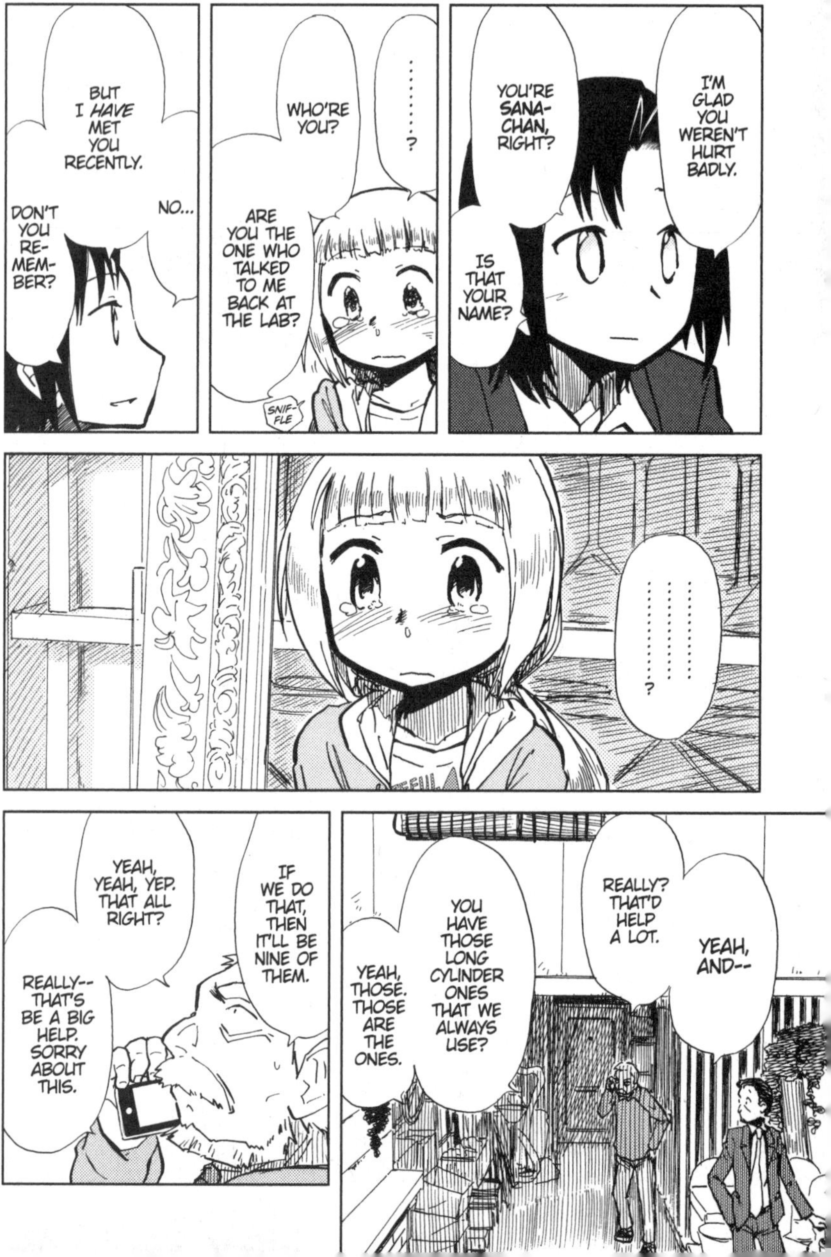
I'M GLAD YOU WEREN'T HURT BADLY.
YOU'RE SANA-CHAN, RIGHT?
IS THAT YOUR NAME?
......?
WHO'RE YOU?
ARE YOU THE ONE WHO TALKED TO ME BACK AT THE LAB?
SNIF-FLE
NO...
BUT I *HAVE* MET YOU RECENTLY.
DON'T YOU RE-MEMBER?
......?
YEAH, AND--
REALLY? THAT'D HELP A LOT.
YOU HAVE THOSE LONG CYLINDER ONES THAT WE ALWAYS USE?
YEAH, THOSE. THOSE ARE THE ONES.
IF WE DO THAT, THEN IT'LL BE NINE OF THEM.
YEAH, YEAH, YEP. THAT ALL RIGHT?
REALLY-- THAT'S BE A BIG HELP. SORRY ABOUT THIS.

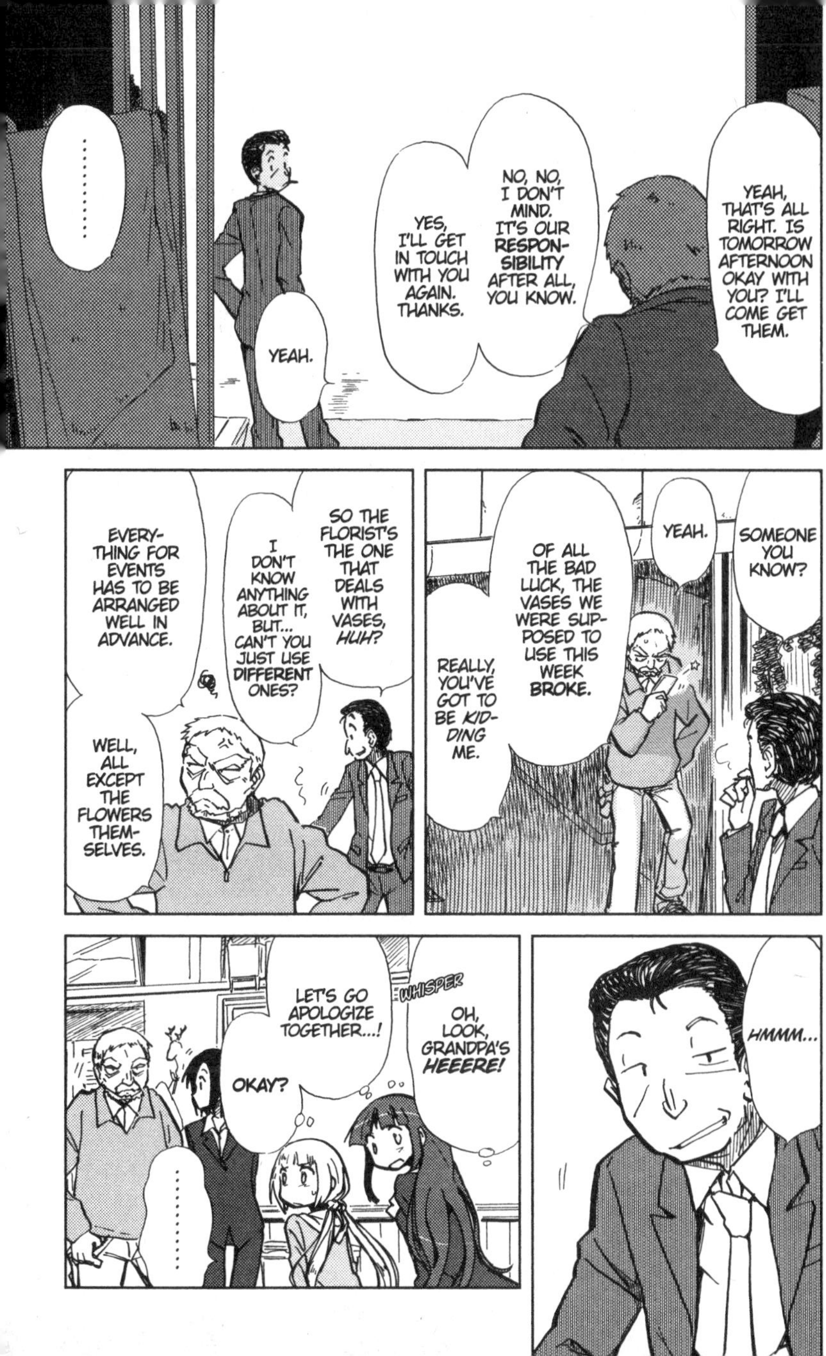
YEAH, THAT'S ALL RIGHT. IS TOMORROW AFTERNOON OKAY WITH YOU? I'LL COME GET THEM.
NO, NO, I DON'T MIND. IT'S OUR RESPONSIBILITY AFTER ALL, YOU KNOW.
YES, I'LL GET IN TOUCH WITH YOU AGAIN. THANKS.
YEAH.
......
SOMEONE YOU KNOW?
YEAH.
OF ALL THE BAD LUCK, THE VASES WE WERE SUPPOSED TO USE THIS WEEK BROKE.
REALLY, YOU'VE GOT TO BE KIDDING ME.
SO THE FLORIST'S THE ONE THAT DEALS WITH VASES, HUH?
I DON'T KNOW ANYTHING ABOUT IT, BUT... CAN'T YOU JUST USE DIFFERENT ONES?
EVERYTHING FOR EVENTS HAS TO BE ARRANGED WELL IN ADVANCE.
WELL, ALL EXCEPT THE FLOWERS THEMSELVES.
HMMM...
OH, LOOK, GRANDPA'S HEEERE!
WHISPER
LET'S GO APOLOGIZE TOGETHER...!
OKAY?
......

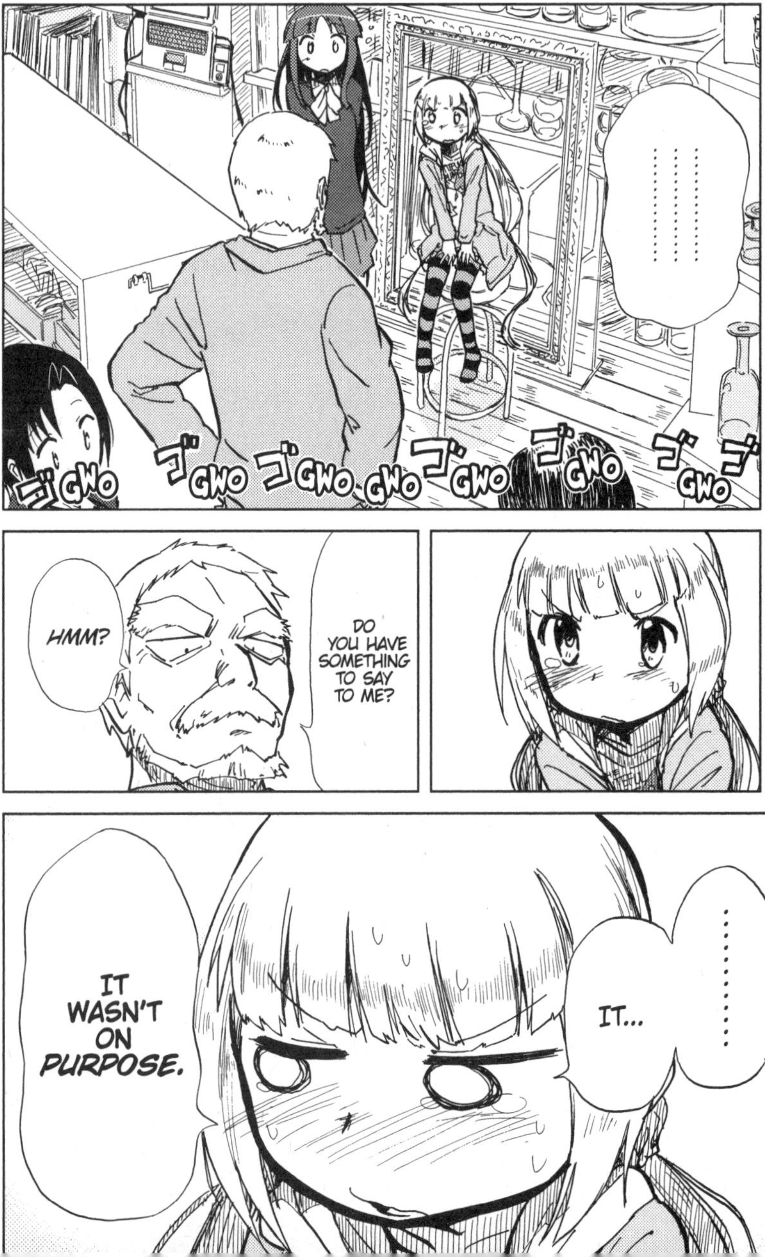
......
ゴ GWO ゴ GWO ゴ GWO GWO ゴ GWO ゴ GWO ゴ GWO ゴ
DO YOU HAVE SOMETHING TO SAY TO ME?
HMM?
......
IT...
IT WASN'T ON PURPOSE.

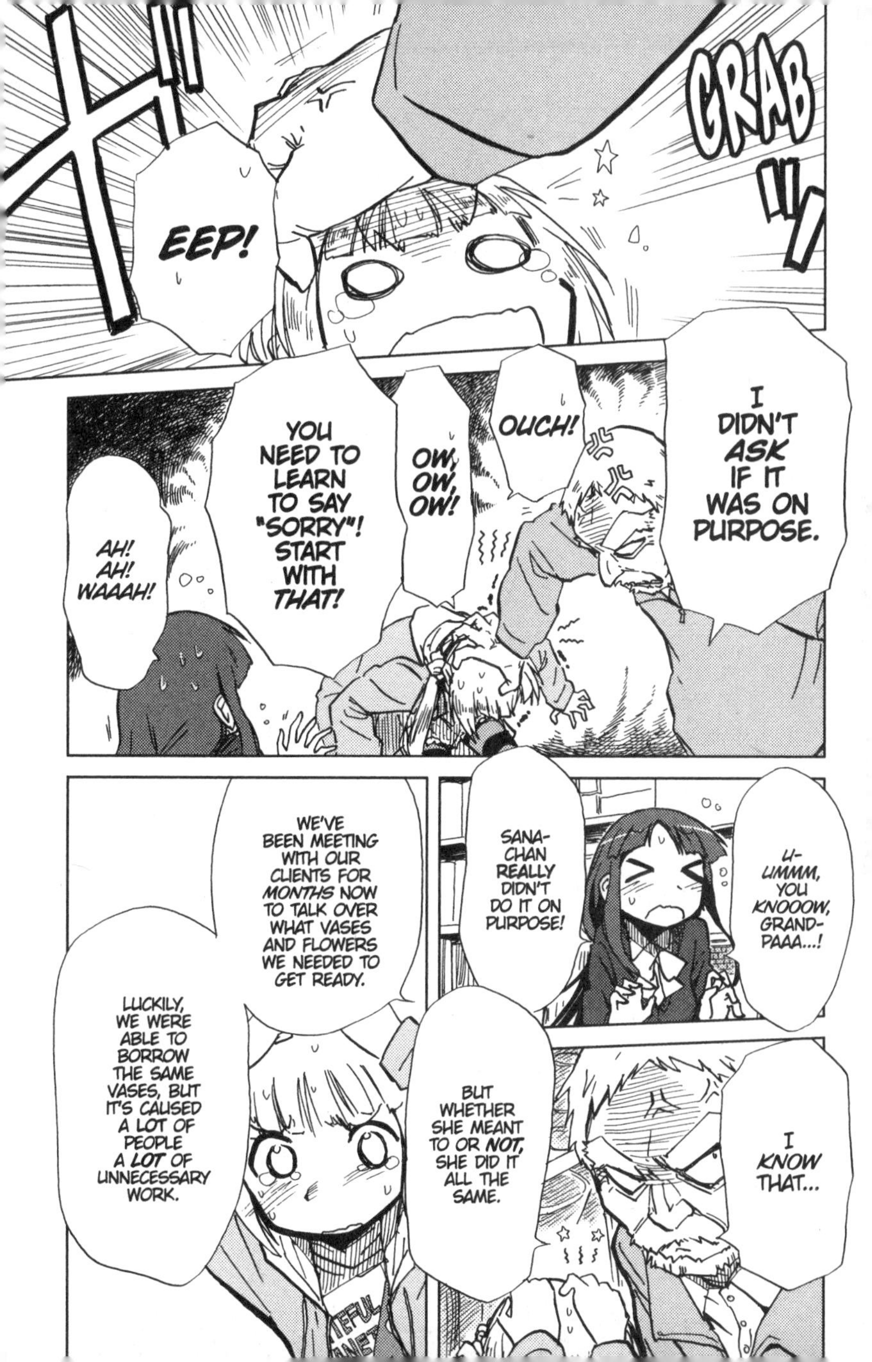

GRAB
EEP!
I DIDN'T ASK IF IT WAS ON PURPOSE.
OUCH!
OW, OW, OW!
YOU NEED TO LEARN TO SAY "SORRY"! START WITH THAT!
AH! AH! WAAAH!
U-UMMM, YOU KNOOOW, GRAND-PAAA...!
SANA-CHAN REALLY DIDN'T DO IT ON PURPOSE!
I KNOW THAT...
BUT WHETHER SHE MEANT TO OR NOT, SHE DID IT ALL THE SAME.
WE'VE BEEN MEETING WITH OUR CLIENTS FOR MONTHS NOW TO TALK OVER WHAT VASES AND FLOWERS WE NEEDED TO GET READY.
LUCKILY, WE WERE ABLE TO BORROW THE SAME VASES, BUT IT'S CAUSED A LOT OF PEOPLE A LOT OF UNNECESSARY WORK.

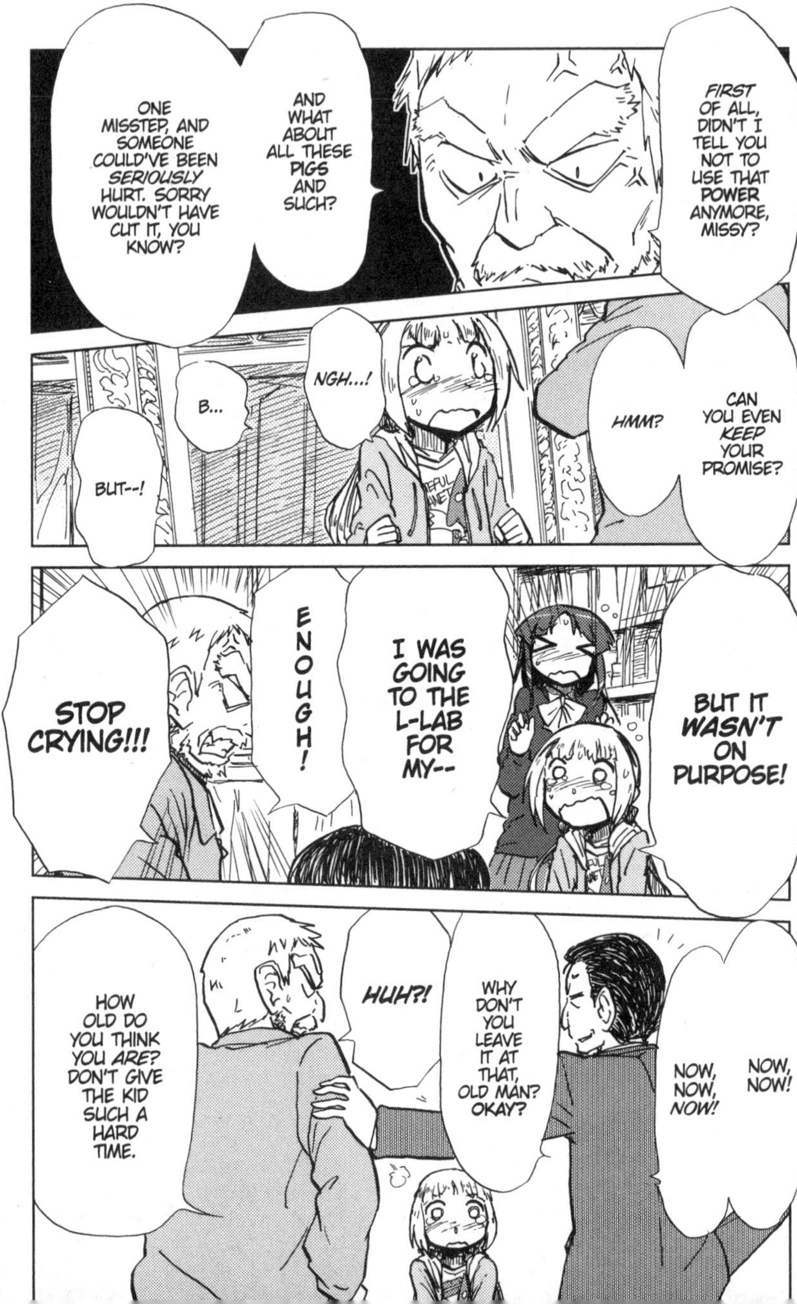
FIRST OF ALL, DIDN'T I TELL YOU NOT TO USE THAT POWER ANYMORE, MISSY?
AND WHAT ABOUT ALL THESE PIGS AND SUCH?
ONE MISSTEP, AND SOMEONE COULD'VE BEEN SERIOUSLY HURT. SORRY WOULDN'T HAVE CUT IT, YOU KNOW?
CAN YOU EVEN KEEP YOUR PROMISE?
HMM?
NGH...!
B...
BUT--!
BUT IT WASN'T ON PURPOSE!
I WAS GOING TO THE L-LAB FOR MY--
ENOUGH!
STOP CRYING!!!
NOW, NOW!
NOW, NOW, NOW!
WHY DON'T YOU LEAVE IT AT THAT, OLD MAN? OKAY?
HUH?!
HOW OLD DO YOU THINK YOU ARE? DON'T GIVE THE KID SUCH A HARD TIME.

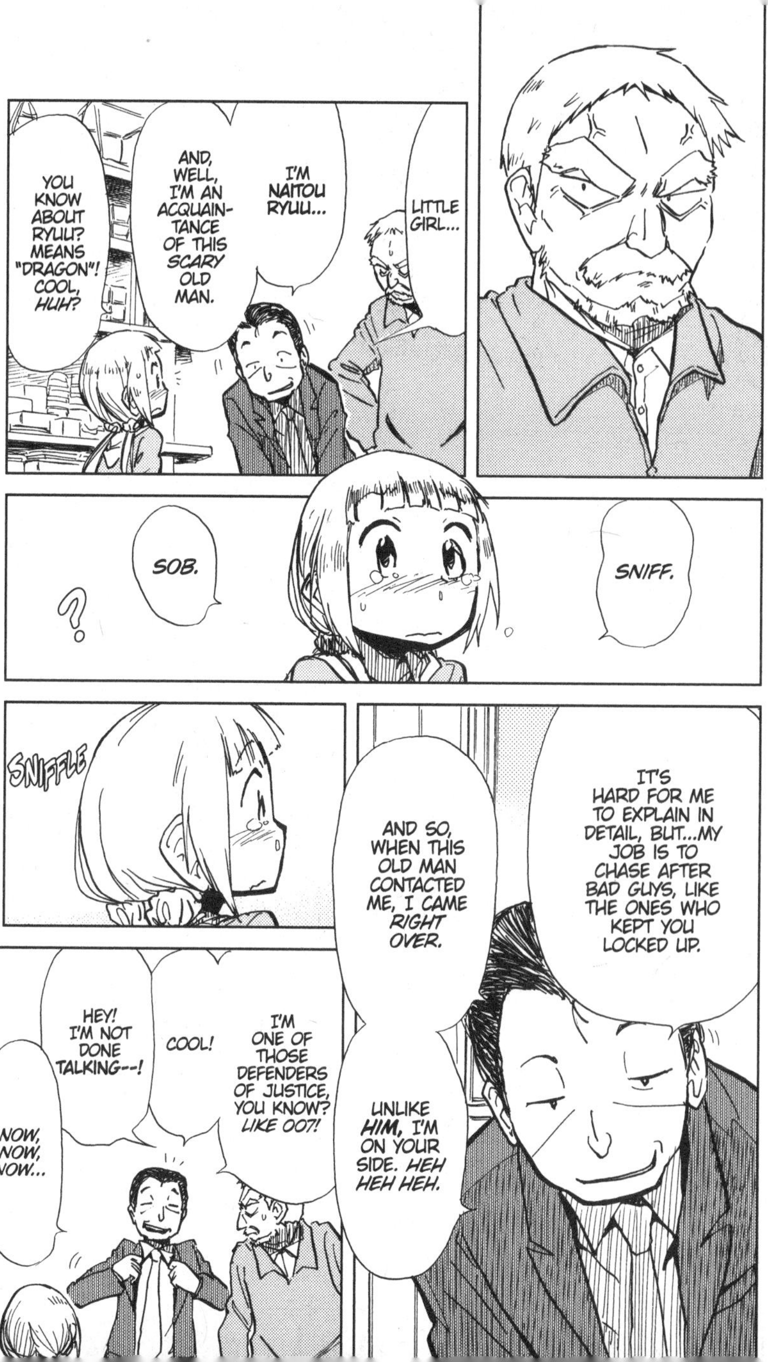
LITTLE GIRL...
I'M NAITOU RYUU...
AND, WELL, I'M AN ACQUAIN-TANCE OF THIS SCARY OLD MAN.
YOU KNOW ABOUT RYUU? MEANS "DRAGON"! COOL, HUH?
SNIFF.
SOB.
?
IT'S HARD FOR ME TO EXPLAIN IN DETAIL, BUT...MY JOB IS TO CHASE AFTER BAD GUYS, LIKE THE ONES WHO KEPT YOU LOCKED UP.
AND SO, WHEN THIS OLD MAN CONTACTED ME, I CAME RIGHT OVER.
UNLIKE HIM, I'M ON YOUR SIDE. HEH HEH HEH.
SNIFFLE
I'M ONE OF THOSE DEFENDERS OF JUSTICE, YOU KNOW? LIKE 007!
COOL!
HEY! I'M NOT DONE TALKING--!
NOW, NOW, NOW...

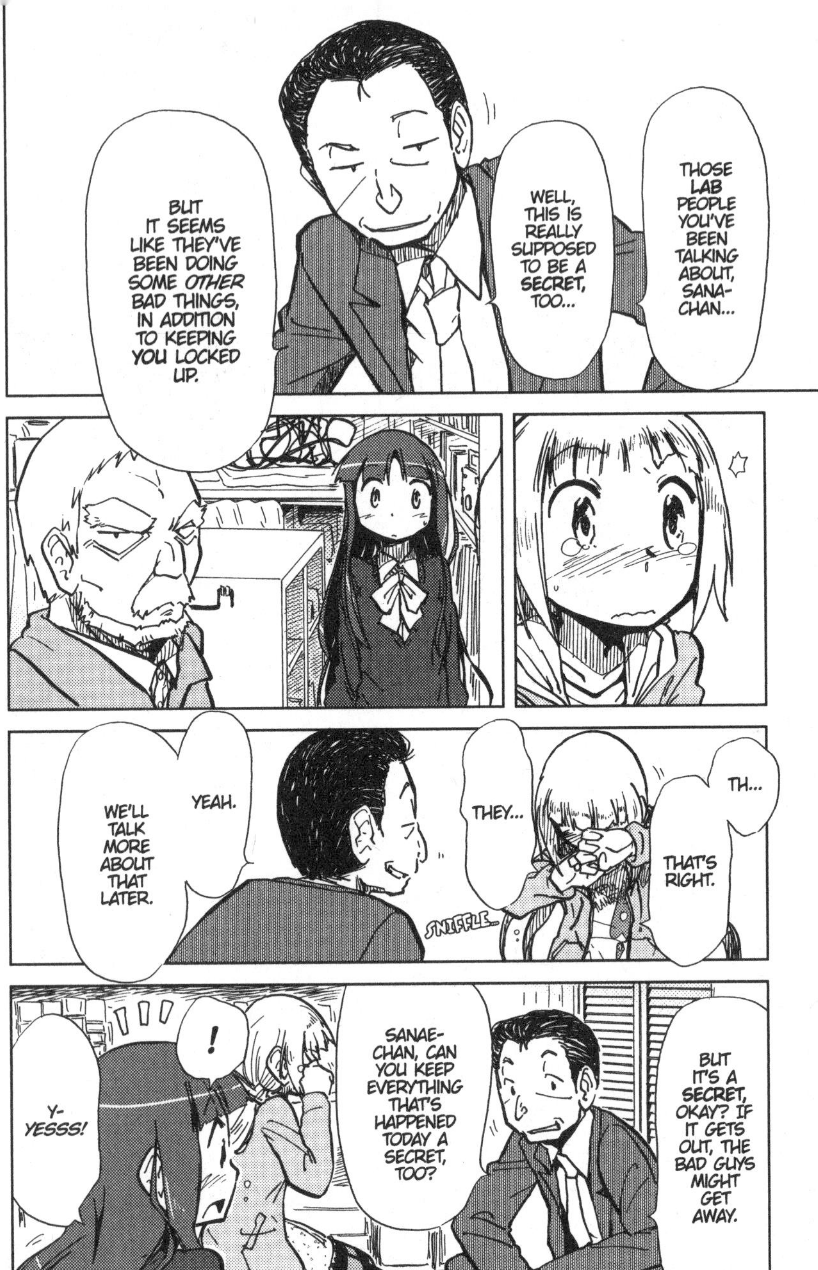
THOSE LAB PEOPLE YOU'VE BEEN TALKING ABOUT, SANA-CHAN...
WELL, THIS IS REALLY SUPPOSED TO BE A SECRET, TOO...
BUT IT SEEMS LIKE THEY'VE BEEN DOING SOME *OTHER* BAD THINGS, IN ADDITION TO KEEPING YOU LOCKED UP.
TH...
THAT'S RIGHT.
THEY...
SNIFFLE...
YEAH.
WE'LL TALK MORE ABOUT THAT LATER.
BUT IT'S A SECRET, OKAY? IF IT GETS OUT, THE BAD GUYS MIGHT GET AWAY.
SANAE-CHAN, CAN YOU KEEP EVERYTHING THAT'S HAPPENED TODAY A SECRET, TOO?
!
Y-YESSS!

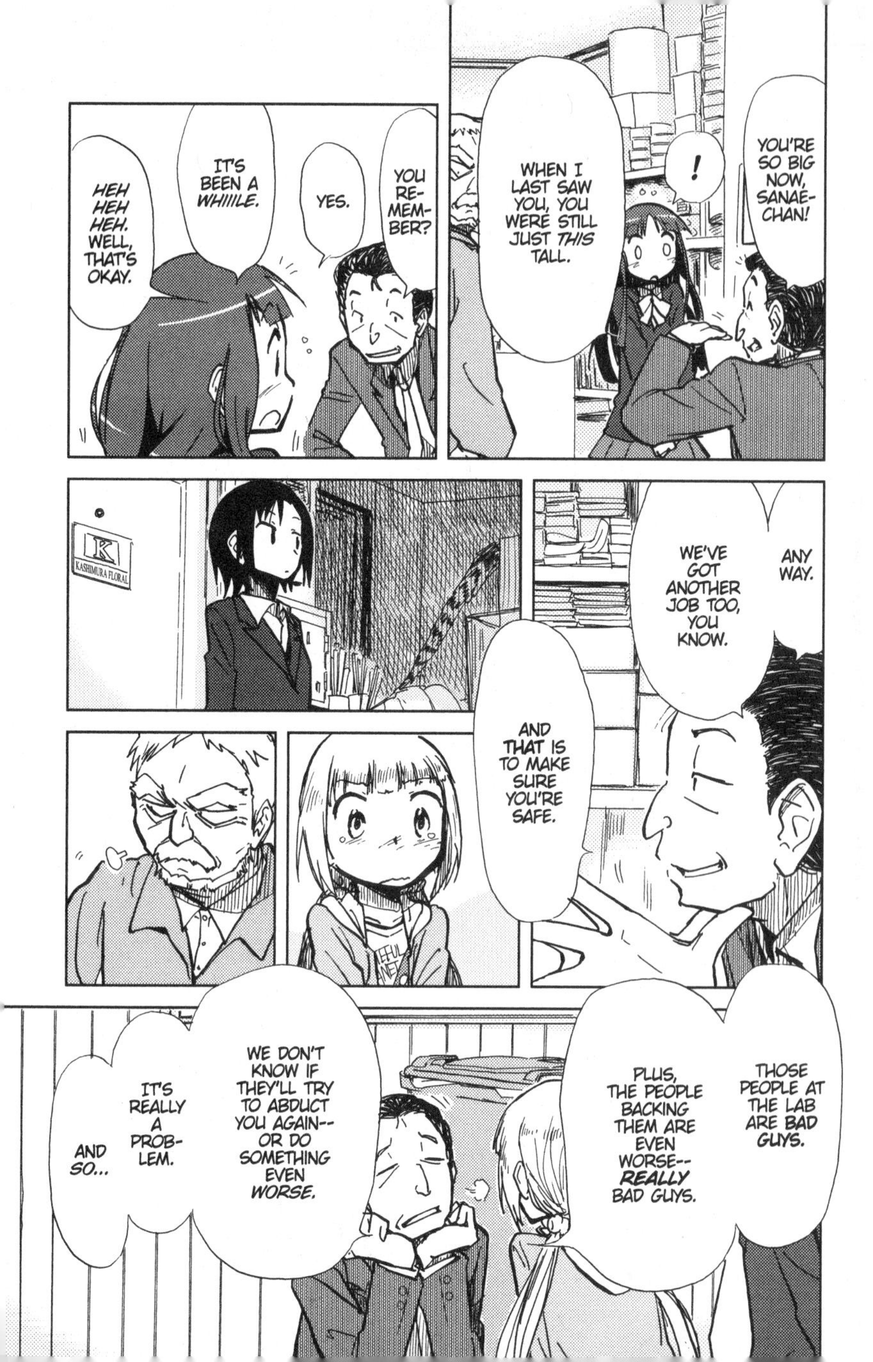
YOU'RE SO BIG NOW, SANAE-CHAN!
!
WHEN I LAST SAW YOU, YOU WERE STILL JUST *THIS* TALL.
YOU RE-MEM-BER?
YES.
IT'S BEEN A *WHIIILE.*
HEH HEH HEH. WELL, THAT'S OKAY.
ANY WAY.
WE'VE GOT ANOTHER JOB TOO, YOU KNOW.
AND **THAT** IS TO MAKE SURE YOU'RE SAFE.
K
KASHIMURA FLORAL
THOSE PEOPLE AT THE LAB ARE BAD GUYS.
PLUS, THE PEOPLE BACKING THEM ARE EVEN WORSE-- ***REALLY*** BAD GUYS.
WE DON'T KNOW IF THEY'LL TRY TO ABDUCT YOU AGAIN-- OR DO SOMETHING EVEN *WORSE.*
IT'S REALLY A PROB-LEM.
AND SO...

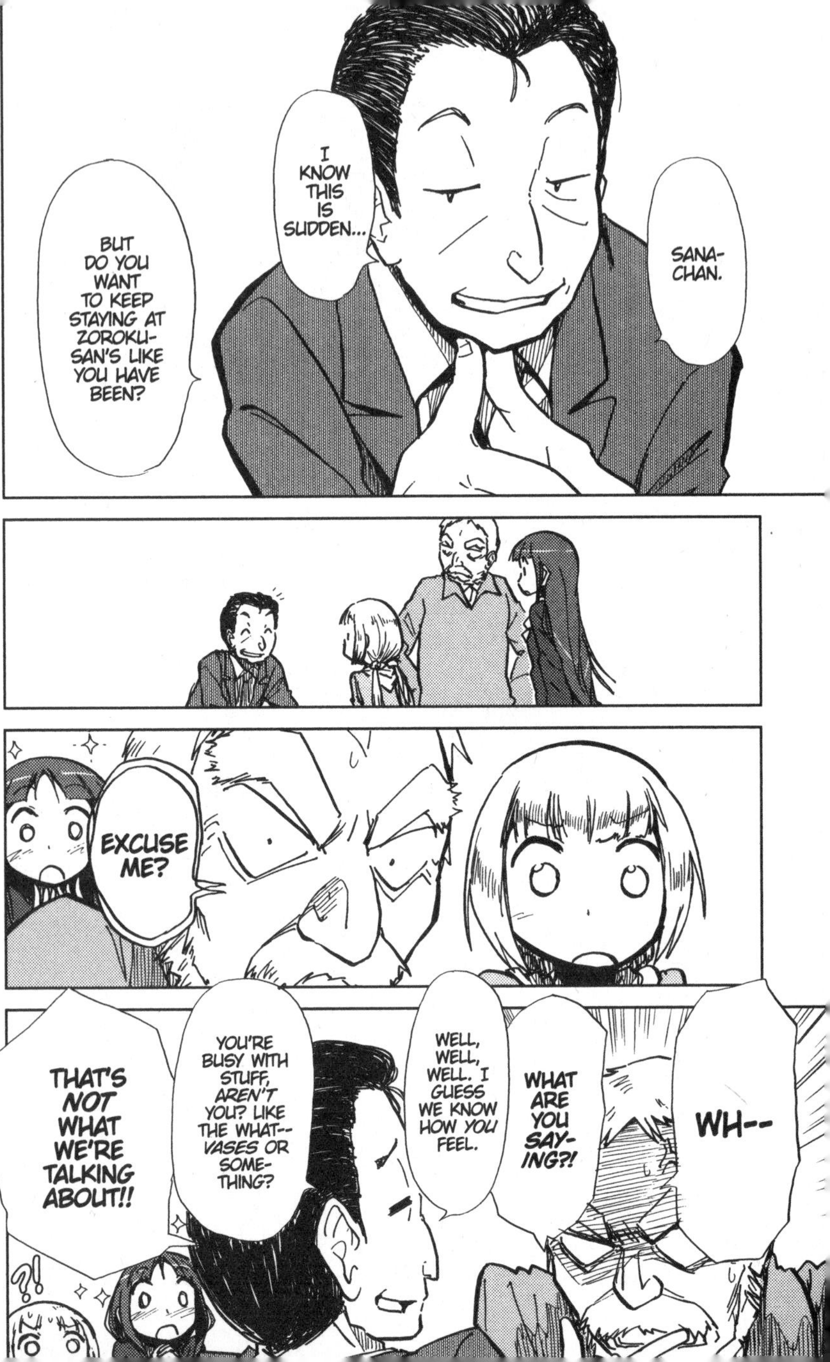
SANA-CHAN.
I KNOW THIS IS SUDDEN...
BUT DO YOU WANT TO KEEP STAYING AT ZOROKU-SAN'S LIKE YOU HAVE BEEN?
EXCUSE ME?
WH--
WHAT ARE YOU SAYING?!
WELL, WELL, WELL. I GUESS WE KNOW HOW *YOU* FEEL.
YOU'RE BUSY WITH STUFF, *AREN'T* YOU? LIKE THE WHAT--*VASES* OR SOMETHING?
THAT'S *NOT* WHAT WE'RE TALKING ABOUT!!
?!

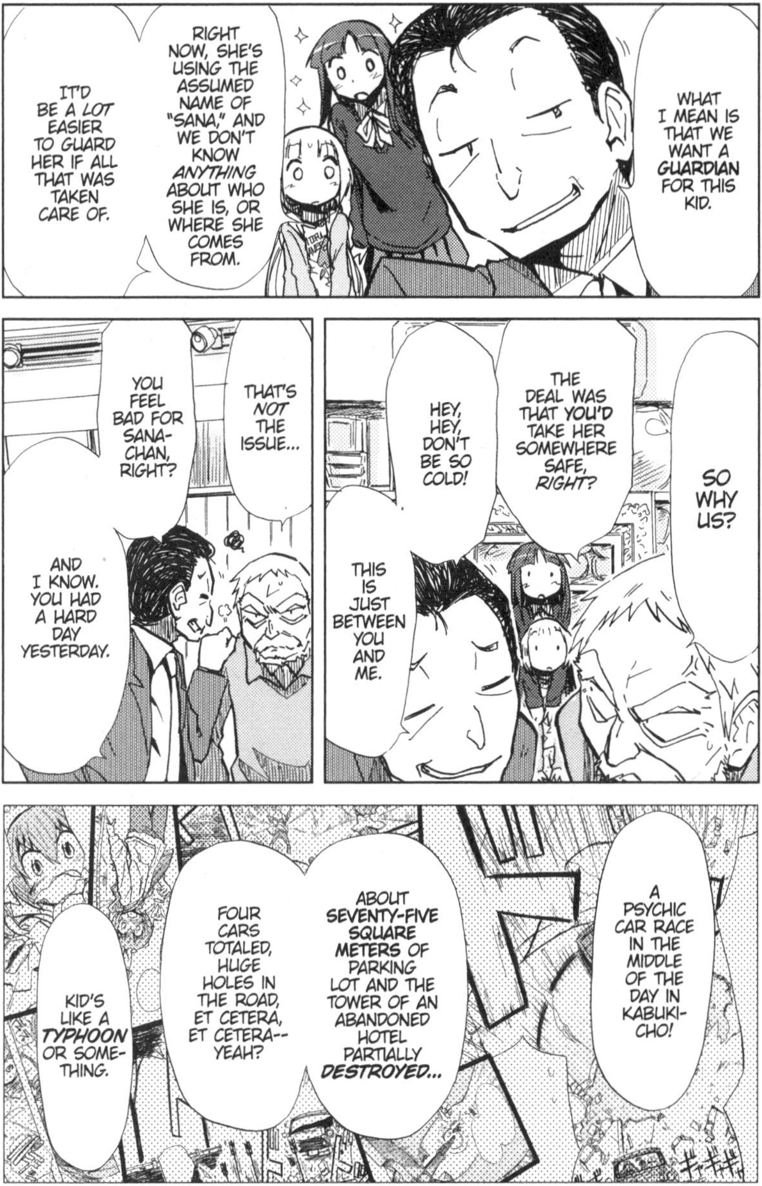

WHAT I MEAN IS THAT WE WANT A GUARDIAN FOR THIS KID.
RIGHT NOW, SHE'S USING THE ASSUMED NAME OF "SANA," AND WE DON'T KNOW ANYTHING ABOUT WHO SHE IS, OR WHERE SHE COMES FROM.
IT'D BE A LOT EASIER TO GUARD HER IF ALL THAT WAS TAKEN CARE OF.
SO WHY US?
THE DEAL WAS THAT YOU'D TAKE HER SOMEWHERE SAFE, RIGHT?
HEY, HEY, DON'T BE SO COLD!
THIS IS JUST BETWEEN YOU AND ME.
THAT'S NOT THE ISSUE...
YOU FEEL BAD FOR SANA-CHAN, RIGHT?
AND I KNOW. YOU HAD A HARD DAY YESTERDAY.
A PSYCHIC CAR RACE IN THE MIDDLE OF THE DAY IN KABUKI-CHO!
ABOUT SEVENTY-FIVE SQUARE METERS OF PARKING LOT AND THE TOWER OF AN ABANDONED HOTEL PARTIALLY DESTROYED...
FOUR CARS TOTALED, HUGE HOLES IN THE ROAD, ET CETERA, ET CETERA--YEAH?
KID'S LIKE A TYPHOON OR SOMETHING.

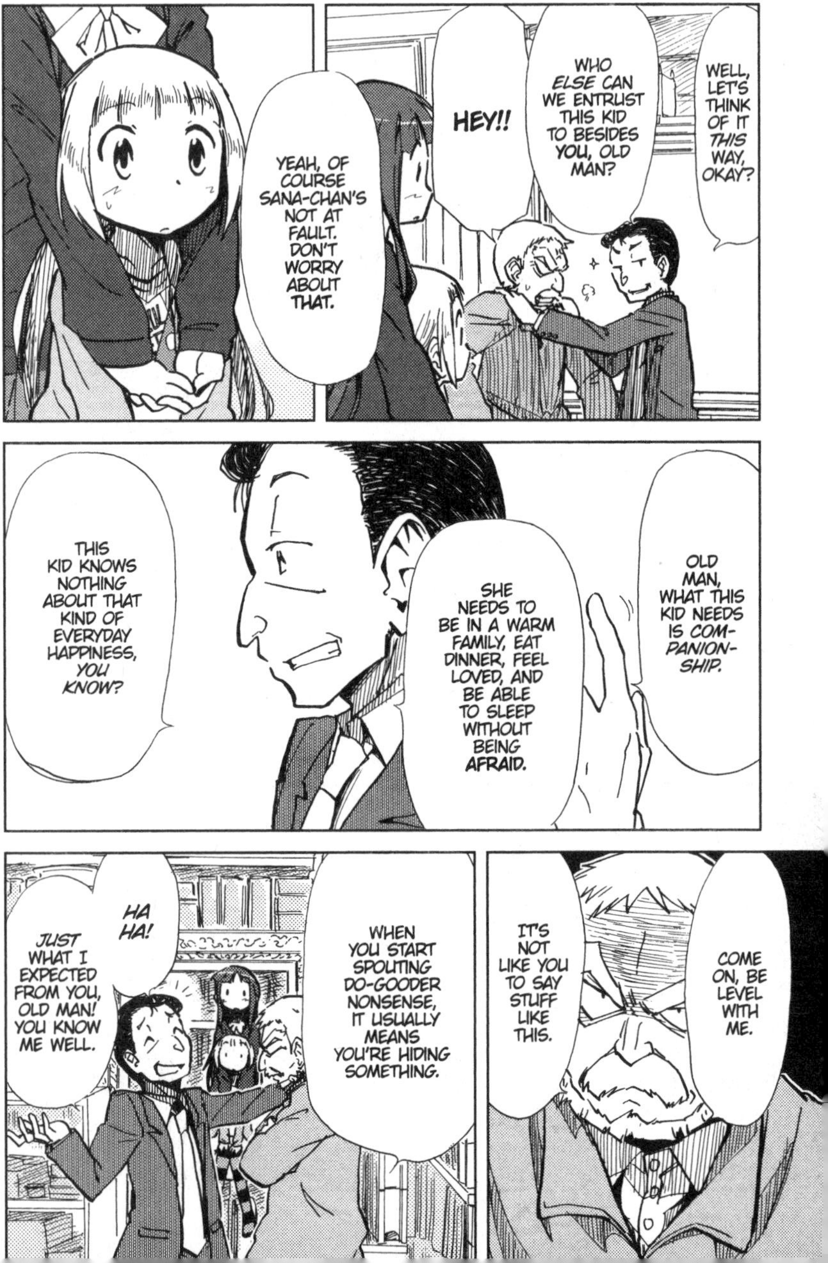
WELL, LET'S THINK OF IT *THIS* WAY, OKAY?
WHO *ELSE* CAN WE ENTRUST THIS KID TO BESIDES **YOU**, OLD MAN?
HEY!!
YEAH, OF COURSE SANA-CHAN'S NOT AT FAULT. DON'T WORRY ABOUT THAT.
OLD MAN, WHAT THIS KID NEEDS IS *COMPANIONSHIP.*
SHE NEEDS TO BE IN A WARM FAMILY, EAT DINNER, FEEL LOVED, AND BE ABLE TO SLEEP WITHOUT BEING **AFRAID.**
THIS KID KNOWS NOTHING ABOUT THAT KIND OF EVERYDAY HAPPINESS, *YOU KNOW?*
COME ON, BE LEVEL WITH ME.
IT'S NOT LIKE YOU TO SAY STUFF LIKE THIS.
WHEN YOU START SPOUTING DO-GOODER NONSENSE, IT USUALLY MEANS YOU'RE HIDING SOMETHING.
HA HA!
JUST WHAT I EXPECTED FROM YOU, OLD MAN! YOU KNOW ME WELL.

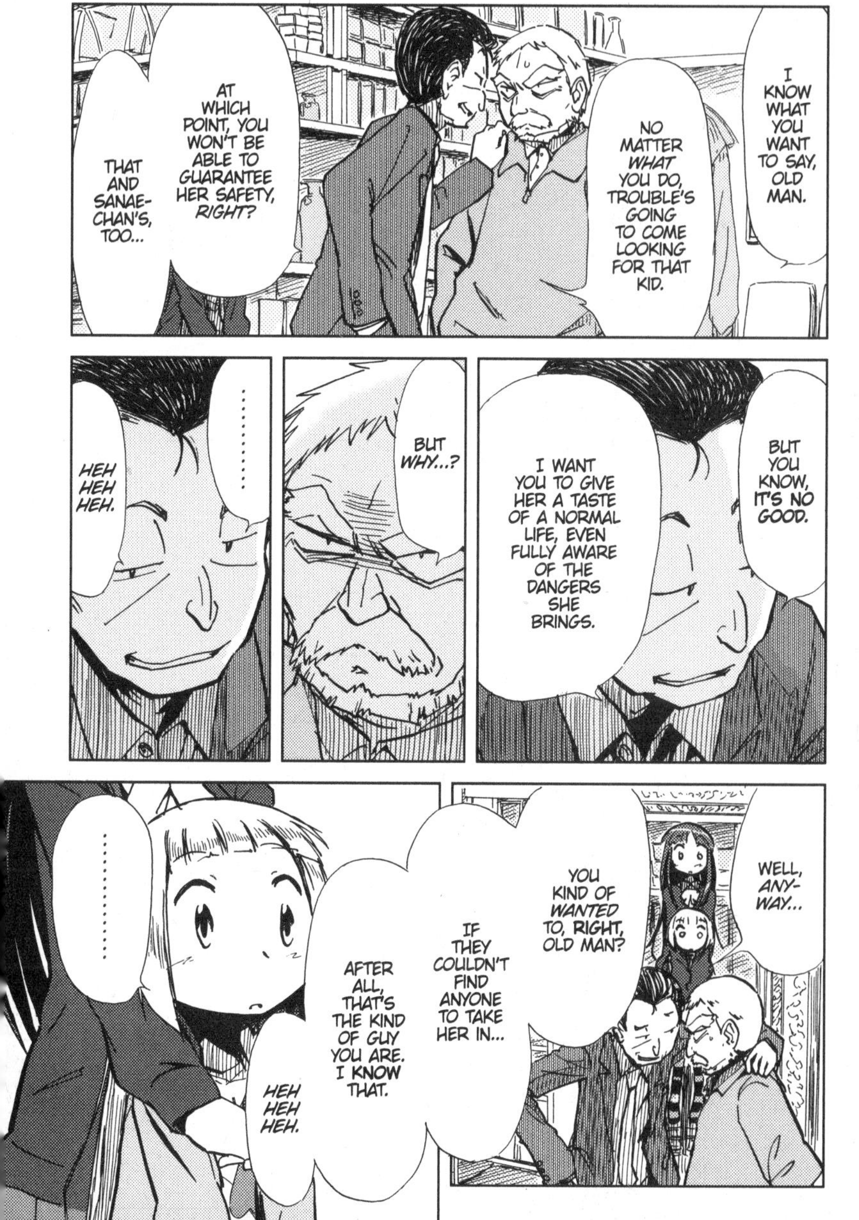
I KNOW WHAT YOU WANT TO SAY, OLD MAN.
NO MATTER *WHAT* YOU DO, TROUBLE'S GOING TO COME LOOKING FOR THAT KID.
AT WHICH POINT, YOU WON'T BE ABLE TO GUARANTEE HER SAFETY, *RIGHT?*
THAT AND SANAE-CHAN'S, TOO...
BUT YOU KNOW, IT'S NO GOOD.
I WANT YOU TO GIVE HER A TASTE OF A NORMAL LIFE, EVEN FULLY AWARE OF THE DANGERS SHE BRINGS.
BUT *WHY...?*
......
HEH HEH HEH.
WELL, *ANY-WAY...*
YOU KIND OF *WANTED* TO, RIGHT, OLD MAN?
IF THEY COULDN'T FIND ANYONE TO TAKE HER IN...
AFTER ALL, THAT'S THE KIND OF GUY YOU ARE. I KNOW THAT.
HEH HEH HEH.
......

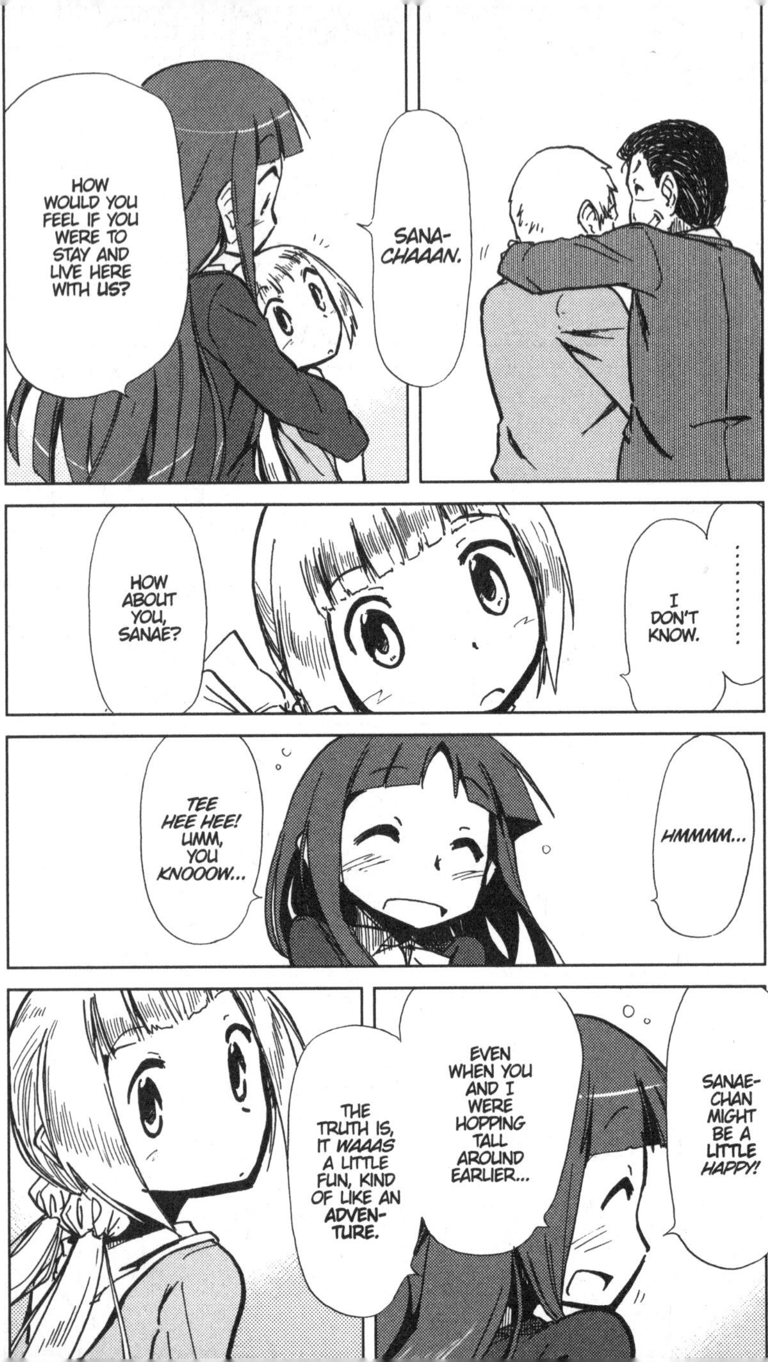
SANA-CHAAAN.
HOW WOULD YOU FEEL IF YOU WERE TO STAY AND LIVE HERE WITH US?
......
I DON'T KNOW.
HOW ABOUT YOU, SANAE?
HMMMM...
TEE HEE HEE! UMM, YOU KNOOOW...
SANAE-CHAN MIGHT BE A LITTLE *HAPPY!*
EVEN WHEN YOU AND I WERE HOPPING TALL AROUND EARLIER...
THE TRUTH IS, IT *WAAAS* A LITTLE FUN, KIND OF LIKE AN ADVEN-TURE.

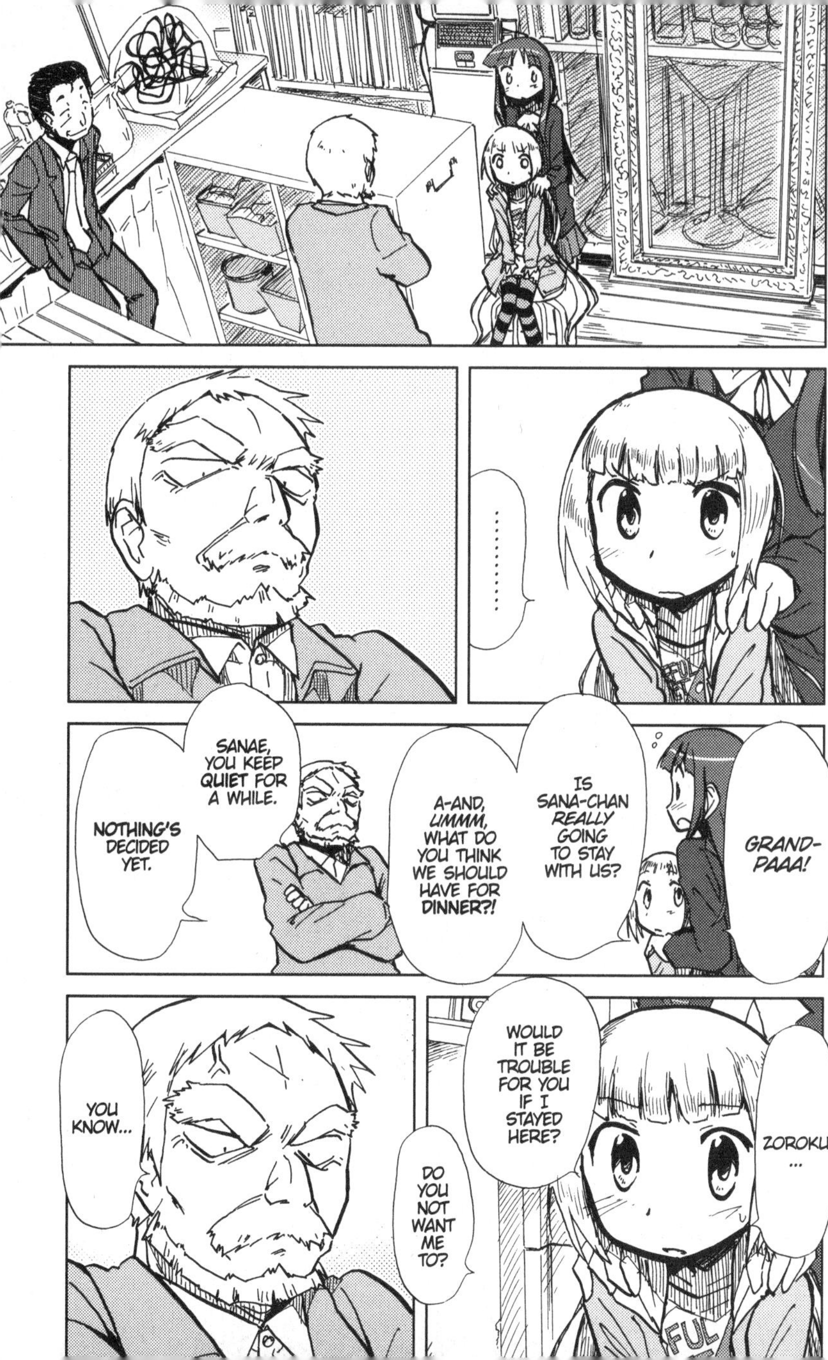
......
GRAND-PAAA!
IS SANA-CHAN REALLY GOING TO STAY WITH US?
A-AND, UMMM, WHAT DO YOU THINK WE SHOULD HAVE FOR DINNER?!
SANAE, YOU KEEP QUIET FOR A WHILE.
NOTHING'S DECIDED YET.
ZOROKU...
WOULD IT BE TROUBLE FOR YOU IF I STAYED HERE?
DO YOU NOT WANT ME TO?
YOU KNOW...

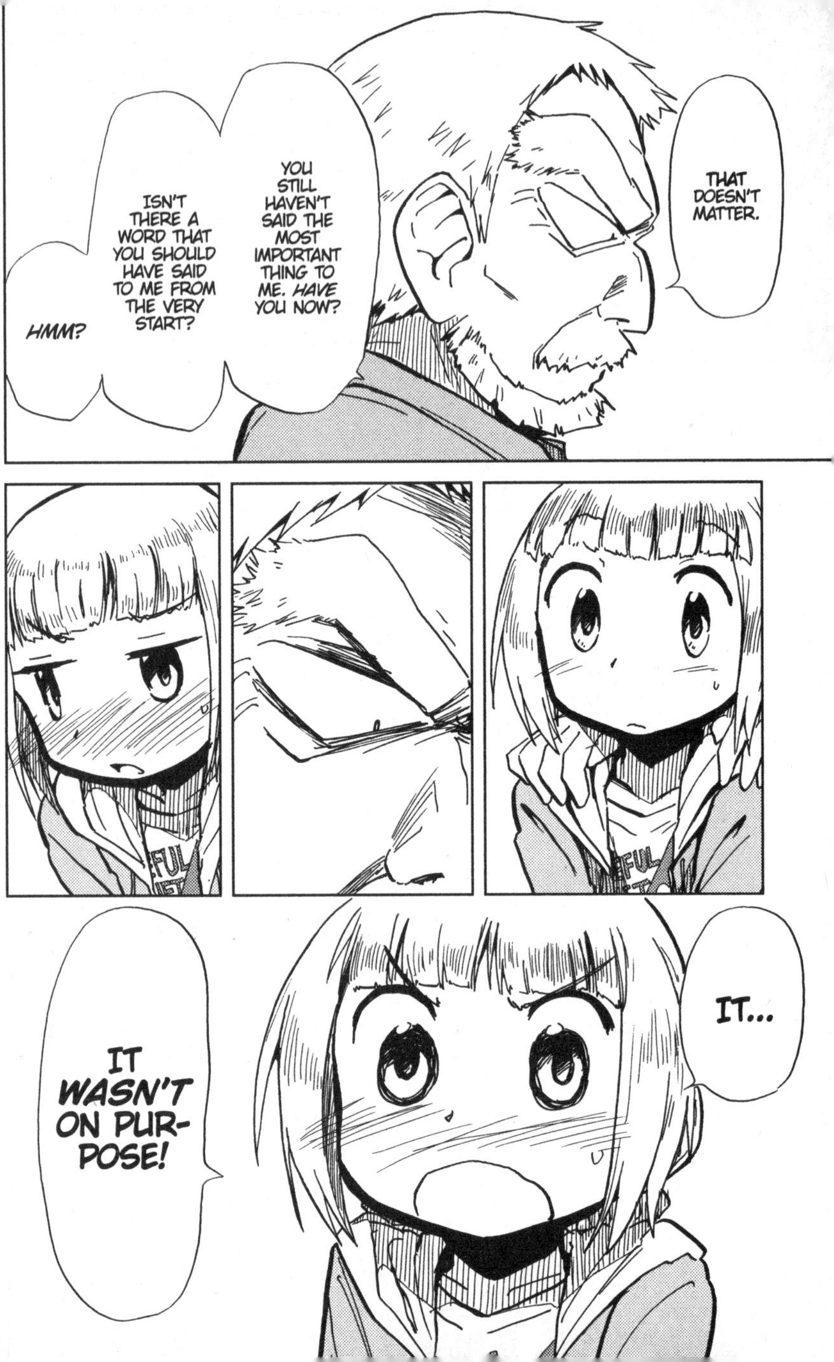
THAT DOESN'T MATTER.
YOU STILL HAVEN'T SAID THE MOST IMPORTANT THING TO ME. *HAVE* YOU NOW?
ISN'T THERE A WORD THAT YOU SHOULD HAVE SAID TO ME FROM THE VERY START?
HMM?
IT...
IT *WASN'T* ON PUR-POSE!

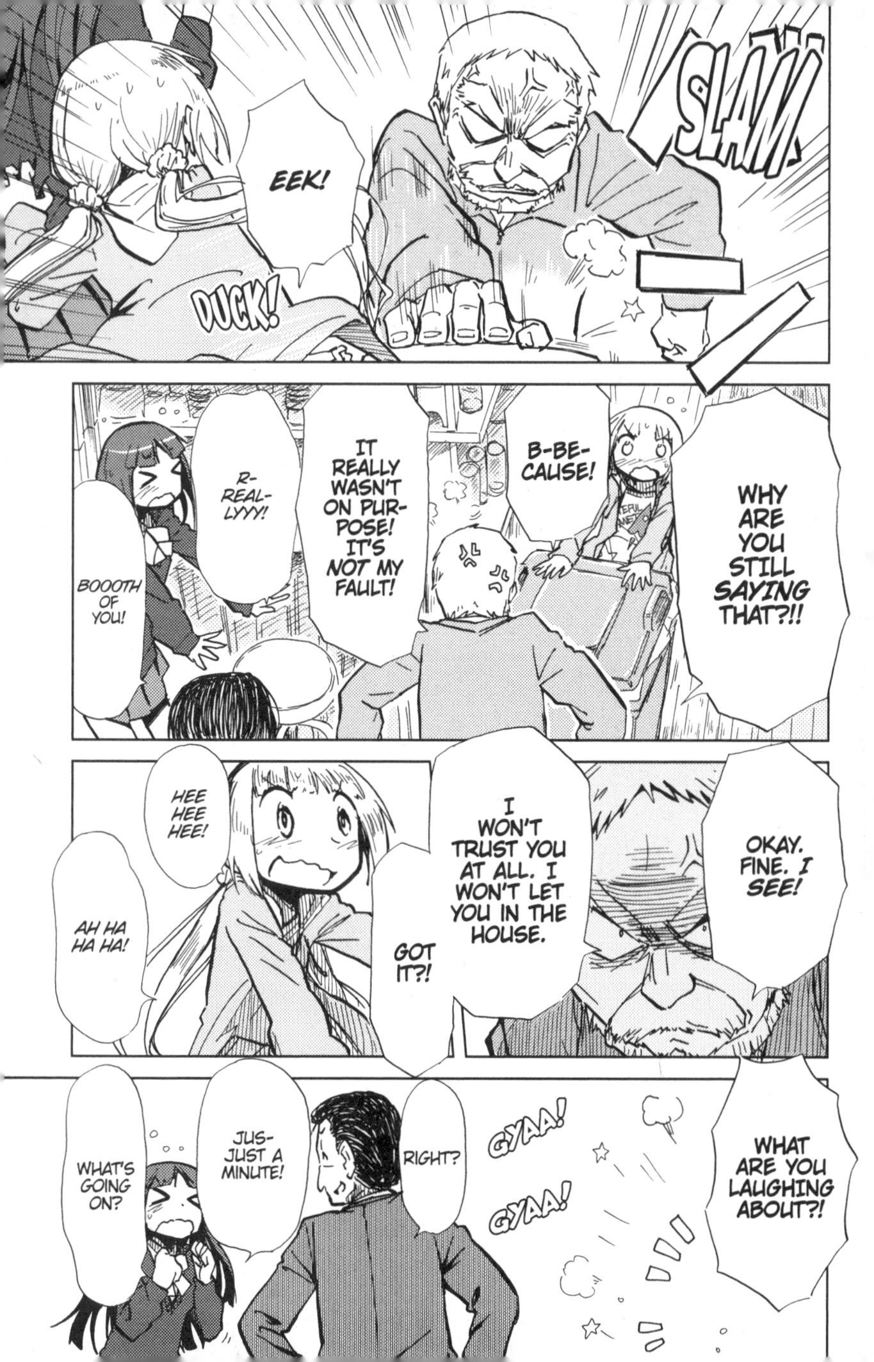
SLAM
EEK!
DUCK!
WHY ARE YOU STILL SAYING THAT?!!
B-BE-CAUSE!
IT REALLY WASN'T ON PUR-POSE! IT'S NOT MY FAULT!
R-REAL-LYYY!
BOOOTH OF YOU!
OKAY. FINE. I SEE!
I WON'T TRUST YOU AT ALL. I WON'T LET YOU IN THE HOUSE.
GOT IT?!
HEE HEE HEE!
AH HA HA HA!
WHAT ARE YOU LAUGHING ABOUT?!
GYAA!
GYAA!
RIGHT?
JUS-JUST A MINUTE!
WHAT'S GOING ON?

THIS IS A STORY FROM WHEN I COULD STILL GO FREELY TO THE LAND OF DREAMS.

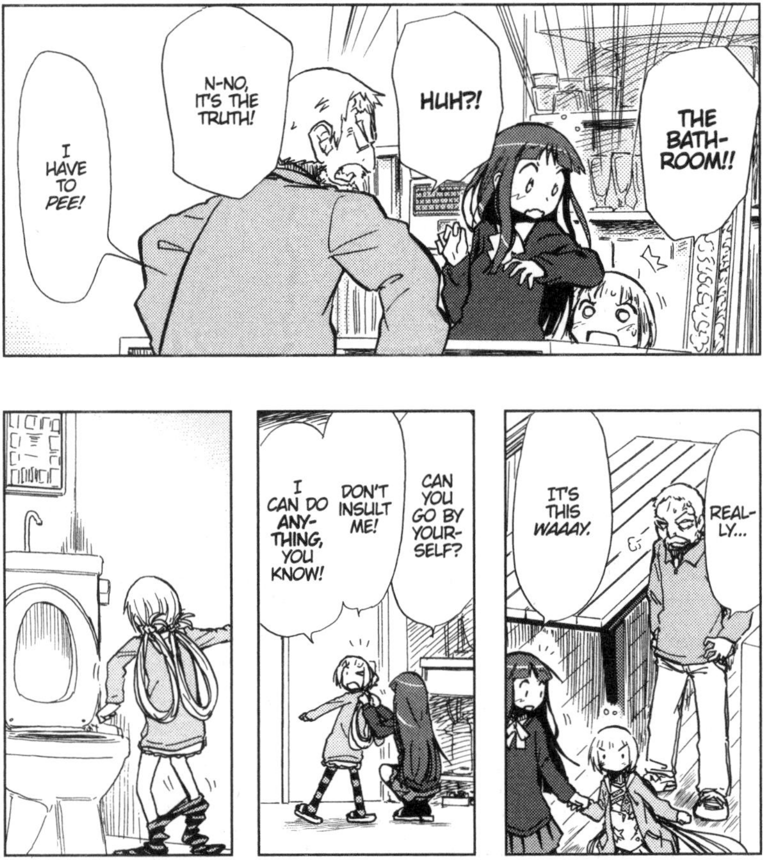
THE BATH-ROOM!!
HUH?!
N-NO, IT'S THE TRUTH!
I HAVE TO PEE!
REAL-LY...
IT'S THIS WAAAY.
CAN YOU GO BY YOUR-SELF?
DON'T INSULT ME!
I CAN DO ANY-THING, YOU KNOW!

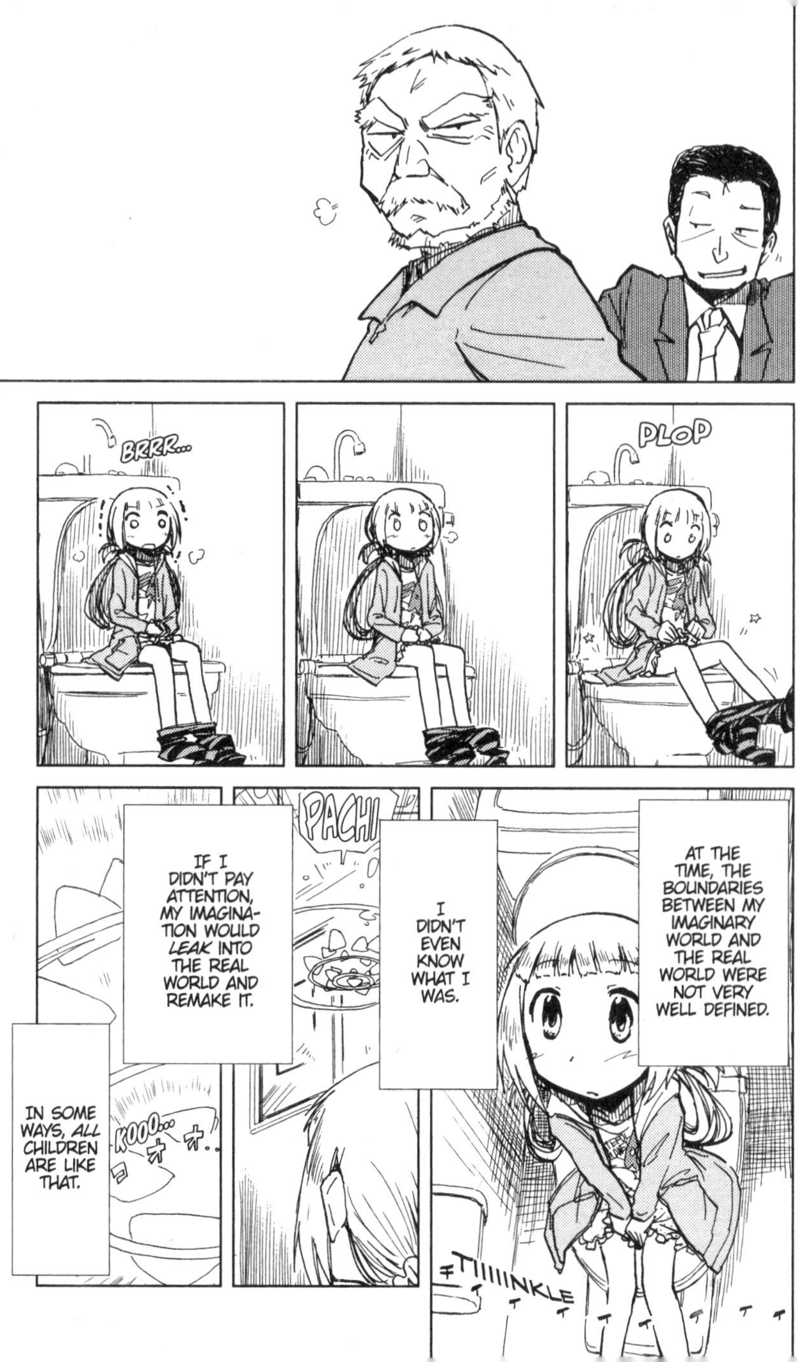
PLOP
BRRR...
AT THE TIME, THE BOUNDARIES BETWEEN MY IMAGINARY WORLD AND THE REAL WORLD WERE NOT VERY WELL DEFINED.
I DIDN'T EVEN KNOW WHAT I WAS.
TIIIIINKLE
PACHI
IF I DIDN'T PAY ATTENTION, MY IMAGINATION WOULD *LEAK* INTO THE REAL WORLD AND REMAKE IT.
KOOO...
IN SOME WAYS, *ALL* CHILDREN ARE LIKE THAT.

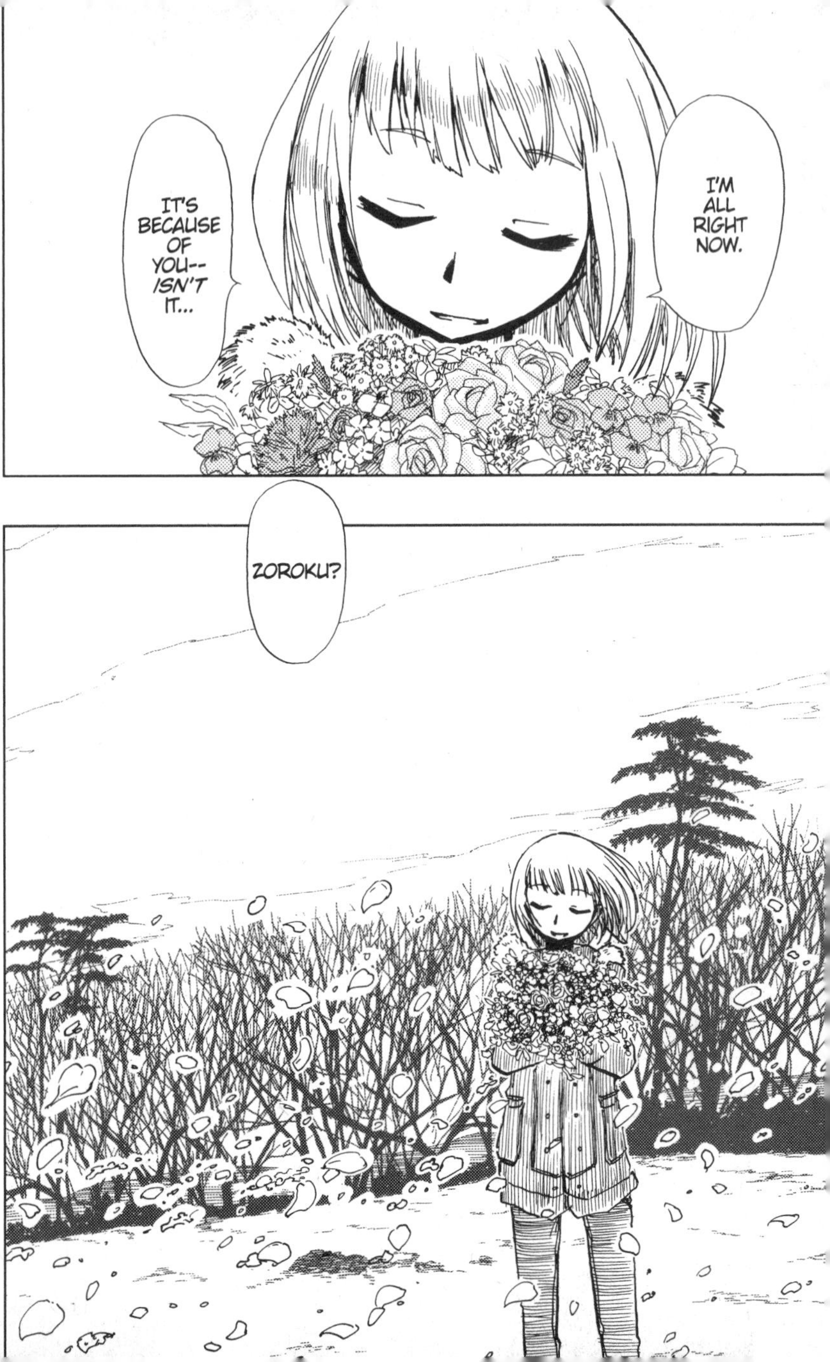
I'M ALL RIGHT NOW.
IT'S BECAUSE OF YOU-- ISN'T IT...
ZOROKU?

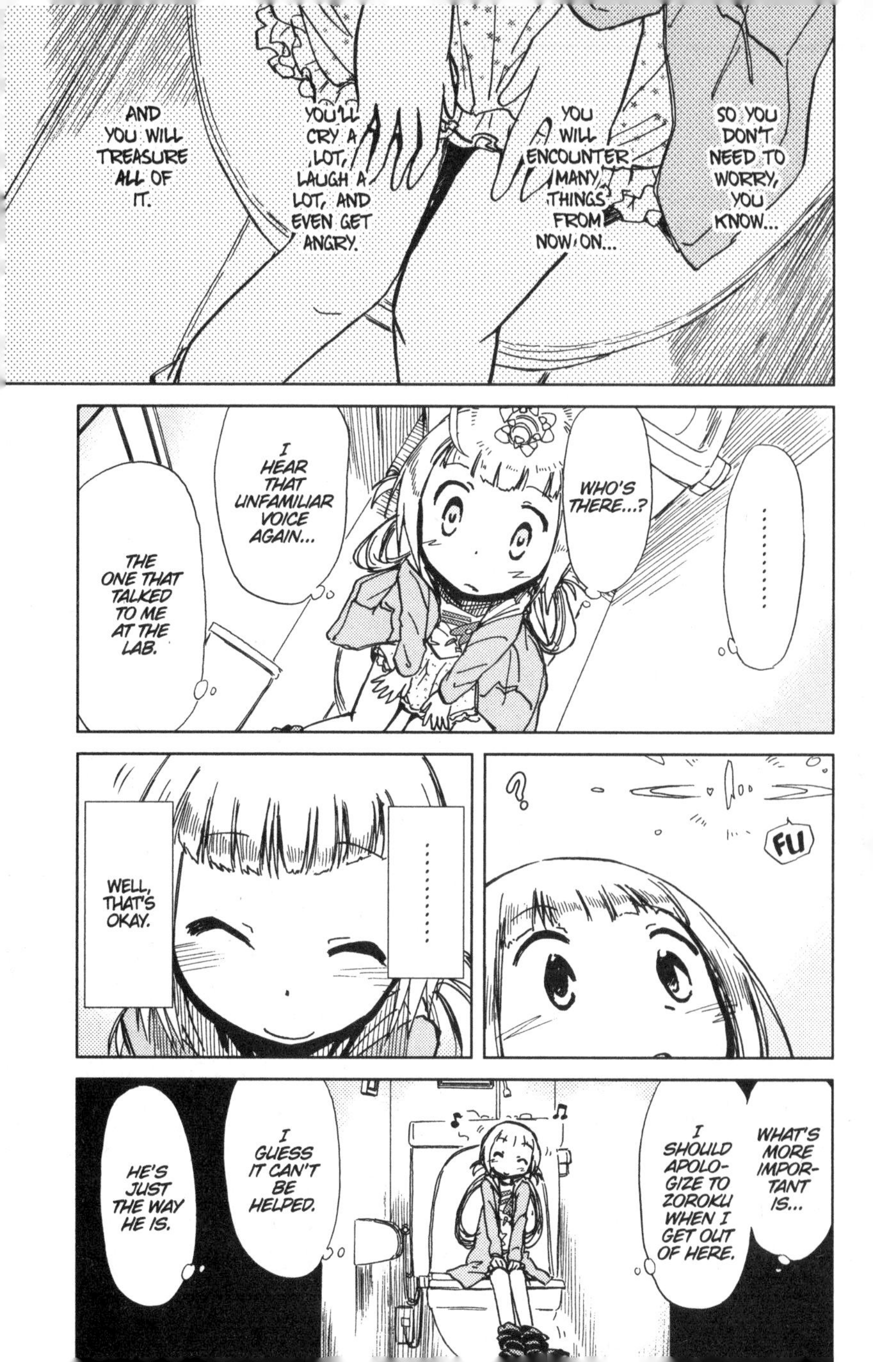
SO YOU DON'T NEED TO WORRY, YOU KNOW...
YOU WILL ENCOUNTER MANY THINGS FROM NOW ON...
YOU'LL CRY A LOT, LAUGH A LOT, AND EVEN GET ANGRY.
AND YOU WILL TREASURE ALL OF IT.
......
WHO'S THERE...?
I HEAR THAT UNFAMILIAR VOICE AGAIN...
THE ONE THAT TALKED TO ME AT THE LAB.
FU
......
WELL, THAT'S OKAY.
WHAT'S MORE IMPORTANT IS...
I SHOULD APOLOGIZE TO ZOROKU WHEN I GET OUT OF HERE.
I GUESS IT CAN'T BE HELPED.
HE'S JUST THE WAY HE IS.

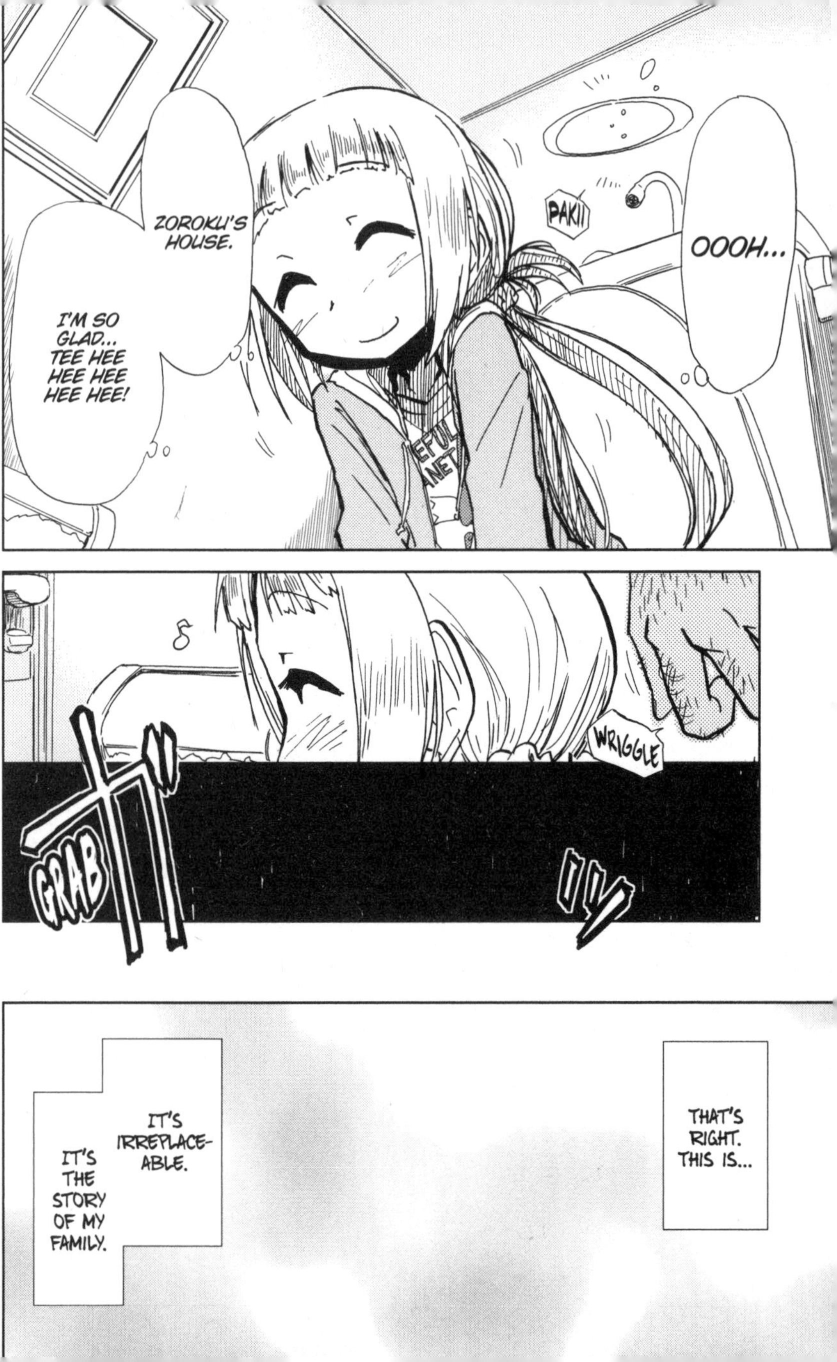
OOOH...
PAKII
ZOROKU'S HOUSE.
I'M SO GLAD... TEE HEE HEE HEE HEE HEE!
WRIGGLE
GRAB
THAT'S RIGHT. THIS IS...
IT'S IRREPLACE-ABLE.
IT'S THE STORY OF MY FAMILY.

Alice & Zoroku

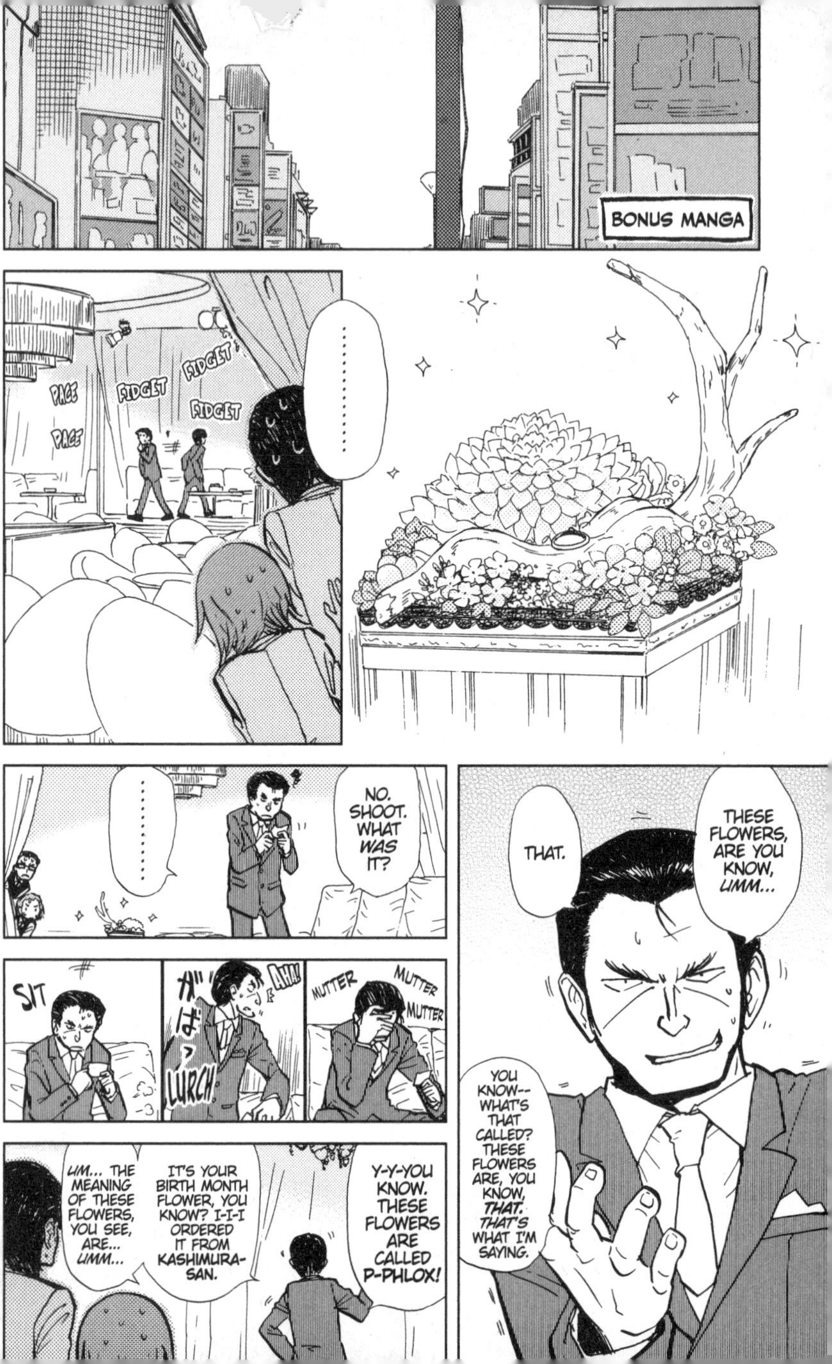
BONUS MANGA
......
FIDGET
FIDGET
FIDGET
PACE
PACE
THESE FLOWERS, ARE YOU KNOW, *UMM...*
THAT.
YOU KNOW-- WHAT'S THAT CALLED? THESE FLOWERS ARE, YOU KNOW, ***THAT.*** ***THAT'S*** WHAT I'M SAYING.
NO. SHOOT. WHAT *WAS* IT?
......
MUTTER
MUTTER
MUTTER
AHA!
がば
LURCH
SIT
Y-Y-YOU KNOW. THESE FLOWERS ARE CALLED P-PHLOX!
IT'S YOUR BIRTH MONTH FLOWER, YOU KNOW? I-I-I ORDERED IT FROM KASHIMURA-SAN.
UM... THE MEANING OF THESE FLOWERS, YOU SEE, ARE... *UMM...*

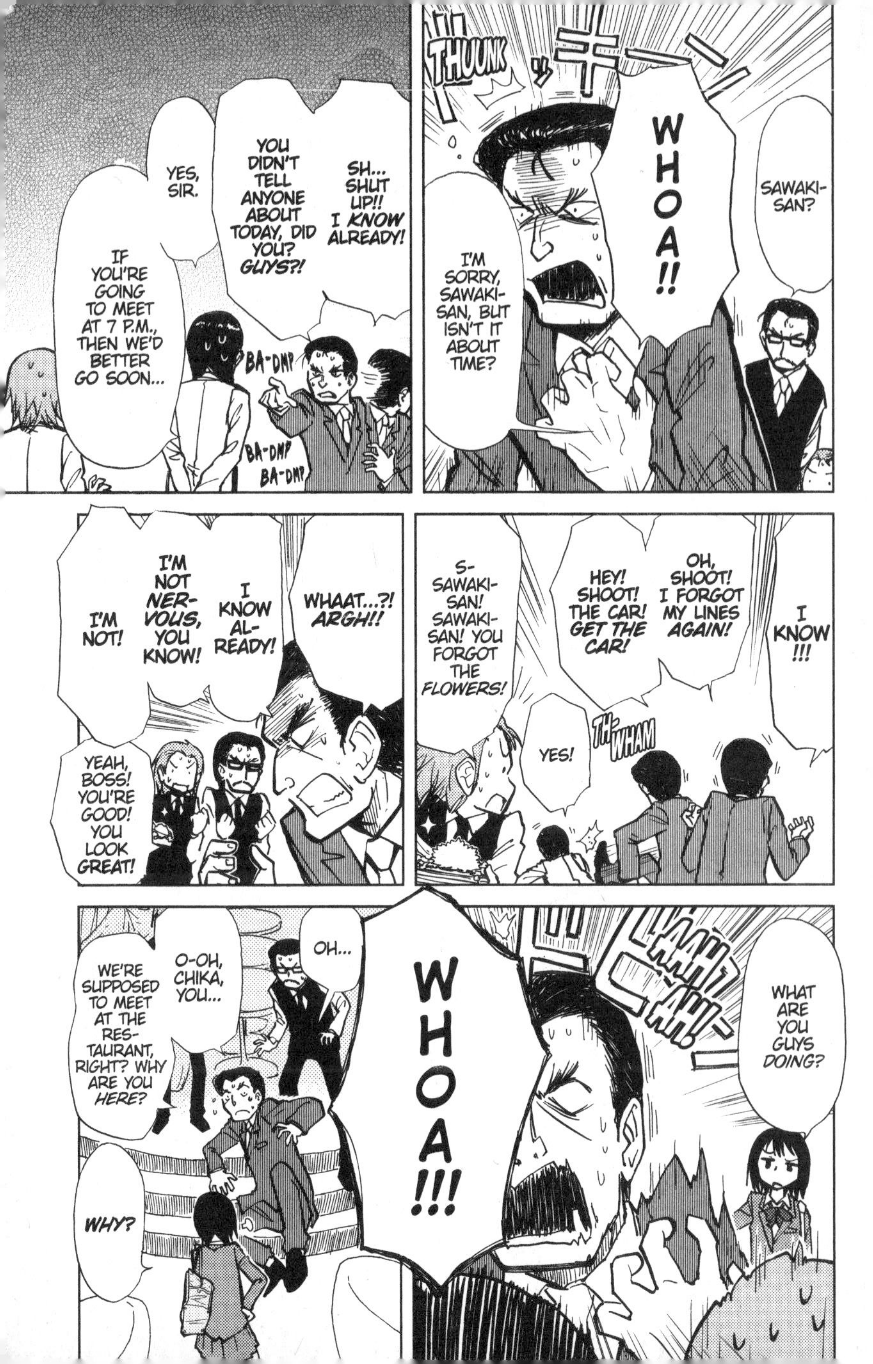
SAWAKI-SAN?
WHOA!!
THUUNK
I'M SORRY, SAWAKI-SAN, BUT ISN'T IT ABOUT TIME?
SH... SHUT UP!! I KNOW ALREADY!
YOU DIDN'T TELL ANYONE ABOUT TODAY, DID YOU? GUYS?!
YES, SIR.
IF YOU'RE GOING TO MEET AT 7 P.M., THEN WE'D BETTER GO SOON...
BA-DMP
BA-DMP
BA-DMP
I KNOW!!!
OH, SHOOT! I FORGOT MY LINES AGAIN!
HEY! SHOOT! THE CAR! GET THE CAR!
S-SAWAKI-SAN! SAWAKI-SAN! YOU FORGOT THE FLOWERS!
TH-WHAM
YES!
WHAAT...?! ARGH!!
I KNOW ALREADY!
I'M NOT NERVOUS, YOU KNOW!
I'M NOT!
YEAH, BOSS! YOU'RE GOOD! YOU LOOK GREAT!
WHAT ARE YOU GUYS DOING?
WHOA!!!
OH...
O-OH, CHIKA, YOU...
WE'RE SUPPOSED TO MEET AT THE RESTAURANT, RIGHT? WHY ARE YOU HERE?
WHY?

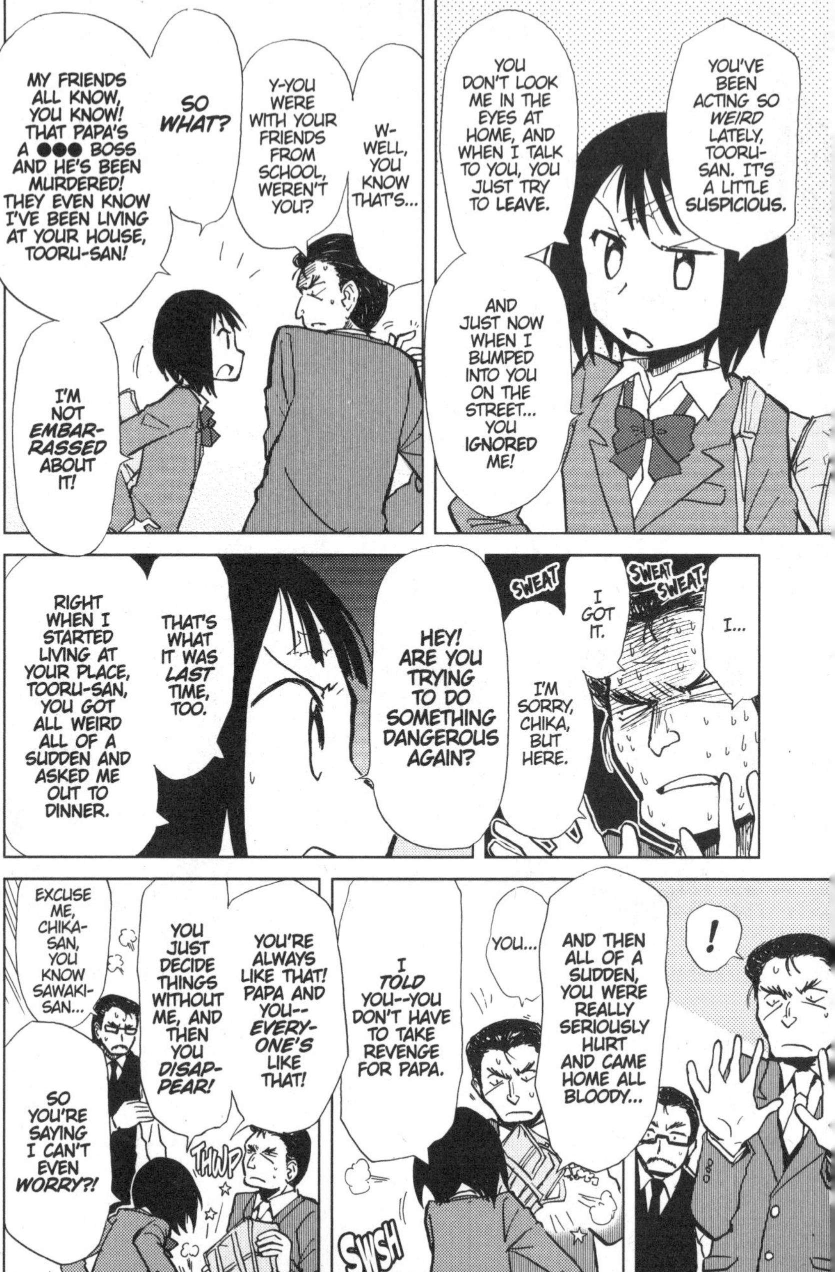
YOU'VE BEEN ACTING SO WEIRD LATELY, TOORU-SAN. IT'S A LITTLE SUSPICIOUS.
YOU DON'T LOOK ME IN THE EYES AT HOME, AND WHEN I TALK TO YOU, YOU JUST TRY TO LEAVE.
AND JUST NOW WHEN I BUMPED INTO YOU ON THE STREET... YOU IGNORED ME!
W-WELL, YOU KNOW THAT'S...
Y-YOU WERE WITH YOUR FRIENDS FROM SCHOOL, WEREN'T YOU?
SO WHAT?
MY FRIENDS ALL KNOW, YOU KNOW! THAT PAPA'S A ●●● BOSS AND HE'S BEEN MURDERED! THEY EVEN KNOW I'VE BEEN LIVING AT YOUR HOUSE, TOORU-SAN!
I'M NOT EMBARRASSED ABOUT IT!
I...
SWEAT SWEAT
SWEAT
I GOT IT.
I'M SORRY, CHIKA, BUT HERE.
HEY! ARE YOU TRYING TO DO SOMETHING DANGEROUS AGAIN?
THAT'S WHAT IT WAS LAST TIME, TOO.
RIGHT WHEN I STARTED LIVING AT YOUR PLACE, TOORU-SAN, YOU GOT ALL WEIRD ALL OF A SUDDEN AND ASKED ME OUT TO DINNER.
!
AND THEN ALL OF A SUDDEN, YOU WERE REALLY SERIOUSLY HURT AND CAME HOME ALL BLOODY...
YOU...
I TOLD YOU--YOU DON'T HAVE TO TAKE REVENGE FOR PAPA.
SWSH
YOU'RE ALWAYS LIKE THAT! PAPA AND YOU--EVERYONE'S LIKE THAT!
YOU JUST DECIDE THINGS WITHOUT ME, AND THEN YOU DISAPPEAR!
THWUP
EXCUSE ME, CHIKA-SAN, YOU KNOW SAWAKI-SAN...
SO YOU'RE SAYING I CAN'T EVEN WORRY?!

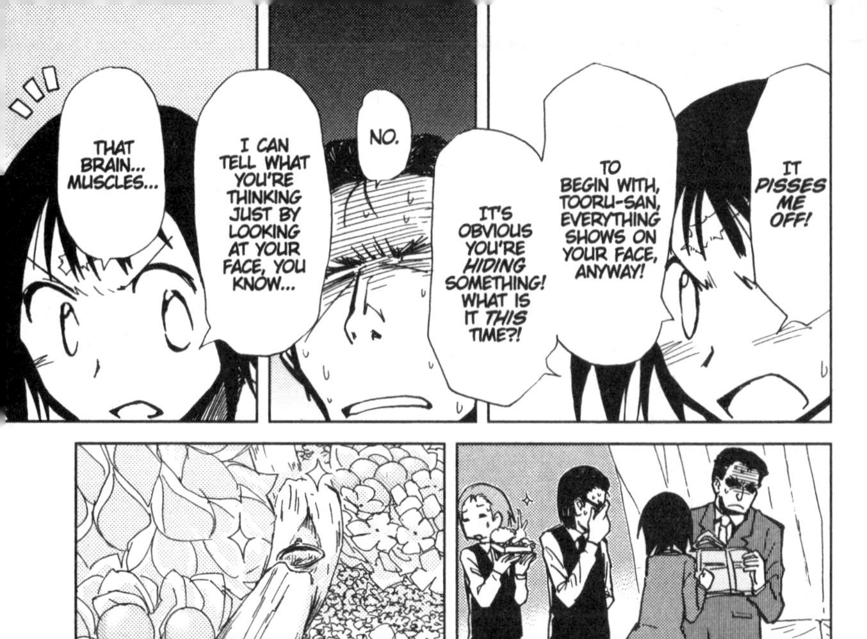
IT PISSES ME OFF!
TO BEGIN WITH, TOORU-SAN, EVERYTHING SHOWS ON YOUR FACE, ANYWAY!
IT'S OBVIOUS YOU'RE HIDING SOMETHING! WHAT IS IT THIS TIME?!
NO.
I CAN TELL WHAT YOU'RE THINKING JUST BY LOOKING AT YOUR FACE, YOU KNOW...
THAT BRAIN... MUSCLES...
ARE YOU AN IDIOT...?
I-IT'S TOO EARLY.

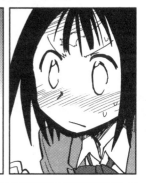

Alice and Zoroku①
Author: Tetsuya Imai
Editor: Mikio Ikai
(COMIC RYU Editorial Department)
Design • Formatting: Afterglow

Research Cooperation:
Everyone at
Massa & Artists

Illustration Assistants:
Siz Takayuki (#1, 3)
Yuzuko Amanatsu (#1)
Special Thanks: Shigeki Mikami

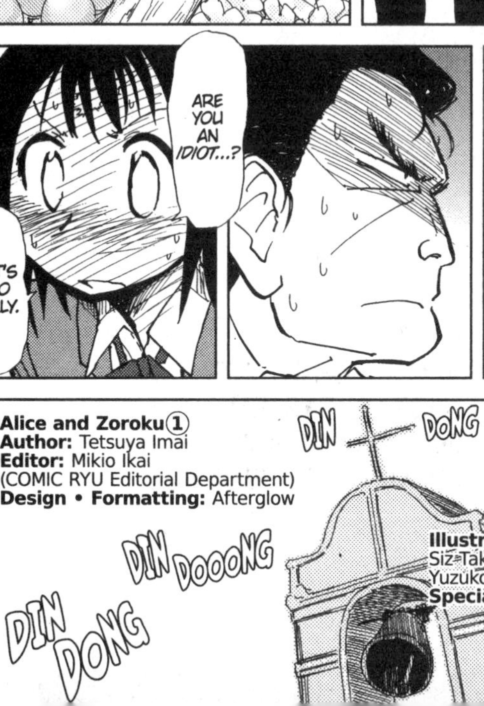
DIN DONG
DIN DOOOONG
DIN DONG

Alice & Zoroku

SEVEN SEAS ENTERTAINMENT PRESENTS

Alice & Zoroku

story and art by TETSUYA IMAI

VOLUME 1

TRANSLATION
Beni Axia Conrad

ADAPTATION
Maggie Cooper

LETTERING
Ludwig Sacramento

COVER DESIGN
Nicky Lim

PROOFREADER
Janet Houck

ASSISTANT EDITOR
Jenn Grunigen

PRODUCTION ASSISTANT
CK Russell

PRODUCTION MANAGER
Lissa Pattillo

EDITOR-IN-CHIEF
Adam Arnold

PUBLISHER
Jason DeAngelis

ALICE TO ZOROKU VOLUME 1
© TETSUYA IMAI 2013
Originally published in Japan in 2013 by TOKUMA SHOTEN PUBLISHING
CO., LTD., Tokyo. English translation rights arranged with TOKUMA SHOTEN
PUBLISHING CO., LTD., Tokyo, through TOHAN CORPORATION, Tokyo.

Seven Seas books may be purchased in bulk for promotional, educational, or
business use. Please contact your local bookseller or the Macmillan Corporate
and Premium Sales Department at 1-800-221-7945, extension 5442, or by
e-mail at MacmillanSpecialMarkets@macmillan.com.

Seven Seas and the Seven Seas logo are trademarks of
Seven Seas Entertainment, LLC. All rights reserved.

ISBN: 978-1-626926-48-6

Printed in Canada

First Printing: July 2017

10 9 8 7 6 5 4 3 2 1

FOLLOW US ONLINE: www.gomanga.com

READING DIRECTIONS

This book reads from *right to left*, Japanese style.
If this is your first time reading manga, you start
reading from the top right panel on each page and
take it from there. If you get lost, just follow the
numbered diagram here. It may seem backwards at
first, but you'll get the hang of it! Have fun!!

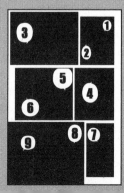